HERMENEUTISCHE UNTERSUCHUNGEN ZUR THEOLOGIE

Herausgegeben von
HANS DIETER BETZ · GERHARD EBELING
MANFRED MEZGER

22

Pseudepigraphy and
Ethical Argument
in the Pastoral Epistles

by

Lewis R. Donelson

J.C.B. Mohr (Paul Siebeck) Tübingen

CIP-Kurztitelaufnahme der Deutschen Bibliothek

Donelson, Lewis R.:
Pseudepigraphy and ethical argument in the pastoral epistles /
by Lewis R. Donelson. –
Tübingen : Mohr, 1986.
   (Hermeneutische Untersuchungen zur Theologie ; 22)
   ISBN 3-16-145009-4
   ISSN 0440-7180
NE: GT

Typeset by Sam Boyd Enterprise in Singapore; printed by Gulde-Druck GmbH in Tübingen; bound by Heinrich Koch KG in Tübingen.

Printed in Germany.

Preface

This study was submitted originally as a dissertation to the faculty of The Divinity School of The University of Chicago in January, 1984. Several changes have been made for publication in order to clarify and complete the work.

A special thanks is appropriate to Hans Dieter Betz, my doctoral advisor at The University of Chicago. He has participated in the development of this study from its inception to its completion. I have incorporated into the final form of this study many of his suggestions, especially those concerning which documents and issues were necessary or unnecessary to the course of the argument. In the entire process, it always was and still is pleasant and productive to work with him.

My teacher, David L. Bartlett, perceived the potential for a dissertation in a short paper and provided me with the initial impetus to undertake this topic. Robert M. Grant contributed an indirect but important influence because I knew that his cool historical eye would one day read the manuscript. Manfred Mezger, who is on the editorial committee for the series "Hermeneutische Untersuchungen zur Theologie," read the manuscript with care, offered numerous corrections in Greek accents, and made several suggestions about clarification and expansion of arguments. Many of the changes in this manuscript from the form it took as a dissertation have come from his comments. My gratitude is due to each one of them.

My student assistants, Dale Ratheal and John Williams, and my wife, Linda Team, did careful and accurate jobs of proofreading the manuscript. And my student assistant, Sally Fauth, did much of the work on the indices.

Thanks are due to The Divinity School of The University of Chicago, Austin Presbyterian Theological Seminary, and Holly Grove Presbyterian Church for their personal and institutional support.

Mr. Georg Siebeck of J. C. B. Mohr (Paul Siebeck), on the advice of the editorial committee of the series "Hermeneutische Untersuchungen zur Theologie," graciously offered to publish this volume.

Finally, there has been a conscious effort to render in English the masculine orientation of the language of the ancient texts which are consulted in this study. This means that "he," 'him," and "his," are employed in this manuscript because the ancient texts, more often than not, use this same gender-exclusive style. This includes, on occasion, the use of masculine pronouns for the deity.

Contents

Introduction

This dissertation does not attempt to fill a gap in New Testament scholarship or to undertake arduous historical spadework as a basis for later work but rather itself builds upon the foundations laid and directions implied by others and essays a synthetic hermeneutic on the Pastoral Epistles. Thus this study offers a new reading of three New Testament letters which have been read many times before. Its justification lies only in the hope that the reading proferred here is more adequate and thus in some sense more correct than previous interpretations.

More than many studies on New Testament documents, this study has emerged naturally and nonstrenuously from movements and directions in previous scholarship. It is as though scholarship on the Pastorals had asked that just such a reading be attempted. Although it was as long ago as 1807 that Friedrich Schleiermacher introduced the notion of non-Pauline authorship of the Pastorals to modern New Testament scholarship, it has not been until the last twenty or thirty years that interpretations of the Pastorals have begun to escape the Pauline shadow[1]. Perhaps because debate over authorship was and is still so animated and because opinions about that question have seemed so tenuous and subjective, scholars, even when convinced of non-Pauline authorship, implicitly compared and contrasted the thinking in these three letters to the Pauline corpus. The Pastorals have suffered badly in such comparisons, for the argumentation in the Pastorals lacks the vigor, clarity, excitement, and depth of what we detect in Paul. And this study does not pretend to find another theological genius lurking in these rather pedestrian letters. However, the growing confidence that the author was not Paul and the waning pressure to re-argue the question of authorship have permitted several scholars to perceive consistency, coherence, and even system in the Pastorals. Those inchoate perceptions are the foundation of this study.

Among the many commentaries on the Pastorals which presupposed non-Pauline authorship, it was above all those of Dibelius-Conzelmann in 1955 and Norbert Brox in 1969 which convinced subsequent scholars that the letters' religious and ethical concepts along with the interpretation of

---

[1] Friedrich Schleiermacher, *Sendschreiben an J. C. Gass: Über den sogenannten ersten Brief des Paulos an den Timotheos* (Berlin: Realschulbuchhandlung, 1807). For a history of modern scholarship on the Pastorals see Peter Trummer, *Die Paulustradition der Pastoralbriefe*, Beiträge zur Evangelischen Theologie 8 (Frankfurt am Main: Peter Lang, 1978), pp. 15–56.

them are clearly non-Pauline[2]. At the same time, no interpreter before Victor Hasler in 1977 made the sustained argument that the Pastorals contain systematic and consistent theological thinking[3]. His study and those of Oberlinner, Trummer, and Lips have begun to track down the theology of the letters[4]. Prior to these recent analyses, every exploration into the theology of the Pastorals concluded for one reason or another that the Pastorals had no real theology[5]. The letters were understood as a pastiche of traditional material which was more or less incoherently pasted together. Thus the Pastorals provided scholars, under this reading, with a rich mine of early Christian tradition but did not display a single thinker or a creative mind behind them. And, I suppose, compared with Paul, that judgment is nearly correct. However, the more recent studies seem to have detected the shadows of theological thinking in these letters. For instance, it has become clear that the author adheres to an epiphany Christology consistently throughout the letters and that he is making an organized argument about church order[6].

Although we have begun to perceive thinking and order in the Pastorals, no attempt has been made to incorporate all the diverse materials and forms of argumentation into one hermeneutical point of view. In attempting this hermeneutic, we shall presuppose non-Pauline authorship and shall raid previous scholarship for the enormous grammatical, semantic, and history-of-religion contextual resources which have been accumulated over the last hundred years. In doing this, even though our presuppositions represent only the non-Pauline school of Pastoral scholarship, the work done by defenders of Pauline authorship will on occasion be of assistance. And, while no argument against Pauline authorship shall be articulated, if the reading of the letters presented here is at all persuasive, then a further vindication of the presupposition of non-Pauline authorship will be accomplished.

---

[2]Hans Conzelmann revised the second edition of Martin Dibelius, *Die Pastoralbriefe*, Handbuch zum Neuen Testament 13 (Tübingen: J. C. B. Mohr [Paul Siebeck], 1931). The English translation is Martin Dibelius and Hans Conzelmann, *The Pastoral Epistles*, trans. Philip Buttolph and Adela Yarbro, Hermeneia (Philadelphia: Fortress Press, 1972); Norbert Brox, *Die Pastoralbriefe*, Regensburger Neues Testament (Regensburg: F. Pustet, 1969).

[3]Victor Hasler, "Epiphanie und Christologie in den Pastoralbriefen," *Theologische Zeitschrift* 33 (1977): 193–209.

[4]Lorenz Oberlinner, "Die 'Epiphaneia' des Heilswillens Gottes in Christus Jesus," *Zeitschrift für die neutestamentliche Wissenschaft* 17 (1980): 192–213; Hermann von Lips, *Glaube, Gemeinde, Amt: Zum Verständnis ·der Ordination in den Pastoralbriefen*, Forschungen zur Religion und Literatur des Alten und Neuen Testaments, Vol. 122 (Göttingen: Vandenhoeck & Ruprecht, 1979); Trummer, *Die Paulustradition der Pastoralbriefe* (1978).

[5]See p. 129, nn. 37–39; p. 130, n. 40.

[6]On the epiphany christology see Oberlinner, "Die 'Epiphaneia' des Heilswillens Gottes in Christus Jesus," and Hasler, "Epiphanie und Christologie in den Pastoralbriefen." On church order see Lips, *Glaube, Gemeinde, Amt*.

Historical hermeneutics inevitably relies upon processes of analogy. That is to say, we can only read ancient documents by imposing upon them a structure external to them. Often times modern theories of language or politics or sociology or religion are used to probe the documents, and the necessary misreading that is done thereby is obvious. But even attempts to let the documents generate their own structure cannot escape this misreading, for they merely hide the external provenance of the perceived structure in subjective judgments about what organizes what. At its best, historical hermeneutics creates a dialogue and even a confrontation between the text and the interpretive structure, allowing the text to reject or alter the structure as it must. The hermeneutic of the Pastorals proffered here is based upon a series of analogies in which structures derived from other sources are used to probe the letters and to organize the arguments into a coherent system. In one sense, I want to protest that the Pastorals themselves generated these structures, for I began by detecting peculiar processes in the Pastorals and then enlisted the assistance of analogous processes. But, in fact, what we have is a dialogue between the text and a series of analogies. The analogies employed here all come from the general historical miliéu of the Pastorals and this may lessen their arbitrariness; however, their adequacy ultimately depends upon one's evaluation of whether they help us understand the Pastorals.

There are three key analogies in this study. The first is based upon the assumption that the letters are pseudepigraphical. If Paul did not write the letters, then someone wrote three letters in his name. Thus our first move is an attempt to understand what a pseudepigraphical letter is and how it works. The Greco-Roman world produced many pseudepigraphical letters which provide a rich context for interpreting the Pastorals, and our study begins with an analysis of those letters which lie closest in literary form to to the Pastorals. I am not attempting hereby to define the pseudepigraphical letter as a genre but to collect clues for how various literary phenomena in the Pastorals should be understood.

The second analogy addresses an old conundrum of Pastoral scholarship. It is clear that the author of the letters does not make sustained arguments which move logically from one topic to another. Instead he seems to juxtapose unrelated materials without logical connections. However, I think that he does in fact create logical interdependencies, although he does so in a peculiar way. Aristotle's analysis of the logic of rhetorical argument, when supplemented by a few categories derived from the procedures of Greco-Roman ethicists, provides a system for comprehending and organizing all the argumentative forms in the Pastorals. The author of the letters is arguing as a good Greco-Roman ethicist would.

The third analogy does not take up a separate chapter but in some ways is the controlling assumption of the whole dissertation. The author of the Pastorals is best understood as a Greco-Roman ethicist, who may color the commonplace ethics of the Roman empire with a Christian hue but who also constructs an ethical system with warrants and forms of argumentation analogous to what we find in Epictetus, Seneca, and other

contemporary ethicists. He builds an ethic not as Paul did or as a twen-
tieth-century ethicist would but in a fashion similar to many of his contemporaries.

These three analogies provide a set of glasses for reading the Pastorals.
The third chapter presents the system which results from such a reading. I
am using and will use the term "system" in its most general sense to refer
to the fact that all the parts relate to a whole; the term does not imply
rigor or profundity but only consistency and structure. Given this definition, the thesis of this dissertation is that the author of the Pastorals uses
the pseudepigraphical letter and the canons of Greco-Roman ethics to
make an ethical and theological argument to his church and that his argument combines the fictionalizing of Pauline history with his ethical and
theological system.

Although this study is designed as an exercise in historical hermeneutics
which attempts only to unravel the logic and system of three ancient letters, the processes of ethical argumentation which are detailed here have,
I think, applicability to discussions of contemporary ethical and political
discourse. Whenever argumentation moves into the public forum, has
ethics and morality as its topic, and wants to persuade more than prove,
the rules for its structure and style must be adjusted accordingly. In short,
the peculiar method of argumentation found in the Pastorals could help
us understand the logic and style of modern political and ethical debate.
The specifics of how modern political and ethical discourse might be addressed are not included here; however, this study suggests that the first
two books of Aristotle's *Rhetoric* would provide fruitful categories from
which to begin such a discussion.

Finally, two recent dissertations on the Pastorals came into my hands
after this manuscript was completed. Benjamin Fiore's study of the personal example in the Socratic and Pastoral epistles supplements at several
points my own discussion of the paradigm[7]. Fiore has done enormous
work in collecting and analyzing both the theoretical discussions and actual usage of ethical paradigms in Greco-Roman and Pauline literature;
and the thoroughness alone makes his work useful. Although I do not
find his analysis of how paradigms are structured particularly helpful, his
description of how diatribe uses paradigms in combination with other
argumentative forms corroborates and supplements my own analysis.
Fiore does not attempt a synthetic reading of the theology or system of
the letters except to take up Malherbe's suggestion that the author of the
Pastorals comes out of Cynic circles. Fiore argues that the Socratic and
Pastoral epistles come out of similar groups and situations. I consider
that unlikely.

David C. Verner has used household imagery as his key for a sociologi-

---

[7] Benjamin Fiore, "The Function of Personal Example in the Socratic and Pastoral Epistles,"
Ph.D. dissertation, Yale University, 1982 (Ann Arbor, Mich.: University Microfilms, 1983).

cal analysis of the Pastorals[8]. I think that his description of social conditions in the Greco-Roman world which encouraged usage of Haustafeln in
parenesis and his account of how household norms are used in argumentation in the Pastorals constitute major contributions. Certainly, he gives us
the most coherent and systematic account of the function of household
norms in the Pastorals. His account, in fact, does not controvert the few
remarks I make about hierarchy and order in the letters but rather provides more solid evidence for those remarks. Like Fiore, Verner does not
attempt a synthetic reading which relates the theological remarks in the
letters to the ethical but instead generalizes from one phenomenon.
Therefore, my major complaint with Verner is not just that he does not
attempt to address the theological system of the letters but that he mis-
understands the fictional nature of the argument. He reads the descriptions of order and hierarchy as reflecting more or less accurately the
actual conditions in the community of the Pastorals, while I, in taking
seriously the nature of the pseudepigraphical letter, regard those descriptions as idealized accounts or wishes rather than fact.

Despite these caveats, I regard both of these dissertations as important
contributions and, therefore, regret that I could not draw more deeply
upon the resources in them for this study. Of course, neither attempts to
analyse or comprehend the theological and ethical system in the letters,
and thus they do not address the major thesis of this study.

---

[8]David C. Verner, *The Household of God: The Social World of the Pastoral Epistles,* Society of
Biblical Literature Dissertation Series 71 (Chico, Calif.: Scholars Press, 1983).

Chapter I

The Pseudepigraphical Letter

This study takes up as a working assumption the thesis that the Pastorals are pseudepigraphical and that continued attempts to perceive the author as some form of mollified, muffled or transformed Paul are fruitless, as are those attempts to find our author among the names of other early Christian writers. Neither Paul nor Luke nor Polycarp was the author. The theology of the Pastorals owes its framework to none of those sources, for the Pastorals proffer a unique and original perception of Christian theology. Whoever the author was, he was not anyone we know, even though he pretended to be Paul.

That is to say, the Pastorals are pseudepigraphical letters, written under the name of Paul by someone who wanted to convince his readers that Paul had written the letters. In so doing the author availed himself of the common Greco-Roman literary device of pseudonymity[1]. In assuming this state of affairs, it is incumbent upon us to ascertain what the pseudepigraphical letter is and what the procedure tells us about the intentions of of the author.

The most recent studies of Greco-Roman pseudepigraphy agree that the inchoate and uncertain state of scholarship in this area precludes many firm generalizations about what pseudepigraphy is or is not. The extensive surveys by Speyer and Brox[2] have managed to expand and com-

---

[1]Scholarship on ancient literature which carries the wrong name as author has tended to use "pseudonymity" and "pseudepigraphy" as interchangeable terms. If there is a distinction between the two, pseudonymity focuses more upon the authorial act and pseudepigraphy upon the character of the literary product, but this is an occasional distinction. In addition pseudonymity may at times refer to the innocent use of a pen name and at other times to the deception of forgery. I will employ the general term pseudepigraphy unless attention is being drawn to the authorial act, in which case I will use the term pseudonymity. The use of neither term in itself should be taken to imply anything about the author's motivation.

[2]Wolfgang Speyer, *Die literarische Fälschung im heidnischen und christlichen Altertum: Ein Versuch ihrer Deutung*, Handbuch der klassischen Altertumswissenschaft, Vol. 1, pt. 2 (Munich: C. H. Beck, 1971) (hereafter cited as *Fälschung*); Norbert Brox, *Falsche Verfasserangaben: Zur Erklärung der frühchristlichen Pseudepigraphie*, Stuttgarter Bibelstudien 79, ed. Herbert Haag et al. (Stuttgart: Katholisches Bibelwerk, 1975). See also less extensive surveys in Alfred Gudemann, "Literary Frauds among the Greeks," in *Classical Studies in Honor of Henry Drisler* (New York: Macmillan, 1894), pp. 52–74; Bruce Metzger, "Literary Forgeries and Canonical Pseudepigrapha," *Journal of Biblical Literature* 91 (1972): 3–24; Gustav Bardy, "Faux et fraudes littéraires dans

plexify our view of pseudepigraphy so that we can no longer blithely pronounce many significant assumptions about an individual pseudepigraphon just because it is pseudonymous[3]. Instead, we must investigate each pseudepigraphon on its individual merits in order to discover where it falls in the diverse and complex world of pseudepigraphy. The Recent scholarship, by way of these surveys, has amassed an impressive collection of ancient pseudepigrapha, ready for investigation, even if it cannot yet provide large-scale theories sufficient to systematize the whole corpus. This collection creates a highly informative context in which to approach the Pastorals. We will discover that although the Pastorals are not exactly like any other known pseudepigraphon there is not anything totally unique or unexpected in the forms and techniques employed by the author. Therefore, we can make progress in understanding the pseudepigraphical devices used by the author of the Pastorals by analyzing how those devices are used elsewhere. For example, what function does the choice of the pseudo-author have? Why was Paul chosen and what influence does he as an historical and legendary figure have over the letters? It will be easier to answer those questions if we understand how the pretended author normally influences a pseudepigraphical letter. Thus we can anticipate that the manner in which the legendary and historical character of Socrates influences the shape and content of the Socratic letters will be informative for how the figure of Paul influences the Pastorals. That is to say, in order to understand the Pastorals better, we need to appreciate the exigencies and potentialities of the Greco-Roman pseudepigraphical letter.

It is of course beyond the needs and abilities of this study to present a complete analysis of Greco-Roman pseudepigraphy nor even one of the pseudepigraphical letter. Therefore, this survey will entertain only those forms and only those questions which intersect our concerns with the Pastorals. This means we will focus above all on the religious, pseudepigraphical letter, especially those which lie closest in both form and function to the Pastorals. Naturally, in order to examine adequately the form and function of the pseudepigraphical letter, we must understand where this particular genre fits into the diverse world of pseudepigraphy. We will therefore begin with a brief examination of the state of affairs in scholarship on general pseudepigraphy and then proceed to the particulars of the letter, which is after all a sub-species of Greco-Roman pseudepigrapha.

As we begin this examination, a forewarning is in order concerning the one-sided nature of this scholarship, that it has heretofore focused primarily upon psychological questions and not literary ones. This infatuation

---

l'antiquité chrétienne," *Revue d'histoire ecclésiastique* 32 (1936): 5–23, 275–302; and Martin Rist, "Pseudepigraphy and the Early Christians," *Studies in New Testament and Early Christian Literature*, Essays in honor of Allen P. Wikgren, ed. D. E. Aune (Leiden: E. J. Brill, 1972), pp. 75–91.

[3]See tentative conclusions in Speyer, *Fälschung*, pp. 307–312, and Brox, *Falsche Verfasserangaben*, pp. 128–29.

with psychology has not only encouraged groundless guesswork about motivations but has also distracted attention from techniques of composition, which are of course more observable and concrete. Even though literary factors will prove to be more helpful for interpreting the Pastorals as well as a corrective foundation from which to engage in psychological guesswork, we shall undertake a short detour through this scholarship not only because it is the only extant work available but also because it creates an informative context from which to begin our own analysis. An investigation into the aesthetics of literary techniques naturally gives rise to questions of the motivations and intentions behind those techniques, so that, when our discussion moves into such questions, this psychological guesswork will make a contribution. It is, however, my intention that an analysis of literary patterns and techniques will direct and control our suggestions about motivations, thus keeping fanciful excesses to a minimum.

A. Current Discussion on Pseudepigraphy

The debate on canonical pseudepigraphy centers upon the question of whether it was licit or illicit, and if illicit, how the psychology of the author can be justified[4]. F. C. Baur articulated the original defense of canonical pseudepigraphy by arguing that the pseudonymous device was a common practice in antiquity and that it was really not intended to deceive[5]. Ever since then scholars have been attracted to this argument[6]. Pseudonymity, it is argued, was an innocent and transparent literary procedure. One imitated the style and thinking of a respected figure in

---

[4]For a full bibliography on pseudepigraphy current to 1970 see Speyer, *Fälschung*, pp. xii–xxiv. See also Norbert Brox, ed., *Pseudepigraphie in der heidnischen und jüdisch-christlichen Antike*, Wege der Forschung, Vol. 484 (Darmstadt: Wissenschaftliche Buchgesellschaft, 1977), pp. 335–42.

[5]Cited in Donald Guthrie, "The Development of the Idea of Canonical Pseudonymity in New Testament Criticism," *Vox Evangelica* 1, ed. Ralph P. Martin (London: Epworth Press, 1962), pp. 43–59. See F. C. Baur, *Die sogenannten Pastoralbriefe des Apostels Paulus aufs neue kritisch untersucht* (Stuttgart: Cotta, 1835).

[6]For the general import of this concept in the history of scholarship see Speyer, *Fälschung*, esp. pp. 13–108; Guthrie, "Canonical Pseudonymity," pp. 43–59; and Metzger, "Literary Forgeries and Canonical Pseudepigrapha," pp. 15–22. Cf. Burton Scott Easton, *The Pastoral Epistles* (New York: Charles Scribner's Sons, 1947). Easton is typical of modern commentators who follow this line: "He [the author] was of course in no sense a 'forger'; as Harrison observes the Pastorals were not first produced on worn papyri and in archaic script to give a false impression of age. Their first recipients knew perfectly well who wrote them and not infrequently had been taught by the author in person. ... Behind pseudonymity, in fact, may well have lain only modesty: 'Whatever I have I owe to Paul; let the credit be given not to me but to him!' " (p. 19). This interpretation continues to be influential among interpreters of the Pastorals.

antiquity in order to express his thoughts to a contemporary audience. The audience knew immediately that the document was pseudepigraphical and accepted it as such. The collections of Pythagorean writings and Jewish apocalyptic are enlisted as a major milieu[7]. In both collections we have documents which manifestly were written by later disciples who referred in deference and respect to that figure in antiquity that influenced them the most. Out of personal modesty and admiration for their master they attributed their thought to him. So C. L. Mitton could write,

> If the writer deliberately derived what he wrote from the epistles which Paul had written, and did so that he might more faithfully represent Paul to a subsequent generation, it might well have been the less honest in his case to pass the results off under his own name than to acknowledge it as Paul's[8].

It is undeniable that one of the primary motivations behind ancient pseudepigrapha was respect for figures of the past, but there is sparse evidence for the concomitant theory that these were executed innocently and openly[9]. The appeal to Jewish apocalyptic is tenuous. The anachronistic dates in the beginning of Judith have been seen as a signal to its readers that the document is a pretense[10]; but other examples are hard to come by. We cannot conclude therefore that Jewish apocalyptic provides any hard evidence of nondeceptive pseudepigrapha[11]. Such school productions as the Pythagoreans, Cynics, Neo-Platonists, and Christians authored under the name[12] of their respective progenitors are of a diverse and uncertain nature[12]. In no case can it be deduced with certainty that this was

---

[7]See discussion in Guthrie for examples of recourse to this literature ("Canonical Pseudonymity," pp. 47–50).

[8]C. Leslie Mitton, *The Epistle to the Ephesians* (Oxford: Clarendon Press, 1951), pp. 259–60, as cited in Guthrie, "Canonical Pseudonymity," p. 50.

[9]The evidence for respect for a figure of the past being sufficient and primary motivation for pseudonymity is overwhelming. Of special interest in this regard is the Neo-Pythagorean literature which was written many years after Pythagoras' death by disciples who had the unfortunate problem that Pythagoras left nothing behind in writing. On their motivations see Iamblichus, *De vita Pythagorica* 158, 198. See discussion in Brox, *Falsche Verfasserangaben*, pp. 71–74, who notes later complaints by Porphyry and others about the disarray in the Pythagorean corpus. See also Gudemann, "Literary Frauds among the Greeks," pp. 62ff.

[10]Luis Alonso-Schökel, "Narrative Structures in the Book of Judith," Protocol of the Colloquy of the Center for Hermeneutical studies in Hellenistic and Modern Culture (Berkeley, Calif.: Center for Hermeneutical Studies, 1975).

[11]Morton Smith, "Pseudepigraphy in the Israelite Tradition," in *Pseudepigrapha I: Pseudopythagorica — Lettres de Platon — Littérature pseudépigraphique juive*, Fondation Hardt, Entretiens sur l'antiquité classique, 18 (Vandoeuvres-Genève: Fondation Hardt, 1972), pp. 191–227 (hereafter cited as *Pseudepigrapha I*); Brox, *Falsche Verfasserangaben*, pp. 41–45.

[12]On the Pythagorean literature see Holger Thesleff, *An Introduction to the Pythagorean Writings of the Hellenistic Period*, Acta Academiae Aboensis, Humaniora, ser. A. Vol. 24, No. 3 (Åbo: Åkademi, 1961); idem, "Doric Pseudo-Pythagorica," in *Pseudepigrapha I*, pp. 59–87; Alfons Städele, *Die Briefe des Pythagoras und der Pythagoreer*, Beiträge zur klassischen Philologie 115 (Meisenheim am Glan: Hain, 1980); and W. Burkert, "Hellenistische Pseudopythagorica," *Philologus* 105 (1965): 17–28. On the Platonic letters see U. v. Wilamowitz-Möllendorff, "Unechte Briefe," *Hermes* 33 (1898): 492–98 and *Kleine Schriften* 3 (1969): 186–92. See other articles in

done innocently with no intention to deceive[13].

In fact, in many cases the contrary can be demonstrated[14]. No one ever seems to have accepted a document as religiously and philosophically prescriptive which was known to be forged. I do not know a single example[15]. We have instead innumerable examples of the opposite. Both Greeks and Romans show great concern to maintain the authenticity of their collections of writings from the past, but the sheer number of pseudepigrapha made the task difficult. When the great libraries emerged, hungry for documents from famous writers, the temptation to forgery was great, so that philosophic, historical, and religious literature all suffered from the onslaught of forgeries[16]. But, even though the literary world was inundated by pseudepigrapha, we have no known instance of a pseudepigraphon recognized as such which acquired prescriptive and proscriptive authority as well. If discovered, it was rejected[17]. The same holds true in Christian circles[18]. As Candlish has pointed out, no writing known as pseudepi-

---

Pseudepigrapha I, esp. Norman Gulley, "The Authenticity of the Platonic Epistles," pp. 105–30. For a general introduction to Neo-Platonic literature and further bibliography see P. Merlan, *From Platonism to Neo-Platonism*, 2d ed. (The Hague: M. Nijhoff, 1960), and R. Baine Harris, ed., *The Significance of Neo-Platonism*, Studies in Neo-Platonism: Ancient and Modern, Vol. 1 (Norfolk, Va.: Old Dominion University Press, 1976).

[13]Speyer has suggested a distinction between pseudepigrapha written as a literary exercise, which would include many school exercises, and religious pseudepigrapha, which make a claim towards authority. See discussion below and Speyer "Religiöse Pseudepigraphie und literarische Fälschung," in *Pseudepigraphie in der heidnischen und jüdisch-christlichen Antike*, pp. 195–263, and "Echte religiöse Pseudepigraphie," in *Pseudepigrapha I*, pp. 333–66.

[14]Every major treatment in recent years admits that many pseudepigrapha intend to deceive and we need only consult any of the studies in p. 7, n. 2, for numerous examples, many of which are cited below in this chapter. Furthermore, the treatment of the pseudepigraphical letter in this chapter in itself provides many examples. The only real point of contention is how pervasive deception was in the world of pseudepigraphy, especially whether it extended into the New Testament canon.

[15]Gudemann for one has noticed that several Greek forgeries were executed innocently with no real effort at deception and that those documents still received a rather favorable reading ("Literary Frauds among the Greeks," pp. 58ff.). But in the examples he cites we have artistic pieces which were not seeking the authority to be gained from the use of the name of a revered figure in a religious or philosophical community. The suggestion of G. Quispel that the writer of the pseudepigraphical letter of Paul to the Laodiceans is proclaiming in his stylized prologue that the "Paul of Galatians" is the pretended author is not convincing. Quispel is cited by Wilhelm Schneemelcher, "The Epistle to the Laodiceans," in *New Testament Apocrypha*, ed. Edgar Hennecke and Wilhelm Schneemelcher, trans. A. Higgins et al., 2 vols. (Philadelphia: Westminster Press, 1963–1965) 2:131. And to my knowledge the surveys of Brox, Rist, Speyer, Gudemann, and Metzger contain no significant example.

[16]Speyer, *Fälschung*, pp. 133–34; Gudemann, "Literary Frauds among the Greeks," pp. 73–74; Metzger, "Literary Forgeries and Canonical Pseudepigrapha," pp. 5–6.

[17]There are many examples in Speyer, *Fälschung*, pp. 112–27 and Brox, *Falsche Verfasserangaben*, pp. 71–80.

[18]Rist, "Pseudepigraphy and the Early Christians," pp. 75–90; Speyer, *Fälschung*, pp. 179–209; Metzger, "Literary Forgeries and Canonical Pseudepigrapha," pp. 12–15; Brox, *Falsche Verfasserangaben*, pp. 71–81.

graphical waš ever accepted as authoritative in the early church[19]. The history of the New Testament canon illustrates this clearly[20]. The Muratorian canon for instance rejects both the *Letter to the Laodiceans* and the *Letter to the Alexandrians* since they were suspected of being forgeries. Eusebius frequently employs this criterion for rejecting writings[21].

The weight of this evidence necessitates a different view of the matter. Candlish, Guthrie, Torm, and others have admitted the deceptive nature of pseudonymity but then have denied that any significant canonical or authoritative Christian material was pseudepigraphical[22]. Instead they believe pseudonymity was a deception employed only in extraordinary circumstances mostly by heretics. It could not have been a major device of orthodoxy. According to Torm, there is no possible psychological justification for a pseudonymous author of the Pastorals[23]. After all, the Pastorals are only general ethical exhortation and rules for church order, so there was no pressing need to employ Paul's name in an act of intentional deception. Thus he cannot imagine an author without a profound need to do so who shortly after Paul's death fabricates three "dramas" in his name[24]. The letters must be genuine. Torm obviously poses the psychological problem forcefully even if he proves to be off base on the question of authorship[25].

Whenever the device of pseudonymity is perceived as extending into the canon and into the domain of early Christian orthodoxy, this encourages many scholars to search for some explanation for the psychology behind these deceptions. In this regard, Aland has tried to find the key in the

---

[19]J. S. Candlish, "On the Moral Character of Pseudonymous Books," *The Expositor*, ser. 4 (1891), p. 103.

[20]See Rist, "Pseudepigraphy and the Early Christians," pp. 84–90, for a treatment of the development of the canon which focuses upon this question.

[21]Eusebius *Ecclesiastical History* 3.25.6; 9.51; 7.1; 9.10,12; 1.9.2–3.

[22]See Guthrie, "Canonical Pseudonymity," pp. 43–59, for a history of the problem. See also Frederik Torm, "Die Psychologie der Pseudonymität im Hinblick auf die Literatur des Urchristentums," in *Pseudepigraphie in der heidnischen und jüdisch-christlichen Antike*, pp. 11–48, und Gottfried Holtz, *Die Pastoralbriefe*, Theologischer Handkommentar zum Neuen Testament 13 (Berlin: Evangelische Verlagsanstalt, 1972), esp. pp. 12–13.

[23]Torm, "Die Psychologie der Pseudonymität im Hinblick auf die Literatur des Urchristentums," pp. 141–46.

[24]"Es scheint mir, dass diese Auffassung der Briefe, sie seien ein mit ethischen Zwecken und mit raffinierter Berechnung erdichtetes Drama in drei Akten, uns eine Verfasserpersönlichkeit vorführt, die psychologisch nicht fassbar ist. Ein so sonderbarer Mensch hat niemals gelebt" (Torm, "Die Psychologie der Pseudonymität im Hinblick auf die Literatur des Urchristentums," p. 146).

[25]For further treatments of the psychology of the ancient forger see Leonard H. Brockington, "The problem of Pseudonymity," *Journal of Theological Studies* 4 (1953): 15–22; Candlish, "On the Moral Character of Pseudonymous Books," pp. 91–107, 262–99; Arnold Meyer, "Religiöse Pseudepigraphie als ethisch-psychologisches Problem," in *Pseudepigraphie in der heidnischen und jüdisch-christlichen Antike*, pp. 90–110, and "Besprechung von: Frederik Torm, "Die Psychologie der Pseudonymität im Hinblick auf die Literatur des Urchristentums," in *Pseudepigraphie in der heidnischen und jüdisch-christlichen Antike*, pp. 149–53; Speyer, *Fälschung*, pp. 94–98; and Brox, *Falsche Verfasserangaben*, pp. 81–104.

phenomenon of anonymity and in the gradual and nearly imperceptible transition from anonymity to pseudonymity[26]. The early Christian writers were not writing for themselves or under their own volition but under the sway of the spirit. Therefore, their own names were irrelevant. Furthermore, against Baur, Aland maintains that Christian pseudepigraphy does not originate from the intentional deployment of a literary device in which an author consciously attempts to emulate the style and thought of his or her master and to proclaim thereby what the apostle might have said if still alive. Rather we have the genuine activity of the spirit — "a real revelation".

For Aland the *Didache* provides the paradigmatic use of pseudonymity in early Christian literature. The author of the *Didache* thought of himself as charismatic and his audience recognized him as such. Without this recognition by both author and audience of the primary role of the spirit it is difficult to conceive how the document could have been published. The author must have read it openly before his congregation, all of whom understood the document as determined by the same spirit which inspired the twelve.

> The one who, in those days, instructed Christian society did so according to the Spirit. He was but the pen moved by the Spirit. ... In my opinion we do not have to explain or justify the phenomenon of anonymity or pseudonymity in early Christian literature. It is the other way round: we need an explanation when the real author gives his name[27].

This appears to be considerably overstated, since there are so many instances of Christian authors using their own names even when they possessed a strong understanding of the spirit[28]. Furthermore, in many instances of Christian pseudepigraphy, the Pastorals in particular, we do not have a concept of the spirit which allows an explanation of this kind. Aland himself admits that New Testament apocryphal works are largely conscious attempts at imitation which border on the "fantastic" and that the Pastorals may belong to an early stage of this fantastic literature[29].

Although Jewish apocalyptic as a genre does not provide working models for the formal elements of Christian pseudepigrapha as literary documents, the theological predicament which inspired Jewish apocalyptic is remarkably similar to that of early Christian pseudonymity. Therefore, the observations of Russell, Mowinckel, and Burkitt, who write

---

[26]Kurt Aland, "The Problem of Anonymity and Pseudonymity in Christian Literature of the First Two Centuries," *Journal of Theological Studies* 12 (1961): 39—49.

[27]Ibid., p. 45.

[28]See discussion in Metzger, "Literary Forgeries and Canonical Pseudepigrapha," pp. 16—18. Clearly a strong understanding of the working of the spirit does not necessarily produce anonymity or pseudonymity as both Ignatius and Polycarp illustrate. See also Speyer, *Fälschung*, pp. 25—27, 176—79; esp. Speyer's analysis in "Religiöse Pseudepigraphie und literarische Fälschung im Altertum," in *Pseudepigraphie in der heidnischen und jüdisch-christlichen Antike*, pp. 195—263, and in "Fälschung, pseudepigraphische freie Erfindung und 'echte religiöse Pseudepigraphie,' " in *Pseudepigrapha I*, pp. 333—66.

[29]Aland, "The Problem of Anonymity and Pseudonymity," pp. 47—48.

primarily on the origins of Jewish pseudepigrapha might shed light on Christian pseudepigraphy[30]. Relying on H. Wheeler Robinson's idea of corporate personality[31], Boman's observations on contemporaneity in the Hebrew vocal system[32], and Pedersen's theory that the inheritance of a progenitor's name includes inheritance of his character[33], Russell attempts to vindicate Jewish pseudepigraphy from the charge of deception. The apocalyptist wrote under the name of a patriarch in order to express his spiritual dependence on his predecessors and his accord with true Old Testament tradition. "In this way pseudonymity is to be explained in terms both of tradition and of inspiration which in turn are to be understood in terms of that peculiar Hebrew psychology to which the apocalyptists had fallen heir."[34]

Unfortunately, this thesis contains nothing beyond those of Aland or advocates of innocent and open forgery, except an appeal to "that peculiar Hebrew psychology." Against this sort of explanation Morton Smith has pointed out that the normal Hebrew pattern for inspired literature was anonymity. In fact he suggests that it was only by way of contact with Greco-Roman literature that Jews began to employ the device of pseudonymity[35]. If so, then no "peculiar Hebrew psychology" was determinative. Furthermore, Smith suggests that the idea of inspiration only clouds the issue, since apocalyptists are only inspired by angels and never by the patriarchs themselves. A revelation by Michael or Raphael or some other angel does not explain how the name of Moses or Enoch or some other patriarch came to be affixed as author[36]. Smith's suggestion that Jewish literature learned the pseudonymous device from Greco-Roman literature is supported by the close formal characteristics which the Christian pseudepigraphical letter shares with Greco-Roman ones and the relatively few affinities with Jewish materials[37]. As a genre the Christian pseudepigra-

---

[30]See Russell for an analysis of the contributions of Mowinckel and Burkitt: D. S. Russell, *The Method and Message of Jewish Apocalyptic*, The Old Testament Library (Philadelphia: Westminster Press, 1964), esp. pp. 127–29.

[31]H. Wheeler Robinson, "The Hebrew Conception of Corporate Personality," in *Werden und Wesen des Alten Testaments*, Beihefte zur Zeitschrift für die alttestamentliche Wissenschaft 66 (1936): 46ff.

[32]Thorleif Boman, *Hebrew Thought Compared with Greek*, trans. Jules L. Moreau (Philadelphia: Westminster Press, 1960).

[33]J. Pedersen, *Israel: Its Life and Culture*, 2 vols. (New York: Oxford, 1926) 1:254–59.

[34]Russell, *The Method and Message of Jewish Apocalyptic*, p. 89.

[35]Smith, "Pseudepigraphy in the Israelite Tradition," pp. 191–227.

[36]Smith, in discussion of Speyer's article, "Fälschung, pseudepigraphische freie Erfindung und religiöse Pseudepigraphie,'" in *Pseudepigrapha I*, pp. 370–71.

[37]A few authors have located the origins of Christian pseudonymity in Jewish apocalyptic. Most notable is Meyer, "Religiöse Pseudepigraphie als ethisch-psychologisches Problem," pp. 90–110. But see Guthrie, "Canonical Pseudonymity"; M. Smith, "Pseudepigraphy in the Israelite Tradition"; Brox, *Falsche Verfasserangaben*, pp. 41–45, and Speyer, esp. in *Fälschung*, pp. 150–70. But cf. Martin Hengel, "Anonymität, Pseudepigraphie und 'Literarische Fälschung' in der jüdisch-hellenistischen Literatur," in *Pseudepigrapha I*, pp. 229–308. The combined analyses of Brox, Smith and Speyer indicate that the influence Jewish apocalyptic had on Christian pseud-

phical letter must be classified as a species of Greco-Roman pseudepigrapha and not Jewish apocalyptic. Of course, it is likely that influence of Greco-Roman literature was occasionally mediated by Jewish literature, but the primary milieu of Christian pseudepigraphy, and especially of pseudepigraphical letters, remains Greco-Roman and not Jewish. We will notice below that R. H. Charles' observations on the motivations behind Jewish apocalyptic are applicable to Christian pseudepigrapha, but these observations are limited to questions of motivation and theological predicament and do not apply to forms of argument and literary techniques. In any case, the arguments of Russell et al. do not mark an advance on the question of deception in Christian pseudepigraphy.

For such an advance we must turn to Speyer, who in addition to his encyclopedic work of collecting and analyzing an enormous number of ancient pseudepigrapha has suggested three categories for understanding the psychology of the writers of pseudepigrapha[38]. Religious pseudepigraphy takes three forms. (1) *Die echte religiöse Pseudepigraphie*: in these cases we are not dealing with an intention to deceive. Instead we have instances where the authors believe the spirit of God has forcibly invaded them so that words which they write are no longer their own words but the words of the spirit. These documents come from a "mythisch-religiöses Erleben." When Speyer enumerates actual examples of this type of pseudepigrapha the number is strikingly small. He limits the category to a few Jewish apocalypses and notes that this phenomenon has nothing to do with Christian pseudepigraphy[39]. (2) *Gefälschte religiöse Pseudepigraphie*: these are documents written under the name of an authority figure in a religious tradition with the intention to deceive its audience. Christian literature belongs to this category. The devices and techniques of this genre will receive our attention in much of what follows. (3) *Fiktive religiöse Pseudepigraphie*: these are pseudepigrapha written primarily as an artistic form, as an exercise in literary style. Speyer also finds very few of these and none among the Christian corpus.

Speyer's three categories of pseudepigrapha mark a genuine advance in clarifying the diverse phenomena which fall under the aegis of pseudonymity. By distinguishing deceptive pseudonymity from inspired pseudonymity and from the simple exercise of a literary experiment, he eliminates

---

epigraphy happened only because Jewish literature first fell under the spell of Greek literature. Thus to understand the essence of pseudepigraphy we must look first to Greco-Roman literature, as they all do, and then to Jewish as a species of it. My own investigation of the pseudepigraphical letter confirms this, because I was unable to find any Jewish letter which appears to be of the same genre as the Pastorals.

[38]Speyer, "Religiöse Pseudepigraphie und literarische Fälschung im Altertum," pp. 195–263, and "Fälschung, pseudepigraphische freie Erfindung und 'echte religiöse Pseudepigraphie,' " pp. 333–66.

[39]Even the few documents Speyer places in this category do not convincingly display this dramatic sense of inspiration. See the rather negative reactions of the respondents to this theory in *Pseudepigrapha I*, pp. 367–71.

the obfuscating presence of innocent pseudepigraphy from our study of the much more common genre of deceptive pseudepigraphy. We are forced to admit that in Christian circles pseudonymity was considered a dishonorable device and, if discovered, the document was rejected and the author, if known, was excoriated. We are further forced to admit, given the enormous amount of evidence collected by Speyer, Rist, Brox, and others, that the disreputable practice was extremely common in early Christianity. As Rist points out, of the twenty-seven books of the New Testament only nine are correctly attributed, the remaining eighteen are pseudonymous by incorrect ascription or by a false claim made in the writing itself. Whatever one's count on a question like that, the influence of pseudepigraphy in early Christianity was obviously enormous[40].

Speyer, Rist, and Brox have further shown that the techniques employed in the world of religious literature in order to mislead about who the author might be are of various kinds[41]. Rist discovers interpolation and deletions to an existing text, false attribution to an existing work, and false attribution by the work itself. For our purposes only the last need concern us, for it is this technique above all which applies to the Christian pseudepigraphical letter. Furthermore, the motivations behind false attributions in the document itself prove to be so diverse that we cannot learn much about the author's particular motives just because he employs the device[42]. A few examples should suffice.

Eusebius, in an attempt to denigrate the value of the *Acts of Pilate*, claimed they were composed by a violent anti-Christian in order to slander the character of Jesus through the pretended eyes of Pilate[43]. Anaximenes composed letters containing vitriolic attacks against three Greek cities under the name of his rival Theopompus in order to ruin his reputation in those cities[44]. In the opposite extreme, we find innumerable cases of works composed at least in part out of respect for a great figure of the past. Among the many examples of this sort we might mention the Neo-Pythagorean literature, the Platonic Epistles, the letters of Apollonius of Tyana, and the pseudo-Pauline letters, though in each of these instances

---

[40]Rist, "Pseudepigraphy and the Early Christians," p. 89.

[41]Brox, *Falsche Verfasserangaben*, esp. pp. 57–62; Speyer, *Fälschung*, esp. pp. 44–84, and Rist, "Pseudepigraphy and the Early Christians," pp. 76–78. Although Speyer and Brox detail a larger diversity of basic pseudepigraphical techniques, the three highlighted by Rist were certainly the most common.

[42]The motivations behind ancient forgery are nearly as numerous as the documents themselves. See Speyer, *Fälschung*, passim, and Gudemann, "Literary Frauds among the Greeks." Metzger, "Literary Forgeries and Canonical Pseudepigrapha," pp. 5–12, catalogues eight different motivations.

[43]Eusebius *Ecclesiastical History* 9.5.1; 7.1; 9.10.12; 1.9.2–3. See discussions of *Acts of Pilate* in Rist, "Pseudepigraphy and the Early Christians," p. 86; Metzger, "Literary Forgeries and Canonical Pseudepigrapha," p. 7.

[44]Pausanius *History of Greece* 6.18.2ff. See discussions in Metzger, "Literary Forgeries and Canonical Pseudepigrapha," p. 6, and Gudemann, "Literary Frauds among the Greeks," p. 67.

other less laudable motives may have played a part[45]. The creation of the great libraries in Alexandria and Pergamum, which searched and paid for literature from the hand of famous people, encouraged forgery in the desire for financial gain[46]. On the surface, the Christian letter of Paul to the Laodiceans seems to have little purpose beyond a desire to fill a gap in the Pauline corpus[47]. For our purposes the analyses of Speyer, Rist, Brox, and Metzger merely serve to demonstrate that the motives seem to be as diverse as the documents themselves. Therefore, as Speyer and Brox both conclude, it is incumbent upon scholarship to withhold any sweeping generalizations about motivation and instead to deduce motives about an author only after careful examination of each individual pseudepigraphon[48].

Nevertheless, it is possible to make a few hesitant generalizations about Christian pseudepigraphy, since its motivations seem to be less diverse than those of Greco-Roman pseudepigraphy in general. Christian pseudepigraphy found its main impetus in doctrinal disputes, the endless argument between orthodoxy and heresy[49]. Apparently both sides in these doctrinal disputes produced pseudepigrapha so that early Christianity soon became flooded with documents of uncertain origin espousing all sorts of doctrines. If a document could be discovered as forged, that would be sufficient grounds for rejection, but this was rarely possible. Therefore, the criterion of doctrinal correctness became the primary basis for judgment[50]. This procedure inevitably led to the theses that there can only be one orthodoxy, that every apostolic document is orthodox, and even that every orthodox document was apostolic[51]. Thus we

---

[45]See the surveys in Brox, Speyer, Gudemann, Bardy for further examples. Also see the discussion which follows.

[46]See p. 11, n.16.

[47]Cf. the analysis of the pseudepigraphical letter which follows in this chapter.

[48]See p. 8, n. 2.

[49]Speyer's work on this seems irrefutable. See esp. his treatment in *Fälschung*, pp. 218–303. For further evidence see Brox, *Falsche Verfasserangaben*, pp. 105–10; and Walter Bauer, *Orthodoxy and Heresy in Earliest Christianity*, English edition ed. R. Kraft and G. Krodel (Philadelphia: Fortress Press, 1971), pp. 147–94.

[50]This is a well documented phenomenon in early Christianity and cannot be adequately explored here. See the general histories of the New Testament canon such as Hans von Campenhausen, *The Formation of the Christian Bible*, trans. J. A. Baker (Philadelphia: Fortress Press, 1972) and accounts in Speyer, *Fälschung*, pp. 179–209, and Brox, *Falsche Verfasserangaben*, pp. 71–80, 120–28, which are specifically focused upon the relationship between orthodoxy and forgery. See also the discussion which follows in this chapter.

[51]Couched in this form this is of course an exaggeration, but see the comments of Speyer, *Fälschung*, p. 201: "Bei ihrer Kritik sahen die christlichen Schriftsteller hauptsächlich darauf, ob eine Schrift, die von einem anerkannten Kirchenschriftsteller zu stammen schien, rechtgläubig war oder nicht. Von diesem Gesichtspunkt aus mussten sie alle jene Bücher ablehnen, die unter dem Deckmantel eines rechtgläubigen Namens, sei es Jesu selbst, der Apostel, ihrer Schüler oder der späteren Bischöfe und Kirchenschriftsteller ketzerische Lehren verkündeten. ... Die Kritik der Christen war also dogmatisch bestimmt. Ihre Echtheitskritik arbeitete so fast ausschliesslich mit den Begriffen 'Rechtgläubig' und 'Häretisch.' Dadurch war aber eine partielle Blindheit gegeben, so

can understand how Tertullian reacts to the discovered forgery of the *Acts of Paul*[52]. The author of the pseudepigraphon pleaded that it was only his great love for the apostle which moved him to forge his account. Tertullian, however, believed that the author was justly deposed from his ministry primarily because he had expressed belief in the right of a woman to preach and baptize and not simply because he had perpetrated a forgery. Again, Bishop Serapion of Antioch in 200 C.E. initially permitted the reading of the *Gospel of Peter* in the church at Rhossus, until he had a chance to read it, discovered unorthodox parts, and then declared the letter a "pseudepigraphon"[53]. His only working criterion was whether the document was orthodox in his eyes or not.

Since orthodox authorities by this process declared their own pseudepigrapha to be apostolic, even while rejecting its opponents' pseudepigrapha as forgeries, the early church has bequeathed us many forgeries under the guise of apostolic origins. We can assume that if the heterodox had been the victors in the battle for church power then they would have bequeathed us just as many. The inability of the various camps to detect forgeries on independent grounds coupled with the enormous value placed on the apostolic witness meant that pseudepigraphy would flourish and that its techniques in producing verisimilitude could become quite sophisticated. Speyer's collection illustrates throughout how this state of affairs encouraged the use of any form of deception no matter how underhanded. For instance, in the *Apostolic Constitutions* we discover a warning against the books of Simon, Cleobius, and their followers which they are accused of forging under apostolic names[54]. What makes this warning intriguing is that it occurs in a document which itself is forged under apostolic names. Rist in fact argues that if 2 Thessalonians is pseudepigraphon then we might have an instance in 2 Thess. 2.1-2 where a pseudepigraphon attempts to reject an authentic letter[55]. If the reference to a "letter purporting to be from us, to the effect that the day of the Lord has come" refers to 1 Thessalonians, which the author apparently knew, then this may indeed be the case. In any event it appears that in Christian circles the art of pseudepigraphy reached new heights and that any device, no matter how outrageous, would be employed if effective. Thus Torm's question of psychology remains and in fact becomes more pressing. How can we justify this intentional deception on the part of people who must have thought they were doing the right thing?

Brox offers the suggestion that Plato's concept of the good lie and rhetoric's permissive attitude towards useful deceptions and exaggerations

---

dass die Christen Fälschungen, die aus Kreisen kamen, die mit ihnen die gleichen Glaubensanschauungen teilten, nicht entlarven konnten."

[52]Tertullian *De Baptismo* 17.

[53]Eusebius *Ecclesiastical History* 6.12.3–6.

[54]*Apostolic Constitutions* 6.16.

[55]Rist, "Pseudepigraphy and the Early Christian," p. 82.

determined the Christian understanding of pseudepigraphy[56]. Plato rejects the true lie, but accepts the lie which is useful for the health of the one lied to. Likewise Cicero notes that rhetoric permits a lie if something sagacious is said thereby[57]. Identical ideas frequent Christian circles. Clement of Alexandria, referring to Christ himself, says,

> For he not only thinks what is true, but he also speaks the truth, except it be medicinally, on occasion; just as a physician, with a view to the safety of his patients, will practice deception or use deceptive language to the sick, according to the sophist[58].

Origen in his argument with Celsus declares that Celsus himself must admit that a lie is necessary on occasion for the health of the one lied to[59]. A lie is permissible if the goal is to heal or save. These lies are a rightful part of the οἰκονομία — they are pedagogical lies. After all one cannot always speak openly to the crowd. The Greco-Roman receptiveness to this idea has been further documented by Momigliano in his study of Greek biography, where he underlines the near indifference of Greek biography towards the distinction between truth and fiction. For instance, Xenophon's *Cyropaedia* may never have been intended to be a true account of a real person's life, and similarly Polybius insists that a proper encomium demanded a somewhat exaggerated account of a man's achievements[60]. In short, if one had a cause which was important enough and a lie could assist, then it is "permissible" to employ a lie. However, this does not mean that the lie could be carelessly executed so that it might be easily discovered. To the contrary, the justification for the lie requires that it remain undetected, for any defense of its use resides in its successful deception of the audience, which is helped thereby. If this is so, then we can understand how excesses and sophisticated techniques emerged.

For our purposes the particular lie is to falsely attribute one's own creation to the hand of a great figure from the past. We need have few doubts as to why this was done. R. H. Charles expressed the motivation succinctly many years ago. Although writing on the rise of pseudonymity in Jewish apocalyptic, his remarks apply equally well to the emergence of pseudepigrapha in Christian circles, and in fact have been less controverted in regard to Christian pseudepigraphy than Jewish[61]. Charles says that pseudonymity emerged in Jewish circles because the supremacy of the law had precluded prophetic inspiration. Direct inspiration belonged only to figures of the past; therefore, if one wanted to say anything new, anything

---

[56]Brox, *Falsche Verfasserangaben*, pp. 83f; Plato *Republic* 2.376e–382b; 3.389b, 414c–e.

[57]Cicero *Brutus* 9.42.

[58]Clement of Alexandria *Stromateis* 7.53.

[59]Origen *Contra Celsum* 4.19. Origen in fact quotes Plato *Republic* 3.389b.

[60]Arnaldo Momigliano, *The Development of Greek Biography* (Cambridge: Harvard University Press, 1971), pp. 55, 82.

[61]R. H. Charles, "Eschatology," *Encyclopaedia Biblica*, Vol. 2 (London, 1901), cols. 1335–92. See discussion of the reception of his ideas in the realm of Jewish apocalyptic in Russell, *The Method and Message of Jewish Apocalyptic*, pp. 130ff.

inspired, one needed to place that inspiration in a time when inspiration was legitimate. Consequently, one wrote under the pseudonym of one of the patriarchs. Similarly, in early Christianity the apostolic time became a special time in which the complete and accurate Christian message was conveyed to the apostles. Therefore, when doctrinal disputes began to trouble the church, both sides looked to apostolic times for guidance and vindication of their own views. You wrote in the name of an apostle simply because that apostle had greater credence than you or any contemporary did and by so doing your own ideas or the ideas of your sect were given greater credibility. We have few instances where there is even the slightest evidence that the authors believed themselves to be so filled with the spirit that they were actually writing under direct spiritual contact with an apostle. Rather it appears that intentional deception, recognized as potentially blameworthy, was employed because the need for the good lie was so great. We must assume that the fever of doctrinal disputes reached such a pitch that many Christians, whom we must assume thought they were doing the right thing, decided it was in the best interest of the church to deceive it. Furthermore, as we noted earlier, the history of the New Testament canon and the many arguments between the orthodox and heterodox demonstrate that the early church equated all truth with apostolicity. If true, it must be apostolic[62]. Thus writers of a pseudepigraphon, naturally believing their own ideas to be true, would infer from their orthodoxy that their ideas had roots in apostolic times. But this is perhaps to strain too hard to make the disreputable reputable.

At this point this is the best answer scholarship has given us to Torm's insistent moral stance: in the swirl of doctrinal and organizational debate and disagreement the apostolic times provided every faction with the illusion of reliability and credibility, and this illusion became a frequent and effective weapon in these debates. There are many examples collected by Rist, Speyer, Brox, and Metzger which illustrate this situation, but one is particularly informative — Salvian's Ninth Letter[63].

---

[62]This neat equation does not remove the charge of deception against a forger. To believe oneself to be in accord with apostolic doctrine is not identical to believing oneself to be Paul or Peter. It does permit us to entertain the possibility that a forger thought he was saying what an apostle would indeed say if alive. More than likely, different forgers took different attitudes towards this question. Some may indeed have thought their deceptions were above criticism. Nevertheless, whatever their individual psychology on this point, they were still consciously employing a lie which they knew was potentially damaging if discovered. Thus we cannot conclude that forgery was ever innocently or naively done. Furthermore, we have seen that this equation is somewhat overstated, because when a document was somehow discovered to be forged then it was rejected, even if doctrinally correct. Thus proper doctrine serves only to protect a document from rigid scrutiny (see Speyer's comments on p. 17, n. 51 above) and does not redeem it once it is known as a forgery. For similar conclusions see Candlish, "On the Moral Character of Pseudonymous Books," pp. 262ff.

[63]For a translation of Latin text see Alfred E. Haefner, "A Unique Source for the Study of Ancient Pseudonymity," *Anglican Theological Review* 16 (1934): 8–15. For representative exam-

About the year 440 C.E. a pamphlet appeared entitled *Timothei ad Ecclesiam* (Libri IV) which addressed avarice in the church. This pamphlet, which we still have, parades itself as an epistle written by Timothy to the Church Catholic. When Bishop Salonius saw the document he apparently guessed who wrote it and demanded of Salvian an explanation of his act of forgery. Salvian does not admit the authorship, although there is perhaps a veiled confession at the end of his letter. Instead he writes a letter to Salonius defending the author in the third person. It is this letter we shall discuss here.

Salvian's defense, which is fascinating for its subtlety and inherent contradictions, casts a helpful light upon the motivations of a forger, the attitude of the public towards forgery and apostolicity, and the importance of being undetected in any forgery.

Salvian begins by admitting the importance of the task assigned him by Salonius "on the ground that a work of greatest merit may be less highly valued if people are in doubt about its authorship." At the same time he decries this condition.

> For in the case of every book we ought to be more concerned about the intrinsic value of its contents than about the name of its author. ... Since the name is immaterial, there is no use asking about the author's name so long as the reader profits from the book itself.

Although this defense is somewhat indirect it is clear what Salvian is thinking. The public looks quickly at authorship, while the true value of a book lies in its intrisic worth.

> For a statement is commonly taken to be worth what its author is worth. For people nowadays are so trivial and worthless that when they read, they are more concerned about the author than about what they are reading; they are more interested in the author's reputation than in the force and vigor of his words.

When these statements are distilled to their real substance they amount to an appeal to the old argument of the good lie. These days we have to lie to the people because that is the only way to get them to hear the higher truth. No longer does anyone evaluate a book on its own merits but only on the reputation of the name affixed to it. Therefore, "the author wisely selected a pseudonym for his book for the obvious reason that he did not wish the obscurity of his own person to detract from the influence of his otherwise valuable book."

This is the heart of Salvian's defense although he makes two other less convincing pleas. First, he appeals to the author's admirable humility. He refuses to use his own name, because God wants us "to avoid every pretense of vainglory." We must do everything in secret — "the writer, in his own words, is humble in his own sight." Second, Salvian notices a play on words similar to what Luke employed in naming his addressee Theophilus,

---

ples of the influence of this document on modern scholarship see Rist, "Pseudepigraphy and the Early Christians," p. 90, and Metzger, "Literary Forgeries and Canonical Pseudepigrapha," pp. 7—8.

"love of God" [*sic*]. So in this case the writer is following this excellent example by writing under the name of Timothy, which means "honor of God" [*sic*]. These last two arguments are hardly convincing. Surely Salvian intended his readers to understand Timothy not as a play on the etymology of the name but as a reference to the historical Timothy, the companion of Paul. Furthermore, the appeal to humility is obviously inadequate since all humility requires is anonymity not pseudonymity.

Given these reservations, Salvian's defense still tells us much about the milieu of pseudepigraphy and how that milieu encouraged so many forgeries in the name of apostles. As Salvian says, the general church population evaluates a document solely on the basis of the credibility of the writer and not on the usefulness and power of the ideas in the work. There are so many echoes of this attitude that we must assume that this rather facile fascination with apostolicity or non-apostolicity was the norm. But if this was the prevailing attitude among Christian churches, a peculiar predicament was forced upon all writers who had something new and personal to say. If they publish their ideas under their own obscure names, they stand little chance of a fair hearing. So if they believe their ideas to be true (the opposite is nearly a psychological impossibility), then perhaps they should avail themselves of that common literary device of pseudonymity. It is interesting that we do not encounter the expressed claim that if something is true it must be apostolic, rather we hear only that if the cause is important enough then a lie is forgivable.

Finally, the detection of Salvian's deception by Salonius emphasizes the paramount need for success in deceiving the readers. Salvian was clumsy in his pseudepigraphical technique (all he did was affix Timothy's name) and, now that his letter has been uncovered as a forgery, his ideas will get little hearing. A detected forgery discredits the ideas more than would anonymity or ascription to a relative unknown. Thus if one takes the risk of forging a document, the deception must be complete. These things must be done skillfully.

This brief account of the current scholastic discussion on pseudepigraphy and of the few generalizations which can be made about Greco-Roman and Christian pseudepigraphy suggests several probable assumptions we might essay about the Pastorals. Naturally these assumptions will be subject to further scrutiny. However, we might anticipate the following.

The Pastorals were witten in response to heresy. The vigor of the heresy and the problems it was creating necessitated, in the author's opinion, the use of the good lie. Our author needed to add force and credibility to his arguments so he pretended that Paul wrote three letters to two famous co-workers. His intention was to deceive his readers, and therefore he employed whatever means were necessary to accomplish that deception. As we shall see, he does it skillfully. The appeal to Paul is made on the basis of Paul's unique authority in the early church, for he is a legendary figure whose life and teachings are prescriptive. If Pagel's description of the gnostic use of Paul is correct, then the author may have possessed the secondary motive of rescuing Paul from the hands of gnostics[64]. But this is uncertain.

The singular gap in all the foregoing analyses of pseudepigraphy is the lack of attention to literary techniques and conventions. The fascination over the psychology of pseudepigraphy has not encouraged research into how pseudepigrapha are constructed, how the deception is accomplished, what role the pseudo-author has in the structure of the arguments, or any other literary questions. Yet I believe it is here, in questions of literary technique, that the most fruitful research can be done. Focusing upon literary questions relieves us of the highly subjective task of guessing at motivations, even though attempting to ascertain common literary patterns among various pseudepigraphical letters is in itself an aesthetic exercise. We cannot, of course, appeal to some known genre structure for pseudepigraphical letters on which all these writers depended, because no such standard existed. The Platonic, Socratic, and deutero-Pauline letters all manifest different structures. This is to be expected since, for instance, deutero-Pauline letters should look like genuine letters of Paul and certainly not like some imaginary pseudepigraphical letter genre. Given this caveat, the pseudepigraphical letters we shall examine manifest recognizable literary techniques and patterns. Attention to these techniques and patterns will divulge useful information about how these letters work, why they were written, and what the authors believed.

B. The Pseudepigraphical Letter in the Greco-Roman World

The final court of appeal for all defenders of Pauline authorship has always been the personal sections in 2 Tim. 4.6—22 and Tit. 3.12—15, because these theologically irrelevant personal remarks are seen as *prima facie* evidence of authenticity[65]. The argument contends that these per-

---

[64]Elaine Hiesey Pagels, *The Gnostic Paul: Gnostic Exegesis of the Pauline Letters* (Philadelphia: Fortress Press, 1975).

[65]Most modern commentaries include a discussion of the crucial relationship between personalia and the question of authorship. For thorough discussions by commentators who adhere to Pauline authorship see Joachim Jeremias, *Die Briefe an Timotheus und Titus*, Das Neue Testament Deutsch 9 (Göttingen: Vandenhoeck & Ruprecht, 1975), pp. 1—10; Ceslaus Spicq, *Les Épîtres Pastorales*, Études Biblique 4th ed., 2 vols. (Paris: J. Gabalda, 1969), pp. 157—214; and J. N. D. Kelly, *A Commentary on the Pastoral Epistles*, Black's New Testament Commentaries (London: Adam & Charles Black, 1963), pp. 27—34. See also C. Spicq, "Pèlerine et Vêtements," *Mélanges Eugène Tisserant* 1 (Vatican City: Biblioteca apostolica vaticana, 1964), pp. 389—417. Many scholars convinced of non-Pauline authorship of most of the letters but unable to accept forgery of the personalia take recourse to a theory of genuine Pauline fragments incorporated into pseudepigraphical letters. See e.g., P. N. Harrison, *The Problem of the Pastoral Epistles* (London: Oxford University Press, 1921), pp. 87—135; Anthony Tyrrell Hanson, *The Pastoral Letters*, The Cambridge Bible Commentary (Cambridge: Cambridge University Press, 1966), pp. 10—14, who changes his mind in his more

sonalia are a slice from the mundane affairs of Paul's life, showing him
with ordinary needs and with genuine warmth toward his friends. Moreover, these offhand remarks contribute nothing meaningful to the theology of the letters and thus do not seem to be the kind of thing a forger
would forge. Psychologically it is nearly impossible to imagine an author
who exhorted such high ethical behavior in his letters and would stoop to
such underhanded methods to perpetrate a fraud. Moreover, these personalia are clumsily executed if they are fake, since they fit with no
known moment in Paul's life and, even worse, contain inherent contradictions[66]. We are being asked to imagine an author who would drop such
incredibly subtle touches as the request for parchments and the cloak he
left behind and at the same time stumble into these awkward contradictions. Such a personality split is unlikely. Furthermore, these personalia
have the feel of authenticity; they are too life-like in their simplicity and
concreteness. The mention of such irrelevancies as parchments and winter
cloaks cannot be the style of a forger, for this would require too much
duplicity on his part. They must simply be the mundance requests generated by a real life.

> It is one thing to publish under the name of Paul or some other apostle a treatise, whether in
> the form of a letter or of something else, which the author sincerely believes to express the
> great man's teaching, or which he even believes to have been disclosed to him by the self-same
> Spirit which used the great man as his mouthpiece. It is quite another thing to fabricate for it a
> detailed framework of concrete personal allusions, reminiscences, and messages, not to mention
> outbursts of intensely personal feeling, which one knows to be pure fiction but which one puts
> together with the object of creating an air of verisimilitude[67].

Of course, it is my contention that the author did just that; in the interest
of deception he fabricated all the personal notes, all the fine moments of
deep piety, and all the careless but effective commonplaces in the letters.
Furthermore, ideas of inspiration offer no reprieve, since the pseudonymous author is normally under no delusions about ecstatic revelations
from the spirit. To the contrary, he is quite self-consciously employing
pseudonymity in order to deceive and, because of the necessity of avoid-
ing detection, he will use whatever effective means occur to him. Brox,
Speyer, Rist, and others have gathered convincing evidence from the general milieu of pseudepigraphy showing what extreme means were employed in the aggressive and bitter battles between factions in the world of
Greco-Roman religion and philosophy. But there is more evidence. The

---

recent commentary, *The Pastoral Epistles*, The New Century Bible Commentary (Grand Rapids,
Mich.: Wm. B. Eerdmans, 1982), pp. 10—11. For the best discussion of how the personalia can be
squared with pseudonymity see Brox, *Die Pastoralbriefe*, pp. 60—65, and "Zu den persönlichen
Notizen der Pastoralbriefe," *Biblische Zeitschrift* 13 (1969): 76—94. See also J. L. Houlden, *The
Pastoral Epistles*, Pelican New Testament Commentaries (New York: Penguin Books, 1976), pp.
32—35. But cf. the curiously ambiguous treatment by Dibelius-Conzelmann, *The Pastoral Epistles*,
pp. 127—28.
[66]2 Tim.4.11,12,16.
[67]Kelly, *The Pastoral Epistles*, p. 33.

particular genre of the pseudepigraphical letter displays in abundance the exact type of deception we find in the Pastorals. The careless references to mundance affairs of daily life, the specific requests for ordinary and seemingly insignificant objects to be delivered, and even the attempt to display personal feelings are all fully documented in other letters. It is to this evidence that we now turn. It will be obvious as the argument proceeds that no attempt to survey the entire field of Greco-Roman pseudepigraphical letters will be made. Rather the world of pseudepigraphical letters is seen through the eyes of the Pastorals and examples are engaged here only because they cast light on the situation of the Pastorals themselves. Thus a great deal of material is left out; in particular the pseudepigraphical letters incorporated into Jewish histories and apocalypses are not analyzed since they seem to have such different form and function from the Pastorals[68].

The twelfth and thirteenth letters of Plato display efforts at verisimilitude equal to that of the Pastorals, both containing detail which seems to have no philosophical, ideological, or historical intent, but which contributes to the appearance of genuineness[69]. The motivation behind *Epistle 12* is easier to ascertain than that of *Epistle 13,* since it seems to have been written to add credence and good reputation to certain false Platonic treatises which had come down through the hands of Archytas[69a]. In the letter Plato begins by acknowledging to Archytas the receipt of writings from him and then refers to a Trojan colony in Italy. It is likely that both of these remarks have absolutely no basis in fact and really do nothing to contribute to the ultimate argument of the author; they seem to be there merely to set the stage for Plato's concluding remarks.

> As to those treatises of mine about which you wrote, they are not as yet complete, but I have sent them to you just in the state in which they happen to be; as concerns their preservation we are both in accord, so there is no need to give directions.

The deception here is remarkable especially if we can presume that the forger of the letter is the present possessor of the false Platonic writings. Our forger first of all establishes the authenticity of the Platonic writings in his possession, but which he knows to be forged and in fact might even have forged himself, by having Plato declare that he has sent them to him even though they are unfinished. And if that is not enough, the

---

[68]See p. 14, n. 37.

[69]On the authenticity of the Platonic epistles see Wilamowitz-Möllendorff, "Unechte Briefe," and Norman Gully, "The Authenticity of the Platonic Epistles," in *Pseudepigrapha*, 1:105–30. Translations of the Platonic Epistles are from the Loeb Classical Library, trans. R. G. Bury. For a basic introduction see J. Harward, *The Platonic Epistles* (Cambridge: Cambridge University Press, 1932). Holger Thesleff, "Okkelos, Archytas, and Plato," *Eranos* 60 (1962): 8–36, claims that these letters were written by a Pythagorean in the second century in order to portray Plato's *Timaeus* and *Critias* as dependent on memoirs of Pythagorean teachings compiled by a Lucanian named Okkelos. The usual interpretation, Thesleff admits, is that the letters attempt to authenticate the false Okkelos tractate.

[69a]Diogenes Laertius 8.80.

forger then forestalls any objections about how such important documents could have remained unknown and intact all this time. He does this
not by describing how this has happened but by simply intimating that
Plato and Archytas had devised a method to preserve them. And with a
nice touch Plato remarks that, since they have already worked out the
details of this preservation, there is no need to discuss it further, thereby
saving the forger the difficult task of dreaming up a plausible explanation
for how the preservations might have been accomplished. Thus we get a
hint of how the difficult problem of publishing forgeries could be addressed[70], and in any case this constitutes one example of a forger who
was cognizant of the awkwardness of getting his pseudepigraphon before
the public, yet managed a workable solution. The motives of the author
of this pseudepigraphical letter are surprisingly easy to ascertain and the
techniques he utilizes in service of these motives are both unscrupulous
and effective. He wants to validate documents he knows are forged so he
writes another forgery. In his forged letter he includes apparent irrelevancies, which I assume are intended to mask his true motives by making his
crucial sentence appear to be just another offhand remark. He also adds a
clever bit of evidence to use against any accusation that no document of
such import could have remained unknown to everyone but Archytas.

The motives of the author of *Epistle 13* are not so easy to decipher, but
his techniques are remarkable. The letter reads like an expanded edition of
the personalia of the Pastorals, for it is all mundane, commonplace, and
personal. Philosophy and ideology are absent. Instead the letter portrays
Plato as submerged in the marketplace, worried about his and Dionysius'
finances, making offhand remarks about insignificant people, and arrang-
ing the transport of such momentous things as a jar of honey. If one is
forced to guess at the motives of the author, then one might assume it
wàs simply to describe Plato as concerned and competent in everyday
affairs and to provide some biographical detail about Plato to a public
which remained curious about the man[71]. Whatever his motives might
have been, his literary techniques are illuminating. The letter is nothing
but the mundane and personal, and a few quotes should suffice to demonstrate this.

> As regards the things you wrote me to send you, I have had the Apollo made and Leptines is
> bringing it to you. It is by a young and good craftsman named Leochares. He had at his shop
> another piece which was, as I thought, very artistic; so I bought it with the intention of present-
> ing it to your wife ...[72].

---

[70]Aland, "The Problem of Anonymity and Pseudonymity," p. 44, thinks the excessive awkwardness of pretending to have found an old document and the enormous difficulties in getting
the document published mitigates against any linkage of pseudonymity and deception. See also
Harrison, *The Problem of the Pastoral Epistles*, p. 12.

[71]See Harward, *The Platonic Epistles*, pp. 230–34, for a discussion of authenticity and the
possible motives suggested by various scholars.

[72]Plato *Epistle* 13.361a.

I am also sending you twelve jars of sweet wine for the children and two of honey. We arrived too late for the storing of the figs, and the myrtle-berries that were stored have rotted; but in the future we shall take better care of them. About the plants Leptines will tell you[73].

In this same mundane vein we encounter references to unimportant gifts being sent to unimportant people, such as a hoplite's corselet to Cratinus and three tunics of seven cubits to the daughters of Cebes[74]. At the end of the letter we recognize a concern for explaining how this irrelevant letter was preserved in the admonition to Dionysius to preserve the letter[75].

The Platonic letters are informative because they, like the Pastorals, are successful pseudepigrapha; they were believed by many to be geniune. They succeed due to the consummate skill of their authors in using apparently extraneous detail in the same way any person would employ such detail in a real letter to a friend. The detail does not attract attention because of any suspicious-looking ideological slant, rather the detail appears to be natural and unrehearsed. It is simple and therefore effective deception. While *Epistle 12* displays the motives of the author, *Epistle 13* displays technique. The latter is in fact superior to the Pastorals in versimilitude. The commonplaces and personalia are woven into a plausible and convincing portrait of everyday life which is much more extensive and complex than what the Pastorals manage. This makes the personalia of the Pastorals much less convincing as evidence of genuineness.

The *Epistles of Anacharsis* contain a few historical or legendary references to the life of Anacharsis but use them in remarkably different ways than the Platonic letters do[76]. Anacharsis, we read, was uncultured by Greek standards and had been categorized as a barbarian by the Athenians. The author of the pseudepigraphical letter of Anacharsis to the Athenians[77] uses this uncultured background of Anacharsis and the Athenians' elitist reaction to him to propagate his own Cynic notions about the irrelevancy of high culture. The letter begins by having Anacharsis recall to the Athenians that they laughed at his speech because he did not pronounce Greek correctly. After this quick historical reference the letter proceeds to argue about the difference between appearance and reality and the relativity of all culture. The crux of the argument is that "a speech is not poor if good intentions stand behind it and good actions follow upon the words. But the Scythians judge a speech poor only when its argument is poor." The manner in which the author slides from legendary events into philosophical discourse reveals the ultimate purpose of these letters: they are occasions for philosophical discourse. In most of the letters the author makes no pretense of an historical occasion inspiring the

---

[73]Ibid., 13.361b.
[74]Ibid., 13.363a.
[75]Ibid., 13.363e.
[76]For bibliography on *Epistles of Anacharsis* see Abraham J. Malherbe, *The Cynic Epistles*, Society of Biblical Literature Sources for Biblical Study 12 (Missoula, Mont.: Scholars Press 1977), pp. 6–9. Text, translation, and letter numbers are from Malherbe.
[77]*Epistles of Anacharsis* 1.

latter; instead he leaps right into philosophy and ethics[78]. Because of this overpowering concern for promulgating Cynic philosophy, the letters actually make little pretext of being real letters. In form and style they read more like epistles, as defined by Deissmann and as distinguished from letters[79]. Nevertheless, for our purposes they are still useful because they demonstrate how amenable the pseudepigraphical letter was for promulgating one's own ideas.

We find more of the same in the *Epistles of Crates*[80], where biographical and personal remarks do not seem to have the function so much of lending verisimilitude but of giving a context for praising and expounding Cynic philosophy. The letter to his wife, Hipparchia, quoted in full, is typical.

> Return quickly. You can still find Diogenes alive (for he is already near the end of his life; yesterday, at any rate, he all but expired) in order to greet him for the last time and to learn how much philosophy can do even in the most terrifying circumstances[81].

In this fashion everyday events are utilized only to illustrate philosophical truths. Furthermore, a slight change in technique is discovered in these letters. The character of the recipient of the letter is actually more important than that of the sender. The sender, in this case Crates, is simply portrayed as a Cynic philosopher without any striking peculiarities or idiosyncracies. As we shall see, it is not really possible to distinguish the doctrines of Crates from those of Anacharsis, Diogenes, or any other Cynic whose name appears on pseudepigraphical letters. If legend or history is used, it is only to spark discussion not to clarify the personal and unique doctrines of any particular author. Crates is just an empty vessel into which the author pours his own Cynic ideas.

Thus it is more the needs and biases of the pseudo-recipient which determine the subject matter of each individual letter. Crates writes to his students, to his wife, to the wealthy, to Diogenes, to the Athenians, and to many others; and in each case the letters contain philosophical remarks appropriate for the recipient. Therefore, when Crates writes to his students, he gives general instruction in the Cynic lifestyle[82], when he writes to Diogenes, he discusses the enslaving nature of fame[83], and when he writes to the wealthy, he greets them with "go hang yourself"[84]. Oc-

---

[78]Ibid., 3, 4, 5, 6, 7, 8 are all typical.

[79]Adolf Deissmann, *Light from the Ancient East*, trans. Lionel R. M. Strachan (Grand Rapids, Mich.: Baker Book House, 1978), pp. 227–33. But cf. analysis of William G. Doty, *Letters in Primitive Christianity* (Philadelphia: Fortress Press, 1973), pp. 1–19. Although Deissmann's categories have been proven to be imprecise, his original distinction between letters and epistles is still valid even if oversimplified.

[80]For bibliography see Malherbe, *The Cynic Epistles*, pp. 10–13. Text, translation, and letter numbers come from Malherbe.

[81]*Epistles of Crates* 1.

[82]Ibid., 2, 3, 5, 6, 11, 15, 16, 17.

[83]Ibid., 8.

[84]Ibid., 7.

casionally our author will create a specific situation as a pretended cause for Crates to write. The letter to Lysis is a good example. It begins, "I have heard, Lysis, that you have been constantly drunk ever since the contest in Eretria"[85]. From there, appropriately enough, Crates gives a discourse on the value of temperance (ἐγκράτεια).

The motivations behind this kind of pseudepigrapha are transparent; the author desires to address his Cynic notions to specific kinds of people and specific kinds of behavior. In order to do this, he employs the name of a famous Cynic philosopher who writes letters to people who happen to have the exact problem our author is worried about. We cannot honestly determine if he thought Crates himself would have said the same thing; but in any case he recognizes no distance between his own beliefs and those he attributes to Crates, since we discover no indications of the specific doctrines of Crates having any influence[86]. The genre of the pseudepigraphical letter enables the author to address whomever and whatever he wants without any strictures on his ideas but with the protection and glamor of a famous name. For instance, we can detect his wish to speak out on the poor conditions of ordinary people and the sad state of affairs in his own world when he addresses letters to cities as a whole and to whole classes of people[87]. Thus to the Athenians, he writes:

> I hear that you are in need of money. Therefore, sell your horses and you will have money. Then, whenever there is a need for horses, vote that your asses are horses. For this has become your custom in every matter: not to do what is proper for your needs but to do what has been voted upon[88].

The only time these letters make any real pretense towards verisimilitude is in the letters of Crates to Hipparchia, his wife[89]. For the most part the letters are like all the others in that they are primarily occasions for philosophic discourse and not greetings and conversation between friends, but several of the letters to Hipparchia go beyond expounding on the role of women in general and use a pretended event as the cause for the letter. On two occasions Crates writes because Hipparchia has sent him a tunic which she has woven for him.

> I am returning the tunic that you wove and sent to me because those of us who live a life of perseverance are forbidden to wear such things, and I do so in order that I may cause you to desist from this task you have undertaken with much zeal so that you might appear to the masses to be someone who loves her husband[90].

Of course, Crates moves from there into a reminder that he married her not to get a loving wife but for the sake of philosophy. Another letter to

---

[85]Ibid., 10.
[86]Malherbe, *The Cynic Epistles*, esp. pp. 10—11.
[87]See e.g., *Epistles of Crates* 7, 25, 26, 27.
[88]Ibid., 25.
[89]Ibid., 1, 28, 29, 30, 31, 32, 33.
[90]Ibid., 30. But cf. 32.

Hipparchia begins, "I hear that you have given birth"[91]. What follows however is not a tender exchange between husband and wife that the birth of a child might ordinarily evince, but again philosophy, in this case on the value of exercise during pregnancy and the proper treatment of infants. After all, philosophy is the sole reason these letters were created and detail is never extraneous, included merely for verisimilitude; it is always the springboard to philosophy. Nevertheless, we do notice that this author (or authors) does not hesitate to fabricate circumstances if he has any use for them.

The *Letters of Apollonius of Tyana*[92] are noteworthy for the wide variety of recipients. Most of the letters are sent to pretended disciples, but Apollonius also writes to the chief councillors of different cities, to Domitian, to philosophers of every stripe, to priests at assorted temples, to the Peloponnesians, to the presidents of the Olympic games, to rulers of various countries, to the Roman Quaestors, to a legislator, to the scribes of the Ephesians, to the Milesians, to the Platonists, to those who think they are wise, and to a multitude of others. The critical role played by the recipient is obviously highlighted in this collection. Furthermore, these letters do not pretend to epistolary style. They are normally quite short, consisting of a single saying or a few quick remarks, and they possess no marks of a real letter, for there is nothing in them but philosophy. Actually the determination and characterization of genre in these cases is quite complex, because both here and in some of the Platonic letters we might have genuine letters actually written by Apollonius or Plato mixed with the pseudepigraphical. If so, then we must assume a type of philosophical letter which eschewed personal detail and which contained nothing but philosophy and ethics. Therefore, a forger could fabricate a letter which also lacked personal detail and still be attempting to make his letter look real. In any case, we have in the *Letters of Apollonius* further evidence for the critical role of the pseudo-recipient.

The *Epistles of Diogenes*[93] contain a particularly fine example of how choosing the right recipient allows the author to address those philosophical problems closest to his own heart. What could be better for a Cynic than the opportunity to compose a letter from Diogenes to Alexander the Great or to Plato? In the latter case, of course, Diogenes and Plato are not talking but our author, a Cynic philosopher, and contemporary Platonists.

> You scorn my rough cloak and wallet as though they were burdensome and difficult, and my way of life as of no benefit, doing no good. Now they are burdensome and difficult to you, for you learned to take your fill without moderation from the tables of a tyrant, and to adorn

---

[91]Ibid., 33.

[92]Text and translation in Philostratus, *The Life of Apollonius*, trans. F. C. Conybeare, Loeb Classical Library, 2:408–81. See Robert J. Penella, *The Letters of Apollonius of Tyana*, (Leiden: E. J. Brill, 1979).

[93]For bibliography see Malherbe, *The Cynic Epistles*, pp. 14–21. Text, translation, and letter numbers come from Malherbe.

yourself with the bellies of sheep, but not with the virtue of the soul. But as for me, as I practiced these things with virtue ...[94].

Although this particular letter to Plato has no basis in fact or legend, the
life of Diogenes was filled with shadowy, potentially fascinating events
which were a perfect breeding ground for pseudepigraphy. Of course, the
best known is the encounter between Diogenes and Alexander which in-
spires two letters from Diogenes to Alexander and a third to Phanomachus
which recounts the meeting in detail[95]. We also have a legendary account
of a meeting between Diogenes and Socrates in which Socrates bestows
upon Diogenes the meager vessels required for a true philosopher, namely,
the double cloak, the wallet, a cup, a bowl, and a staff, along with instructions appropriate to each item[96]. In all these cases the genre of the letter
drifts towards that of biography, for not only are the specific fabrications
of the author accomplished more in the interest of legend and historical
detail and less towards the verisimilitude of a letter, but also this biographical material in its own way promulgates philosophy and needed instruction. The role of imitation in Greco-Roman philosophy is well documented; and these philosophic letters reflect the pervasiveness of the concept in their recollections and, in some cases, fabrication of events from
the lives of these great men. As the letter of Crates to Aper declares, "But
if the life of Socrates and Diogenes pleases you leave the writings of the
tragic poets to others and devote yourself to emulating those men (σαυτὸν
ἐπάνηκε ἐπὶ τὸν ἐκείνων ʹ ζῆλον)"[97]. Of course, all this closely parallels
the fascination of the Pastorals with the life of Paul.

One further observation on the *Epistles of Diogenes* should be made,
although a full discussion of this phenomenon will be postponed until
later. The letters contain two curious, and apparently contradictory, remarks on the function of a letter. Writing to Hipparchia, Diogenes encourages her to write, "for letters are worth a great deal and are not inferior to
conversation with people actually present (δύναται γὰρ αἱ ἐπιστολαὶ πολλὰ
καὶ οὐχ ἥττονα τῆς πρὸς παρόντας διαλέξεως)"[98]. But elsewhere, writing to Antalcides, he says,

Letters might preserve the memory of those who are no longer alive, but would not reveal the
virtue of those alive but not present (ἃ μνήμας μὲν ἂν σώζοι τῶν οὐκ ὄντων, ἀρετῆς δὲ
ζώντων καὶ οὐ παρόντων οὐκ ἂν εἴη δηλωτικά). I am obliged to write this to you, so that you
will not address me through inanimate means (ἀψύχων), but will be present in person (παρὼν
αὐτός)[99].

The discussion hinges upon how well letters substitute for the actual
presence of a person. At this point, we need only remark that letters ob-

---

[94]*Epistles of Diogenes* 46.
[95]Ibid., 24, 40, 33.
[96]Ibid., 30. 3.
[97]*Epistles of Crates* 35.
[98]*Epistles of Diogenes* 3.
[99]Ibid., 17.

viously desired to stand in place of the author, to present his or her thoughts or character by way of the written word. It appears there was some debate on how well a letter could actually do this.

The *Epistles of Heraclitus*[100] have little new to add though they reinforce some of our observations. We witness again the quick elevation of a minor event into philosophy, when a discussion of disease suddenly becomes one of the superiority of the soul to the body[101]; and we recognize the importance of the recipient's character in the exchange of letters between Heraclitus and King Darius[102]. But the most fascinating moment in these letters is the forced apology for Heraclitus in the letter to Hermodorus[103]. Heraclitus had apparently been accused of impiety because he erected an altar and wrote his own name on it, thus making himself a god. The letter responds with a brief digression on the folly of idols but then rewrites the story in order to excuse Heraclitus of the crime.

> I enscribed on the altar the words "Heracles the Ephesian," not "Heraclitus," thus making the god your fellow citizen ('Ηρακλεῖ ἐπέγραψα τῷ 'Εφεσίῳ τὸν βωμὸν πολιτογραφῶν ὑμῖν τὸν θεόν, οὐχ 'Ηρακλείτῳ)[104].

From that point the letter moves to philosophy, but the intentions and concerns of the author are manifest: he is trying to alter a bad story about Heraclitus in order to rescue him from the calumniations it attracted. It would be extraordinarily difficult to argue that our author believed his reworked account was true. At best, we might imagine that the author found the original story unconscionable (intimating thereby the great softening in the attitude towards religion and the gods by later Cynics), assumed there must be some mistake and some plausible explanation for this impossible story, and then devised this rather clever changing of the name from Heraclitus to Heracles. But whatever his thinking might have been, it is clearly a case of juggling accounts in order to deceive.

The Pythagorean letters illustrate the use of mundane and realistic events as the pretended occasion for letters and as platforms for philosophical discourse[105]. For instance, the letter of Theano to Eubule begins with Theano claiming to have heard that Eubule is spoiling her children. The letter then gives a discourse on child-rearing. Theano's letter to Nikostrate begins with the note that Nikostrate's husband is mad, moves into an analysis of marriage, and finally gives advice on how to survive hard times. We find the use of trivial events and realistic detail in the discussion of a

---

[100]For bibliography see Malherbe, *The Cynic Epistles*, pp. 22–26. Text, translation, and letter numbers come from Malherbe.

[101]*Epistles of Heraclitus* 5.

[102]Ibid., 1, 2, (3).

[103]Ibid., 4.

[104]Ibid., 4.2.

[105]On the Pythagorean letters see Städele, *Die Briefe des Pythagoras und der Pythagoreer*, and Thesleff, *An Introduction to the Pythagorean Writings of the Hellenistic Period* and *The Pythagorean Texts of the Hellenistic Period*, Acta Academiae Aboensis, Humaniora, Ser. A., Vol. 30, no. 1 (Åbo: Åbo Akademi, 1965).

broken bed in the letter of Theano to Eukleides, the doctor, and in the concern over Plato's book, entitled "Ideas or Parminides," in Theano's letter to the philosopher Rhodope. Both of these letters also use the character of the pretended recipient creatively by addressing questions of health to a doctor and comments about a Platonic book to a philosopher. Melissa's letter to Klearata and Myia's to Phyllis address peculiarly feminine problems by having one woman write another. In the former Melissa discusses the difficulties of a woman being a philosopher; in the latter the occasion of Phyllis giving childbirth elicits a discourse on motherhood. Finally, we must note the strong paradigmatic role Pythagoras plays in his letter to Hieron. He is portrayed as the ideal philosopher. There were hints of this phenomenon in the letters by Anacharsis, Crates, Diogenes, and Heraclitus. Crates in particular appears to be portrayed as an ideal. But 'Pythagoras' aggressive claim in this letter of possessing αὐτάρκεια clearly puts him in the special category of being a wise man. The idealization of the pretended author and the concomitant use of the author as an ethical paradigm, which is only lightly drawn here, becomes a major method of argumentation in the Socratic letters and, as we shall see, in the Pastorals.

The *Epistles of Socrates and the Socratics*[106] expand both the biographical interest and the attempt to make the letters look like real letters. Thus we encounter long, novelistic, rather prosaic recollections about Socrates' life as well as a multitude of extraneous detail and mundane, trivial information appropriate to unpretentious private letters between friends. In short the letters are personal; Socrates refers constantly to both the minutiae and notabilia of his own life and to those of family and friends; people are depicted travelling back and forth between cities; people send greetings to one another; and people express apparently genuine affection for one another. Of course, the letters paint this realistic scene primarily as a backdrop for their higher goal of promulgating Cynic philosophy, and therefore we rarely find instances of pure isolated personalia but of personalia which drifts easily and logically into philosophical comment. The personalia and other devices of verisimilitude not only lend credence to the genuineness of the letters but also provide an immediate, lifelike context for philosophical analysis.

Nevertheless, there are some examples of personal remarks and extraneous detail which seem to have no purpose other than to create an aura of real life in the letters.

I gave Euphron of Megara six measures of barley meal and eight drachma and a new coat for you so that you can make it through the winter[107].
I do not yet have any of the things to send to Syracuse which you said that Archytas wanted to receive from you. But we shall send them to you very soon[108].

---

106 For bibliography see Malherbe, *The Cynic Epistles*, pp. 27—34. Text, translation and letter numbers come from Malherbe.
107 *Epistles of Socrates and the Socratics* 21.1.
108 Ibid., 24.1.

But I do not have enough paper to write down the rest of his excuses, such a scarcity of paper did the king create for us by taking Egypt[109].

I will send you large white lupines so that you will have something to eat[110].

Put away some dried figs so that you might have some for the winter, and get some Cretan bread, for these things seem to be better than money, and both bathe and drink from the Nine Sprouts, and wear the same filthy cloak summer and winter, as is fitting for a free man living democratically in Athens[111].

The last citation illustrates how easily insignificant detail is suddenly given significance by placing it in a philosophical context. This same tension between using something for its effectiveness in creating an atmosphere of real life and using the same thing as an occasion for philosophic discourse is noticeable in the numerous personal greetings and references to named people. Sometimes proper names are employed simply to display Socrates as an ordinary if virtuous person with many friends.

Apollodorus, who is called the mad-man, and Dio praise you[112].

Send Philistion and strengthen me in whatever manner you can[113].

Xanthippe and the children are doing well[114].

Your son Gryllus has already sent Geta to you, who told you everything that happened to Socrates during the trial and at his death[115].

As things are now well with you, your family affairs in Athens, too, are according to God's will. Write us again about your bodily health, for we know that because of your understanding and virtue you are healthy in soul. And if you need anything that is yours, write us, for my possessions, Plato, are by all rights yours, even as they were Socrates'[116].

You wrote to me that since you did not wish to cause me grief, you concealed that you are about to move further away, but by Zeus the Olympian, I am beginning to miss you[117].

And I have written to both my son Gryllus and to my friend to help you if you need anything. I wrote to Gryllus, seeing that already during your childhood you used to attach yourself to him, and used to express your love for him[118].

Therefore, accept these things and know that Eucleides and Terpsion are very good and noble men who have good will toward both you and Socrates. When the children should want to come to us, do not stop them, for the trip to Megara is not long. And let the abundance of tears you have shed suffice[119].

For as long as I and the other friends have the power to help you, you will lack nothing[120].

In fact, the majority of the letters in the Socratic collection contain personal references of some sort whether they are benign and are used only for verisimilitude or they are specific occasions for philosophical comment. We obviously cannot cite them all here, but it is sufficient to add to the

---

[109] Ibid., 28.14.
[110] Ibid., 9.4.
[111] Ibid., 9.2.
[112] Ibid., 21.3.
[113] Ibid., 33.3.
[114] Ibid., 4.
[115] Ibid., 14.1.
[116] Ibid., 26.2.
[117] Ibid., 25.1.
[118] Ibid., 19.
[119] Ibid., 21.1.
[120] Ibid., 21.3.

above examples the note that several letters contain nothing but such personal remarks and seem to have no other purpose than simply display-ing friendship and hospitality on the part of the author[121]. The short letter of Socrates to Xenophon, quoted here in full, exemplifies this.

> You are not ignorant of the care I have bestowed on Chaerophon and now he has been chosen by the city as ambassador to the Peloponnesus, and he will probably come also to you. Hospi-tality (τὰ τῶν ξενίων) is easily supplied to a philosopher; but travel conditions are unsafe, espe-cially now, because of the troubles which have arisen there. If you take care of him, you will have both saved a friend and also shown the greatest kindness to me[122].

No hidden philosophical agenda can be detected in letters such as this; apparently they were created simply to display the Socratics as warm, friendly people.

However, it is possible that later debate and animosity among the philosophical schools encouraged the use of these personal notes for more aggressive purposes. Certain people needed to be placed correctly; either on Socrates' side or not. In reference to Socrates' death we read:

> And the friends who were present with him when he died were myself [Aeschines], Terpsion, Apollodorus, Phaedo, Antisthenes, Hermogenes, and Ctesippus. But Plato, Cleobrotus, and Aristippus did not come; for Plato was ill and both of the others were in Aegina[123].

Similary the elaborate commendation given to some people in the letters may be intended to raise their stock with later generations.

> Greet Simon the shoemaker and commend him, because he continues to devote himself to the teachings of Socrates and uses neither his poverty nor his trade as a pretext for not doing phil-osophy, as certain others do who do not want to understand fully or to admire Socrates' teach-ings and their contents[124].
>
> Antipater who brings this letter is a native of Magnesia, but he has for some time in Athens been writing a Greek history. He says that he has been unjustly treated by someone in Magne-sia. Therefore listen carefully to his story and help him as actively as you can. ... The bearer of this letter was the only person who first gave credible accounts about the land of the Oly-thians[125].
>
> I thought I should write you about my physical condition, and also because I think that if you come to the Academy you will keep the School together. ... He [Plato] confirmed at his death that he held you in high regard. He enjoined all of us who belong to his household, if something should happen to you, to bury you next to thim, for he thought that you would not at all sep-arate yourself from the Academy[126].

On the other hand, we may be seeing the shadows of ancient debates in the occasional calumniations[127]. Simon begins a vitriolic and sarcastic ex-change of letters with Aristippus with the words, "I hear that you ridicule our wisdom in the presence of Dionysius"[128]. Simon then admits that he

---

121 Ibid., 2, 3, 4, 10, 11.
122 Ibid., 2.
123 Ibid., 14.9.
124 Ibid., 18.2.
125 Ibid., 28.1.
126 Ibid., 30.1,2.
127 See e.g., ibid., 14.1; 28.
128 Ibid., 12.

is a lowly shoemaker who must cut straps of leather for his shoes, adding pointedly that he would gladly cut some more straps to admonish foolish men who purport to be following the precepts of Socrates but actually live in luxury. In his own letter Aristippus replies sarcastically that he in fact admires Simon since he used to persuade such wonderful men as Socrates and others to sit with him and even today attracts the company of Antisthenes[129]. Further Simon should in fact prefer him to Antisthenes, since he is a wearer of shoes and thus makes Simon's profession something to be admired, while Antisthenes goes about barefooted and persuades others to do so and thus makes Simon idle and without income. This same Aristippus emerges again as a rather benign antagonist in a fanciful debate among Aeschines, Dionysius, and Plato in the marketplace of Syracuse[130]. Aristippus gets Aeschines, the writer of the letter, a favorable hearing by Dionysius for one of his writings, but after the reading, Plato, who was also present, admits to Aeschines that when Aristippus is present he, Plato, hesitates to speak freely. Aeschines ends the letter by recalling that he admonished Plato and Aristippus to stop their jesting ($\pi\alpha\iota\delta\iota\dot{\alpha}$). It becomes clear from this that our author could not completely overcome the historical animosity among certain of his Cynic predecessors, although he tries mightily to depreciate the severity by calling it $\pi\alpha\iota\delta\iota\dot{\alpha}$. We might surmise that the author is trying to smooth over all the disagreements in the Socratic school (which includes Cynics and Platonists) but that all appearances of genuineness would be sacrificed if he wrote letters which ignored or contradicted well-known disagreements. The ability to transform the face of history without giving oneself away as a forger takes a delicate touch and we will see the same struggle in the Pastorals.

The one overwhelming impression created by the Socratic letters is that the original circle of Socrates' disciples had deep affection for one another and managed lives which were intricately intertwined with one another. More important than any specific remarks in the letters for producing this impression is the simple existence of friendly letters written by members of the Socratic school to one another. In this way the letters make Xenophon, for instance, an unmistakable hero not by calling him one in so many words but simply by having him receive friendly letters from Socrates and send friendly letters to others in the Socratic circle[131]. A philosophical pantheon is created by the rather straightforward act of affixing the correct names as senders and recipients of these letters.

The frequency and effectiveness with which the Socratic letters employ the pseudepigraphical devices of extraneous detail and personal references vitiate any arguments about the Pastorals which insist that no pseudepi-

---

[129] Ibid., 13.

[130] Ibid., 23.

[131] Xenophon is recipient in *Epistles of Socrates and the Socratics* 2, 5, 14 and sender in 15, 18, 19.

graphical letter could contain such mundane remarks about parchments and winter cloaks or such intimate greetings among friends. In fact, the scale on which the aura of verisimilitude is carried out in the Socratic letters makes the Pastorals look rather tame. And since the personalia and even the extraneous detail can be used for purposes other than verisimilitude when the occasion warrants, the naming of friends and enemies in the Pastorals might well be done in order to draw careful lines among the author's contemporaries. The author of the Pastorals may be creating his own leadership pantheon in all the personal greetings in his letters.

Most of the personal situations manufactured in the Socratic letters go beyond building an artifice of real life and provide contexts for philosophical discussion. Aristippus' letter to his daughter, Arete, illustrates how skillfully these letters can manage the interplay between a private discussion and general philosophic ethics[132]. Aristippus writes a moving response to his daughter's request that he return immediately to Cyrene, which never ventures beyond what a father would say to his daughter and yet which succeeds in becoming paradigmatic for a general public. Aristippus apologizes for his delay, excusing himself because he has become ill; but then he slips in a stunning remark which indicates how sick he actually is when he gives advice to her on how to take care of his will. Suddenly the letter becomes a farewell from father to daughter. He gives fatherly advice about her husband, notes that she is financially secure because of the two gardens and the property in Berenice, and suggests that she might go live with Xanthippe, Socrates' wife, just as he used to live so pleasantly with Socrates himself. Finally, about children, he encourages her to share her goods with Lamprocles, the son of Socrates, if he comes to Cyrene, and to treat him as her own son. In order to get help raising children she might adopt the daughter of Eubois, "whom you called by my mother's name, Mika, when you wanted to please her, indeed, I too, often called her Mika." Most of all he adjures her to take care of little Aristippus "so that he may be worthy of us and of philosophy. That is the real inheritance I leave him ... ." The letter ends with a gentle admonition to follow the philosophic life.

> But concerning philosophy you have not written me that anyone has robbed you of it. So, my good woman, rejoice greatly in the wealth which you have accumulated and make your son, whom I would like to have as my own, its possessor. Since I shall die without enjoying him, I trust you will guide him on a course of life that is customary for good men. Farewell, and do not be distressed about us.

This touching forgery stays within the natural confines of a farewell letter from father to daughter, but at the same time becomes paradigmatic for all parents. Provide adequate financial options for your children, though not necessarily luxury, monitor the familial relationships and give gentle

---

[132] Ibid., 27.

advice about them, and most of all encourage your children towards the philosophic life, which is the only life worth living.

The major pedagogical tool of the Socratic letters, which is even more frequently used than direct ethical admonitions, is the proffering of biographical sketches as paradigms for virtuous behavior[133]. Socrates himself naturally provides the usual subject for these studies, but all of the Socratics who appear in the letter corpus do so in paradigmatic fashion, as we noticed above with Aristippus. In one letter an unnamed Lacedaemonian youth is even used as a contrast to the evil behavior of Anytus and Meletus, who championed the accusations against Socrates at his trial[134]. This Lacedaemonian out of love for Socrates journeys to Athens only to discover that Socrates has been put to death. In remorse he found the grave, wept over it, slept over it through the night, and kissed it repeatedly the next morning. When the Athenians learn of his devotion and compare it to the despicable deeds of Anytus and Meletus they are so filled with regret over Socrates' death that they execute Anytus and Meletus. Thus the letter imagines them coming to their senses about Socrates by seeing the two possible attitudes to him embodied in the two paradigmatic models: the Lacedaemonian youth embodies piety and devotion to Socrates and Anytus and Meletus embody enmity and evil. The point being that one learns by witnessing good behavior in others (Ἐκίνησε δὲ αὐτοὺς μάλιστα καὶ τὸ τοῦ νεανίσκου τοῦ λακεδαιμονίου πάθος).

It is with this pedagogical model in mind that Socrates' life and death are constantly called upon in these letters. In one sense Socrates becomes an empty vessel into which Cynic virtues are poured; but in another sense his historical or legendary implacability in the face of death and disdain towards the normal human affection for ease, wealth, fame, and power have exerted an irresistable influence on all subsequent Cynic doctrines. This tension between fidelity to accurate memories of the historical Socrates and the need to portray him as a modern Cynic underlies all the biographical references to him. After all, it was not just historical curiosity which encouraged repetition of his virtues in life and death but also a desire to discern in him virtues that could be emulated.

Aeschines' letter to Xenophon[135] rehearses the events of Socrates' death in a way that teaches subsequent generations the essential virtue of the philosophic life. The letter begins by creating a real life situation as the context for the letter: Xenophon, engaged in a military expedition, has missed Socrates' trial and death, and although his son Gryllus has already sent word to him, Aeschines repeats the events from his point of view. He begins with an excoriation of Anytus and Meletus,

---

[133]See Fiore, "The Function of Personal Example in the Socratic and Pastoral Epistles," pp. 182–303.

[134]*Epistles of Socrates and the Socratics* 17.3.

[135]Ibid., 14.

these two abominable men [who] persisted in wickedness until the end of things, and when we
thought that they were ashamed of their wiles, and had stopped, they proceeded to inflict still
more evil upon us.

Once their horrible behavior has been enumerated and condemned, Aeschines proceeds to recount the incredible and admirable demeanor of Socrates throughout the trial. We learn that Socrates smiled throughout and
could have been acquitted if he had taken recourse to flattery or entreaty
but opted instead to speak truthfully and justly, and in so doing actually
condemned his accusers.

And after he had been condemned, he went out laughing, and during the time he was in prison,
he enjoyed conversing with us even more than before. ... And for that reason, he used to say
that prison where he found himself and his chains forced him to practice philosophy, "for,"
he said, "I was always distracted in the marketplace by certain people."

Socrates' demeanor was so convivial that his admirers would often forget
that he was in prison and so would forcefully try to remind themselves
that these were unhappy circumstances. Socrates, of course, rebuked their
sadness. In fact, so many beautiful things did Socrates say and so much
contentment did he show in the face of death that "we could no longer
weep for Socrates because he was about to die, but we rather envied him
and wept for ourselves." The final lesson being that

the philosopher does nothing other than to die, since he disdains the demands of the body and
is not enslaved by the pleasure of the body; and this is nothing other than the separation of the
soul from the body, and death is nothing other than the separation of the soul from the body.
And in this he was very persuasive.

This same utilization of Socrates' behavior as a paradigm is even more
apparent in the letters ostensibly written by Socrates himself. For instance,
in a letter which pretends to be written in response to a request by an unnamed ruler that Socrates come help him rule in return for promised
money, material goods, and power, Socrates not only responds by saying
to this ruler that he could not know Socrates at all if he thinks that he
would teach for money, but also uses the occasion to condemn in no uncertain terms those philosophers who do teach for financial reward[136]. A
reader is thus presented with a choice of being like Socrates or like those
he condemns — both possibilities are presented. In this same letter we encounter a series of biographical allusions which teach the reader that there
is no other reasonable course in life than to do whatever task God (ὁ
θεός) has assigned you. Socrates insists that he cannot leave Athens because God has placed him there and "he knows better than I what is
sound (τὸ ὑγιές), seeing that when I asked about going to you, he forbade
me to go." To disobey the will of God is to court disaster and Socrates
recalls an event from his own life to illustrate the point. When he was a
participant in the battle of Delium, he was in retreat with a large company

---

[136]Ibid., 1. Surely this letter has in mind Plato's aborted stay in Syracuse.

when his "daimon" warned him against a certain route. Most of the company became angry and treated his warning to them as a joke and took that route anyway. They soon encountered the enemy cavalry in pursuit and all were destroyed. The reader is left to draw his own conclusions, but Socrates himself remained in Athens and did not cross his "daimon" this time either.

Again we can see the pedagogical function of Socrates' life in a letter in which he responds to certain criticisms the recipient has made about his poverty and insufficient monetary provisions for his family[137]. The letter begins with a quick note displaying Socrates' hospitality. "I have taken care of the two visitors, as you urged me to do, and I have sought out one of our companions who will plead their cause before the people." Then Socrates argues that one must expect people to make fun of his poverty because his life is so contrary to what most people want. He constantly refuses gifts and "it is not surprising that other people consider one who is thus inclined to be insane." After all, philosophers are different in so many ways from ordinary persons.

> I am satisfied to have the plainest food and the same garment summer and winter, and I do not wear shoes at all, nor do I desire political fame except to the extent that it comes from being prudent and just. But those who pursue the luxurious life forego nothing in their diet, and they seek to wear different garments not only during the same year, but even in the same day, and they take great delight in forbidden pleasures.

We have two contrasting lifestyles, but only one can make you happy (εὐδαιμονία), for only one can make you self-sufficient (αὐτάρκης) like the gods. The life of poverty as exemplified in Socrates is the only happy life. Socrates then denies that he has not provided well for his children, for he has provided them friends who can take care of them emotionally and financially and most of all he has given them encouragement towards the philosophic life. After all his sole hope for his children is to bequeath them right thinking (φρονεῖν εὖ). We have seen this kind of argument before in Aristippus' letter to his daughter: bequeath philosophy, not wealth, to your children.

On numerous occasions the letters expressly admit to holding the pedagogical theory of imitation of great people, but this is not surprising since this was such a common Greco-Roman point of view.

> And it is indeed reasonable that he is wise who copies himself after the wisest, and he is happiest who assimilates himself as much as possible to one who is happy (καίτοι σοφώτερόν τε εἶναι εἰκός, ὅστις ἑαυτὸν ἀπεικάζει τῷ σοφωτάτῳ... τῷ μακαρίῳ)[138].
> We must truly become good men and praise him because he lived wisely, devoutly, and piously (ἐβίωσε σωφρόνως καὶ ὁσίως καὶ εὐσεβῶς), but we must also accuse and blame fortune and those who conspired against him[139].
> So, take courage, Xanthippe, and do not discard any of the good instruction of Socrates, since

---

[137] Ibid., 6.
[138] Ibid., 6.4.
[139] Ibid., 15.1.

you know how important that man was to us, and meditate on how he lived and how he died (ἐπινοεῖ αὐτὸν ὁποῖα ἔζησε καὶ ὁποῖα ἐτελεύτησε). On my part, I think even his death was great and noble, if one views it in the way one should[140].
Indeed, he says in his Rhetoric that one should present family members and well-known persons as examples (παραδείγματα) but then he neglects the rule and uses strangers and the most wicked men as examples ...[141].

The pseudepigraphical techniques in the Socratic letters have proven to be diverse and sophisticated. A complex artifice is structured by depicting Cynic philosophers writing warm, encouraging, and frequent letters to one another. The letters create the appearance of the first Cynic philosophers belonging to one enlarged family, treating each other lovingly, almost as brothers and sisters, and taking on one another's burdens as their own, whether that burden was financial, political, or personal. They even treated each other's children as their own. The techniques used to paint this beguiling portrait have been noted above. They greet each other by name; they refer casually and innocently to mundane affairs; they carry out each other's commissions; friendship, concern, and love are penned into the letters; they share the intimate details of their own lives; and they discuss the philosophic life. All this transcends the efforts at fabricating a milieu and style for the letters which makes them appear genuine, though it does that as well, because the personalia and detail are integral elements in the philosophical and ethical promulgations of the letters. If Socrates was implacable and even happy in the fact of death, so should you be also; in fact, this castigates your agitation in the face of less terrifying events than death. When you see how the first Socratics managed the philosophic life, learn from them, and manage your own endeavors the same way. If you want the best life, study the lives of the best people, watch how they lead the virtuous life, do the same, and you will be happy.

The letters were written to propagate the philosophic life. All the techniques of pseudepigraphy are directed toward that task. Socrates himself was perceived as a rare gem, an instance of the perfect philosopher, whose life was unique for its virtue. It would be a terrible tragedy to lose or forget or tarnish that gem. Thus Socrates' style of living was paradigmatic and even canonical for later Cynics. He is the Jesus and Paul of Cynic circles; whatever he did was prescriptive and philosophically impeccable and, moreover, whatever is correct in today's philosophy was already anticipated and perfectly embodied in him. The task of later Cynics, our authors, was to preserve, and perhaps interpret, a perfect record of this perfect man.

I think that we certainly need to record what that man [Socrates] said and did. And this would be the best apology for him, both for now and the future, if instead of contending in a court of law; we rather set forth his life and virtue for all time (ἀλλ' εἰς ἅπαντα τὸν βίον παρατιθέντων τὴν ἀρετὴν τἀνδρός). And I say that we shall do an injustice to our common friendship and, as he said, truth, if we do not willingly write about him[142].

140Ibid., 21.3.
141Ibid., 28.10.

But this is not an easy task. It takes a skillful hand and, more, it takes an orthodox hand.

> But as to my writings, I do not yet have anything of the sort that I would have the confidence to show to others without being there myself. ... It is impossible to take back a writing once it has reached the hands of the public. Truly, Plato is able to have great influence through his writings. ... I must think about Socrates, that he not be endangered by my doing a poor job of describing his virtue in the Memorabilia. And I believe that it makes no difference whether one defames someone directly or writes things which seem to be unworthy of the virtue of the one he is writing about[143].

Socrates' reputation must be protected against all traducements, rescued from incompetent or unorthodox hands, and promulgated as the one reliable paradigm from which every philosopher can learn. We must wonder if the author of the Pastorals is not doing the same thing with Paul's reputation in his letters.

C. The Pseudepigraphical Letter in Early Christianity

Although the techniques employed in the Greco-Roman pseudepigraphical letters and the expressed purposes, such as proffering models adequate for imitation, parallel the techniques and purposes of New Testament pseudepigraphical letters, it is not until we move into the domain of Christian pseudepigraphy that we can recognize at first glance that a non-canonical pseudepigraphon and a canonical one belong to the same genre. This is so in large part because the raw material is suddenly the same. When we enter the world of Christian literature, differences in language and subject matter from one document to another are minimized, because everyone is dependent upon a common heritage, even if that heritage contains diversity. Therefore, even when we encounter a rather facile pseudepigraphon like the *Epistle to the Laodiceans* the affinity in form with the Pastorals is manifest and unmistakable.

Schneemelcher considers the *Epistle to the Laodiceans* a clumsy forgery, the purpose of which is simply to fill out a gap in the Pauline corpus created by the mention of a letter to the Laodiceans in Col. 4.16[144]. He regards Quispel's efforts to perceive even minor literary pretentions in the letter as giving far too much credit to the "worthless patching together of Pauline passages and phrases"[145]. Finally with a devaluation of the letter of this magnitude he confesses amazement that the letter ever survived in Christian manuscripts.

142Ibid., 15.2.

143Ibid., 22.1, 2.

144Schneemelcher, "The Epistle to the Laodiceans," in *New Testament Apocrypha* 2:131.

145Knopf-Krüger, quoted by Schneemelcher, *New Testament Apocrypha* 2:129. On Quispel see p. 131.

But Schneemelcher's refusal to admit any literary pretensions and his insistence that the letter has no theological purpose are overdone. The letter enjoyed considerable dissemination among Latin-speaking Christians and may have lost its canonical status only because of a mistaken identification with a Marcionite letter of the same name[146]. In any event, the simplicity of form and the undeniable prosaism of the theology enable us to perceive clearly the purpose of the letter.

The letter imitates and in fact quotes the Pauline language from Philippians and Galatians[147]. It contains two major admonitions: beware of heretics and devote yourself to the ethical life. In support of these two expressed hopes the letter enlists the authority of Paul's unique reputation. Other than affixing his name to the letter and quoting or paraphrasing his known letters, the letter also refers casually to Paul's suffering. Paul's joy and perseverance in the face of suffering becomes the single biographical detail which recurs in the pseudo-Pauline corpus, as the Pastorals themselves illustrate. Unless we are compelled to dismiss as misleading the explicit statements of the letter itself for reason of their mundaneness, which of course we are not, then the letter states clearly what its purpose is. Heterodoxy is undermining the tranquility and morality of the church and the author avails himself of the power of Paul's reputation by way of the common device of pseudonymity in order to admonish his readers to orthodoxy and morality. That the letter is executed without much intensity or any profundity not only explains why the letter dropped out of consideration for canonical status without much of a struggle but also illustrates how an orthodox Christian could take recourse to the good lie of a pseudepigraphon without much cause and with little genuine effort.

The battle between orthodoxy and heterodoxy noticed above receives a more sophisticated treatment in *3 Corinthians* in the *Acts of Paul*[148]. This letter of Paul to the Corinthians is in response to a letter they sent him questioning the orthodoxy of Simon and Cleobius who have come into their company teaching new things (or so the fiction goes).

> Two men are come to Corinth, named Simon and Cleobius, who pervert the faith of many through pernicious words, which you shall put to the test. For never have we heard such words, either from you or from the other apostles; but what we have received from you and from them, we hold fast. ... Do you write or come to us.

Heterodox teachers are depicted as having arrived in Corinth. The Corinthians respond to their presence with impeccable behavior; they hold only

---

146The *Muratorian Canon* reads, "There is current also [an epistle] to the Laodiceans, another to the Alexandrians, forged in Paul's name for the sect of Marcion, and several others, which cannot be received in the catholic Church; for it will not do to mix gall with honey" (*New Testament Apocrypha* 1:44).

147See list of quotes and allusions provided by Schneemelcher in notes to text (ibid., 2:131–32).

148*Acts of Paul*, trans. R. McL. Wilson, in *New Testament Apocrypha* 2:322–89, esp. 374–77.

to what they have heard already from Paul. That the teaching of Simon and Cleobius is heterodox is clear.

> We must not, they say, appeal to the prophets, and that God is not almighty, and that there is no resurrection of the flesh, and that the creation of man is not God's, and that the Lord is not come in the flesh, nor was he born of Mary, and that the world is not of God, but of angels. Wherefore, brother, make speed to come hither.

Just as in the Cynic and Socratic letters where an imaginary situation is created as the occasion for philosophical analysis, this arrival of heterodox teachers and the appeal by the Corinthians moves Paul, being in prison and unable to come in person (luckily), to write a letter, which is the next best thing to his being there. Paul's letter to the Corinthians typifies the widespread retreat to apostolic authority and established doctrinal tradition whenever confronted with any creative theological speculation. The Corinthians themselves behave paradigmatically, for when faced with doctrinal uncertainty they take recourse to apostolic authority. Paul's letter reiterates in various ways the wisdom of this attitude. The heart of the argument in the letter is the assertion that the apostles delivered the full message in the beginning; there is nothing new to be said about Christian theology. "For I delivered to you in the beginning what I received from the apostles who were before me, who at all times were together with the Lord Jesus Christ"[149]. The letter then repeats an orthodox version of salvation history[150], or at least what our author thought was orthodox, with some regard for answering the specific propositions of Simon and Cleobius. What will prove to be important for us is not just that a rather tame and non-speculative version is given, but that the author of this letter is implying that there is nothing new which can ever be added to the old established formulae. The full revelation has already been given. The Pastorals will echo this stodgy argument.

After Paul has addressed the heretical claims of Simon and Cleobius and rehearsed his orthodox position he concludes the letter in a manner which betrays clearly the crux of the motivation for the author's recourse to pseudepigraphy.

> But if you receive anything else, do not cause me trouble; for I have these fetters on my hands that I may gain Christ, and his marks in my body that I may attain to the resurrection from the dead. And whoever abides by the rule which he received through the blessed prophets and the holy gospel, he shall receive a reward (and when he is risen from the dead shall obtain eternal life). But he who turns aside therefrom — there is fire with him and with those who go before

---

[149]Cf. 1 Cor. 15.3.

[150]The account is orthodox in the sense that it is devoid of the fantastic. The cosmic speculations which frequent gnostic circles were rejected as heterodox and unsound by orthodox authorities. See e.g., 1 Tim. 1.4; Tit. 1.14; 3.9. Of course, all references to orthodoxy in this survey of pseudepigraphical letters must be mitigated by Bauer's demonstration that the terms are anachronistic, imposed upon church history by the doctrinal victors. It is more correct to understand these debates as occurring between two church factions (or more), both of which considered themselves orthodox.

him in the way, since they are men without God, a generation of vipers; from these turn away in the power of the Lord.

The appeal to the specific statements of the prophets and apostles is non-sense unless there is some form of nascent canon, which certainly included genuine Pauline letters and maybe even the Pastorals themselves[151]. In any case this reliance upon the past can only be maintained if there was extant a written corpus of some kind. This written corpus is placed over against any new revelation coming by way of oral tradition or directly from the spirit. It becomes more complicated when we recognize that this written corpus was not inviolable and could obviously be added onto by way of the device of forgery, as the existence of *3 Corinthians* itself attests. Given this orthodox corpus the pseudonymous author tries to make an addition to it using whatever techniques are necessary to achieve his deception. Paul is enlisted as the author for reasons of his special authority. If there are other reasons for picking Paul in particular they cannot be detected, for the only item peculiar to him is a perfunctory reference to his suffering. His character does not color the theology of the letter in any way that I can discover[152]; he is only employed as an apostolic figure of great import who wrote letters, might have written others not heretofore known, and had an historical association with Corinth. Thus Paul is chosen as the author because of the larger concerns of the *Acts of Paul* and not for the argumentative needs of the letter. For the author of our letter it appears there is an explicit and absolute choice between orthodoxy and heterodoxy, since he does not feel compelled to argue theologically in any real detail, but simply opposes the old to the new, remarking as he does that the old has an authority and surety that the new can never have. Choose the old way, Paul's way, the apostles' way, the way of life; or choose the new way, the unknown way, the way to death.

Among the remarkable things about the *Correspondence of Seneca and Paul* is the intriguing fact that Jerome considered the letters genuine[153]. This is surprising not because of any special facility on Jerome's part in detecting forgeries but because these letters are rather facile pseudepigrapha which essay an improbable friendship without using any elaborate, surreptitious techniques. Apparently early Christians were quite eager to admit the genuineness of a document if it suited their sense of orthodoxy,

---

[151]In spite of the many allusions to the Pauline corpus in this letter there is none I can detect to the Pastorals. This might be further evidence that the Pauline corpus circulated in some areas without the Pastorals well into the latter half of the second century.

[152]See the list of allusions to the Pauline corpus provided by Wilson in the notes to the text (*New Testament Apocrypha* 2:375–77). However, it is clear that the citations from Paul are taken without any genuine understanding of Pauline thought.

[153]Jerome *De viris illustribus* 12, reads "L. Annaeus Seneca from Corduba ... lived a very abstemious life. I would not receive him into the list of saints were I not made to do so by those epistles which are read by very many, of Paul to Seneca and Seneca to Paul." Quoted by A. Kurfess, "Correspondence of Seneca and Paul," in *New Testament Apocrypha* 2:134.

and Jerome certainly would have enjoyed believing in historical rapprochement between Seneca and Paul.

The letters do contain a few casual references to everyday minutiae which contribute nicely to a sense of verisimilitude. In *Epistle 1* Seneca recalls walking in Sallust's garden, refers to the conversation he had there with Lucilius, about which he assumes Paul has already heard, and confesses how much he longed to meet Paul in person after reading his letters. Again in *Epistle 2* the aura of real life is enhanced by Paul's reference to his joy in receiving Seneca's letter and his declaration that "I would have been able to answer it at once had the young man whom I purposed to send to you been at hand." Surely there is no other purpose for such a remark than to make the letters seem as life-like as possible. Of the same status is Seneca's remark in *Epistle 9* that he has sent Paul a book on verbosity (*de verborum copia*).

In a more skilled fashion, the letters manufacture a friendship and display a desire for the letters to substitute for the person's own presence, which are essential to Greco-Roman letters and thus integral to the artifice of genuineness in a good pseudepigraphon.

> As often as I hear your letters, I think of your presence and imagine nothing other than you are always with us. As soon then as you set about coming, we shall see one another and do so at close quarters[154].
>
> Your staying away, being all too long, distresses us. What then is wrong? What keeps you away[155]?

The deference they pay to one another culminates in Paul's insistence, in defiance of proper literary conventions, on placing his name second in all the letters he addressed Seneca[156], to which Seneca replies by insisting on Paul's worthiness[157]. The primary impression which this correspondence creates is of a budding friendship between Seneca and Paul which is by force limited to the exchange of letters. Their admiration for one another makes them desirous of a meeting, but because of the danger to Paul, letters must take the place of any face-to-face confrontation.

As pseudepigrapha these letters illustrate several qualities frequent to the genre. They employ extraneous detail for no other discernible purpose than verisimilitude; they imagine and successfully create life-like situations giving rise to the letters; they illustrate how letters were conceived as substitutes for the actual presence of the person; they presuppose a friendliness which lies at the heart of Greco-Roman letter writing; and in an unequalled way they demonstrate how pseudepigraphical letters can make a forceful argument for the friendship or animosity be-

---

154*Correspondence of Seneca and Paul* 4.

155Ibid., 5.

156Ibid., 10: "As often as I write to you and set my name behind yours ..." occurs in all the letters except 14, which may be a later addition to the collection.

157Ibid., 12: "You can believe then you are not unworthy to be named first in the letters. ... For I desire that my place be yours with you (in your letters) and that yours be as mine."

tween or among people who may have had no historical contact with one another.

The Abgar legend contains an exchange of letters between the toparch Abgar of Edessa and Jesus[158] which exemplifies the ancient understanding of a letter being capable of conveying the presence of the person. In this case the letter, according to Bauer, is treated as having magical power by later Christians in Edessa[159]. The story goes that Abgar writes to Jesus saying that he has heard about his miracles and believes them, and asking him to come and heal him. Jesus responds in letter by praising Abgar's faith even though he has not seen. And though Jesus says he cannot come, he promises to send someone in his place. "And when I am taken up, I will send to you one of my disciples, that he may heal your afflictions and give life to you and them that are with you." The purpose of the letter is to get the power of Jesus himself to Edessa. This is accomplished on one level by the sending of Thaddeus after Jesus' death. He comes in power and heals Abgar, thus completing the promise of the letter. But on another level Jesus' power is conveyed by the letter itself. Bauer collects several references to the legendary power of this letter, concluding that,

> Very early people placed themselves under the protection of the sacred document. Thus the Bishop of Edessa told Aetheria that Abgar and many others after him, when a siege threatened, brought Jesus' letter to the gate, there read it, and immediately the enemy dispersed. Later the people of Edessa for this reason fastened the precious document in transcript on the city gates. He who possessed a copy could feel secure before the judges, on a journey, or against sickness and misfortune[160].

Whatever the value of these observations might be, they do demonstrate the prevalence of the idea and complete the picture of how a letter from Jesus could convey his healing power even after he was gone. It was done by his emissary (in other letters this is usally the bearer of the letter) and by the letter itself or even a copy, and surely not always magically but sometimes just by the force of argument.

The *Epistula Petri*, a letter of Peter to James, which is recorded in the *Kerygmata Petrou*[161] along with a narrative describing the impact of the letter, raises the level of deception and duplicity to a new height and idealizes in the narrative how a supposedly genuine apostolic letter should be treated. In this letter we get a glimpse into the aggressiveness of the world of pseudepigraphy in early Christian circles. Peter's reputation has been under attack, perhaps by Paul himself in Galatians, so the author forges a

---

158 Walter Bauer, "The Abgar Legend," in *New Testament Apocrypha* 1:437—43.

159 Of course, the magical papyri include many examples of the inherent and effective power of a letter and Hans Dieter Betz has detected the influence of the concept on the Pauline corpus itself. Paul's letter to the Galatians, according to Betz, is a magical letter in that it imposes upon its readers both the curse in Gal. 1.8—9 and the blessing in Gal. 6.16. "Reading the letter will automatically produce the 'judgement' " (Hans Dieter Betz, *Galatians*, Hermeneia [Philadelphia: Fortress Press, 1979], p. 25).

160 *New Testament Apocrypha* 1:439.

161 G. Strecker, "Kerygmata Petrou," ibid., 2:102—27.

letter to rescue Peter from these attacks and must use elaborate deception to do so.

Peter complains that "even while I am alive people have distorted my words" and that "these people wish to give my opinions as if they knew them better than I do myself"[162]. Therefore, Peter has forwarded to James books of his preaching, which contain his own words, undiluted and pure, along with this letter, with instructions on how to take care of the books. The books are to be handed over to worthy people and not to Gentiles or anyone of dubious reputation. "Hand over the books of my preaching in the same mysterious way [as Moses did] to our seventy brethren. ... For if we do not proceed in this way, our work of truth will be split into many opinions"[163]. Thus they should entrust the books to someone only when they have been "examined and found to be worthy."

James' response is exemplary and certainly intended for imitation. He accomplishes Peter's requests by establishing a vow that must be said by all who receive the books, which includes the following:

> He shall not copy the books himself or allow any one else to copy them[164].
>
> When on a journey or when about to die, I shall not take the books with me or leave them behind in my house, or entrust them to my son, but shall give them to a bishop who is of the same faith[165].

And James closes with this admonition:

> If we pass on the books to all without discrimination and if they are falsified by audacious men and are spoiled by interpolation — as indeed you have heard that some have already done — then it will come to pass that even those who earnestly seek the truth will always be led into error[166].

The letter reflects a religious, literary milieu in which genuine documents are subjected to alteration and forged documents compete with them for a hearing. In such an environment no document could be considered reliable. Therefore, the *Epistula Petri* both takes advantage of the turmoil by adding to the numbers and attempts to protect the doctrines in the rest of the *Kerygmata Petrou* from suspicions of inauthenticity. Here, the reader is told, is the preaching of Peter, not handed on carelessly, not oral tradition, not even copied, and thus not vulnerable to the meddling of unworthy people, but the pure, sound, utterly reliable words of Peter. They were first written down and attested to by Peter himself, passed on to James, a man of unimpeachable morals, who in turn made absolutely certain that they were entrusted to worthy men in such a way that no possible change of any kind could sully them. Not even the error of a copyist is possible. The audacity of this ruse far exceeds the preten-

---

162*Kerygmata Petrou* 1.2.4.

163Ibid., 1.3.1—2.

164Ibid., 2.2.1.

165Ibid., 2.3.3.

166Ibid., 2.5.1.

sions of the author of the Pastorals. The author condemns others who falsify documents and makes elaborate assurances that in this case no falsification has taken place, even while he is surreptitiously disseminating his own forgery. The use of proper names and the quaint requests for material employed by the author of the Pastorals seem calm by comparison, though they have been considerably more effective. Above all, the extremes encountered in the *Epistula Petri* demonstrate how aggressive and competitive the world of Christian literature became in this era. There seems to be no sense of fair play or honesty but only a sense of orthodoxy and heresy; and orthodoxy, according to the orthodox, must be defended and articulated whatever the cost in forthrightness.

The complexity and subtlety of the pseudepigraphical letter in the New Testament canon preclude anything more than a few cursory remarks, although, since the canonical pseudepigrapha prove to be normal species of Greco-Roman epistulary pseudepigraphy, there will be nothing surprising about the methods employed. In fact, excepting the Pastorals themselves, we discover few of the more sophisticated deceptions we have seen elsewhere. It may be that the Pauline corpus so dominated the rest of the canonical epistles that the major canonical pseudepigraphical device was a slavish imitation of Pauline language and style[167]. This is likely to be the case for Ephesians, Colossians, and 2 Thessalonians[168], but even Jude, the Petrine Epistles, and the Pastorals appear on the surface to be more like Pauline letters than any other letter type in the ancient world. Nonetheless, the latter group does illustrate how the same problems and methods encountered in non-canonical pseudepigrapha occur just as readily in the canon.

Jude is a rather facile pseudepigraphon but still is *prima facie* evidence of how important apostolic authority became in early Christianity[169]. The author of Jude had a theological statement to make and considered apostolic authority, and therefore deception, necessary for a positive hearing. The "Jude" chosen by the author as a pseudonym obviously was in-

---

[167]Barnett has articulated the most thorough analysis of Paul's literary influence on the rest of the New Testament (Albert E. Barnett, *Paul Becomes a Literary Influence* [Chicago: University of Chicago Press, 1941]). But cf. Doty, *Letters in Primitive Christianity*, pp. 65–81, who sees a more uneven influence on post-Pauline canonical and non-canonical Christian letters than does Barnett. And even Barnett admits Paul's popularity fluctuated.

[168]To my mind the circumstances and motivations behind 2 Thessalonians have not yet been adequately explained. But see Brox, *Falsche Verfasserangaben*, pp. 24–25, and John A. Bailey, "Who Wrote II Thessalonians?" *New Testament Studies* 25 (1975): 131–45.

[169]Jude can only very loosely be called a letter for its seems to have no origin and no destination. It is more of a literary tractate or treatise to which epistolary trappings are added. It is addressed τοῖς ἐν θεῷ πατρὶ ἠγαπημένοις καὶ Ἰησοῦ Χριστῷ τετηρημένοις κλητοῖς, which is hardly a specific destination. It closes with a doxology and not with Pauline-style greetings. But its authenticity was generally uncontested in the early church and it was a member of the Muratorian canon. The major doubters in antiquity seem to have been Origen (Eusebius, *Ecclesiastical History* 6.25) and Eusebius, under Origen's influence (ibid., 2.23,25).

tended to be understood as Jude, the brother of James, and thus the brother of Jesus[170]. Nothing is known about this Jude other than his pedigree; his specific character and beliefs are and probably were then a mystery, but he sits in impressive proximity to the apostolic origins of the church. This combination of being unknown and apostolic suits the needs of our author perfectly. He is now free to present his own theology without the restraints of any known history or legend attached to the pretended author, and at the same time his theology accrues apostolic weight. To accomplish this he needed only to prefix to his letter the salutation, "Jude, a servant of Jesus Christ, and brother of James." No other pseudepigraphical devices are used.

In both thought and style 1 Peter lies very close to the Pastorals, although as a pseudepigraphon it is much less sophisticated[171]. Both use the figure of an apostle to authenticate their teachings. Peter's function as the pseudo-author in 1 Peter is to give credence to $\tau a \hat{v} \tau a$, which probably refers to the teachings contained in 1 Peter[172]. Like the Pastorals, 1 Peter is primarily an exhortation to ethical behavior; it contains similar allusions to suffering, and employs the idea of imitation as a primary pedagogical model[173]. Nevertheless, Peter serves a less complicated function in 1 Peter than does Paul in the Pastorals. Peter acts simply as a name to give apostolic authority to arguments which could have been made by anyone or attributed to anyone. There is nothing in the letter that is tied to some peculiarity of Peter's life and teachings. In only one instance is the unique position of Peter used. In 1 Pet. 5.1, as an eyewitness to Jesus' life, he is in a unique position to authenticate Jesus' sufferings and to enjoin that pattern of suffering onto the readers[174]. But, other than that, Peter functions as any apostle would. The real author pens in Peter's name as author and creates a nice impression of genuineness by having Silvanus and Mark send personal greetings at the close of the letter. Of course, we have seen

---

[170]See Werner Georg Kümmel, *Introduction to the New Testament*, founded by Paul Feine and Johannes Behm, trans. A. J. Mattil, 14th ed. (New York: Abingdon Press, 1966), pp. 300–1, for a discussion of Jude's identity.

[171]Of the many similarities, we might mention the intimate linkage of ethics and Christology. In 1 Peter this linkage occurs primarily in anticipation of Jesus' return, while the Pastorals find ethical warrants both in Jesus' return and in his first appearance. On 1 Peter see, e.g., 1.13; 2.12; 3.9ff.; 4.5,7. 1 Peter prefers ἀποκαλύπτειν (1 Pet. 1.5,12; 5.1) and ἀποκάλυψις (1 Pet. 1.7; 4.13) to the Pastorals ἐπιφαίνειν and ἐπιφάνεια.

[172]The use of $\tau a \hat{v} \tau a$ in 1 Peter is comparable to the use of παραθήκη in the Pastorals, for just as in the case of παραθήκη it is not necessary to imagine certain unknown and unnamed Christian traditions. In fact, both ταῦτα and παραθήκη refer to the doctrines inculcated in the letters themselves.

[173]See e.g., 1 Pet. 1.15; 2.21: "For to this you have been called, because Christ also suffered for you, leaving you an outline (ὑπογραμμός), that you should follow in his step." Here following means to suffer as Christ suffered, while in the Pastorals one is to suffer as Paul suffered. However, in 1 Pet. 5.9 other Christians (ἀδελφότης) are proffered as good examples of suffering.

[174]μάρτυς τῶν τοῦ Χριστοῦ παθημάτων.

too many of these forged personal remarks to be surprised or impressed with them any longer. On the whole 1 Peter illustrates for us the pervasive importance of apostolic authority along with the pedagogical concern with imitation and the growing reliance upon sound traditions.

2 Peter is uniquely important for understanding the genre of the Christian pseudepigraphical letter. Its adherence to New Testament norms in its stylized prescript and greeting and its consistent awareness of being subject to earlier tradition, when combined with its pseudepigraphical origins, make the letter crucial for understanding the genre[175]. Of all the New Testament pseudepigraphical letters only 2 Peter approaches the Pastorals in the aggressiveness with which it employs pseudepigraphical techniques[176].

A rigid understanding of inspiration and tradition in 2 Peter elevates the role of the pseudo-author into an integral, irreplacable link in the salvation process, which goes far beyond the simple need for apostolic credibility we encountered in Jude and 1 Peter. According to Ernst Käsemann, revelation in 2 Peter has become "a piece of property which is at the community's disposal" and which has been handed down complete by the earliest apostles[177]. The full revelation was given in the past and the author's function today is simply to remind the readers of the truth which they have already heard[178]. Käsemann argues persuasively that "only one who has been an eyewitness and hearer of this particular history can be the guarantor of the tradition of the Church"[179]. In the fact of enthusiasts who appeal to the spirit and individual revelation, our author projects the sanctity and completeness of tradition. There is no new revelation. Thus, "The messenger of the Gospel has become the quarantor of the tradition, the witness of the resurrection has become the witness of the historica sacra"[180]. Käsemann proffers the suggestion that the author of the letter portrayed Peter as about to die so that the letter could become Peter's last will and testament[181] and another instance of the complete revelation of Jesus Christ, which is guaranteed by an eye-witness and only needs to be handed on to subsequent generations. Perhaps the author

---

[175]See Doty, *Letters in Primitive Christianity*, on epistolary conventions in early Christianity. He includes only an offhand observation (p. 70) that 2 Peter does indeed follow normal procedure. I know of no detailed treatment of 2 Peter's relationship to Pauline letter formulae.

[176]Brox, *Falsche Verfasserangaben*, pp. 18–19, says, "Man erkennt also, wie die Reklamation apostolischer Autorität für diesen Brief weit stärker und sogar qualitativ anders als in den ersten Beispielen literarisch durchgehalten ist und 'erfinderisch' wird bzw. die sich anbietende Möglichkeit der Fälschung detaillierter und entschlossener ausschöpft."

[177]Ernst Käsemann, "An Apologia for Primitive Christian Eschatology," in *Essays on New Testament Themes*, trans. U. J. Montague, Studies in Biblical Theology (Naperville, Ill.: Alec R. Allenson, 1964), pp. 169–95, esp. 174.

[178]2 Pet. 1.12–13.

[179]Käsemann, "An Apologia for Primitive Christian Eschatology," p. 176.

[180]Ibid., p. 177.

[181]2 Pet. 1.13ff.

justified his forgery by imagining himself as the executor of Peter's testament.

Käsemann is certainly correct that the revised concept of revelation and the concomitant elevation of tradition place a new burden upon the function of the pseudo-author. 2 Peter cannot have just any apostolic witness since it needs someone especially close to Jesus himself to authenticate beyond question the doctrines contained in the letter. The pseudo-author must be one of the twelve. And more than that the author's recourse to pseudonymity exceeds the need for the increased weight an apostolic name can give, because the ethics enjoined by the author has no discernible Christological warrant other than what is provided by the historical witness of Peter himself[182]. Therefore, if the artifice of pseudepigraphy is broken the entire argumentation of the letter collapses. In 2 Peter the deception must be successful.

2 Pet. 1.12—15 summarizes the motivation behind this pseudepigraphon.

> Therefore I shall always remind you of these things, though you know them and are established in the truth you have. I think it is right, as long as I am in this tent, to arouse you by way of reminder, knowing that the putting off of this tent of mine is soon, as our Lord Jesus Christ made clear to me. And I will try to see to it that after my departure you may be able at any time to recall these things.

From this quote we can reconstruct both the necessity for the forged letter and the intended results. We notice that the full revelation has already been given and only needs to be recalled[183]. Nothing new is articulated. Therefore, as his last will and testament, immediately before the death he saw coming, Peter left behind a permanent reminder of that deposit of truth. The intention expressed in 2 Pet. 1.15 to continue to remind the readers of this truth is accomplished in the writing of the letter itself, which will serve as a permanent reminder, not subject to death. We can understand this expressed intention as the closest thing we have in the canon to an apology for pseudepigraphy. Christians need permanent reminders of the final truth revealed by Jesus himself and passed on by the first apostles[184].

The same motivation finds expression in 2 Pet. 3.1—2.

> This is now the second letter that I have written to you[185], beloved, and in both of them I

---

[182]This is of course contra 1 Peter, the Pastorals, and even Paul and more like post-canonical works such as the *Epistula Petri* and *3 Corinthians*.

[183]Käsemann, "An Apologia for Primitive Christian Eschatology," argues that the main theological task enjoined on Christians in 2 Peter is "to recall"; thus the letter places heavy emphasis upon μιμνῄσκεσθαι and its cognates.

[184]In the same way as 1 Tim.6.20 Timothy is ordered to guard the traditions, a task which the author of the Pastorals is himself performing by forging and disseminating his letters.

[185]On the question of whether the author of 2 Peter knew 1 Peter see G. H. Boobyer, "The Indebtedness of 2 Peter to 1 Peter," in *New Testament Essays: Studies in Memory of T. W. Manson*, ed. A. Higgins (Manchester: Manchester University Press, 1959), pp. 34—53.

have aroused your sincere mind by way of a reminder; that you should remember the predictions of the holy prophets and the commandment of the Lord and Savior through your apostles.

The line of succession is clearly articulated, from the Old Testament prophets and Jesus himself their traditions are passed on through the apostles. Therefore, 2 Peter contains not only the correct doctrine and ethics as preached by Jesus but also the correct exegesis of the Old Testament prophets. The problems of interpretation and the conflicts among early Christians about how to read the Old Testament are obviously the instigation of this claim. This need to authenticate the scriptural interpretations of the letter as the only correct interpretations receives a final warrant in Peter's biographical recollections of the transfiguration. In 2 Pet. 1.16—21 our author uses Peter's unique history to full advantage. Peter was one of only three people who witnessed Jesus' transfiguration and this special status is extended to include special status for Peter as an exegete. Peter has seen the glory of God the Father and because of that vision he has received special insight into the meaning of scripture.

For it is not by following cleverly constructed myths that we have made known to you the power and presence of our Lord Jesus Christ, but in being eyewitnesses of his greatness (2 Pet. 1.16).

No clear explanation is given as to how this is accomplished; it is simply stated as true.

We have the prophetic word, which is more certain; you do well to hold to it, as to a lamp shining in a dingy place, until the day dawns in light and the morning star rises in your hearts. But first, know this, that no prophecy in scripture is subject to one's own interpretation; for prophecy did not ever come by the will of man, but men, carried along by the holy spirit, have spoken from God (2 Pet. 1.19—21).

In this way Peter arrogates to himself the sole right to correct scriptural interpretation because some kind of special inspiration took place at the transfiguration. With this stunning claim the author can present the exegesis in 2 Peter as uniquely inspired. I find this to be a rather effective use of pseudepigraphy.

Further use of Peter's unique position in early Christianity is discernible in the caveat about Paul's letters.

As our beloved brother Paul wrote to you according to the wisdom given him, speaking of these things as he does in all his letters, in which there are some things hard to understand, which the ignorant and unstable twist to their own destruction, as they do the other scriptures (γραφάς) (2 Pet. 3.15—16).

In addition to Peter's special status as an interpreter of scripture, which is here enlarged to include the Pauline corpus, the author also uses Peter's incomparable prestige in the early church to put a lid on Paul's influence. Paul is declared to be dangerous, regardless of the scriptural status of his letters. Perhaps in all of early Christianity only Peter enjoyed a reputation sufficient to the task of opposing Paul effectively. Once again, we see how carefully Peter has been chosen as the pseudo-author. Our author needed as a pseudonym one of the twelve in order to properly authenticate his static traditions, someone who possessed unparalleled inspiration into the meaning of scripture, and someone of sufficient prestige to counterbalance the influence of the Pauline corpus. Only Peter could fill all these requirements and even he needed to have his portrait filled out with a fictional account of an exegetical ability bestowed at the trans-figuration.

Therefore, the author of 2 Peter produced a credible framework for his ideas only because he used the potentialities of pseudepigraphy to the ful-lest. Unlike 1 Peter or Jude, or even Ephesians, Colossians, and 2 Thessal-onians, the logic of 2 Peter collapses if the forgery is detected. 1 Peter, Jude, Ephesians, Colossians, James, and 2 Thessalonians could easily have circulated without a pseudonym without vitiating the theological argu-ment of the letters. Pesudonymity was employed in these cases primarily because apostolic and especially Pauline authority was useful. It is true that the deutero-Pauline letters perceive themselves as Pauline in thought and spirit and thus require Paul's name if any pseudonym is used at all, but this is more like the allegiances of a philosophic school, and they could have circulated anonymously or with the author's real name without unravelling the theological logic of the letters. This is not the case with 2 Peter, which would lose essential components of its arguments if Peter's name were removed. The letter lacks the personal greetings and extraneous detail common to many pseudepigraphical letters but it uses biographical reminiscences and the prestige of the pseudoauthor with good effects.

D. The Pastorals as Pseudepigraphical Letters

The Pastorals conform beautifully to the pseudepigraphical letter genre. They hold no surprises in either form or function. This ready conformity vitiates any argument for the Pauline authorship of the letters based on the presence of extensive personalia, the occasional warmth and sincerity of Paul's tone, or the seemingly careless references to mundane affairs. None of these things lies beyond the normal scope of ancient pseudepi-graphy; in fact, the techniques in the Pastorals now look rather tame com-pared to some of the radical devices we have examined. But even more important for an analysis of the Pastorals is the information we have gain-ed about how pseudepigraphical techniques function as conveyors of in-formation and argument. We are now able to move beyond limited debate about motivation into that of hermeneutics. We are closer to understand-ing what the Pastorals as pseudepigraphical letters can tell us about the theological concerns of the author. Personalia, false biographical detail, the choice of the pseudo-author and the pseudo-recipient, and all the pseud-epigraphical techniques do more than deceive; they provide clues to the author's milieu; they are vessels through which he articulates his theology. It is not enough to say what literary genre the Pastorals might be, we must also ask what theology, what specific view of the Christian reality, the author of the letters is attempting to promulgate by these fictional means. As a prelude to that question, we must of course be clear about what pseudepigraphical techniques our author employs. Then we can what he means to say.

At the outset we notice that our author does not tip his hand. He is not employing pseudepigraphy as an exercise either in literary convention or in simple deference to Paul; he is trying to deceive. At no point does he break the spell of verisimilitude and allow his own face to show; to the contrary, he weaves a life-like world in which Paul, Timothy, and Titus carry on the personal and public business of Christian apostles. We have seen the disastrous results of discovery in such cases as Salvian's letter. We have seen several examples showing how aggressive and convoluted the literary war between competing factions could be. We have further seen how elaborate and devoid of scruples pseudepigrapha can be. Therefore, we can expect our author to employ any device he might deem necessary to accomplish his deception. Facile forgeries do not normally last[186]. The abundance of Christian pseudepigrapha which failed to achieve canonical status proves that. If our author has something important to say, he must structure his forgery well.

The author of the Pastorals produced a fairly credible sense of real life in his letters by using the usual pseudepigraphical techniques. There is nothing new or especially creative in what he has done. The contention that his artifice is so convincing that we must doubt that anyone in the first or second century "would be likely to possess the sure psychological touch and consummate artistry to introduce, for example, the noble farewell charge contained in 2 Tim. 4.6ff." is clearly overstated[187]. Compared to what we have seen elsewhere, the personalia, the extraneous detail, the sense of friendship and finally the overall framework of verisimilitude is of rather modest proportions. We must not give the author too much credit for being some kind of profound artist when most of what he does literarily is pedestrian and commonplace. He is writing fiction and it is not difficult to include a few life-like moments.

---

[186] The success of Jude and 1 Peter, neither of which shows any sophistication in its attempts to deceive, in convincing the early church that they were apostolic merely shows how readily the orthodox would grant canonical status to a document they considered orthodox. Thus it was their orthodoxy and not any verisimilitude which determined their friendly reception. Colossians and Ephesians accomplished verisimilitude by imitating Paul's style, language, and thought. We might speculate that James succeeds because it sounds Jewish-Christian.

[187] Kelly, *The Pastoral Epistles*, p. 33. This is an extremely popular argument among defenders of authenticity and advocates of the fragment theory, but I fail to see its substance. See, e.g., Harrison, *The Problem of the Pastoral Epistles*, pp. 57–59; C. K. Barret, *The Pastoral Epistles*, The New Clarendon Bible (Oxford: Clarendon Press, 1963), pp. 16–17. But we have demonstrated in our survey of other pseudepigraphical letters how easy it was to fabricate personal notes even more elaborate than 2 Tim. 4.6ff., although this passage is admittedly as effectively drawn as any we have seen.

The personalia in 2 Tim. 4.9—22 and Tit.3.12—15 are reminiscent of the greetings throughout the Pauline corpus. Greetings are sent to specified persons in the company of the recipient, and specified people in the company of the sender send personal greetings to the recipient. In addition "Paul" passes on personal information on the whereabouts of many of his companions, as if it would be of interest to Timothy and Titus. They both read pretty much like Rom. 16 and Col. 4.7—18, producing an impression of Christians scattered throughout the Roman world who had genuine affection and concern for one another. The parallels to the Socratic letters are nearly exact. We can surmise that historically both Socratics and Christians did feel personal attachment to others of the same philosophical or religious stripe in other cities whom they might have met earlier[188]. It is logical, therefore, that if the author of the Pastorals or the Socratic letters wants his letters to appear life-like, then he must reproduce this environment in the letters. And to do so is rather simple; it takes no consummate artist to write either 2 Tim.4.9—22 or Tit.3.12—15.

Paul himself is portrayed not only as a preacher of the orthodox kerygma but also as a normal man with everyday concerns. Thus he asks in 2 Tim.4.13 that Timothy bring with him the cloak he left behind with Carpos in Troas, his books, and especially his parchments. This detail is comparable to the figs and jars of honey in the Socratic letters, but the items may not have been chosen haphazardly since $\beta\iota\beta\lambda\iota\alpha$ and $\mu\epsilon\mu\beta\rho\acute{\alpha}\nu\alpha\iota$ are peculiarly appropriate materials for a travelling apostle who likes to write letters[189]. On two occasions in particular "Paul" speaks eloquently of the structure of his own private faith. In 1 Tim.1.12—17 he recalls his sinful past, being the foremost of all sinners[190], who persecuted the church,

---

[188] Adolf Harnack, *The Mission and Expansion of Christianity in the First Three Centuries*, trans. and ed. James Moffatt (New York: Harper & Bros., 1962), pp. 375—76, in his excursus, "Travelling: The Exchange of Letters and Literature," declares "These data are merely intended to give an approximate idea of how vital was the intercourse, personal and epistolary and literary, between the various churches, and also between prominent teachers of the day. It is not easy to exaggerate the significance of this fact for the mission and propaganda of Christianity. The cooperation, the brotherliness, and moreover the mental activity of Christians, are patent in the connection, and they were powerful levers in the extension of the cause. Furthermore, they must have made a powerful impression on the outside spectator, besides guaranteeing a certain unity in the development of the religion and insuring the fact that when a Christian passed from East to the West, or from one distant church to another, he never felt himself a stranger."

[189] This is reminiscent of *Epistles of Socrates and the Socratics* 28.14 where the author complains that he cannot write any more because of the scarcity of $\beta\iota\beta\lambda\acute{\iota}o\nu$. Paul's request, therefore, expresses a common concern among those who must write letters, so common, in fact, that the request becomes a useful artifice in pseudepigrapha.

[190] W. M. Ramsay, "A Historical Commentary on the Epistles to Timothy," *Expositor*, ser. 7, 8 (1909): 270—71, finds in this phrase conclusive evidence of authenticity: "Had he so carefully thought out the imposture as to invent a touch of religious feeling, which has gone direct to the heart of thousands: Who can invent such a wonderful expression of religious emotion except one who feels it himself? And how could the impostor feel it in his assumed character? And how could the imposter so accurately gauge the character of his readers as to know that they would recognize in them the character of Paul? ... In every direction, the theory of false authorship of

and yet received God's mercy so that God might show his patience as an example (ὑποτύπωσις) to later Christians. And in 2 Tim. 4.6—8 he anticipates his death with unflinching confidence and hope: "I have fought the good fight, I have finished the race, I have kept the faith. Finally the crown of righteousness is set aside for me ... ." The lofty heights of the language and sentiment expressed here have encouraged many commentators to insist that no forger could have done this[191], but only Paul, as if a forger could not be bright and clever with words, or as if Paul were the only intelligent person in early Christianity. In any case both citations use these biographical reminiscences for grander purposes than mere verisimilitude since Paul always serves a paradigmatic function. 1 Tim. 1.16 expressly describes God's treatment of Paul as being πρὸς ὑποτύπωσιν τῶν μελλόντων πιστεύειν and in 2 Tim. 4.8 "Paul" insists that the crown of righteousness will be awarded "not only to me but to all who have loved his epiphany." Biographical reminiscences inevitably do this in pseudepigrapha; they cross the border between verisimilitude and teaching; the actions, thoughts, and words of a revered founder are unavoidably prescriptive and paradigmatic to his successors. Recollections about Socrates' trial and death, whether done by "Socrates" or one of the Socratics, teach his followers how to face life's difficulties. Again, we can recall the paradigmatic function of Peter and James in the *Epistula Petri* or even Aristippus in the letter to his daughter. So Paul's personal recollections are just good pseudepigraphical technique.

Paul's intimacy with Timothy and Titus is well established in the Pauline corpus. According to Paul's own letters no one stood in closer proximity to Paul than Timothy. He is, in fact, the co-sender of the letters to Corinth (2 Corinthians), Philippi, Colossae, Thessalonica (1 and 2 Thessalonians), and Philemon. Paul calls him "my fellow worker (ὁ συνεργός μου)" and "my beloved child (μου τέκνον ἀγαπητόν)" and sends him as his representative to carry out special apostolic tasks to both Corinth and Thessalonica[192]. Therefore the Pastorals are simply continuing and expanding upon a well-known intimacy between the two.

> I give thanks to God whom I serve with a clear conscience, as did my ancestors, as I remember you continuously in my prayers. Night and day I long to see you, remembering your tears, so that I may be filled with joy. I am reminded of your unfeigned faith, which dwelt first in your grandmother Lois and your mother Eunice, and I am convinced now also in you. On account of which I remind you to rekindle the gift of God, which is in you through the laying on of my hands (2 Tim. 1.3—6).

---

these four words breaks down, for any one who can appreciate their religious quality. And literary criticism loses all reason and wanders into a pathless jungle of fancies, unless it proceeds on the principle that a great illuminative or creative saying is to be credited to the author who wrote it as the result of his own genius, and not to be reckoned as the result of his blundering exaggeration of some other person's words."

191See p. 23, n. 65, and p. 55, n. 187 above, but also any commentary which supports authenticity.
192Rom. 16.21; 1 Cor. 4.17; 16.10; 1 Thess. 3.2, 6.

Our author uses Paul's usual procedure of beginning his letters with a prayer for the recipients and applies it to Timothy. In so doing, he confirms Timothy's orthodoxy (ἀνυπόκριτος πίστις), and adds a nice personal touch of giving the names of his mother and grandmother, implying thereby that Paul is an old acquaintance of the family. Furthermore, the author claims it was Paul himself who ordained Timothy with the laying on of his hands, which of course does not square with 1 Tim. 4.14 where it is the presbyters (πρεσβυτέριον) who lay hands on Timothy[193]. In addition to expressing his desire to see Timothy in the foregoing quote, on two other occasions "Paul" urges Timothy to come to see him soon (2 Tim.4.9,21). "Paul" calls Timothy "genuine child in faith (γνήσιον τέκνον ἐν πίστει)" (1 Tim.1.2) and "beloved child (ἀγαπητὸν τέκνον)" (2 Tim.1.2) and admonishes him with the gentle advice to drink not only water but also wine for his stomach and frequent ailments (1 Tim.5.23). Our author also takes the trouble to include some personality traits for Timothy himself. Beyond the remark about his weak health which needs wine for medicine, he is reported to have been raised from his youth in the scripture (2 Tim 3.15), he must be exhorted to shun the dangerous passions which afflict the young (2 Tim.2.22), yet he is reminded that he should not brook any disrespect because of his youth (1 Tim.4.12)[194]. In fact, the bulk of 1 and 2 Timothy consists of detailed instructions and exhortations for the task assigned him by "Paul," as though he needs careful monitoring and encouragement. In short, as a paradigm, he is very human.

Titus receives more perfunctory treatment but the same tendencies are manifest[195]. "Paul" calls him "genuine child according to shared faith (γνήσιον τέκνον κατὰ κοινὴν πίστιν)" (Tit.1.4), pleads with him to meet him in Nicopolis (Tit.3.12), and of course sends him a letter full of careful instructions for the carrying out of his commission.

The result of the foregoing is an aura of friendship among Paul, Tim-

---

[193]Brox, *Falsche Verfasserangaben*, pp. 22—23, interprets this contradiction as a seam in the fabric of verisimilitude, showing the author contradicting himself because he is creating facts as he needs them and is not dependent upon any real history. But cf. Kelly, *The Pastoral Epistles*, pp. 106—8; Donald Guthrie, *The Pastoral Epistles*, Tyndale New Testament Commentaries (Grand Rapids, Mich.: Wm. B. Eerdmans, 1957), p. 98. The alternate translation of 1 Tim 4.14 as "elder-ordination" rather than "ordination by elders" is possible but slightly strained and not necessary. The old suggestion that Paul was one of the elders or even the leader of the presbytery is sufficient to eliminate any contradiction, even a fictional one.

[194]Brox, *Falsche Verfasserangaben*, p. 23, argues, "Der Grund dafür ist der, dass der angebliche Adressat den Typ für alles abgeben muss, was der Verfasser kennzeichnen will, also für das Ideal und für die Unzulänglichkeit, für den vorbildlichen Vorsteher und für den Schüler und möglichen Versager, der erst am Anfang seiner Bewährung steht." This may well be the case, but we must wonder whether the author has not reproduced Paul's ambiguous treatments of Timothy in 1 Corinthians. There Timothy is also the trusted companion who carries out Paul's commission (1 Cor. 4.17), but Paul also seems diffident about his success when he admonishes the Corinthians to put Timothy at ease when he arrives (1 Cor. 16.10).

[195]Titus occurs in the Pauline corpus primarily in 2 Corinthians where he successfully calms the troubles there. But he is also among Paul's entourage at the apostolic council (Gal. 2.1).

othy, and Titus. We have already seen how important the idea of friendship can be in pseudepigraphical letters, for example, in the *Correspondence of Seneca and Paul* and throughout the *Socratic Epistles*. The Pastorals thus reflect the customary procedure of pseudepigraphical letters as
well as the historical realities witnessed in Paul's own letters.

All these devices of verisimilitude conform closely to those used in
pseudepigraphical letters throughout the Greco-Roman world; therefore,
in order to ascertain in the intentions of the author, and as a prelude to
investigating his theology, we must try to determine how he uses these
commonplace pseudepigraphical techniques and why he chose pseudonymity in general and Paul in particular as his pseudonym. That is to say,
we must try to understand how the pseudepigraphical letter, with both its
strictures in form and its capacity to convey information, helps and hinders
our author in expressing his own theology.

Without a doubt it was the battle with heresy which moved our author
to pseudonymity[196]. Disruption in his church caused by church members
he considered immoral and heterodox moved him to draw upon Paul's authority to authenticate and elevate his own rather conservative view of the
Christian life. "For there are many insubordinate men, empty talkers and
deceivers, especially those of the circumcision, who must be silenced,
since they are upsetting whole families by teaching what one should not
for shameful gain" (Tit. 1.10–11). Time and again he issues warnings and
pronounces judgment against the heterodox[197]. There is nothing unique
in this; taking recourse to forgery became a common procedure in early
Christianity in the battle among the various factions; nor is there anything
unique in appealing so stringently to a fixed, familiar doctrine to oppose
an opponent's teaching, which an author finds fanciful and dangerous.
This is the primary milieu of pseudepigraphy and in itself tells us little
about the author except that he was immersed in the doctrinal disputes
which frequented the early church. We must ask further questions about
how he employs that tradition, what the tradition is, what the doctrines
of his opponents might actually be, and what he considers legitimate and
illegitimate as theological warrants. Most of that must wait until later.

In the same way, the personalia by their mere presence tell us very little.
Some of the personal remarks might have no purpose beyond lending an
air of verisimilitude. The bulk of 2 Tim. 4.9–13 and the personal greetings
at the end of both 2 Timothy and Titus probably fall into this category.
But we have seen how these personal remarks sometimes disguise the alternative motive of locating the author's contemporaries as being either in

---

[196]This is generally uncontested in scholarship on the Pastorals, especially among those who
consider the letters pseudepigraphical. See e.g., Easton, *The Pastoral Epistles*, p. 2: "The Pastor
wrote first of all to protect the faith and morals of the Church against a corrupting invasion of
'false teaching' ... ."

[197]1 Tim. 1.3–7, 19, 20; 4.1–10; 2 Tim. 1.15; 2.14–3.9; 4.3, 4; Tit.1.10–16; 3.9–11.

accord or discord with the pseudo-author[198]. Thus we must wonder if the condemnations of Hymenaeus, Alexander, Phygelus, Hermogenes, Philetus, and Demas might not be aimed at the author's contemporaries who are somehow connected with these names[199]. And the excessive praises lavished upon Onesiphorus are readily explicable only if the author is thereby flattering and vindicating to his readers some of their contemporaries, perhaps even himself (2 Tim.1.16—18).

Modern supporters of the theory of pseudonymity usually describe the author as a good Paulinist who out of deference for the apostle and out of need for his authority affixed Paul's name to his own letters. Perhaps, it is suggested, Paul's name had to be chosen because our author needed to rescue Paul from the mistreatment and heterodox interpretations of gnostic-tinged opponents[200]. He wanted desperately to bring Paul back into the approved arena of the orthodox. The difficulty with this interpretation begins when these authors note how poorly the author understood Paul. He appears to be a Paulinist not in theology but only in name; he is defending a man he knows mostly by reputation and legend. He is basically ignorant of Paul's unique version of Christian salvation and thus passes on a handful of catch phrases which sound like Paul but which do not inform the author's thinking in any substantive way.

Of course, we have seen that this ambiguous relationship between author and pseudo-author is the normal state of affairs in pseudepigraphical letters. The range is considerable. People like Anacharsis, Crates, Diogenes, and Heraclitus function merely as empty vessels into which the authors pour their own Cynic notions, while Socrates' character, especially his implacability in the face of death and his loyalty to a native city which was going to kill him, impinges upon the later author's portrait of him. It is likely that in cases where certain legends were common knowledge, such as Socrates' death, any extensive tampering with the facts would destroy the aura of historicity and unveil the document as a forgery. If pervasive legends tied an author's hand, we can understand the penchant for creating completely new and imaginary conditions rather than rewriting and modifying old ones. The *Correspondence of Seneca and Paul, 3 Corinthians*, the Abgar legend, and the *Epistula Petri* all fabricate new situa-

---

[198]E.g., *Epistles of Socrates and the Socratics* 14.9; 18.2; 28.1; 30.1, 2; 14.1; 12; 13; 23. Perhaps also Simon and Cleobius in *3 Corinthians* should be included.

[199]1 Tim 1.20; 2 Tim 1.15; 2.17; 4.10.

[200]Barrett, *The Pastoral Epistles*, pp. 16—17, declares, "The purpose of the Pastorals was practical. Paul was assailed: to Jewish Christians he was 'the enemy,' and to many Gentile Christians he was suspect, or was in danger of becoming suspect, because he was in favor with the gnostics. Those who held fast to the doctrine they had received from their master were under the necessity to publish, to represent in their own generation the genuine Pauline voice."

[201]See discussion in Dibelius-Conzelmann, *The Pastoral Epistles*, pp. 15, 16, 126, 127, 152—54. But cf. Guthrie, *The Pastoral Epistles*, pp. 16—24. Recourse to a second imprisonment theory is simply to admit that the historical allusions cannot be harmonized with the events in Paul's life as we know them.

tions rather than modify old ones. If this is the favored procedure in early Christianity we can understand why all attempts to fit the personal remarks in the Pastorals into known frameworks from the other Pauline letters or Acts have been so unsuccessful[201]. It is much more likely that our author has not tried to conform his remarks to any specific and known situation in Paul's life but is simply making up new ones. On the other hand, Paul is not simply an empty vessel; nor is he a mere purveyor of authority like Jude. The legends surrounding Paul, especially those of his suffering, get considerable play in the Pastorals[202]. Furthermore, Paul's unique history as a travelling apostle makes the fabricated situation of all three letters believable. Paul loved to write letters to churches he had founded and showed a constant pastoral concern for them even after he was gone. His long association with Ephesus would make the two letters to Timothy, who is in Ephesus, quite believable. And although only Acts 27 mentions Crete and Paul in the same breath, and there he is under arrest and does not appear to have started any churches, there may have been other legends extant which we do not know about. But even if not, there is nothing fantastic about assuming Paul did missionary work on Crete. The roles of Timothy and Titus, as we have seen, function effectively in the author's attempt toward verisimilitude. In the other Pauline letters, Paul frequently entrusts members of his entourage with missionary tasks, sometimes even Timothy and Titus themselves[203]. The Pastorals thereby become wholly believable pseudepigrapha, since the pseudo-author and the pseudo-recipients all behave in a fashion consistent with what the author and his readers knew about them.

Furthermore, a combination of Paul as author and Timothy and Titus as recipients creates a volatile situation resplendent with opportunities. When Cynic authors dreamed up letters written by Diogenes to Plato, or Diogenes to Alexander the Great, when early Christians dreamed up letters from Paul to Seneca and Seneca to Paul, from Peter to James, or from Paul to Timothy and Titus, it was the unique combination of pseudo-author and pseudo-recipient which created the unusual potentialities. The Pastorals pretend to be private communications from Paul to two of his most trusted confidants. If anything secret was ever handed down by Paul it would certainly be here in private communications of this sort. Therefore we can believe that these letters contain the complete, unaltered, wholly reliable teachings of Paul. When else would Paul ever express his complete mind, unguarded and untempered, except in private admonitions to Timothy and Titus?

Paul, Timothy, and Titus do more than convey authority or lend credibility to fabricated situations, they also function as paradigmatic models.

---

[202] 2 Tim. 1.12, 15–18; 2.8–10; 3.10–12; 4.6–18.

[203] On Timothy: 1 Cor. 4.17; 16.10; Phil. 2.19; 1 Thess. 3.2, 6. On Titus: 2 Cor. 7.6; 8.16, 17, 23.

The role of imitation in early Christian thought is well documented and does not need to be rehearsed here[204]; moreover, we have seen how pervasive the idea is in pseudepigraphy. The close association between imitation and pseudepigraphy flows quite naturally from that deep reverence for the past which is shared by both author and reader. The neat equation, apostolicity equals orthodoxy, may be slightly too facile, but it indicates the enormous deference given to apostolic people and their teachings in the doctrinal disputes of post-apostolic Christianity. In such a milieu the common Greco-Roman affection for imitation receives new import. As it was said in regard to Socrates: "And it is indeed reasonable that he is wise who copies himself after the wisest, and he is happiest who assimilates himself as much as possible to one who is happy"[205]. To which we might add, "and he is orthodox who copies the orthodox."

Therefore, all the biographical detail given to Paul, Timothy, and Titus must be seen as doing more than providing verisimilitude, for those biographical remarks are idealized portraits of heroes to be imitated. This is, in fact, expressly stated in the letters themselves[206].

Show yourself in all things a model (τύπος) of good works (Tit.2.7).

Do your best to present yourself to God as one approved, an unashamed worker, who makes straight the word of truth (2 Tim.2.15).

Now you have observed by teaching, my conduct, my plan, my faith, my patience, my love, my steadfastness ... (2 Tim.3.10).

For this gospel I was appointed preacher and apostle and teacher, and therefore I suffer these things. But I am not ashamed, for I know whom I have trusted, and I am convinced that he is able to guard my traditions until that day. Follow the pattern (ὑποτύπωσις) of sound words which you have heard from me (2 Tim.1.11–13).

The author of the Pastorals in this way combines effectively two common practices in pseudepigraphical letters. Doctrinally, the historical Paul has little influence. He is used more for his authority than for his idiosyncratic view of Christian theology. Occasional hints of Pauline language[207] and the possibility that our author made an unsuccessful attempt to understand Paul (after all, no one seems to have understood Paul in the second century) preclude our equating Paul with an empty vessel for the author's ideas. Nevertheless, the theology of the Pastorals has little to do with the theology of Paul. In fact, as we shall discover, our author articulates a theological system unique in early Christianity. Biographically, however, Paul has considerable influence. In fact, all the characters in Pastorals, not just Paul, Timothy, and Titus, might be portraits painted for pedagogical purposes. Thus the harsh contrast between Hymenaeus et al.

---

[204]Hans Dieter Betz, *Nachfolge und Nachahmung Jesu Christi im Neuen Testament*, Beiträge zur historischen Theologie 37 (Tübingen: J. C. B. Mohr [Paul Siebeck], 1967).

[205]*Epistles of Socrates and the Socratics* 6.4.

[206]In addition to citation given below, see 1 Tim. 1.16 and 2 Tim. 4.8.

[207]For an extensive list of passages in the Pastorals which reflect language of the Pauline corpus see Adolf Schlatter, *Die Kirche der Griechen im Urteil des Paulus* (Stuttgart: Calwer Verlag, 1936), p. 15.

and Onesiphorus might serve the same function as the contrast between the unnamed Lacedaemonian youth and the despicable pair of Anytus and Meletus, who are paradigmatic of the correct and incorrect attitude towards Socrates.

The concept of a fixed, permanent, complete revelation of the truth handed over by apostles to their followers seems to be almost unique to Christianity, because the attitude of the philosophic schools towards tradition seems to be much more complex. It is only in Christian circles that we find such elaborate attempts to prove that a certain doctrine comes directly and unscarred from apostolic times. The counterposing of reliable tradition and unreliable innovations displayed in *3 Corinthians* is typical, while the impeccable procedure inaugurated by James on the occasion of his receipt of a letter from Peter is more radical and indicates how crucial the concept became in later years. The position of the Pastorals stands somewhere between these radical claims of later years and the loose allegiances of Paul to the past or of the authors of Ephesians and Colossians, who express their allegiance primarily through doctrinal fidelity. 2 Peter, which is more or less contemporary with the Pastorals, illustrates how easily a pseudepigraphical letter can employ this idea. When the author of 2 Peter divested himself of all possibility of future revelations, he elevated Peter's role above that of an authority figure to a guarantor of tradition. Knowledge of the truth depends upon the sole authority of Peter and his teachings. Thus in the Pastorals the crucial function played by tradition ($\pi\alpha\rho\alpha\vartheta\acute{\eta}\kappa\eta$) requires that the link from Paul to Timothy and Titus to present day church leaders be carefully forged and remain unbroken. Thus the friendship among Paul, Timothy, and Titus does more than add verisimilitude, it guarantees the traditions. A full treatment of $\pi\alpha\rho\alpha\vartheta\acute{\eta}\kappa\eta$ in the Pastorals must wait until a later time, but we need to be cognizant at this point that recourse to a fixed, reliable tradition was a frequent and almost omnipresent tactic of Christian pseudepigraphy. The crucial question for the Pastorals will be what the author means when he refers to the "tradition which you have received."

Looking beyond the internal devices of the pseudepigraphical letter, we have noticed that the letter itself, as a finished product, an object, carries special abilities to convey information from one person to another. A letter is more than a collection of formal devices and arguments, more than a treatise, more than a document without origin or destination, of value only because of the ideas it contains. A letter creates personal contact between sender and recipient.

We have seen reflections of this capacity to create personal contact throughout our survey of pseudepigraphical letters. Diogenes writes to Hipparchia "for letters are worth a great deal and are not interior to conversation with people actually present"[208]. In *3 Corinthians* Paul's letter is treated as a viable alternative to his actual presence. In the *Correspond-*

---

[208]*Epistles of Diogenes* 3.

ence of Seneca and Paul, Paul's letters serve throughout as a substitute
for his actual presence, and Paul writes to Seneca, "As often as I hear
your letters, I think of nothing other than that you are always with us."
And most of all in the Abgar legend we saw how the letter actually conveyed Jesus' presence magically so that the letter was tacked to the city
gates to defend it. All this suggests that the letters were understood as able
to convey the actual presence of the sender to the recipient of the letter.
At least this is so in ideal terms, for admittedly we noticed in Diogenes'
letter to Antalcides a complaint about having to address him in "inanimate means" rather than being present in person[209], and Paul and Seneca
seem to chafe under the limitation imposed by letter-writing. Nevertheless, it is safe to conclude that letters, pseudepigraphical letters included,
attempted to convey the presence of the sender to the recipient even if
their success was partial.

Koskenniemi has identified three basic characteristics of the Hellenis-
tic letter[210]. First and foremost, $\varphi\iota\lambda\circ\varphi\rho\acute{o}\nu\eta\sigma\iota\varsigma$, or friendship, forms the
foundation of all Hellenistic letters[211]. Letters express friendship between
two persons and are ways of maintaining and nurturing that friendship.
Second, letters function as a mode of $\pi\alpha\rho\circ\nu\sigma\acute{\iota}\alpha$ or presence, attempting to
convey the presence of one friend to another who is separated from
the sender[212]. Third, letters are a form of $\delta\iota\acute{\alpha}\lambda\circ\gamma\circ\varsigma$ or homily, in which
previous conversation between friends is continued in literary form[213]. As
we have seen, the applicability of these characteristics to pseudepigraphical
letters, especially the Pastorals, is obvious[214].

Funk has interpreted Koskenniemi's findings as a hermeneutical key to
the Pauline corpus[215]. Paul attempts to establish his apostolic presence in
three ways: the letter, the apostolic emissary, and his own personal presence. Funk believes that Rom. 15.14—33 and 1 Cor. 4.17 contain the basic
formulae for conveying presence through those means. He further notes

---

[209]Ibid., 17.

[210]H. Koskenniemi, *Studien zur Idee und Phraseologie des griechischen Briefes bis 400 n. Chr.*,
Annales Academie Scientiarum Fennicae, Ser. B. Vol. 102, No. 2 (Helsinki: Suomalaisen Tiedeak-
atemie, 1956).

[211]Demetrius *On Style* 231: "A letter is designed to be the heart's good wishes ($\Phi\iota\lambda\circ\varphi\rho\acute{o}\nu\eta\sigma\iota$)
in brief."

[212]Ibid., 227: "The letter, like the dialogue, should abound in glimpses of character ($\mathring{\eta}\vartheta\iota\kappa\acute{o}\nu$).
It may be said that everybody reveals his own soul in his letters. In every other form of composi-
tion it is possible to discern the writer's character, but in none so clearly as the epistolary."

[213]Ibid., 223: "Artemon, the editor of Aristotle's letters, says that a letter ought to be written
in the same manner as a dialogue ($\delta\iota\acute{\alpha}\lambda\circ\gamma\circ\varsigma$), a letter being regarded by him as one of two sides of
a dialogue."

[214]Gustav Karlsson, "Formelhaftes in Paulusbriefen?" *Eranos* 54 (1956): 138—41, shows that
the motif, "absent in body, but present through letter," can be traced from the beginning of the
Christian era into the Middle Ages.

[215]Robert W. Funk, "The Apostolic 'Parousia': Form and Significance," in *Christian History
and Interpretation: Studies Presented to John Knox*, ed. W. R. Farmer et al. (Cambridge: Cambridge University Press, 1967), pp. 249—68.

that, for Paul, letters serve as an awkward and temporary substitute for his actual presence. In fact, at times it seems that Paul values the emissary sent in his behalf more highly than the letter written by him.

Finally Stenger has applied the findings of both to the Pastorals, arguing that the author did not receive the model for his letters from general Greco-Roman literature but directly from Paul's own letters[216]. Furthermore, Stenger suggests that if the author had wanted merely to validate his own teaching or put Paul's stamp upon it he would have used the testament genre[217], but he chose the letter genre because he wanted to overcome the temporal distance between apostolic teachings and his own church. He needed to convey Paul's own presence into the doctrinal debates of his church. Only a letter can do this, because only a letter attempts "Die ἀπουσία zur παρουσία zu machen." His basic text is, of course, 1 Tim. 3.14—15:

> I hope to come to you soon, but I am writing these things to you so that, if I am delayed, you might know how one ought to behave in the house of God, which is the church of the living God, the pillar and foundation of truth.

Stenger argues further that the double pseudonymity of the letters, where both author and recipient are fictitious, enables Paul to also be present via the tasks completed by his emissaries. Thus, Paul is present in the letters themselves and in the teaching the letters promulgate, but equally Paul is present in the activity of the proper church officers who were appointed by Timothy and Titus and who are therefore trustworthy men. One can theoretically contact Paul by contacting the present-day church leadership.

The capacity of the Hellenistic letter to overcome the distance between friends and to make the absent present seems to be highlighted in pseudepigraphical letters. Moreover, in the pseudepigraphical letter, the letter is not an awkward and temporary substitute for an eventual meeting of sender and recipient, because such a meeting will never take place. The letter itself must carry the full and final presence of the sender.

In any event the Pastorals clearly manifest all of Koskenniemi's characteristics. We have noticed how carefully our author has structured the relationships among Paul, Timothy, and Titus and also how Paul's authority has been specifically handed over. Not only do the exigencies of Paul's permanent absence place a special weight on this transfer of his authority, but also the theological stance of eliminating new relevations and the concomitant emphasis on tradition place the full burden of any knowledge of Christian truth upon this successful embodiment of Paul's thought and person into his letters and emissaries.

---

[216]W. Stenger, "Timotheus und Titus als literarische Gestalten: Beobachtungen zur Form und Funktion der Pastoralbriefe," *Kairos* 16 (1974): 252—67.

[217]This is not necessarily true. We have seen in the instance of Jude and many of the Cynic epistles that the pseudepigraphical letter was flexible enough to use the pseudonym strictly as a conveyor of authority. Moreover Paul was known for writing letters not his testament.

E. Conclusion

If the Pastorals hereby prove to be fine examples of the pseudepigraphical letter genre, this does not mean that the pseudepigraphical letter is a genre in any formal sense, as if there were certain rules and regulations imposed upon all respectable forgers. It would be absurd to imagine someone defending the credibility of his pseudepigraphon because he had followed the accepted norms for the pseudepigraphical letter. It is more correct to say that the pseudepigraphical letters we have examined contain certain common characteristics. And these common characteristics result more from the exigencies of deception and the shared milieu of doctrinal debate among religious or philosophical factions than from structural requirements. Of course a pseudepigraphical letter must look like a real letter and thereby is subject to certain restrictions. For instance, the Pastorals must imitate the structure and style of the Pauline letter if they are to look genuine. Thus a pseudepigraphical letter functions more by providing possibilities than by prescribing restrictions. It provides the author with a specific way of participating in the doctrinal debates going on around him. It is a set of tools and the author of the Pastorals uses them as effectively as anyone in antiquity.

We have demonstrated that the Pastorals are typical pseudepigraphical letters, for they do not employ a single device of deception or literary technique which cannot be paralleled elsewhere. Furthermore, the Pastorals seem to share a religious milieu with other pseudepigrapha which is dominated by excesses of the doctrinal debates among competing factions. The retreat to reliable traditions along with a proscription against new revelations forces the authors of many pseudepigrapha into certain common theological positions which our author shares. His concentration upon the traditions handed over by way of an unbroken line of succession from Paul to certain living church officers, along with the paradigmatic function of each figure along the line, is a commonplace theological stance for someone who reacts to doctrinal diversity as he does. Moreover, these tenets of his theology are logical and nearly automatic companions of the genre itself. This link between genre and theology is inescapable and we have only sketched the bare outlines of both here. In fact, only an analysis of the Pastorals which holds genre and theology in focus together can discover the meaning of the letters. We shall find that the author has a cogent and consistent theological system which finds expression easily, naturally, and almost without any strictures through this genre, and that his theological system is built upon arguments and fictions which only the pseudepigraphical letter could have permitted him.

Chapter II

Forms of Argument

The Pastorals are composed out of an extensive array of literary forms[1]. The arguments move from doctrinal pieces to exhortations to biographical reminiscences to virtue and vice lists to household rules. Some sections are created out of concise imperatives combined with brief warrants for those imperatives. Other sections contain larger blocks of material, such as household rules or virtue and vice lists. This method of composition has been read by scholarship as evidence of the lack of literary design or of an inability to systematize disparate sources[2]. A. T. Hanson is representative of this interpretation of the literary structure of the letters when he divides the Pastorals into nine "distinct types of material"[3]. In his commentary he analyzes each separately without trying to comprehend a connection between these literary elements or to discover any argumentative structure in the letters. He remarks, "The Pastorals are made up of a miscellaneous collection of material. They have no unifying theme; there is no development of thought"[4].

Commentators on the Pastorals simply do not detect any logical interplay among the types of literary material. Dibelius-Conzelmann, Brox, Easton, and others who affirm non-Pauline authorship understand the au-

---

[1]The literature on the literary and liturgical sources in the Pastorals is extensive. This has been the primary focus of all scholarship on the Pastorals, equal in weight to the concern over authorship. The most thorough treatments are given in Dibelius-Conzelmann, *The Pastoral Epistles*; Brox, *Die Pastoralbriefe*; Robert Falconer, *The Pastoral Epistles* (Oxford: Clarendon Press, 1937). Besides these commentaries, there are monographs on the individual literary forms. On these, see references in the next chapter.

[2]For example, Houlden, *The Pastoral Epistles*, p. 31, declares that the Pastorals are "the work of a man who leans upon Paul but has not properly absorbed his teaching ... and, indeed, has his own almost technical means of treating his source-material. ... [There is] the reiterated use in the relatively meager and segregated doctrinal passages of a small number of ideas... ." Easton, *The Pastoral Epistles*, p. 14, in a similar vein remarks "But there is no sustained thought beyond the limits of the separate paragraphs, from paragraph to paragraph — and sometimes even within paragraphs — the topic changes without preparation and sometimes apparently without motive."

[3]Hanson, *The Pastoral Epistles*, pp. 42—47. Hanson's list includes extracts from a church order, domestic codes, liturgical fragments, confessional or homiletic statements, lists of sinners or sins, historical details about Paul's life, transposed Pauline passages, midrash or haggada on scripture, direct exhortation and instruction.

[4]Ibid., p. 42.

thor as an unsystematic thinker, a dogmatist, who combined a variety of distinct literary elements into a disorganized collage[5]. They do not try to follow the logic of the arguments. It might seem that defenders of Pauline authorship would want to detect clear argumentation in the letters, but Spicq, Jeremias, Kelly, and others do not do this in commentaries[6]. All commentaries proceed pretty much the same way: they analyze the various types of material in the letters, try to determine the original provenance of that material along with the redactional activity of the author on that material; and then, if they want to discuss the religious ideas of the author, they do so in terms of these literary types. Since there are doctrinal pieces, they discuss the author's theology and Christology by examining those pieces; since there are household rules, they discuss his ideas on church order; since there are references to Paul's past, they discuss his relation to Pauline traditions. This is done with each kind of material. Even the recent monographs, which have made significant strides in unfolding the author's theology, do not pay attention to the interplay of these materials within the letters[7]. In short, the Pastorals are dissected into pieces and then each piece is examined in turn. The kind of commentary one finds on a Pauline letter, where great care is taken to detail the flow of the argument and to place each statement into that flow, does not yet exist on the Pastorals.

In fact, very little is ever said about the literary style of the author, except perhaps to note that his mode of argumentation is lifeless compared with Paul's[8]. A. T. Hanson makes as direct a comment as one can find in this literature, noting that the author alternates his material skillfully, because

> It would not have done to put all his church order material, or all his Pauline transpositions, or all his liturgical material together in one block. That would have looked too like a manual of church order, or an exposition of Paul, or a book of worship, and he wanted to give the impression that he was writing letters[9].

Robert J. Karris' short commentary is perhaps the one exception. The topical format of the commentary, its brevity, and its intention to address "a wide audience" precluded any extensive treatment of the author's

---

[5]Dibelius-Conzelmann, *The Pastoral Epistles*, esp. pp. 8–10; Brox, *Die Pastoralbriefe*, esp. pp. 49–55; Easton, *The Pastoral Epistles*, pp. 22–30.

[6]Spicq, *Les Épitres Pastorales*; Jeremias, *Die Brief an Timotheus und Titus*; Kelly, *The Pastoral Epistles*. Kelly for instance, focuses his analysis not so much on sources but on the place of individual tenets in the Pastorals within the Pauline corpus of ideas. Thus he creates an interesting dialogue between the Pastorals and other Pauline letters, but does not trace the progression of arguments within the Pastorals themselves.

[7]See Oberlinner, "Die 'Epiphaneia' des Heilswillens Gottes in Christus Jesus"; Trummer, *Die Paulustradition der Pastoralbriefe*; Lips, *Glaube, Gemeinde, Amt*; Hasler, "Epiphanie und Christologie in den Pastoralbriefen."

[8]See, for example, Brox, *Die Pastoralbriefe*, pp. 47–48, where he denigrates the Pastorals for lacking the "explosive style" and "energy" of the Pauline letters.

[9]Hanson, *The Pastoral Epistles*, p. 46.

style[10]. Nevertheless, it is clear that Karris believes the author of the Pastorals has organized his material with care. For instance, Karris' short analysis of the exhortatory style of Tit. 1.10—16, where he shows how various catchwords and concepts play off one another, is without parallel in Pastoral scholarship[11]. Throughout the commentary Karris notes the interrelationships of various arguments in the letters. His work is a step in the right direction, but much more is needed[12]. Karris has done little more than suggest that certain possibilities are there.

It is the thesis of this chapter that the parenetic style of the Pastorals is in accord with the canons of Greco-Roman ethical argument and that other Greco-Roman ethical documents provide analogies and categories for understanding the eclectic pastiche of material which make up the Pastorals. We shall begin with a tight focus, looking at how individual propositions combine with others to form ethical arguments, and then broaden our focus gradually, looking at the role of Paul as a paradigm and at the composition of larger blocks of material. At each step in this process other Greco-Roman ethical documents will provide tools for analysis. In the end, the Pastorals appear to present carefully structured arguments which follow the parenetic canons of their day.

A. The Enthymeme

The initial problem in evaluating the method of argumentation in the Pastorals resides in the nature of ethical logic. The lack of the Pauline style which shifts in fairly organized fashion from one subject to another does not mean, of course, that no coherence exists in the argumentation of the Pastorals. The author of the Pastorals places imperatives next to indicatives without detailing the connection between them; thus these juxtapositions seem to lack a logical basis. However, when we consult the treatments of ethical logic in antiquity and compare the canons established there to the actual procedure in the Pastorals, a close correspondence is discovered.

In order to locate treatments of ethical logic in antiquity we cannot go

---

[10]Robert J. Karris, *The Pastoral Epistles*, New Testament Message 17 (Wilmington, Del.: Michael Glazier, 1979).

[11]Karris, *The Pastoral Epistles*, pp. 108—9.

[12]Verner, *The Household of God*, pp. 112—25, and Fiore, *The Function of Personal Example in the Socratic and Pastoral Epistles*, have recently gone beyond Karris in detecting order and coherence in the arguments of the Pastorals. Both find many analogies to the author's method in other Greco-Roman ethicists. And, therefore, although they organize and analyze the letters along different lines than I do, they confirm the essential point that the author's parenetic methods are typical for his day. Verner finds the best analogies in Seneca, while Fiore looks to the Socratic letters.

to the philosophical treatments of scientific logic but must consult the
rhetorical handbooks, where the logic of rhetorical argument is analyzed[13]. The system of Aristotle, as outlined in the *Art of Rhetoric*, proves
to be the most fruitful for unpacking the logic in the Pastorals and thus
the Aristotelian categories will be used here. However, since Quintilian
and Cicero lie closer in time to the Pastorals, some explanation is required as to why Aristotle is more helpful. James H. McBurney's survey of the origin of the Aristotelian enthymeme and its subsequent
influence on the history of rhetoric demonstrates that it was Aristotle
above all who injected the study of logic into the study of rhetoric, which
had theretofore concentrated on the proper order of a speech and how to
appeal to the emotions[14]. Further, McBurney suggests that post-Aristote-
lian rhetorical theory tended to separate logic from appeals to passion and
character and to relegate logic to that part of the speech devoted to
proofs[15]. And in fact Quintilian has little to say about logic; and what he
does say is said more clearly and with more detail by Aristotle[16]. On the
other hand, Cicero devotes considerable energy to the logic of rhetoric in
both *De Inventione* and *Topica*[17]. Yet there are problems with using

---

[13]This distinction between scientific and rhetorical reasoning is a basic tenet of the *Rhetoric*
where Aristotle carefully defines the differences; see Aristotle *Rhetoric* 1354al–1358a35. See E.
M. Cope, *An Introduction to Aristotle's Rhetoric* (London: Macmillan, 1867), pp. 67–133. Larry
Arnhart, *Aristotle on Political Reasoning: A Commentary on the "Rhetoric"* (Dekalb, Ill.: Northern Illinois University Press, 1981) devotes much of his commentary to the distinction between
scientific and rhetorical reasoning. He notes that the distinction in Plato among dialectic, rhetoric,
and sophistry is not maintained in the same way for Aristotle, because he changes the definitions
of both dialectic and rhetoric. See also Lloyd Bitzer, "Aristotle's Enthymeme Revisited," in *Aristotle: The Classical Heritage of Rhetoric*, ed. Keith V. Erickson (Metuchen: Scarecrow Press, 1974),
pp. 141–55; and Sally Raphael, "Rhetoric, Dialectic, and Syllogistic Argument: Aristotle's Position in 'Rhetoric' I–II," *Phronesis* 19 (1974): 153–67.

[14]James H. McBurney, "The Place of the Enthymeme in Rhetorical Theory," in *Aristotle: The
Classical Heritage of Rhetoric*, pp. 117–40. See also Friedrich Solmsen, "The Aristotelian Tradition in Ancient Rhetoric," in *Aristotle: The Classical Heritage of Rhetoric*, pp. 278–309. Aristotle
at the beginning of the *Rhetoric* notes that previous compilers of the arts of rhetoric had devoted
themselves to the arousing of emotions, which Aristotle sees as being outside the real subject matter, which is the enthymeme, the rhetorical deductive proof (1354a11–1354a18).

[15]McBurney, "The Place of the Enthymeme in Rhetorical Theory," pp. 132–34. Cicero begins
his *Topica* with a reference to Aristotle's works which "contained a system developed by Aristotle
for inventing arguments," and laments that Aristotle is ignored except by a few philosophers
(*Topica* 1.1.2–3). Cicero is implying that the Aristotelian system of rhetorical logic had dropped
into disuse. See also Cicero *Topica* 1.2.6–8, where Cicero says Aristotle originated both the invention and judgment of arguments but Stoics concern themselves only with the latter.

[16]Quintilian *Institutio Oratoria* 5.8,9,10; 5.14. Quintilian gives an interesting review of the confusion over the enthymeme, but for the most part seems to follow Aristotle's view closer than
Cicero. In 5.32 Quintilian complains about the mixing of logic and rhetoric. He thinks the enthymeme (*ratiocinatio*) and the kind of argument useful for the orator mix poorly and work at all
only in the *probatio*.

[17]*De Inventione* was intended to be the first part of a five part work on rhetoric by Cicero (*De
Inventione* 1.7.9), but it was the only part completed. Cicero defines invention as "the discovery
of valid or seemingly valid arguments to render one's cause plausible." Thus whatever Cicero in-

Cicero. Cicero confines his analysis of rhetoric more to the courtroom than does Aristotle (although the court is the primary milieu for Aristotle as well) and thus his categories seem more slanted to that setting and less useful for the generalizations necessary to analyze the Pastorals[18]. Cicero's treatment of the common topics in his *Topica* does not seem to mark any advance on Aristotle; in fact, he treats them more as a storehouse for ready-made arguments than as logical patterns from which one can create arguments[19]. Even more limiting is his general confinement of logic in *De Inventione* to the *confirmatio* and the *refutatio*[20]. Thus for Cicero logic comes to the fore in a speech when it is time to make precise arguments or to refute them, while for Aristotle each moment of the speech is grounded in logic. Finally, and perhaps most importantly, Aristotle's treatment of the role of logic is more thorough and systematic than anything else in antiquity. His system provides all the categories necessary for an analysis of the Pastorals and those of Cicero and Quintilian simply do not. Admittedly there are instances when Cicero's comments help to explain certain structures in the Pastorals[21]. That will be noted when appropriate.

It is highly improbable that the author of the Pastorals had first-hand acquaintance with Aristotle's *Rhetoric*. And even though ancient education patterns make it possible and indeed probable that the author would have known the general canons of rhetoric, the author does not appear to be consciously using the logical categories which are described in what follows. Thus, the use of Aristotle's enthymeme to explain the structure of deductive logic in the Pastorals is not intended to imply that the author is attempting to conform his argumentative logic to some known ideal

---

tended to say on rhetorical logic is probably contained herein. He also introduces his *Topica*, being in conscious imitation of Aristotle, as places (*loci*) where an orator can find arguments.

[18]Nearly every example in both *De Inventione* and *Topica* comes out of the courtroom. Aristotle's *Rhetoric* makes a striking contrast, for he has few illustrations directly from the court; his setting is more the public and political forum. Arnhart argues that the common topics are arranged in the *Rhetoric* as an apology for Socrates against the Athenians (Arnhart, *Aristotle on Political Reasoning*, pp. 147–54).

[19]From *De Oratore* 2.163–73 and *Topica* 1.2.6–8 it seems that Cicero comprehended accurately what Aristotle meant by τοπικά and yet his own concern seems more to have been to prepare a list of arguments which an orator can keep ready to use. On this see Solmsen, "The Aristotelian Tradition in Ancient Rhetoric," pp. 289 and 305, n. 74.

[20]Cicero *De Inventione* 1.34–96. Book 2 of *de Inventione* (2.11) is described by Cicero as an attempt to give "concrete examples of arguments to be used in confirmation and refutation of each kind of case."

[21]The most important modification is the expansion of the three-fold enthymeme into a five-fold *ratiocinatio*. The additions consist of individual proofs for each of the premises. Cicero claims that this five-fold structure is adherred to by Theophrastus and the Peripatetics. Solmsen, "The Aristotelian Tradition in Ancient Rhetoric," pp. 287–89, points out that Cicero is following the form of the ἐπιχείρημα developed by the Peripatetics and Hermagoras. Quintilian agrees with Cicero and gives an analysis of the variety of terms and usages of what is for him basically one kind of rhetorical proof (*Inst. Or.* 5.8,9,10). Just as the enthymeme can be formally incomplete, the five-fold schema recommended by Cicero can be also. However, this complexification of the logical structure helps to explain some of the more elaborate arguments in the Pastorals.

but merely that the kind of logic Aristotle describes can be found in the Pastorals. Thus the system proposed here is something that is imposed from outside the text, even though it attempts to track structures within the text.

Aristotle's analysis of rhetorical logic is presented in the first two books of the *Art of Rhetoric*. Recourse to the *Organon* is really not necessary except to clarify certain distinctions in terms, since the *Organon* treats scientific and dialectic logic not rhetorical logic[22]. Aristotle takes care in the *Rhetoric* to differentiate between the logic devoted to science and that logic appropriate to rhetoric, noting that the former is based on first principles and is structurally complete while the latter is not[23]. This difference will be clarified in what follows.

Aristotle calls rhetoric the counterpart ($\dot{\alpha}\nu\tau\acute{\iota}\sigma\tau\rho o\varphi o\varsigma$) of dialectic, meaning that it is a tool which can be applied to any subject[24]. He defines it more precisely as "the faculty ($\delta\acute{\upsilon}\nu\alpha\mu\iota\varsigma$) of discovering the possible ways of persuasion for any subject"[25]. This immediately distinguishes it from a science, since it focuses upon persuasion ($\pi\iota\theta\alpha\nu\acute{o}\varsigma$) and not proof[26]. Therefore, the formalism of a science is out of place, for such rigor is not persuasive to a general audience[27]. Aristotle notes that the tendency to pile up syllogisms in a speech is the reason why the educated are less persuasive than the uneducated with a crowd, for the former use formal premises ($\tau\dot{\alpha}\ \kappa o\iota\nu\dot{\alpha}\ \kappa\alpha\grave{\iota}\ \kappa\alpha\theta\acute{o}\lambda o\upsilon$), while the latter speak of what they know and what is near ($\dot{\epsilon}\xi\ \ddot{\omega}\nu\ \ddot{\iota}\sigma\alpha\sigma\iota,\ \kappa\alpha\grave{\iota}\ \tau\dot{\alpha}\ \dot{\epsilon}\gamma\gamma\acute{\upsilon}\varsigma$)[28]. Or again, in the *Nicomachean Ethics* he uses in the midst of a larger argument the proposition that "demanding logical demonstrations from a teacher of rhetoric is clearly

---

[22]Both Cope and Arnhart use the *Organon* on occasion in their commentaries, but systematic attempts to harmonize the two create problems. See Donovan J. Ochs, "Aristotle's Concept of the Formal Topics," *Speech Monographs* 36 (1969): 419–25, who believes the *Rhetoric* was composed in sections and collates it with the *Topics*. The tendency to dissect the *Rhetoric* goes back to Friedrich Solmsen, *Die Entwicklung der Aristotelischen Logik und Rhetorik* (Berlin: Weidmannsche Buchhandlung, 1929). See also Raphael, "Rhetoric, Dialectic, and Syllogistic Argument," pp. 153–67.

[23]Aristotle *Rhetoric* 1357a13–17, 22–36.

[24]Ibid., 1354a1. See Cope, *An Introduction to Aristotle's Rhetoric*, pp. 67–99; Arnhart, *Aristotle on Political Reasoning*, pp. 3–5, 17–21; Theresa M. Crem, "The Definition of Rhetoric According to Aristotle," in *Aristotle: The Classical Heritage of Rhetoric*, pp. 52–71. Raphael, "Rhetoric, Dialectic, and Syllogistic Argument," pp. 153–67, believes that the confusion in the *Rhetoric* results from a failure on Aristotle's part to distinguish rhetorical logic from dialectical logic, which Aristotle wants to conflate.

[25]Aristotle *Rhetoric* 1355b25–26. On this definition see Arnhart, *Aristotle on Political Reasoning*, pp. 34–35; Cope, *An Introduction to Aristotle's Rhetoric*, pp. 14–27; Crem, "The Definition of Rhetoric According to Aristotle."

[26]This distinction receives extensive treatment in both Cope and Arnhart, but for the impact of the concept upon the nature of rhetorical logic see Bitzer, "Aristotle's Enthymeme Revisited," pp. 141–55.

[27]See ibid., esp. p. 151; Arnhart, *Aristotle on Political Reasoning*, pp. 40–43; and Crem, "The Definition of Rhetoric According to Aristotle."

[28]Aristotle *Rhetoric* 1395b27–31.

about as reasonable as accepting mere plausibility from a mathematician"[29]. Thus, it is significant that Aristotle changes the terminology for proofs when in the field of rhetoric. Proofs are not called ἀποδείξεις but πίστεις (ἡ δὲ πίστις ἀπόδειξίς τις)[30]. This signals one of the complex conundrums of Aristotelian scholarship: what is the difference between scientific logic and rhetorical logic?

Even a careful Aristotelian scholar like E. M. Cope has difficulty here, for Cope seems to have changed his mind about what the difference was[31]. The problem focuses upon two distinctions which Aristotle expresses in the *Rhetoric*. First, he notes that rhetorical proofs do not proceed from first principles (ἀρχή) as do scientific proofs[32]. First principles are propositions which must be accepted by practitioners of a science as unquestionably valid[33]. Once any analysis begins to argue from such principles it is not dialectic or rhetoric but a science[34]. Rhetorical proofs, in contrast, are composed of probabilities, signs (necessary and non-necessary), and paradigms[35]. The key question here is what Aristotle means by probabilities (εἰκότα). We need to recall at this point that, at the beginning of the *Rhetoric* when Aristotle distinguishes between true rhetoric and that of the sophist, he employs the term ἔνδοξα to analyze the problem of truth in rhetoric[36]. Aristotle is arguing that, since rhetoric deals with per-

---

[29]Aristotle *Nicomachean Ethics* 1094a25—27.

[30]Aristotle *Rhetoric* 1355a6—7. On this term see William M. Grimaldi, "A Note on the πίστεις in Aristotle's *Rhetoric*, 1354—1356," *American Journal of Philology* 78 (1957): 188—92, who distinguishes πίστις as matter and πίστις as form; G. H. Wikramanayake, "A Note on the πίστεις in Aristotle's Rhetoric, "*American Journal of Philology* 82 (1961): 193—96, who claims that Aristotle never uses πίστις in the sense of a source for rhetorical demonstration; and Joseph T. Lienhard, "A Note on the Meaning of ΠΙΣΤΙΣ in Aristotle's Rhetoric,"*American Journal of Philology* 87 (1966): 446—54, who insists with Grimaldi that πίστις in the *Rhetoric* is not univocal.

[31]For an analysis and critique of Cope's change of mind see Bitzer, "Aristotle's Enthymeme Revisited," pp. 148—52. See Cope, *An Introduction to Aristotle's Rhetoric* p. 103, n. 1, where Cope attributes his error to undue deference to Sir W. Hamilton.

[32]Aristotle *Rhetoric* 1355a10—18. Rhetoric shares with dialectic this characteristic of beginning with ἔνδοξα not ἀρχαί (*Topics* 100a30). On the ἀρχαί and dialectic see Aristotle *Topics* 101a37—b4; Raphael, "Rhetoric, Dialectic, and Syllogistic Argument," pp. 154—57; Arnhart, *Aristotle on Political Reasoning*, pp. 17—21.

[33]Arnhart points out that the ἀρχαί "must be taken on trust" (*Aristotle on Political Reasoning*, p. 18).

[34]Aristotle *Rhetoric* 1358a25—26. Raphael, "Rhetoric, Dialectic, and Syllogistic Argument," p. 163, notes that Aristotle gives no hint how one could arrive upon the ἀρχαί of ethics or how one could recognize them if one did; but she points out that in the *Topics* (101a34—b4) they can be arrived at by induction and in the *Nicomachean Ethics* (1098b2) and the *Posterior Analytics* (99b15—100b17) by intuition or perception.

[35]Aristotle *Rhetoric* 1357a32—b25. Discussions on these terms and what they ramify are extensive. Raphael, "Rhetoric, Dialectic, and Syllogistic Argument," pp. 159—60, collates Aristotle's remarks in the *Rhetoric* with his more detailed discussion in the *Prior Analytics*. See also Cope, *An Introduction to Aristotle's Rhetoric*, pp. 169—68; Arnhart, *Aristotle on Political Reasoning*, pp. 43—47. For a fuller bibliography see Arnhart, p. 199, n. 113.

[36]Aristotle *Rhetoric* 1355a17—18. Aristotle makes similar assertions at 1355a27—28, 1395b 31—1396a4, and 1402a33—34.

suasion, the dynamic of belief and disbelief between the orator and the audience determines the probative status of the art[37]. He defines ἔνδοξα in the *Topics* as "things generally admitted by all, or by most men, or by the wise, and by all of most of these, or by the most notable and esteemed"[38]. Aristotle apparently means that a speech requires the consent of the audience and, therefore, the propositions which compose arguments are those statements which the audience will accept as valid. Thus the propositions of a rhetorical proof are neither necessarily true nor false but only what are accepted as true or false by the audience[39]. Aristotle clarifies this further by focusing not upon the credulity of the audience but upon the subject matter of rhetoric. He declares that rhetorical proofs do not deal with necessities but only with accidentals. This is because rhetoric's subject matter is human behavior and human behavior is always contingent. Thus rhetorical proofs are rarely drawn from necessity (ἐξ ἀνάγκης) but from what is generally true (ἐπὶ τὸ πολύ)[40]. Second, Aristotle distinguishes rhetorical proofs from scientific proofs by noting that one of the propositions of the three-fold scientific syllogism is normally suppressed[41]. Thus, in appearance they are formally incomplete. Either one of the propositions or the conclusion can be missing[42]. He concludes that this imperfection actually assists in the persuasion of the crowd, for it encourages them to participate in the speech by completing the argument[43].

The two peculiarities of rhetorical proof, being based on probabilities and being formally incomplete, have inspired much discussion among subsequent readers of the *Rhetoric*[44]. The debate focuses upon whether these idiosyncracies make rhetorical logic invalid and what this does to its probative status. The researches of McBurney, Bitzer, Arnhart, and Sprute on the enthymeme, along with the discussion among Grimaldi, Wikramanayake, and Lienhard on the meaning of πίστις, provide sufficient

---

[37]Bitzer, "Aristotle's Enthymeme Revisited"; Arnhart, *Aristotle on Political Reasoning*, pp. 6–7, 10–11, 28–34, 183–88.

[38]Aristotle *Topics* 100a30. Cf. ibid., 100b21–23.

[39]See p. 73, n. 32 and p. 74, n. 37 above. Therefore, rhetoric shares with dialectic the quality of being a neutral instrument which does not have to hunt the truth but which may. Of course, Aristotle must distinguish rhetoric from sophistry in order for this similarity to exist, which is in fact the first thing he does in Book I. See Eric Weil, "La Place de la logique dans la pensée aristotelicienne," *Revue de metaphysique et de morale* 56 (1951): 283–315. Aristotle argues that the truth is easier to prove and more likely to persuade (*Rhetoric* 1355a20–23, 36–38).

[40]Aristotle *Rhetoric* 1357a22–33.

[41]Ibid., 1357a16–17.

[42]See Cope, *An Introduction to Aristotle's Rhetoric*, pp. 102–5. Cf. Bitzer, "Aristotle's Enthymeme Revisited"; Aristotle *Rhetoric* 1395a21–1396a3.

[43]Aristotle *Rhetoric* 1400b29–34. Cf. Bitzer, "Aristotle's Enthymeme Revisited," p. 151.

[44]For a summary see Bitzer, "Aristotle's Enthymeme Revisited." Cf. Cope, *An Introduction to Aristotle's Rhetoric*, pp. 67–99, 99–108, 160–68; Arnhart, *Aristotle on Political Reasoning*, pp. 13–47; R. C. Seaton, "The Aristotelian Enthymeme," *The Classical Review* 28 (1914): 113–19.

tools for understanding the ramifications of these distinctions[45]. Aristotle is not saying that rhetorical proofs are either illogical or formally defective; rather he is describing what happens to logical arguments when the subject matter is human behavior and the ultimate probative status of the argument resides in its persuasiveness with a general audience. These transformations should be clear in what follows.

A complete exposition of the various categories in Aristotle's system of rhetorical logic is not necessary for a comprehensive analysis of the Pastorals and lies beyond the scope of this dissertation. The outline which follows touches the major distinctions needed to describe the kinds of arguments in the Pastorals and notes the most important categories in the *Rhetoric*.

Aristotle says that there are three kinds of proofs in rhetoric: those based on the character ($\mathring{\eta}\vartheta o\varsigma$) of the speaker, those based on the emotions ($\pi\acute{a}\vartheta o\varsigma$) of his hearers and those based on the speech itself[46]. Logic undergirds all three[47]. While he introduces rhetoric as the counterpart of dialectic, he expands this by defining rhetoric as the offshoot ($\pi a\rho a\varphi v\acute{e}\varsigma$) of both dialectic and ethics, equating the later with politics[48]. This connection with ethics explains his extensive forays into the nature of virtue; and the connection with politics explains his care in defining kinds of government[49]. In any case, the subtle connection established here between rhetoric and ethics creates the basis for finding analogies between the analysis of rhetorical logic found here and the ethical arguments in the Pastorals.

Aristotle compares the demonstrations in dialectic to those in rhetoric. There are two kinds of inference in both: deductive and inductive[50]. This is the primary distinction he makes among all rhetorical arguments, and he changes the terminology for these two forms when they are rhetorical, just as he changed $\grave{a}\pi\acute{o}\delta\epsilon\iota\xi\iota\varsigma$ to $\pi\acute{\iota}\sigma\tau\iota\varsigma$. He says, "I call an enthymeme a rhetorical syllogism, and a paradigm a rhetorical induction ($\kappa a\lambda\tilde{\omega}$ δ'

---

[45] Jürgen Sprute, *Die Enthymemetheorie der aristotelischen Rhetorik*, Abhandlungen der Akademie der Wissenschaften in Göttingen (Göttingen: Vandenhoeck & Ruprecht, 1982); Grimaldi, "A Note on the $\pi\acute{\iota}\sigma\tau\epsilon\iota\varsigma$ in Aristotle's *Rhetoric*," pp. 188–92; Wikramanayake, "A Note on the $\pi\acute{\iota}\sigma\tau\epsilon\iota\varsigma$ in Aristotle's in Aristotle's Rhetoric," pp. 193–96; Lienhard, "A Note on the Meaning of ΠΙΣΤΙΣ in Aristotle's Rhetoric," pp. 446–54.

[46] Aristotle *Rhetoric* 1356a1–20.

[47] Arnhart, *Aristotle on Political Reasoning*, pp. 35–38.

[48] Aristotle *Rhetoric* 1356a20–33, 1359b8–12.

[49] Ibid., 1365b31–1366a16, 1359b19–1360a37, 1360b4–1362a14.

[50] Ibid., 1356a34–b4. Raphael, "Rhetoric, Dialectic, and Syllogistic Argument," believes that Aristotle did not sufficiently examine the fundamental differences between dialectic and rhetoric. She contends that in his desire to establish a logical foundation for rhetoric Aristotle conflated dialectical analysis and syllogistic analysis, which, according to Raphael, are incompatible. Thus the confusion in the *Rhetoric* does not evidence literary layers but Aristotle's mistake in trying to import the dialectical distinction between induction and deduction into rhetorical argument, which is almost always inductive. Against Raphael, I do not think the lack of formal premises necessarily implies that the argument in Aristotle's terms cannot be deductive.

ἐνθύμημα μὲν ῥητορικὸν συλλογισμόν, παράδειγμα δὲ ἐπαγωγὴν
ῥητορικήν)"[51]. He limits all rhetorical proofs to either enthymeme or
paradigm, and nothing else[52]. That is to say, all argument is either deductive or inductive. Aristotle believed that paradigms have probative force
but that they are less effective than enthymemes[53]. In fact, he devotes
very little attention to paradigms; most of his discussion focuses upon the
enthymeme. In what follows we shall trace out the characteristics of the
Aristotelian enthymeme. When we attempt to discuss the paradigms in
the Pastorals we will need to examine other sources of ethical paradigms
in the Greco-Roman world to complete the Aristotelian discussion.

Aristotle proffers a distinction between enthymemes based upon special topics (ἴδιοι τόποι or εἴδη) and those based upon common topics
(κοινοὶ τόποι)[54]. He declares that most arguments are composed out of
special topics, which he defines as propositions which are particular and
special to each subject[55]. He adds the argument that the special topics
useful for ethics are not useful for physics[56]. While special topics are composed out of propositions peculiar to an individual subject, the common
topics are proper to all subjects[57]. Having made this distinction, he proceeds to detail the three kinds (εἴδη) of rhetorical speeches: deliberative,
forensic, and epideictic. He distinguishes each by the role of the hearer,
the subject of the speech, and the timeframe of the speech[58]. He then
analyzes the special topics peculiar to each[59].

This three-fold distinction of the kinds of speeches makes sense only
because Aristotle conceives of politics as the field of rhetoric. The audience of the speech is composed of the judge and the attendant assem-
bly[60]. Although parenesis of the kind in the Pastorals does not coincide
exactly with any of these three, it falls most comfortably under the aegis
of deliberative[61]. Aristotle describes the deliberative as hortatory and dis-
suasive (συμβουλῆς δὲ τὸ μὲν προτροπὴ τὸ δὲ ἀποτροπή): it relates to
the future, concerning what one ought to do[62]. The end (τέλος) is what

---

[51]Ibid., 1356b4—6.
[52]Ibid., 1356b6—8.
[53]Ibid., 1356b23—27.
[54]Ibid., 1358a10—35.
[55]Ibid., 1358a17—18.
[56]Ibid., 1358a18—21.
[57]Ibid., 1358a29—32.
[58]Ibid., 1358a36—b20.
[59]Ibid., 1359a30—1391b6.
[60]Ibid., 1358a36—b8.
[61]In addition to the observations which follow, we can perhaps locate an explanation for this
relationship in the history of ancient genres. Wendland theorized that the diatribe, which clearly
provides the closest stylistic parallel to the Pastorals, emerged from a combination of the philosophic dialogue with the methods of rhetoric (Paul Wendland, Die hellenistisch-römische Kultur,
2d and 3rd eds. [Tübingen: J. C. B. Mohr (Paul Siebeck), 1912], pp. 77—81).
[62]Aristotle Rhetoric 1358b8.

is expedient and harmful (τὸ συμφέρον καὶ βλαβερόν)[63]. Further, it is when discussing the special topics of deliberative rhetoric that Aristotle notes the connection between rhetoric and ethics[64]. And, although he defines the most important subjects as the ways and means of the state, war and peace, defense, imports and exports, and legislation, he also discusses much of what is proper to ethics. Since deliberation deals with how to choose what is useful, Aristotle analyzes what happiness is, dividing it into its component parts, because happiness is useful. He notes that a similar treatment of virtue is in place, but since virtue is more closely connected with epideictic oratory he postpones it. He then discusses how to evaluate the relationship between means and ends, things we choose for their own sake or for something else. He defines the basic elements (στοιχεῖα) of what is good and expedient. Since virtues are good, he gives a brief analysis, postponing details till later. He analyzes the relationship of time to what is good, how to evaluate the greater and lesser among goods, and in fact details a diverse array of subtleties of how to determine what is better than something else[65]. There is no point in trying to trace out the complexities of this enumeration of the special topics of deliberation, but it is important to understand what Aristotle means by the designation "special topic" and what its relationship is to the common topics.

Grimaldi has pointed out that, although this distinction preceded Aristotle and continued in rhetoric afterwards, Aristotle in fact gave this a special reading, unique to him[66]. Grimaldi proposes, as a basis for the Aristotelian distinction, that special topics are the material for propositions while the common topics are the forms of inference of these propositions. Special topics provide the factual information appropriate to a given subject and compose a single proposition to an enthymeme. The common topics are the "forms of inference" or "modes of reasoning"[67]. They are the shape which propositions take. Grimaldi's proposal is helpful. The twenty-eight common topics are indeed concerned with kinds of inference[68]. Grimaldi divides them into those based upon antecedent-consequent or

---

[63]Ibid., 1358b22.

[64]Ibid., 1359b8—12.

[65]Ibid., 1359a30—1366a22.

[66]William M. Grimaldi, "The Aristotelian *Topics*," in *Aristotle: The Classical Heritage in Rhetoric*, pp. 176—93. Cf. Solmsen, "The Aristotelian Tradition in Ancient Rhetoric," esp. pp. 280—82, 287—92.

[67]Grimaldi, "The Aristotelian *Topics*," p. 186. But cf. Sprute, *Die Enthymemetheorie der aristotelischen Rhetorik*, pp. 156—57, who rejects Grimaldi's distinction.

[68]Aristotle *Rhetoric* 1396b19—1400b33. For a summary of the diverse terminology used to describe the nature of common topics see Donovan J. Ochs, "Aristotle's Concept of Formal Topics," in *Aristotle: The Classical Heritage of Rhetoric*, pp. 194—95. For examples of these topics as illustrated in speeches with which Aristotle may have been familiar see Georgiana Paine Palmer, "The ΤΟΠΟΙ of Aristotle's Rhetoric as Exemplified in the Orators" (Dissertation, University of Chicago, 1932).

cause-effect, more-less, and some form of relation[69]. Cicero treats the topics more as deposits of argument, but Aristotle seems to envision them as shapes an argument might take. Furthermore, we do not find full enthymemes among the special topics[70]. Perhaps Grimaldi is correct that the two must be put together. Thus to define a virtue as good does not constitute an argument unless one combines it with a cause-effect or more-less structure. Courage is good, "this" leads to courage, thus "this" is good. Only thus combined do we have an enthymeme.

Yet there are problems with Grimaldi. One must wonder how the commonplaces fit this schema. Also Aristotle expressly says that most ($\tau \dot{a}$ $\pi \lambda \epsilon \hat{\iota} \sigma \tau a$) enthymemes are constructed from special topics, and fewer ($\dot{\epsilon} \lambda \acute{a} \tau \tau \omega$) from the common topics, thereby implying that some enthymemes can be built strictly out of one of the twenty-eight common topics without the material of special topics[71]. Nevertheless, the analyses of Cope and Sprute on the relationship, which seem to be the other major options, do not really clarify all this[72]. It appears from this that the exact relationship is unclear, encouraging some commentators to deny the literary unity of the *Rhetoric*, believing it to be composed in stages and thus to be unharmonized[73]. Given this, Grimaldi's explanation remains the most helpful though it must be accepted with the caveat that some common topics can stand on their own.

Between the special topics and the common topics, Aristotle treats the commonplaces, the paradigms, and maxims[74]. Although we shall return to his treatment of paradigms, we should mention at this point his analysis of maxims. He defines a maxim as a saying ($\dot{a} \pi \acute{o} \varphi a \nu \sigma \iota \varsigma$) which deals not with particulars or with all kinds of universals but with the objects of

---

[69]Grimaldi, "The Aristotelian *Topics*," p. 183. Arnhart, *Aristotle on Political Reasoning*, not only accepts Grimaldi's distinction between special topics and common topics (pp. 47–48), but also his categorization of the common topics into these three patterns (p. 148).

[70]See Raphael, "Rhetoric, Dialectic, and Syllogistic Argument," pp. 162–66, who points out the complications and inconsistencies in the *Rhetoric* over this distinction.

[71]Aristotle *Rhetoric* 1358a26–28.

[72]Cope, *An Introduction to Aristotle's Rhetoric*, pp. 128–29, detects three kinds of topics in the *Rhetoric*, including what Grimaldi and Arnhart call the commonplaces. Although he notes that the special topics are "materials" and that the common topics are "heads of families of similar arguments," he does not attempt to interrelate the two, distinguishing them primarily by the range of subject matter with which they can deal. Sprute, *Die Enthymemetheorie der aristotelischen Rhetorik*, argues that no definition of topics is adequate. Sprute speaks of many different kinds of topics, some of which make enthymemes possible and some of which stand alone. He demonstrates in this way that Aristotle's various comments in the *Rhetoric* cannot be systematized. However, he does not offer an option for comprehending the topics which we can use here. I do not find, in any case, anything in Sprute which contradicts the line taken here.

[73]The theory of literary layers goes back to Solmsen, *Die Entwicklung der Aristotelischen Logik und Rhetorik*. Ochs, "Aristotle's Concept of Formal Topics," pp. 194–204, detects layers for different reasons (see p. 201, n. 15, for further bibliography). Cf. Raphael, "Rhetoric, Dialectic, and Syllogistic Argument," pp. 161–67, for a critique of Solmsen.

[74]Aristotle *Rhetoric* 1391b7–1397a6.

human action and the choice and refusal of certain actions[75]. They are single propositions in an enthymeme and can be either a premise or a conclusion[76]. Thus, he says that a maxim to which the why and wherefore are added (προστεθείσης δὲ τῆς αἰτίας καὶ τοῦ διὰ τί) becomes a complete enthymeme[77]. He gives the following example: " 'There is no man who is really free' is a maxim, but when taken with the next sentence is an enthymeme: 'for he is the slave of either wealth or fortune' "[78]. A maxim is particularly useful for its persuasive powers. First, maxims persuade because of the vulgarity (διὰ τὴν φορτικότητα) of the hearers, who are pleased if an orator hits upon opinions they themselves hold. For instance, a man who has bad neighbors enjoys a maxim which laments the stupidity of neighbors[79]. Secondly, they persuade because they make the speech ethical (ἠθικοὺς γὰρ ποιεῖ τοὺς λόγους)[80]. They accomplish this by making the moral purpose (προαίρεσις) of the speaker clear; for when maxims are good they show the speaker of them to be good[81].

In summary, Aristotle provides several distinctions helpful for comprehending the kind of argumentation which occurs in the Pastorals. His success in analyzing the structure and logical status of rhetorical argument, differentiating it from scientific logic but nevertheless demonstrating its coherent structure and probative status, removes the onus of sloppiness and nonsense from arguments in the Pastorals which are concerned with probabilities not necessities. This non-necessary character of ethical logic, Aristotle surmises, originates from rhetoric's goal of persuasion. Thus while changing to a new terminology, Aristotle provides categories and standards to analyze the sources and structures of rhetorical logic and for distinguishing true enthymemes from fallacious ones.

As noted above, Aristotle calls deductive arguments enthymemes. The propositions of enthymemes are mostly drawn from the special topics of a given subject, but may be drawn from general opinions, maxims, signs, or paradigms, all of which are probable and not necessary[82]. Furthermore, good rhetorical style recommends the suppression of one element of the enthymeme, for it is not persuasive to state the obvious or the foolish. This truncated structure encourages the participation of the audience. Nevertheless, enthymemes are constructed from commonplaces and common topics which are basically sound. That is to say, they are built upon

---

[75]Ibid., 1394a21–25.
[76]Ibid., 1394a26–28.
[77]Ibid., 1394a31–32.
[78]Ibid., 1394a4–6.
[79]Ibid., 1395b1–11.
[80]Ibid., 1395b12–13.
[81]Ibid., 1395b16–17.
[82]The necessary signs (τεκμήρια) are an apparent exception, since Aristotle declares that necessary signs are those signs from which syllogisms can be constructed (ibid., 1357b6–7). See Cope, *An Introduction to Aristotle's Rhetoric*, pp. 160–68, for an analysis of necessary signs and the less than satisfactory examples which Aristotle provides in the *Rhetoric*.

theories of cause-effect, more-less, and forms of relationship which are part of the way people think. The twenty-eight common topics, the four commonplaces, the careful definitions and distinctions within the special topics give enthymemes probative and epistemological status. Aristotle is careful to distinguish rhetoric from sophistry, for, while the latter disregards questions of truth and falsehood, rhetoric is governed by epistemological standards and focuses upon what is "probably" true[83].

In order to analyze the deductive argumentation in the Pastorals, we shall begin with the special topic, noting the kinds and analyzing a few examples along with the relationship of these to the common topics; then we shall investigate the enthymemes which appear to be common topics; and finally we shall consider enthymemes built out of maxims, including scripture. These categories will provide a structure for every enthymematic argument in the Pastorals. Paradigms and inductive arguments will need a further theoretical basis before they can be adequately analyzed.

Just as Aristotle says that most enthymemes are built out of special topics, nearly all the enthymematic arguments in the Pastorals are based upon the peculiar belief system of the author. Therefore most of his arguments would be persuasive only to persons who shared his general religious presuppositions. His arguments are based upon special topics peculiar to a segment of early Christianity. They are, furthermore, deliberative in that they concern decisions about the future, about what is expedient and harmful, and thus about what one ought to do. Of course, the data are not drawn from the dynamics of the state and the role of virtue in public life, as they are in Aristotelian deliberative rhetoric, but from the dynamics of God's plan of salvation, the needs of the church community, and the role of virtues in their private and public ramifications. The complexities and details of this plan of salvation will be analyzed in the next chapter, but at this point we can partition these special topics into several categories, realizing as we do this that some of the propositions in the Pastorals might be classed under a couple of these categories.

The special topics in the Pastorals are drawn from (1) salvation statements, (2) the character of the religious life, and (3) the entrusted traditions. Salvation statements are those propositions which explicitly articulate the relationship between certain human actions and the actions or demands of God. Within this category distinctions need to be made among statements which refer to (a) God or Jesus as actors (creator, savior, or

---

[83]Arnhart's recent commentary focuses upon the partial epistemological status given to rhetoric by Aristotle. His thesis that "rhetoric is a genuine form of reasoning" constitutes in fact the major thesis of his study (Arnhart, *Aristotle on Political Reasoning*, p. 183). It is obvious that Aristotle does intend to distinguish between sophistry and rhetoric since he opens Book I by detailing the differences. In this he is at odds with Plato who only distinguishes dialectic from sophistry, thereby denigrating the latter and rhetoric along with it (cf. Plato *Gorgias* 452E, *Soph.* 222C, *Apol.* 17A, 18D). Thus when Aristotle opens his *Rhetoric* by calling rhetoric the counterpart of dialectic he is trying to move it from its linkage with sophistry, which has no positive connection with truth, into a linkage with dialectic, which has a more positive relationship with truth.

judge), (b) things which lead to salvation because God's plan of salvation is structured in a certain way, (c) the wants or demands of God, (d) prophecies or the activity of the spirit, and (e) the prescriptions of scripture. Appeals to the proper character of the religious life not only seem to presuppose the crucial role of virtues in the processes of salvation but also seem to focus upon (a) their private dimensions or (b) their corporate dimensions. The appeals to the entrusted traditions or the sound teachings examine doctrines and ethical standards by how well they agree with the author's sense of his traditions.

Aristotle's analysis of enthymemes suggests that these materials in themselves do not constitute an argument but must be given a logical shape. The common topics describe the shape these materials might take when they are   incorporated into a full deductive argument[84]. Grimaldi suggests that the common topics are of three kinds: (1) cause and effect (antecedent-consequent), (2) more and less, and (3) some form of relation[85]. This simplification is helpful for analyzing the structure of arguments in the Pastorals since it is very difficult to insist upon exact correspondences. Palmer's attempt to compare the common topics in the *Rhetoric* to the speeches with which Aristotle may have been conversant shows that only in the case of Isocrates can many one-to-one correspondences be found[86]. Recourse to Cicero's *Topica* helps even less since they are so slanted to the courtroom[87]. But, working with Grimaldi's divisions, nearly all the enthymemes in the Pastorals take the shape of "cause and effect." This is so because the author is arguing about what leads to salvation and what does not. Within the umbrella of cause and effect Grimaldi places eight of the twenty-eight common topics[88], and thus we can use this simplification without trying to decide whether a given enthymeme is based, for example, on consequences or causes. All of the enthymemes which follow immediately below are understood as taking the form of inference known as cause and effect. There are a few arguments which seem to relate better to other of the common topics and these will be noted as they occur.

1. Salvation Statements

Salvation statements serve a variety of functions in argumentative structures in the Pastorals and the enthymemes in which they occur can be

---

[84]Grimaldi, "The Aristotelian *Topics*," p. 186.

[85]Ibid., p. 183.

[86]Palmer, "The ΤΟΠΟΙ of Aristotle's Rhetoric as Exemplified in the Orators."

[87]George Alexander Kennedy, *The Art of Rhetoric in the Roman World, 300 B.C.–A.D. 300* (Princeton: Princeton University Press, 1972), gives a comprehensive account of the growth and transformations of rhetoric in the Greco-Roman era.

[88]Grimaldi, "The Aristotelian *Topics*," p. 183.

quite abbreviated or lengthy and complex. The most common form of these statements is in terms of the activity of God or Jesus. Herein I would include 1 Tim. 1.12–17; 2.5–7; 3.16; 4.5, 10; 6.12, 13, 14–16; 2 Tim. 1.8–10, 18; 2.11–13, 19, 25–26; 3.9; 4.1, 10, 14, 17–18; Tit. 1.1– 3; 2.11–14; 3.4–7.

In their simplest form these are structured like 1 Tim. 1.15 which reads, "This saying is reliable and worthy of all acceptance, that Christ Jesus came into the world to save sinners, among whom I am the foremost." The precise argument can be expressed in syllogistic form as follows:

    (A) Major premise: Jesus saves sinners.

    (B) Minor premise: I am a sinner.

    (C) Conclusion: Thus Jesus saved me.

The conclusion was not quoted above but is stated in both 1.13 and 1.16. This logically coherent argument depends upon the author's understanding of who Jesus is and what Jesus does. None of the common topics as defined by Aristotle corresponds exactly to this sort of special topic, although we can imagine how some of the ethical material under special topics of deliberative rhetoric could take this kind of shape when used in an enthymeme[89]. We also note that 1 Tim. 1.15 seems to be, on the one hand, a self-contained enthymeme, but on the other hand, a single moment in a larger argument of 1 Tim. 1.12–17. Quintilian and Cicero both understand the enthymeme (actually the term has changed to $\epsilon\pi\iota\chi\epsilon\iota\rho\eta\mu\alpha$ or *ratiocinatio*) as being five-fold rather than three-fold[90]. Quintilian gives a description of the diversity and complexity of the discussion about the form of the enthymeme, and both he and Cicero describe the five-fold schema as major premise, proof of major premise, minor premise, proof of minor premise, and conclusion[91]. Cicero notes that this full form is often compressed into four elements or less[92]. Actually it would be difficult and ultimately misleading to force the argumentation in 1.12–17 into this schema and yet the author is clearly building argument upon argument. This is typical of the Pastorals: we see some enthymemes so compressed as to appear without logical coherence and others which are caught up in complex arguments. In 1.12–17 complete enthymemes are contained in 1.12–13; 15; and 16; and they seem to reinforce one another.

The enthymeme in 1 Tim. 4.3–5 illustrates the frequent combination in the Pastorals of enthymematic arguments with imperatives. Aristotle connects some of the special topics of deliberative rhetoric with imperatives or at least with choice, and two of his common topics are similarly

---

[89]For examples see Palmer, "The TOΠOI of Aristotle's Rhetoric as Exemplified in the Orators." Aristotle's analysis of special topics for deliberative rhetoric does not consist of composing enthymemes but of detailing the special material from which arguments can be drawn: "Now let us again derive our arguments for exhortation or discussion on these and other questions" (*Rhetoric* 1360b1–3).

[90]See p. 71, n. 21.

[91]Quintilian 5.13; Cicero *De Inventione* 1.57–67.

[92]Cicero *De Inventione* 1.70–77.

connected[93]. Since both deliberative rhetoric and the Pastorals are dealing with good and bad options and with proper behavior, the recourse to imperatives is natural. 1 Tim. 4.3—5 is the second half of a prediction by the spirit of the character of heretics in later times which continues the description by saying,

> ... who prohibit marriage, [telling us] to abstain from food, which God created to be received with thanksgiving by those who believe and know the truth. Because everything created by God is good, and nothing is to be thrown away which is received with thanksgiving, for it is made holy through the word of God and prayer.

The structure of this argument is complex and does not fall readily into syllogistic form, yet it is logically coherent.

(A) Everything God created was created to be used.

(A) Everything God created can be sanctified with prayer.

(B) God created food.

(C) Food ought to be used and be received with prayer.

The contention that the author does not make coherent theological arguments when debating his opponents cannot be squared with passages such as this[94]. The argument is based upon the author's conception of God as creator and its ramifications in daily life. Once again, we must notice that this enthymeme is combined with another in 4.1—2, producing a double-pronged refutation of the ascetic practices of the author's opponents. In this instance, the imperative is only implied, since no verb occurs here in the imperative mood.

The second most frequent form of salvation statement occurs in special topics which rely upon identifying things which lead to salvation because God's plan of salvation is structured in a certain way. Herein I would include 1 Tim. 1.8—10; 2.15; 3.6—7, 13, 14—16; 4.7—8, 16; 5.24—25; 6.9, 17—19; 2 Tim. 2.9, 10, 11—13; Tit. 1.13; 3.3—11.

In its simplest form these come as an assertion that one should do something because it leads to salvation. 1 Tim. 4.7—8 typifies this structure: "Train yourself for piety. For bodily training is helpful only a little, but piety is helpful for everything, having the promise of life now and to come."

(A) Piety leads to life (salvation).

(B) Training can produce piety.

(C) If you want life, train yourself towards piety.

The enthymeme is full and the conclusion comes as an imperative. It is, of course, assumed that life or salvation is desirable. Both premises are based upon the author's special conception of God's plan of salvation and consequently the argument would only be forceful with people who share this vision. Once again, this enthymeme seems to be connected with enthy-

---

[93] See Aristotle's definition of deliberative rhetoric (*Rhetoric* 1358b20—25) and the common topics devoted to exhortation and dissuasion (ibid. 1399a11—29).

[94] See, for example, Brox, *Die Pastoralbriefe*, pp. 39—41.

memes immediately preceding and following. 1 Tim. 4.6 is an enthymeme based upon the premise of the effectiveness of the sound teachings. 1 Tim. 4.9—10 provides an enthymeme to prove the validity of the major premise that piety leads to salvation. This agrees with Cicero's contention that full enthymemes provide separate proofs for their premises. 1 Tim. 4.10 was categorized as a special topic based upon the activity of God. Therefore, the author has constructed here an argument with several tiers, corresponding perhaps to the four member enthymeme (although this structure does not leave room for 4.6).

1 Tim. 6.17—19 proffers a structure of similar complexity.

> Command those who are rich in the present age to not be haughty nor to put their hopes in the uncertainty of riches, but in God, who provides us everything richly for enjoyment, to do good, to be rich in good deeds, to be generous, sharing, storing up for themselves a good foundation for the future so that they may obtain true life.

This enthymeme appeals to the author's belief that richness in good deeds rather than richness in things leads to salvation. The imperative which forms the conclusion grows out of the problem of choice between alternate ways of living. Although he provides a statement about the activity of God, the specific content of that statement does not constitute a premise in the enthymeme. The premises come out of the structure of God's plan of salvation, a structure which is detailed and anchored in God in other parts of the letter.

There are three enthymemes (1 Tim. 2.3—4; 4.4; 5.4) which seem to appeal simply to what God wants, arguing that something should be done because God wants it done without any explicit connections to salvation. Thus 1 Tim. 5.4 says, "If a widow has children or grandchildren, let them learn first of all to be pious towards their own household and to return to their progenitors what is owed, for this is acceptable before God."

Other enthymemes depend upon the activity of the spirit either in prophecy or in other modes. These include 1 Tim. 1.18—19; 4.1—3; 2 Tim. 1.6—7, 14; 3.1; 4.3—4. We have already mentioned 1 Tim. 4.1—3 which is a prophecy by the spirit combined with an enthymeme on the activity of God as creator. 2 Tim. 1.6—7 illustrates this appeal to the spirit outside of its connection with prophecy.

> For this reason I am reminding you to rekindle the gift of God which is in you through the laying on of my hands. For God did not give us a spirit of cowardice but of power and love and moderation.

Although this might be classified as a topic from definition, it actually depends on the author's linkage of the spirit with virtues[95]. The argument is

---

[95]Palmer, "The ΤΟΠΟΙ of Aristotle's Rhetoric as Exemplified in the Orators," p. 29, describes the topic from definition as "to state some particular aspect of the thing under discussion as to make it correspond to something else, and usually to something about which the audience has a settled opinion; or else to give a definition of the other thing which brings it to coincide with that under discussion." Thus the author of the Pastorals addresses the problem of flagging leader-

structured along the lines that the spirit which you have has certain qualities, thus you should act accordingly. This is another example of the intimate and unbreakable connection the author creates between his ethics
and salvation statements.

Finally there are two scriptural passages which fit into the category of
salvation statements, since they define the process of salvation as established by God. The rest of the scriptural citations function more as maxims
and will be considered with them. 1 Tim. 2.11—14 contains an enthymeme with an imperatival conclusion based upon a midrash-style exegesis
of the Adam and Eve story[96].

> Let a woman learn quietly and in all obedience; I do not allow a woman to teach or to have
> authority over a man (or her husband), but to be in silence. For Adam was formed first, then
> Eve; and Adam was not deceived but the woman being deceived fell into transgression.

2 Tim. 3.8 also discovers in scripture the pattern wherein salvation occurs
or does not occur. Whereas the Adam and Eve story provides proof of the
danger of women escaping their proper place and proffers thereby a proscription for the correct order in the church, in 2 Tim. 3.8 the story of
Jannes and Jambres who opposed Moses is used as an analogue for those
who oppose the teaching of the author. In both instances, scripture describes the structure of God's plan of salvation; and in both, the analysis
enables the author to draw conclusions about proper behavior.

Moreover, both of these passages lack full syllogistic form. They leave
unexpressed the major premise which allows the generalization from Eve
to all disobedient women or from Jannes and Jambres to all opponents.
This means that in form they are close to being inductive arguments rather
than deductive and thus function more as paradigms than as enthymemes.
As has often been pointed out, the line between induction and deduction,
when dealing with paradigms or examples, is difficult to draw[97]. Aristotle
himself lists induction as the tenth common topic, which is supposed to
be deductive[98]. The illustrations he gives are difficult to distinguish in
form from his paradigms. They are analyzed here since they do more than
create analogies based on part to part as paradigms do, but furthermore
participate in and articulate the basic structure of the salvation process.

2. The Character of the Religious Life

This category is closely related to those salvation statements which are

---

ship by enlisting the nature of the spirit. For a discussion of the connection between the spirit
and virtues, see the next chapter.

[96]Anthony Tyrell Hanson, "Eve's Transgression: 1 Timothy 2.13—15," *Studies in the Pastoral
Epistles* (London: S.P.C.K., 1969), pp. 65—77.

[97]See especially Raphael, "Rhetoric, Dialectic, and Syllogistic Argument," who declares that
the distinction between induction and deduction, while valid for dialectic, is not valid for rhetoric.

based upon the structure of God's plan of salvation but take the form of straightforward assertions of virtue or descriptions of the pious life (and their opposites). These assertions include virtue and vice lists, which will receive extensive analysis in the next chapter, along with all the enthymemes built upon ethical standards which receive no additional warrant to claims about their salvific impact. Even though explicit linkage to the processes of salvation does not occur in these arguments, other arguments in the letters show that this linkage is presupposed here[99]. Therefore, these special topics based on virtues and good deeds take the form of inference of cause and effect, for these virtues lead to salvation or the lack thereof to judgment. The most frequent form is an imperative to do something because it is a virtue or to refrain from something else because it is a vice.

Although nearly every virtue has both private and public dimensions, most of the special topics based on the value of the pious life focus either upon the private dimension or the public. The enthymemes based on private virtue or vice include 1 Tim. 2,2, 9–10; 3.1–3, 8–10, 11–12; 4.6; 5.6–8, 9, 11–12; 6.4–5, 11; 2 Tim. 2.3, 22–24; 3.2–5, 13, 17; Tit. 1.6–8, 16; 2.2–10.

1 Tim. 5.5–8 contains an enthymeme with an imperatival conclusion which appeals simply to proper and improper behavior of a widow.

> She who is a true widow and is alone has put her hope in God and remains in prayers and petitions night and day, but she who lives profligately has died. Exhort these things so that they might be beyond reproach. But if anyone does not care for his own people especially his own family, that person has denied the faith and is worse than an unbeliever.

The premises which support the conclusion in this argument are derived from the author's opinion of what is appropriate and inappropriate for certain people. He provides no further warrant beyond the preemptive assertion that a true widow behaves in a certain way. Given the acceptance of this premise, the conclusion that widows must be exhorted to behave thus is valid. This is a striking example of what Aristotle means by enthymemes based on common opinions (ἔνδοξα)[100]. If the audience accepts the premise, in this case that widows should behave thus, then the argument is sound. The form of inference is valid; only the premise is tentative. Furthermore, the major premise which involves the salvific effect of being proper to one's place in the community is suppressed. Thus we have a formally incomplete enthymeme based on a probability not a certainty.

2 Tim. 3.17 contains a premise to an enthymeme on the value of scripture. After detailing the pedagogical functions of scripture the author adds

---

See also Gerald A. Hauser, "The Example in Aristotle's *Rhetoric:* Bifurcation or Contradiction?" in *Aristotle: The Classical Heritage of Rhetoric*, pp. 156–68.

[98]Aristotle *Rhetoric* 1398a34–b20.

[99]On this connection see next chapter. Also see, for example, Tit. 2.11–14.

[100]Aristotle *Rhetoric* 1355a17–18; also 1355a27–28, 1395b31–1396a4, 1402a33–34. See also p. 74, nn. 37, 38.

the result clause, "so that the man of God might be complete, equipped for every good work." Thus the enthymeme can be analyzed as follows:

(A) A man of God should do good works.
(B) Scripture equips one for good works.
(C) Therefore, study scripture.

As with many of the enthymemes, the major premise is suppressed, but the reader can readily (unconsciously) supply it. Aristotle argues that a suppressed premise should be easy to discover, and in most cases this is true in the Pastorals.

The enthymemes based upon special topics which are drawn from the qualities of the pious life as they relate to the community are 1 Tim. 1.3–5; 5.4, 10, 13, 16, 20; 6.2; 2 Tim. 2.14, 16–17; 3.6–7; Tit. 1.10–11; 3. 8–9, 14. These enthymemes exhort or discourage behavior on the basis of its impact on the community.

> Remind them of these things, adjuring them before God to not dispute over words, which is useful for nothing but brings destruction on those who hear. Be eager to present yourself as approved, an unashamed worker, who makes straight the word of truth. But avoid profane and empty words for they will make more and more progress towards impiety (2 Tim. 2.14–16).

Especially in v. 14 the premise from which the imperative conclusion is drawn consists of the author's interpretation of the usefulness of debates about words. This same interpretation is employed in v. 16. In both cases a second premise which might justify this interpretation is omitted. Logically we have a two-member enthymeme which is repeated twice with minor variations.

We will note in the next chaper how all the virtue and vice lists seem to be slanted more towards their impact on the community than upon the private dimension, and oftentimes the virtues seem to be strictly communal.

> Let someone be enrolled as a widow, being not less than sixty years old, wife of one man, who is attested by good works, if she has cared for children, was hospitable to strangers, washed the feet of the saints, helped the oppressed, and has pursued every good work (1 Tim. 5.9–10).

The unexpressed major premise for such an enthymeme would declare that these enumerated actions are beneficial to the church. To express this would be to state the obvious and thus would distract from the flow of argument. The reader easily and probably unconsciously supplies the premise.

Within the category of enthymemes based on premises about the pious life a third type must be added to the private and communal, namely, the public. The author appeals to the opinion of outsiders in 1 Tim. 3.7; 5.7, 14; Tit. 2.5, 8. For instance, 1 Tim. 6.1 argues "Whoever are slaves under the yoke, let them consider their own masters worthy of all honor, so that the name of God and the teachings are not blasphemed." A major premise declaring that the work of God should not be blasphemed would be superfluous.

3. The Entrusted Tradition

The third major category of special topics in the Pastorals consists of enthymemes wherein the author appeals to tradition, the sound teachings, or the true gospel. These include 1 Tim. 1.11; 4,6; 6.3, 20; 2 Tim. 2.2, 8–9; 3.14–17; Tit. 1.5, 9; 2.1.

Tit. 1.9 concludes a listing of requisite virtues for a bishop with "who holds fast to the reliable preaching which is in accordance with the teachings, so that he might be able to exhort by the sound teachings and to rebuke those who are opposed." The conclusion that a bishop should do this depends upon the expressed minor premise that adherence to the sound teachings enables the bishop to meet his duties of exhortation and rebuke. A major premise which establishes the place of these teachings in the plan of salvation is unexpressed here, although that connection is established elsewhere in the letters.

When all these kinds of special topics in the Pastorals are compared with the remarks of Aristotle in the *Rhetoric*, it is clear that these enthymemes, which are built out of special topics, have no probative force with people who do not share with the author his unique set of beliefs. Aristotle's tendency to analyze the persuasiveness of rhetorical arguments by concentrating on the ambiguous epistemological status of the probabilities which compose the premises of these arguments explains how the author of the Pastorals can construct enthymemes out of such private premises. As Aristotle points out, all that is needed is that the audience and the speaker can agree on a premise[101]. Once agreement is reached, then the enthymemes have the same epistemological force as any dialectical argument. Thus the Pastorals are addressed to the rather small audience of those who can agree with the author's premises.

Some of the enthymemes in the Pastorals show strong correspondence with some of the common topics in the *Rhetoric*. These enthymemes would appear to be more general or public in that they do not presuppose any private set of beliefs. 1 Tim. 1.15–16; 3.4–5; and perhaps Tit. 1.6 use the form of inference which Aristotle calls "the greater and lesser." 1 Tim. 5.23 depends on the topic of health; 2 Tim. 2.21–22 on the topic of analogy; and 2 Tim. 3.10–13 on the topic of opposites. This list could be expanded if one wanted to be aggressive in these analogies. For instance, the author of the Pastorals seems to argue constantly in terms of contrasts or oppositions between one life-style or set of beliefs and another (his and his opponents) and this method relates to Aristotle's topic of opposites.

1 Tim. 3.4–5 builds an enthymeme out of the common topic of greater and lesser in the midst of a virtue list for bishops, saying "[a bishop ought] to rule his own household well, keeping his children in obedience with all

---

[101]Aristotle, *Rhetoric* 1395b31–1396a3.

dignity. If someone does not know how to govern his own house, how will he care for the church of God?" The logic depends upon the common assumption that inability to accomplish easy things suggests an inability to accomplish harder ones.

Aristotle treats maxims as sayings which can be used as a premise in an enthymeme; thus he considers them as elements in deductive reasoning. The Pastorals use scriptural citations in 1 Tim. 5.17–18 and 2 Tim. 2.19 in the same fashion as they employ non-scriptural maxims in 1 Tim. 4.8; 6.6–8, 10; 2 Tim. 2.4–6; and Tit. 1.12, 15. Whether scriptural or non-scriptural, these maxims are presented as valid premises from which conclusions can be drawn. In this way, they are neither special topics nor common topics but are still constituent parts of an enthymeme. The common topic of previous judgment probably provides the form of inference for enthymemes based on maxims.

1 Tim. 5.17–18 uses two scriptural passages as premises:

> Let elders who rule well be considered worthy of double honor, especially those who labor in speaking and teaching. For scripture says, "You shall not muzzle the ox which treads grain," and "The worker is worthy of his wages."

The enthymeme builds upon the premise provided by the two scriptural passages that workers should be paid for their work. The minor premise establishing the analogy between elders and laborers is unexpressed as such a banal premise should be. Only the conclusion which includes provisions for double payment for double work is puzzling. Perhaps this doubling in the conclusion explains the need for two scriptural passages.

The series of three maxims in 2 Tim. 2.3–7 seems to have the same probative force as scripture.

> Share in the suffering like a good soldier of Christ Jesus. No soldier on service gets entangled in the affairs of everyday life, so that he can please the one who enlisted him. And if someone competes in athletics, he is not crowned unless he competes according to the rules. It is the farmer who does the work who should have his share first of the crop. Think about what I say, for the Lord will give you understanding in all things.

Three maxims are placed back to back without interpretation as premises to the exhortations to be strong in the grace, to entrust the teachings to faithful men, and to share in the sufferings. There is no apparent direct correspondence between the three imperatives and the three maxims, although we must suspect that the tripling of the maxims comes from the existence of three imperatives which need premises. The first maxim obviously picks up on the term soldier, but the other two seem to have no similar correspondence. Thus the logic becomes very general and perhaps not all that easy for the reader to supply. Certainly the three imperatives and the three maxims all deal with people fulfilling their proper duties and being treated accordingly. This suggests an explanation for why an enthymeme that is based on a maxim is normally incomplete, lacking the premise which details the connection between the maxim and the problem at hand. The connection can be difficult to articulate even when the maxim seems appropriate to the author.

The preceding analysis of enthymemes is intended to be comprehensive in that it includes every obvious instance of deductive reasoning in the Pastorals. No doubt, other readers of the Pastorals would want to change his list, either adding or subtracting or moving passages to different categories; therefore, this analysis is not intended to be beyond question in all its details. Nevertheless, the Aristotelian analysis of enthymematic argument provides adequate categories for all the deductive reasoning in the Pastorals. Furthermore, this analysis demonstrates that the author is making an argument or arguments and is not just juxtaposing diverse materials without design. Also in this way, we have seen that the author depends on certain data in order to make his arguments. The special topics come from a wide range of special premises. The system behind this special material will be the subject of the next chapter. Our immediate conclusion, however, is that the individual propositions in the Pastorals are interrelated logically and that Aristotle describes the character of this ethical logic in the first two books of the *Rhetoric*.

B. The paradigm: Inductive and Illustrative

The second major proof in the *Rhetoric* is the paradigm, which Aristotle calls the rhetorical form of induction.

> We have said that a paradigm is a kind of induction and with what kind of material it deals by way of induction. It is neither the relation of part to whole (οὔτε ὡς μέρος πρὸς ὅλον), nor of whole to part, nor of one whole to another whole, but of part to part, of like to like (ὡς μέρος πρὸς μέρος, ὅμοιον πρὸς ὅμοιον), when both come under the same genus, but one of them is better known than the other. For example, to prove that Dionysius is aiming at a tyranny, because he asks for a bodyguard, one might say Pisistratus before him and Theagenes of Megara did the same, and when they obtained what they asked for they made themselves tyrants. All the other tyrants known may serve as a paradigm of Dionysius, whose reason, however, for asking for a bodyguard we do not yet know. All these paradigms are contained under the same universal principle (καθόλου), that one who is aiming at a tyranny asks for a bodyguard[102].

Paradigms do not rely on complete correspondence but only on part to part or like to like. Furthermore, it is only this single point of correspondence which constitutes the moment of logic. Paradigms are refuted by showing that the dissimilarities between the examples outweigh the similarities; thus care must be taken to assure they are of the same genus. Aristotle points out that the first principles which form the major premises of the logic are normally unstated[103]. The logic of a paradigm is actually, as Aristotle himself admits, a combination of induction and deduction[104]. After

102Ibid., 1357b26—36.
103Ibid., 1357a15—25.
104Ibid., 1394a9—16; Cope, *An Introduction to Aristotle's Rhetoric*, p. 106.

all, first principles can eventually be discovered from a long series of in-
ductions[105]. In fact, induction and deduction become almost the same
thing, for conceivably one could list every possible example and thus
could state the major premise in the form of an "all." In the paradigm he
gives above, if every instance of tyranny and asking for a bodyguard were
collected, the premise could be stated as "everyone who is aiming at tyranny always asks for a bodyguard." In the sciences, although first principles are sometimes discovered by intuition, it is preferable to collect as
many examples as possible in order to make the principles inducted from
them more valid. But in rhetoric such a procedure would be unseemly and
unpersuasive. In fact, in rhetoric the speaker does not express the major
premise but moves directly from like to like. Commentators have pointed
out that in many instances the major premise of a paradigm would look
absurd if expressed; thus it is better to suppress it and let the audience
complete the logic unconsciously[106]. The suspect nature of the logic of
paradigms causes Aristotle to treat them as less convincing than enthymemes and, in fact, leads him to subdivide paradigms into inductive
paradigms and illustrative ones.

> If we have no enthymemes, we must employ paradigms as demonstrative proof, for conviction
> (πίστις) is produced by these; but if we have them [enthymemes], paradigms may be used as
> evidence (ὡς μαρτυρίοις) and as a kind of epilogue to the enthymemes. For if they [par-
> adigms] stand first, they resemble induction, and induction is not suitable to rhetorical speeches
> except in very few cases; if they stand last they resemble evidence (μαρτυρίοις) and a wit-
> ness is in every case likely to produce belief (ὁ δὲ μάρτυς πανταχοῦ πιθανός)[107].

This means that Aristotle actually envisions two kinds of paradigms:
one, which is used without an enthymeme, as a form of inductive argument, and another, which is an illustration of the argument contained in
an existing enthymeme. He declares that the first kind "resembles induction" and that it is rarely suitable to rhetorical speeches, while the second
kind resembles evidence, which is more persuasive than induction.
This distinction is crucial for understanding the increased importance of
paradigms in Greco-Roman times. To anticipate the discussion below,
Greco-Roman ethicists contradict Aristotle's assertion that inductive
paradigms do not belong in rhetorical speeches. In fact, the inductive
paradigm, based on ethical prototypes, becomes one of the leading forms
of parenesis.
This distinction between inductive and illustrative paradigms relates to
logical form and parenetic function, but Aristotle makes a further distinction based on the sources for a paradigm. This mirrors his division of enthymemes into special topics (the sources) and common topics (the forms
of inference). He says that there are two major types (εἴδη) of paradigms:

---

[105]See p. 73, n. 34.
[106]Hauser, "The Example in Aristotle's *Rhetoric*," pp. 156—68.
[107]Aristotle *Rhetoric* 1393a9—16.

the historical, which are already in existence and the speaker merely uses, and those he fabricates himself[108]. The latter are further divided into παραβολή and λόγοι[109]. The historical paradigm is illustrated in the passage quoted above where the paradigms of Pisistratus and Theagenes are used to prove that Dionysius aspires to tyranny. Aristotle defines παραβ-ολή as a saying of Socrates (τὰ Σωκρατικά), which makes a comparison; thus it would be a parable "if one were to say that magistrates should not be chosen by lot, for this would be the same as (ὅμοιον γὰρ ὥσπερ) choosing as representative athletes not those competent to contend, but those on whom the lot falls"[110]. The λόγοι are fables, like those of Aesop, and need not concern us[111].

Thus Aristotle makes two major distinctions within the category of paradigms which are essential for comprehending the different shapes and uses of paradigms in ethical argument. Gerald A. Hauser has pointed out that the formal distinction between inductive paradigms and illustrative paradigms goes back to a bifurcation within the processes of all induction in Aristotle's *Organon*[112]. Just as induction receives only cursory treatment in the *Rhetoric* in comparison to enthymemes, induction receives much less attention than the syllogism in the *Organon*. Hauser summarizes,

On the basis of evidence in the *Organon* we may conclude that Aristotle treats *epagoge* as a bifurcated term. "Independent" induction functions as a method whereby universal premises are *discovered*. "Supportive" induction functions as a method whereby universal premises are *verified*[113].

Therefore, according to Aristotle, the inductive paradigm, which exists independently of enthymemes, produces first principles. They are part of the process of discovery whereby a person is led to "see a universal truth with the eyes of his own soul"[114]. On the other hand, the illustrative paradigm proves or exemplifies what one already knows. As best I can tell, both may be historical or created as needed.

Both kinds of paradigms are found in the Pastorals. The Pauline biographical passages are inductive paradigms which present Paul as the prototype of Christian behavior. In his character and experiences can be discovered the ἀρχαί of the Christian life. Once these first principles are comprehended, Christians can extrapolate into their own day and own lives. Out of the Pauline paradigms the author brings forth the ultimate standards by which he instructs and judges his own church. The brief descriptions of opponents and of Timothy and Titus are illustrative paradigms which embody contrary principles of the Christian life. These contrary

---

108Ibid., 1393a28–30.
109Ibid., 1393a30–31.
110Ibid., 1393b4–7.
111Ibid., 1393b8–10.
112Hauser, "The Example in Aristotle's *Rhetoric*," pp. 158–62.
113Ibid., p. 159.
114Ibid., p. 158. Hauser quotes Kapp (n. 10).

portraits illustrate what the author already knows from enthymematic argument. This basic distinction holds into the Greco-Roman era even though the use of paradigms grows immeasurably. Before attempting an analysis of the paradigms in the Pastorals we need to take account of that growth.

The Pastorals do not use the term paradigm but rather refer to Paul as a prototype (ὑποτύπωσις) and Timothy as a type or model (τύπος)[115]. Yet the terms seem to mean the same thing as paradigm[116]; and, in fact, ὑποτύπωσις functions as the inductive paradigm and τύπος as the illustrative paradigm. Considerable work has been done on the role of "example" in Greco-Roman ethics which has shown how comprehensive the idea of imitation of paradigmatic figures became in the Greco-Roman era. Thus the Pastorals were written in a time in which the use of paradigms to give content and shape to an ethic was frequent. Even in the Pastorals' immediate model for letter-writing, Paul three times enjoins himself on his readers as a model (τύπος) to be imitated (1 Thess. 1.6, 7; Phil. 3.7; and 2 Thess. 3.9, the last of which may be pseudepigraphical). The Aristotelian reticence over paradigms is gone.

Without trying to retrace the steps already taken by other scholars, we note that both Epictetus and Seneca, two Greco-Roman authors who only slightly precede the Pastorals in time, provide helpful evidence for how paradigms came to be used. Moreover, both Epictetus and Seneca employ a diatribe-style argumentation which parallels the style of the Pastorals and thus makes their use of paradigms applicable to the use of them in the Pastorals.

We should recall at this point the importance Aristotle places upon the opinion of the wise in the *Rhetoric*. He defines ἔνδοξα as "things generally admitted by all, or by most men, or by the wise, or by all or most of them, or by the most notable and esteemed"[117]. It is this linkage with the wise which gives rhetoric what epistemological status it has. He declares that in the political and ethical realms only the wise have the necessary experience for making reliable judgments. Thus he insists that even if the young can repeat the sayings of their elders in ethical matters, they do not understand what they say[118]. Therefore, concerning virtue and vice,

---

115 ὑποτύπωσις, 1 Tim. 1.16 (2 Tim. 1.13); τύπος , 1 Tim. 4.12; Tit. 2.7.

116A. von Blumenthal, "ΤΥΠΟΣ und ΠΑΡΑΔΕΙΓΜΑ," *Hermes* 63 (1928): 391–414; Willis Peter DeBoer, *The Imitation of Paul: An Exegetical Study* (Kampen: J.H. Kok, 1962), esp. pp. 17–33, 196–200; Leonard Goppelt, *Typos, the Typological Interpretation of the Old Testament in the New*, trans. Donald H. Madvig (Grand Rapids: Wm. B. Eerdmans, 1982); L. B. Radford, "Some New Testament Synonyms: Δεῖγμα, ὑπόδειγμα, τύπος, ὑποτύπωσις, ὑπογραμμός ," *The Expositor*, 5th series, 6 (1897): 377–87; Leonard Goppelt, " τύπος, κτλ.," *Theological Dictionary to the New Testament*, pp. 246, 259. On imitation see Betz, *Nachfolge und Nachahmung Jesu Christi im Neuen Testament*. Further bibliography in DeBoer and Betz.

117Aristotle *Topics* 100a30.

118Aristotle *Nicomachean Ethics* 1142a11–23.

"Things are true which the good man (σπουδαῖος) says are true"[119]. In fact, it is this linkage with the wise man which is the most persuasive dynamic in rhetoric. Of the proofs, Aristotle declares that the character of the speaker is the main mode of persuasion (κυριωτάτην ἔχει πίστιν τὸ ἦθος)[120]. Furthermore, the use of maxims and the topic from previous judgment, both of which can originate from the wise, demonstrates Aristotle's dependence on the knowledge of the wise man[121]. Thus we can conclude that for Aristotle in the area of ethics the opinion of a wise man is crucial.

The increase in the use of paradigms after Aristotle is reflected in the many Stoic discussions over who is the wise man and whether a wise man actually does exist. Thus the focus which Epictetus places upon the question of the identity of the wise man and his extensive use of both inductive and illustrative paradigms is simply one moment in a long debate in antiquity. In fact, Epictetus uses paradigms from his Stoic past so frequently and with such flexibility that even a partial account would be unseemly. Yet the enormous range Epictetus displays in using them indicates what possibilities were available for the author of the Pastorals[122].

Epictetus uses both inductive and illustrative paradigms. Socrates, Diogenes, and other Stoic wise men function as inductive paradigms. They provide content and direction to the ethical life as patterns which should be studied and imitated. They do this via the things they said, their reaction to specific problems, and by their general character. Epictetus finds illustrative paradigms in his students, in people he meets, in himself, and seems to make up others as he needs them. Thus, as Aristotle notes, paradigms can be historical or made up on the spot.

When Epictetus employs paradigms he can only do so by answering in the affirmative the old Stoic question of whether any wise man exists. I can find no instance where he accords this honor to himself or to anyone living in his own day. He uses himself as an illustrative paradigm, but this can be both negative and positive. When he sings hymns to God and invites others to join him in his praise of God and reason, he is clearly a positive example[123]. But he considered himself flawed, still in progress (προκοπή), not yet wise.

---

[119]Ibid., 1113a22–25. Cf. 1099a13, 1166a12, 1170a14, 1176a15f., 1176b25.

[120]Aristotle *Rhetoric* 1356a13.

[121]Ibid., 1394a19–1395b20, 1398b21–1399a6. The topic from previous judgment should be used "if possible when the judgment was unanimous or the same at all times; if not, when it was at least that of the majority, or of the wise, either all or most, or of the good; or of the judges themselves or of those whose judgment they accept, or of those whose judgment it is not possible to contradict, for instance, those in authority, or of those whose judgment it is unseemly to contradict, for instance, the gods, a father, or instructors." This description includes within its range the author's use of Paul (the wise), scripture (the gods), and the Cretan maxim (the judges themselves).

[122]On the growth of examples in the Greco-Roman era see Klaus Döring, *Exemplum Socratis*, Hermes-Einzelschriften 42 (Wiesbaden: Franz Steiner, 1979). On Epictetus see Döring, pp. 43–79.

[123]Epictetus 1.16.15–21.

Are you then free? says someone. By the gods I wish to be, and pray to be, but I am not yet able to look into the face of my masters, I still honor my paltry body. I take great pains to keep it sound, although it is not sound in any case. But I can show you a free man, so that you may never again have to look for an example (παράδειγμα). Diogenes was free[124].

A description of Diogenes' character follows which details his indifference to his body and all externals, whether kindred, friends, or country. Epictetus summarizes Diogenes' character by asserting that he never did anything for the sake of appearance. Then he adds —

And that you may not think I am showing you an example (παράδειγμα) of a man who was solitary, and had neither wife, nor children, nor country, nor friends, nor kinsmen, who might have bent him and diverted him from his purpose, take Socrates and observe a man who had a wife and little children, but regarded them as not his own[125].

A description of Socrates' character follows. It is clear from this that Epictetus believed that the lives of Socrates and Diogenes demonstrated that the ideal Stoic life was possible.

In what will prove to be a striking parallel to the Pastorals, he attributes the existence of such inductive paradigms to his cosmology. Just as Paul, for the author of the Pastorals, receives his status as a prototype from God's plan of salvation, so do Socrates and Diogenes, for Epictetus, owe their existence to the providence (πρόνοια) of God. According to Epictetus, God has sent scouts (κατάσκοποι) into the world to tell people what wisdom is[126].

Does God so neglect his own creatures, his servants, his witnesses, whom he alone uses as examples to the uninstructed (χρῆται παραδείγμασιν πρὸς τοὺς ἀπαιδεύτους), to prove that he both is, and governs the universe well, and does not neglect the affairs of men, and that no evil befalls a good man either in life or in death[127].

Epictetus' inductive paradigms are anchored in God's providence.

Equally important for Epictetus is that his inductive paradigms provide content and direction to this ethic. Events, whether historical or legendary, in the lives of Socrates, Diogenes, and Zeno, and the reaction of these wise men to those events illustrate how everyone should live. Socrates provides a paradigm for facing death and Diogenes for disregarding externals[128]. Yet Epictetus stretches their applicability beyond the pecu-

---

[124]Ibid., 4.1.151–152.

[125]Ibid., 4.1.159.

[126]Epictetus declares that the true cynic "must know that he has been sent by Zeus to men, partly as a messenger (ἄγγελος) in order to show them that in questions of good and evil they have gone astray, and are seeking the true nature of the good and the evil where it is not, but where it is they never think; and partly, in the words of Diogenes, when he was taken off to Philip, after the battle of Chaeroneia, as a scout (κατάσκοπος). For the Cynic is truly a scout, to find out what things are friendly to men and what hostile; and he must first do his scouting accurately, and on returning must tell the truth ..." (3.22.23–25). Cf. 3.21.19.

[127]Ibid., 3.26.28.

[128]On Socrates: Epictetus 1.4.23–25; 1.9.22; 1.12.23; 1.23.31; 1.29.16–21, 29; 2.1.13–15; 2.2.8, 15; 2.6.26; 3.18.4; 3.24.99; 4.1.159–69; 4.4.20–22; 4.7.29. On Diogenes: Epictetus 1.24. 6–10; 3.22.60; 3.22.80; 3.24.68–70; 4.1.30, 114, 152–58.

liarities of their lives by referring to their general character (ἦθος) and applying that to different situations. Thus Socrates provides a paradigm not only for facing death or any danger but for any difficulty life might pose.

> When you are about to meet someone, in particular when it is one of those men who are held in very high esteem, propose to yourself the question, "What would Socrates or Zeno have done under these circumstances?" and then you will not be at a loss to make proper use of the occasion[129].

Epictetus is proposing herein that certain wise men from the past possessed a discernible character, which, when understood, can direct one's behavior in any situation. Thus a major part of his pedagogy is the studying of these men. His advice becomes in effect to ask oneself what the wise man does in this situation.

> And now that Socrates is dead and memory of him is no less useful to men, nay, is perhaps more useful, than what he said or did while he still lived. Study these things, these judgments, these arguments, look at these examples (παραδείγματα), if you wish to be free[130].
> Even if you are not yet a Socrates, still you ought to live as one who wishes to be a Socrates[131].

In Epictetus inductive paradigms function in three ways: they prove the possibility of achieving wisdom, they provide content and direction to the ethical life, and they are the goal to which one aspires.

These wise men provide content to the ethic, not only from stories about their lives or from their imagined character, but also from their sayings (λόγοι). Epictetus' diatribe-style parenesis is rich with sayings from his Stoic wise men. These sayings gain their force and persuasiveness from their origin. They come from the mouths of scouts who have successfully made the journey to wisdom; thus, they are reliable and unique because only the wise man knows what wisdom is. Typical of these sayings is the valorous remark of Socrates before his trial: "Anytus and Meletus can kill (ἀποκτεῖναι) me, but they cannot hurt (βλάψαι) me"[132]. Epictetus can introduce this saying into any dangerous situation as a prescription for how to face it. Its presence in an argument needs no further warrant or explanation for it evokes both the authority and character of Socrates. It is fitting that the *Encheiridion* ends with this saying along with its companion: "Well, O Crito, if so it is pleasing to the gods, let it be"[133]. The four Socratic sayings at the end of the *Encheiridion* have canonical status for Epictetus. They are not just ἔνδοξα but ἀρχαί; one can reason from them with full epistemological confidence. The *Discourses* also contain numerous sayings, maxims, and proverbs which have a lower status and less epistemological force. Thus within Aristotle's category of maxims (or of the topic from previous judgment) Epictetus distinguishes

---

129Epictetus *Ench.* 33.12. See also 1.9.22.
130Ibid., 4.1.169–70.
131Ibid., 51.
132Ibid., 1.29.18; 2.2.15; 3.23.21; *Ench.* 53.
133*Ench.* 53.

between the sayings of good men or people in progress towards wisdom and those which come from Socrates, Diogenes, or Zeno.

Illustrative paradigms in Epictetus usually take the form of negative illustrations of human foolishness. Epictetus does not possess a storehouse of anti-heroes, but finds his negative illustrations from infamous events in history, from encounters in his own life, or from his imaginary portraits of foolish people. These negatives are frequently counterposed to positive paradigms, or the occasion philosophical discourse, as they do in the Cynic epistles.

The diatribe entitled "To those who have set their heart on preferment at Rome" typifies Epictetus' flexible and creative use of illustrative paradigms[134]. He begins his discourse with his students by recalling a discussion he once had with an older man who was a Roman official. This man, while returning to Rome from an assignment, stopped and visited Epictetus to whom he lamented his dissatisfying life, swearing that from now on he would focus upon a life of peace and quiet. Epictetus, who knows the character of such men, expresses his doubts that the man will reform. Then as Epictetus predicts, when letters arrive from Rome with a new commission, the man abandons his intentions for a life of peace and hurries to his new assignment. In this diatribe, the illustration is apparently based on fact; the man is real, even if he remains nameless. This namelessness is repeated for all the imaginary interlocutors who serve as pedagogical foils for Epictetus. They ask foolish questions and embody foolish fears. In some instances these interlocutors appear to have an historical basis, but at others certainly not (sometimes it is difficult to tell). After recounting the conversation, Epictetus uses himself positively and negatively on the question of activity and inactivity. He describes himself as arising in the morning and, as is his custom, beginning to rehearse his duties for the day, but suddenly wondering what the point of it all is and going back to sleep. I cannot tell if Epictetus is concocting here an imaginary scenario or if he is recalling what he did one morning. The diatribe moves from this into an analysis of activity and inactivity.

The diatribe entitled "Against the contentious and brutal" is constructed differently but manifests the same juxtaposition of positive and negative paradigms[135]. Epictetus begins with the assertion that the good man contends with no one and, if able, allows no one else to contend. Then he says, "We have an example (παράδειγμα) before us of this also, as well as of everything else, in the life of Socrates, who did not merely himself avoid contention upon every occasion, but tried to prevent others as well from contending"[136]. An account of the problems Socrates faced and how he dealt with them follows. Epictetus then opposes to the Socratic paradigm not an historical figure but an imaginary one. An imaginary interlocutor

---

134[Ibid., 1.10.
135[Ibid., 4.5.
136[Ibid., 4.5.2.

complains about his treatment by an imaginary brutal man, wishing to respond in kind. Along the way Epictetus fills out his portrait of this imaginary complainer with short descriptions. He declares to this inter-locutor, "If you seek to act like a wolf, you can bite back and throw more stones than your neighbor did, but if you seek to act like a man... ." And he depicts this man as less than human, saying

> Here is one whose sense of self-respect has grown numb; he is useless, a sheep, anything but a human being. Here is a man who is looking for someone whom he can kick or bite when he meets him; so that he is not even a sheep or an ass; but some wild beast.

This analysis could be extended, but these two instances illustrate how Epictetus combines negative and positive paradigms. For each problem the potential wise man faces, he provides paradigms of the proper reaction and the improper. Part of Epictetus' pedagogy consists of building con-trasts which present distinct options to his students. He builds these par-adigms in a variety of ways with little differentiation between real ones and imaginary ones. Only his canonized Stoic heroes have a relatively stable position. Everyone else alternately fails and succeeds.

Even to a greater extent than Epictetus, Seneca builds his parenesis upon paradigms *(exempla)*[137]. Seneca constructs his inductive paradigms primarily out of stories about Socrates and Cato much as Epictetus does. Moreover, he uses himself at times as an inductive paradigm, not of a *vir bonus*, but of one making progress. Thus like Epictetus, Seneca does not place himself in the category of wise men but only as one on the way. He also uses a vast array of illustrative paradigms to clarify his arguments. Cancik divides the paradigms in Seneca into three kinds: (1) the *exemplum*, which is an inductive paradigm based on an historical person and his reaction to an historical situation, (2) the "Beispiel," which is an invented form or situation, (3) the "Vergleich," which consists of metaphors and analogies from the non-human realm[138]. The latter two function as illus-trative paradigms.

Cancik holds that the *exemplum* is the major parenetic device in Seneca. This elevation of paradigms to the level of primacy above enthy-mematic arguments derives from Seneca's understanding of the *vir bonus* and his belief that one must reform the will *(voluntas)* and not just learn the right deed in order to make the soul *(animus)* virtuous. Pedagogically this reformation of the will is accomplished by keeping company with known wise men. *Exempla* and *praecepta* from the wise present the wise man to one who frequents them. Cancik notes that paradigms for Seneca provide content, make the challenge, and prove the possibility (just as they do in Epictetus)[139]. Finally, Cancik believes that the elevation of

---

[137]Döring, *Exemplum Socratis*, pp. 18–42; Hildegard Cancik, *Untersuchungen zu Senecas epistulae morales*, Spudasmata 18 (Hildesheim: Georg Olms, 1967), pp. 23–24.

[138]Cancik, *Untersuchungen zu Senecas epistulae morales*, p. 24.

[139]Ibid., p. 26.

paradigms in Seneca indicates not only that Roman philosophy was more practical and less theoretical than its predecessors but also that Seneca's focus upon "Innerlichkeit" encourages concentration upon people and character rather than ideas[140]. Analysis and theory are not the best roads to take to the inner dimensions of the soul; only the paradigms of others who have reformed their own souls, can lead the way. "Life needs a stock of conspicuous illustrations."[141] Inductive paradigms become the primary pedagogical technique for Seneca.

Seneca's focus upon the inner dimensions of the soul also explains the way he uses himself as an *exemplum* and his choice of the letter for his primary mode of parenesis. His letters are replete with references to the trivia of his own life. He will recount to Lucilius a rather mundane encounter along with his laudatory or blameworthy reaction, then analyze the event and its ramifications in diatribal form. Cancik presents Epistle 76 as typical[142]. Here Seneca recounts to Lucilius his recent experience of attending a school lecture and how he is ridiculed for being an old man who attends school with young boys. Seneca uses this event as an occasion to discourse upon education and the necessity for continual learning, even when one is an old man. He wants to represent himself not as a *vir bonus* but as one who is learning; and therefore his failures, weaknesses, moments of growth and understanding are essential components of the personal paradigm. This self-witness seems to straddle the border between inductive and illustrative paradigms, for his personal experiences contain behavior which one can learn from and on occasion imitate, but they do not contain first principles of the Stoic life.

Cancik points out htat the letter is the ideal genre for the kind of parenesis which depends heavily upon paradigms[143]. Cancik refers to Koskenniemi's study which highlights the unique capacity of the letter for making the writer present to the reader. Thus, when Seneca wants to proffer himself to Lucilius as one learning to be wise, he chooses the one genre which can present the character of one person to another. We have seen this phenomenon in many pseudepigraphical letters and when those examples are coupled with Seneca, we have in hand good analogies for the type of argumentation in the Pastorals. In the Cynic epistles Socrates is constantly presented as an inductive paradigm or in the language of the epistles as a $\pi\alpha\rho\acute{\alpha}\delta\epsilon\iota\gamma\mu\alpha$ [144]. When this paradigmatic capacity is combined

---

[140]Ibid., pp. 121—27.

[141]Seneca *Epistulae morales* 83.13.

[142]Cancik, *Untersuchungen zu Senecas epistulae morales*, pp. 18—22.

[143]Ibid., pp. 46—61. Cancik relies heavily on Koskenniemi's work and combines it with Seneca's attempts at "Selbstzeugnis" in the letters. Cancik points for an analogy to the letters of Horace which "zur Darstellung der eigenen Person und an bestimmten Stellen zur philosophischen Paränese an einen Freund erhöht" (p. 55).

[144]See Döring, *Exemplum Socratis*, pp. 114—28, and Fiore, "The Function of Personal Example in the Socratic and Pastoral Epistles," pp. 182—303.

with the pseudepigraphical genre in letters which pretend to be written by Socrates, the letter genre and the inductive paradigms reinforce one another so that the primary content of the letter is the presence of the paradigmatic Socrates. The Pastorals combine these same elements in much the same way.

Before analyzing the paradigms in the Pastorals, we need to gather our working conclusions about the use of paradigms in Aristotle, Epictetus, Seneca, and the Cynic epistles.

1. There are two forms of paradigms: the inductive and the illustrative. In Aristotle, inductive paradigms are self-sufficient proofs used independently of enthymematic argument, and illustrative paradigms are witnesses or epilogues used to prove what has been deduced through enthymemes.

2. In Greco-Roman parenesis Aristotle's reticence over the use of paradigms disappears. In fact, paradigms are more important than deduction in Seneca and seem to be of equal weight in Epictetus. This reflects Greco-Roman philosophy's fondness for practicality and ethics over theory and analysis.

3. Inductive paradigms owe their persuasive force to the unique epistemological status given to wise men. Only the wise know what is wisdom; thus one can only learn wisdom by studying the lives and teachings of those who have already achieved it. The lives of Socrates and Paul contain the first principles of Stoicism and Christianity respectively; and therefore by studying and imitating their lives one makes progress.

4. Part of Greco-Roman pedagogy is the use illustrative paradigms to embody positive and negative behavior and thus to portray clear ethical options.

5. Paradigms can either be historical (or legendary) or imaginary.

6. The letter and the pseudepigraphical letter, in their ability to convey the presence of the writer to the reader, reinforce the capacity of inductive paradigms to serve as prototypes.

7. Epictetus attributes the existence and function of wise men to the providence of God, arguing that God has provided the world with reliable witnesses to the virtuous life, thus making the achievement of it possible.

1. Inductive Paradigms

Paul is the source of inductive paradigms in the Pastorals. Just as Socrates and other Stoic wise men bestow their epistemological status upon paradigms drawn from their lives, Paul's life, including both his problems and his responses, produces paradigms which contain the first principles of the Christian life. Both 1 and 2 Timothy are letters which articulate a portrait of Paul and then use that portrait as a paradigm which gives content and direction to the parenesis in the letters. These inductive paradigms are therefore self-contained proofs from which conclusions can be derived. In a reversal of Aristotle, these paradigms initiate enthymematic arguments about the principles contained in these paradigms; thus enthymemes and not paradigms are the witnesses or epilogues. The elevation of the wise man, Paul, to a unique epistemological status, makes inductive paradigms the most reliable point of origin for ethical discourse.

As the supposed author, "Paul" has a complex function in the Pastorals as creator and preserver of the traditions, as apostle, evangelist, and teacher, and as guarantor of the ethical pronouncements. However, these functions do not take the formal shape of inductive paradigms; they emerge from the fiction of his authorship. Therefore, they will be taken up by our analysis later.

Two inductive paradigms based on Paul's life are found in 1 Timothy at 1.12–17 and 1.19–20; four inductive paradigms are found in 2 Timothy at 1.11–12; 2.9–10; 3.10–13; 4.6–22; Titus contains none.

The inductive paradigm in 1 Timothy 1.12–17 is combined with enthymematic arguments in order to produce a characterization of Christian reality which becomes the theme of the entire letter. The author's portrait of Paul contains one detail which does not seem to be based upon either Acts or the Pauline letters[145]. He describes Paul as one who persecuted and insulted Christ, but who received mercy. This contains nothing beyond the traditions in Acts or the Pauline letters, but he makes a subtle addition when he introduces the idea of Paul as blasphemer. As the author of a pseudepigraphon, the author must describe Paul in a way consistent with what his readers know about Paul. Any radical transformation would ring untrue and expose the fiction. Thus, alterations must be minor. The question is why Paul is now described as a blasphemer.

The author opens the letter in 1 Tim. 1.3f. with a charge to Timothy to rebuke and set right the heretics. 1 Tim. 1.8–11, which immediately precedes this inductive paradigm, argues for the usefulness of the law in rebuking heretics. And the first chapter ends at 1 Tim. 1.20 with "Paul" describing how he rebuked Hymenaeus and Alexander. Thus, the theme of 1 Timothy seems to be the problem of heretics and how to deal with them.

Therefore, the author composes his portrait of Paul in order to establish his understanding of how heresy should be solved. To do this, Paul is portrayed not only as the persecutor who is converted but also as the prototypical converted heretic. The author places Paul in his former life in the company of those heretics who are presently troubling the church. He is or was a blasphemer, but as a blasphemer he received mercy and was saved. This experience becomes paradigmatic for all who follow.

The capacity of inductive paradigms, when based upon wise men, to produce first principles is active in this passage. The author attaches an enthymematic argument to his paradigm in order to justify the first prin-

---

[145]On the growth of the Pauline legends see Dennis Ronald MacDonald, *The Legend and the Apostle: The Battle for Paul in Story and Canon* (Philadelphia: Fortress Press, 1983).

ciple that "Christ Jesus came into the world to save sinners." Formally, the passage begins with the inductive paradigm which produces the conclusion that Christ saves sinners, then illustrates that conclusion with an illustrative paradigm based on the same Pauline experience. The logic of the passage is not difficult to follow even though it combines three separate logical forms. This interpenetration of paradigms and enthymemes is anticipated by Aristotle when on different occasions he treats paradigms as separate from enthymemes, as proofs of enthymemes, as elements from which enthymemes are built, and even as species of the common topics[146]. This range does not evidence confusion but an awareness of how rhetorical arguments are actually built.

1 Tim. 1.16 states the author's theoretical basis for inductive paradigms based upon Paul: "But for this reason I received mercy, so that in me, the foremost of all, Christ Jesus might show his complete patience, as a prototype of those who will believe in him for eternal life." The interpretation of this passage depends on the meaning of ὑποτύπωσις. The term τύπος is a frequent one in Greco-Roman ethical literature[147]. Although there is some debate over the original etymology of the term, whether in dependence on its cognate τύπτω it means "blows" or the "imprint" left behind by the blow, in ethical contexts it means the latter[148]. According to Goppelt, τύπος means mold, hollow form, and thus in ethical contexts a "model," though he also notes that παράδειγμα is the most common term for an ethical model[149]. In this way τύπος relates to inductive paradigms and not illustrative ones, for it is not an illustration but a pattern to be imitated. Yet the author calls Paul a ὑποτύπωσος, which is rarer than either τύπος or παράδειγμα. Its most common meaning is "outline," used when a short sketch is given instead of a full treatment[150]. In the Pastorals Paul is treated as the "model" which should be imitated, and thus ὑποτύπωσις is clearly equivalent to τύπος; but the author's decision to designate Paul as a ὑποτύπωσις and Timothy as a τύπος suggests that he was attempting a distinction. This has led to the translation of ὑποτύπωσις as "prototype"[151]. This translation picks up the idea of an outline to be filled in later and includes the idea of imitation which is essential to the author's treatment of Paul. Therefore, as the author argues in the enthymeme which is coupled with this inductive paradigm, Paul is more than a model which ought to be imitated; his life creates the pattern of orthodoxy for all Christians and prefigures the lives of those who follow him. In fact,

---

[146]Aristotle *Rhetoric* 1366a34–b11, 1394a9–18, 1398a33–b20.

[147]See p. 93, n. 116.

[148]DeBoer, *The Imitation of Paul*, pp. 17–23; Radford, "Some New Testament Synonyms."

[149]Goppelt, "τύπος," TDNT, 8:248.

[150]Liddell and Scott, *Greek-English Lexicon* (1968), s.v. ὑποτύπωσις. It is interesting that Aristotle uses τύπος as "outline" in the *Nicomachean Ethics* (1104a) to refer to the sketchiness of his analysis.

[151]See, for example, Lips, *Glaube, Gemeinde, Amt*, p. 50, who translates it as "Vorbild"; Falconer, *The Pastoral Epistles*, p. 124; and Dibelius-Conzelmann, *The Pastoral Epistles*, p. 27.

Paul's life articulates the innate character of God's relationship with people. In this way Paul's life is not unique in the sense that his life is without parallel but in the sense that it is the life with numerous parallels. "Outline" is not a misleading translation, for Paul's life creates the framework of the Christian experience which is filled in by those who follow him. Finally, just as Epictetus attributes the presence of reliable wise men to the providence of God, the author of the Pastorals attributes this special role for Paul to the workings of God's plan of salvation[152].

The inductive paradigm recounts Paul's behavior as persecutor and blasphemer to which Christ responds with mercy and grace. The author induces from this that God used Paul to demonstrate how all blasphemers will be treated. The use of the term ὑποτύπωσις emphasizes the unique status of Paul, but that status is also indicated in the designation of Paul as the foremost (πρῶτος) of all sinners[153]. Thus Paul in this scenario was once worse than any of the heretics who are harassing the church in the author's own day. Just as God saved Paul, God may save these heretics. Not only is Paul's behavior and experience repeated in those who follow, but God's behavior will also be repeated. The implication that everyone was once a blasphemer is stated explicitly in Tit. 3.3: "For we ourselves were once foolish, disobedient, led astray, etc." Then Tit. 3.4 recalls how the goodness and kindness of God was manifested and the former sinners were saved. Therefore, Paul is not just the model Christian but the prototype of Christian conversion. Every Christian begins as a blasphemer and becomes something else only by God's tendency to save blasphemers.

1 Tim. 1.19b—20 contains an incomplete inductive paradigm; it is incomplete because the conclusion is not expressed. It builds upon the theme of heresy with "Paul" declaring that "Some people rejecting this have suffered shipwreck concerning the faith. Among them are Hymenaius and Alexander, whom I handed over to Satan in order that they might learn not to blaspheme." Here Paul is no longer the prototypical converted heretic but the prototypical rebuker of heretics. His behavior shows that heretics must first of all be rebuked, but that this is done for purposes of saving them. Today's blasphemers are tomorrow's good Christians. Gentleness and hope for repentance will characterize all rebuke in the Pastorals.

The author places these two inductive paradigms based on Paul at the beginning of 1 Timothy and these set the agenda for the letter. The rest of the letter is almost an exposition of these two paradigms, for the letter focuses upon the problem of heresy and draws its content and direction from the patterns outlined in the Pauline paradigms. The life of Paul thereby presents the author with first principles about the problem of heresy upon which he can build the series of enthymemes which constitute the

---

[152]For details, see the next chapter.

[153]Dibelius-Conzelmann, *The Pastoral Epistles*, pp. 29—30, suggest that πρῶτος should be translated "first" but then also connect it in meaning with ὑποτύπωσις.

rest of the letter. These inductive paradigms define how heretics should
be perceived and how they should be rebuked. The rest of 1 Timothy addresses the rebuke of heretics and the exhortation of the faithful.

The five inductive paradigms in 2 Timothy give a different configuration to the author's image of Paul, yet these paradigms have the same capacity to provide first principles as those in 1 Timothy. The different configuration given to Paul evidences the fact that 2 Timothy addresses a different problem than 1 Timothy. 2 Timothy speaks to abandoned church
leaders and exhorts them to remain faithful to their tasks. Paul is portrayed as a suffering, abandoned, and faithful church leader.

In 2 Tim. 1.11—12 "Paul" says,

> For this I was appointed preacher and apostle and teacher, and for this reason I suffer these
> things. But I am not ashamed, for I know whom I trust, and I am convinced that he is able to
> guard my entrusted traditions until that day.

Herein the author establishes the value of suffering for the gospel, especially for church leaders to suffer for it. This becomes a continual motif
of the letter, so that Timothy is enjoined throughout to stand fast, to endure what is necessary, and to rekindle his gifts for his office[154]. The next
two verses illustrate how inductive paradigms can produce reliable conclusions. In 2 Tim. 1.13—14 "Paul" reminds Timothy "You have an outline
($\dot{v}\pi o\tau\dot{v}\pi\omega\sigma\iota\varsigma$) of the sound teaching which you heard from me in faith
and love which is in Christ Jesus; guard the good traditions through the
holy spirit which dwells in you." The author bases his imperatival conclusion to guard the entrusted tradition upon the paradigmatic behavior
of Paul, who did so in his day, and upon Paul's (and the author's) confidence that God will preserve these traditions. Therefore, this inductive
paradigm functions as does the one in 1 Tim. 1.12—17, for it locates
paradigmatic behavior not only in what Paul did but also in what God did.
Here the term $\dot{v}\pi o\tau\dot{v}\pi\omega\sigma\iota\varsigma$ is applied to teachings and not to what God
does, but as far as the function of the inductive paradigm is concerned the
result is the same.

The inductive paradigm in 2 Tim. 2.8—10 does not occasion an expressed
conclusion with the same straightforwardness as the one above, although
the hymn in 2 Tim. 2.11—13 functions much as one. The paradigm
strikes the same note as 2 Tim. 1.11—12, for the configuration given
Paul is of the bound and imprisoned apostle who endures "all these things
for the sake of the elect, in order that they might obtain salvation." The
hymn picks up the implied faithfulness of both God and Paul and states
the mathematics of human behavior and God's resultant response as first
principles of God's plan of salvation. Pauline inductive paradigms give
rise to reliable first principles.

2 Tim. 3.10—12 articulates the author's theory of how inductive paradigms should be read.

---

[154] 2 Tim. 1.6, 13—14; 2.1, 3, 15, 22; 3.14; 4.1—2, 5.

But you have followed my teaching, my way of life, my purpose, my faith, my patience, my love, my endurance, my persecutions, my sufferings, and whatever happened to me in Antioch, in Iconium, in Lystra, whatever persecutions I have borne; and the Lord rescued me from all of them. And all who desire to live piously in Christ Jesus will be persecuted.

The three dynamics evidenced in the other inductive paradigms are clearly illustrated here. First, the pattern of Paul's life forms the major proposition. This life is to be studied in all its dimensions. Secondly, God's behavior towards Paul comprises part of inductive paradigms in the Pastorals. Third, he states his conclusion in terms of "all" who follow Paul. This paradigm focuses upon Paul's experience of persecution and harassment and then generalizes that experience of persecution into a first principle.

The inductive paradigm in 2 Tim. 4.6—8 also contains these three elements. It first details the particulars of Paul's behavior: "I have fought the good fight, I have completed the race, I have kept the faith." This admirable performance is given the same context as all of Paul's behavior in 2 Timothy, that of suffering. Paul is on the point of death but remains faithful. Secondly, Paul's behavior occasions a reaction from God: "Finally, the crown of righteousness is set aside for me, which the Lord, the righteous judge, will award me on that day." Third, as an inductive paradigm it produces a generalization: "and not only to me but also to all who have loved his epiphany."

Finally the extensive personalia in 2 Tim. 4.9—22, which end the letter, repeat these same themes. They begin by noting that Demas has left Paul; so also have Crescens and Titus. In fact, Paul has sent everyone away or they have abandoned him: "Luke alone is with me." This echoes 1 Tim. 1.15—18, which declares that all in Asia except one have left Paul. Furthermore, Paul lacks his winter cloak and parchments. He asks Timothy to come and bring Mark, as though the few remaining faithful need to gather around Paul. Alexander is mentioned as someone who has done Paul great harm and is still active, capable of hurting all who follow Paul's teachings. The passage concludes with an account of Paul's defense before the court, where once again all abandoned him. This time even the one faithful person is left out; only the Lord remains. "Paul" concludes with the assertion that, even though totally abandoned, the Lord saved him and will always save him. The author does not draw an explicit conclusion from this inductive paradigm; it is formally incomplete as are 1 Tim. 1.19b—20 and 2 Tim. 2.8—10, yet the implied conclusion is not hard to find.

The inductive paradigms in 2 Timothy not only function as the bases for first principles of the Christian life but they also compose a consistent portrait of Paul. He is the prototype of the suffering, harassed, and abandoned church leader. From appearances, he is not the triumphant apostle, because his people have abandoned him. He is treated as a criminal; only a small minority remain loyal. Yet, although he is harassed and deserted, he remains true to his duties and carries out the tasks God has assigned him. In response to his steadfastness in the midst of crises, God preserves and furthers his work. God saves him in this life and in the life to come. From this paradigm the author infers the basic constituents of Christian reality.

Paul's behavior should be imitated; but if one does, one will endure the same mistreatment. This suggests that 2 Timothy is written by the author to encourage other harassed and abandoned church leaders. He is perhaps speaking from a minority position; his opponents rule the hearts and minds of his church. Thus he speaks to those who share his vision of the Christian life, exhorting them to follow Paul, to endure suffering, to remain loyal to the true traditions. And his exhortation contains a promise, for his paradigms also show how God behaves. God let Paul suffer, and lets all who follow suffer; but in the end God saved Paul and will save the author and his friends. Thus it makes sense that 2 Timothy opens with an admonition to Timothy to "rekindle the gift of God which is in you." Abandoned church leaders are exhorted to not lose heart but to rekindle themselves for the tasks and strains of leadership. The author builds 2 Timothy upon these inductive paradigms into a rallying cry to a minority to gather once again around the true Paul, like Timothy bringing Mark and the winter cloak. And there, safe within the arms of Pauline orthodoxy, they can make their stand, knowing that, even if their words go unheeded in the church, God will save them.

2. Illustrative Paradigms

Illustrative paradigms embody positive or negative characteristics; and principles are not derived from them but they from principles. Aristotle says that they follow enthymemes as witnesses to the enthymematic conclusions. Just as inductive paradigms increase in importance in Greco-Roman parenesis, so do illustrative paradigms. Epictetus and Seneca both use them frequently. In the case of Seneca the line between positive *exampla* and inductive paradigms can be difficult to draw, for positive illustrative paradigms can be offered as models for imitation and not just as illustrations[155].

There are four passages which contain illustrative paradigms in which the person or persons in the paradigm are given a name. From our study of pseudepigraphical letters we concluded that the presence of names says little one way or another about the historicity of the paradigm. In 1 Tim. 1.19–20 the author attaches a negative illustrative paradigm to a positive charge to Timothy: "Some rejecting this have suffered shipwreck concerning the faith. Among them are Hymenaeus and Alexander, whom I have handed over to Satan in order that they might learn not to blaspheme." By coupling the charge and the paradigm, the author in effect presents a positive and a negative illustration, though only the negative

---

[155]Cancik, *Untersuchungen zu Senecas epistulae morales*, pp. 75–91, emphasizes Seneca's desire for "Selbstzeugnis" in his letters, so that Seneca himself as a person making progress becomes an *exemplum* to others who want to make progress.

takes the logical form of an illustrative paradigm. The example of Hymenaeus and Alexander is used to show how Paul treats heretics.

2 Timothy 1.15—17 contains a positive and a negative illustrative paradigm, both of which contain the names of persons. First, "All in Asia have abandoned me, among whom are Phygelus and Hermogenes." The form is the same as in 1 Tim. 1.19—20, for in both a general description is given of certain people and then two names are given of the people in that group. This negative is balanced by a positive paradigm. A person named Onesiphorus is described with a behavior which is the opposite of those who abandoned Paul. He refreshed Paul many times, was not ashamed of his chains, and searched for him zealously in Rome. In neither of the passages does the author draw conclusions from them as though they were inductive paradigms. These are illustrations not prototypes.

The illustrative paradigm in 2 Tim. 2.17—18 is attached to a charge to Timothy and thus is formally similar to 1 Tim. 1.19—20. The charge to Timothy is the positive illustration and the paradigm is the negative. In vv. 16—17a the author refers to a general "they" who progress in impiety, then adds "among whom are Hymenaeus and Philetus." Once again, the names are introduced to concretize and perhaps make more plausible a general negative description.

The personalia in 2 Tim. 4.9—15 contain a series of positive and negative paradigms, all of which contain names. Demas and Alexander are negative; Luke, Mark, and Tychicus are positive; Crescens and Titus could be either, depending on whether they should be linked with Demas or not[156]. To this series is attached an inductive paradigm on Paul (2 Tim. 4. 16—18) which begins by noting that no one stood by Paul on his first defense.

All the illustrative paradigms in the Pastorals focus upon loyalty and disloyalty to Paul. They illustrate and embody both possibilities. Obviously the positive illustrations are intended to be imitated; yet these are not inductive paradigms from which the author derives first principles. However, their connection with Paul means that the pattern of loyalty to him by a few and disloyalty by many becomes the paradigmatic reaction to all church leaders who adhere to Paul's traditions.

The Pastorals contain similar illustrative paradigms which function as do the ones above but which do not contain names. These descriptions are couched in general terms, as though the author is describing kinds of people: 1 Tim. 1.3—4, 6—7 ($\tau\iota\nu\epsilon\varsigma$); 1 Tim. 6.3—5 ($\tau\iota\varsigma$); 2 Tim. 3.1—9 ($\H{\alpha}\nu\theta\rho\omega\pi\iota$) ; 2 Tim. 4.3—4 ("they" of a verb); Tit. 1.10—16 ($\pi\iota\lambda\lambda\iota\iota$). Each of these is a negative illustration which is balanced by a positive, though the positive comes in the form of an exhortation to Timothy and Titus or a general description and is not formally an illustrative paradigm.

---

156 I know of no commentator who connects the rebuke of Demas with Crescens and Titus, because the participle $\dot{\alpha}\gamma\alpha\pi\dot{\eta}\sigma\alpha\varsigma$ is singular. Nevertheless, the inclusion of Crescens and Titus in the list of those absent intensifies the impression of abandonment.

In fact, the author alternates throughout his letters between positive and negative descriptions; it is a major component of his style. For instance, 1 Tim. 6.3—5, which describes how some (τις) oppose the sound teachings, produce controversies, and are full of vice, follows immediately upon a series of positive instructions to Timothy on how to teach and instruct in proper fashion. Then, the negative paradigm is itself followed by an analysis of contrasting attitudes towards money and teaching for profit. This positive and negative alternation takes a different shape in Tit. 1.10—16 which is a general description of an unnamed "many." It follows upon a virtue list for presbyters and is itself followed by an exhortation to teach properly.

Therefore, we may conclude that the author envisions two contrasting life-styles which play off one another throughout his letters. In order to describe the negative he employs illustrative paradigms, but for the positive he uses either inductive paradgims, or exhortations to Timothy and Titus, or general accounts of proper behavior. This method of argumentation is reminiscent of the use of positive and negative paradigms in Seneca and Epictetus.

At this point our discussion is moving nearer to questions of style and further from logic. Before making that move, we should note our conclusions.

1. If Aristotle's account of the nature of rhetorical logic is workable, then we can conclude that the Pastorals use logical arguments because they follow methods of argumentation which agree in form with Aristotle's analysis. Therefore, it is incorrect to deduce that the eclectic style of the letters evidences an absence of logical coherence among individual propositions.

2. According to Aristotle's definition of the enthymemes, as the rhetorical form of deduction, the Pastorals contain many logically sound deductive arguments. Most of these are based on special topics drawn from the author's view of God's plan of salvation; but the private origin of principles does not undermine logical processes.

3. In the Greco-Roman era the paradigms grew in importance in ethical argumentation, yet Airstotle's distinction between inductive and illustrative paradigms still holds for the most part. Given these changes the Pastorals also use coherent inductive arguments.

4. In the Pastorals inductive paradigms are built upon the figure of Paul in a manner analogous to the use of Socrates as a paradigm in the Socratic epistles, Seneca, and Epictetus, so that first principles of the Christian life are derived from them. The author then builds further arguments upon the unimpeachable foundation of these principles.

5. Most of the illustrative paradigms in the Pastorals are negative. And these negative illustrative paradigms are usually balanced by a positive description which does not take the logical form of a paradigm.

C. The Organization of Arguments

What has made the argumentation in the Pastorals so easy to misread is the manner in which the author organizes paradigms and enthymemes into larger arguments, for he does not engage in sustained analysis of one question but moves continuously from one topic to another. This constant shift in the focus of the argument is made more noticeable by the diversity of the materials within the paradigms and enthymemes. This combination makes the Pastorals look to some commentators like a farrago of unharmonized, disparate pieces of argument. We have seen that, contrary to appearances, logical coherence does exist among individual propositions; and the thesis of this section is that a similar coherence exists among the larger sections of argument.

The kind of parenesis contained in the Pastorals finds its closest analogy in ancient diatribe. There is debate over whether "diatribe" is the proper term to describe Greco-Roman parenesis and whether diatribe was a genre at all[157]. There is however no debate over the fact that many Greco-Roman ethicists use a simlar form of argumentation. Thus diatribe will refer here to that parenetic style used by Teles, Musonius Rufus, Epictetus, Dio Chrysostom, and Seneca[158]. Given the validity of this list, the Cynic Epistles can be classed as diatribe, and in some moments Paul's style should be included. Seneca, Paul, and the Cynic Epistles, all employ diatribe within the letter framework; therefore, the combination was not an unnatural one. Stanley Stowers has investigated the characteristics of diatribe in these authors[159]. We do not need to rehearse his work here, since, with his focus upon the phenomenon of the interlocutor, much of his analysis does not apply to the Pastorals; but he has noticed that diatribe is eclectic in its choice of material and that its arguments are often uneven. This is because its goal is persuasion and it must be emotive as well as logical. To that end diatribe employs a variety of parenetic devices. Rather than adhering to the order of argumentation as outlined in the rhetorical handbooks, diatribe tends to pile up different parenetic forms, as if the weight and diversity of the collection will persuade. Nevertheless, this is not done haphazardly. The variety masks the system.

157On the criticism of "dialogue" as the proper designation for this style of argumentation see ibid., pp. 47–48, esp. p. 47, n. 79. Cancik believes the lack of a better term in Latin led to the use of *dialogi* for Seneca's work. Actually, Cancik prefers διάλεξις to διατριβή, but even wonders if διάλεξις is a true genre. See also Stanley Stowers, *The Diatribe and Paul's Letter to the Romans*, Society of Biblical Literature Dissertation Series 57 (Chico, Calif.: Scholars Press, 1981), pp. 26–39.

158Stowers' survey of the history of scholarship shows that beginning with Wilamowitz through Wendland to today at least these figures are grouped together, even if one or the other is elevated as the standard by which the others are judged (*The Diatribe and Paul's Letter to the Romans*, pp. 7–48).

159Ibid., pp. 48–78.

Cancik's analysis of the epistles of Seneca has demonstrated that the diatribe-style argumentation in them is logically coherent and carefully organized[160]. The kind of analysis Cancik has undertaken could be done on the writings of any of the authors placed on the list of users of diatribe, but I know of no similar analysis of the structure of the arguments in Epictetus, Teles, Dio Chrysostom, or the Cynic Epistles. Cancik takes such pains to prove the logical coherence of Seneca's thought and the interconnections of his different teaching styles, because, as with the Pastorals, so many people have been led by the encyclopedic look of the material in the letters to conclude that no system or logic among the various parts exists. Cancik admits that the letters contain a variety of indicative and imperative statements, but successfully illustrates how these various elements depend on each other. Seneca has, Cancik says, two major methods of teaching in the letters: the theoretical, which includes proofs and doxography, and the parenetic[161]. The theoretical employs indicative language interspersed with doxographic material, in which Seneca quotes from wise men. In these theoretical sections Seneca occasionally focused upon logical proofs for his ethical theories; and Cancik shows how these proofs provide foundations for his parenesis. Thus in an individual letter a proof creates the logical basis for later arguments. These two foci of his argumentation find expression in Seneca's use of the terms *laudare* (apologetic) and *probare* (proof)[162].

The parenetic sections in Seneca are filled with various kinds of imperatives which Cancik describes as rows of "Gebote, Verbote, Mahnungen, Warnungen, usw."[163]. Cancik notes the frequent combinations of these imperatives with sayings, inferences, and doctrinal pieces which have a variety defying taxonomy. The heart of Seneca's ethical system is formed by paradigms, and he not only places them in the center of his theory of ethical pedagogy, but, when he exhorts, he uses them as the foundation of his arguments. Thus the paradigms are completed by an "exegesis" or an "application," wherein the relevant moment of the paradigm is applied directly to the situation at hand[164]. The imperatives (*adhortatio*) which follow are introduced by *itaque, ergo,* or *ideo*[165]. This demonstrates to Cancik that Seneca constructs a logical relationship between his paradigms and the imperatives, so that the imperatives do not follow "auf" the paradigms but "aus ihnen"[166].

The diatribe in Seneca does not entertain sustained analysis of an ethical

---

[160]Cancik, *Untersuchungen zu Senecas epistulae morales*, pp. 80—88, argues that Seneca's eclecticism originated from a conscious attempt to exercise freedom from the philosophical schools. It is his desire to be original that makes him informal.

[161]Ibid., pp. 16—18.

[162]Ibid., pp. 18—19, quotes *Epistulae morales* 76.7.

[163]Ibid., p. 23.

[164]Ibid., p. 24.

[165]Ibid.

[166]Ibid., p. 25.

question with a dialectical assault such as Socrates undertakes in the Platonic dialogues, but rather uses a diversity of argumentative forms. As Aristotle pointed out, when the goal is persuasion and not just proof, then the emotions and feelings must be engaged as well. Aristotle insists, however, that a passionate appeal is inadequate, for the participation of reason is necessary for belief[167]. The best way to persuade is through variety. Seneca articulates this theory as follows:

> After all what is philosophy but the law of life? But let us assume that laws are ineffective: it does not follow that moral directions are ineffective too. Or else on these grounds you must maintain that consolation, dissuasion, encouragement, reproof, and praise in their several applications are equally so. They are all varieties of moral direction and by their means spiritual perfection is reached[168].

This is a nice apology for diatribe-style parenesis, because Seneca is arguing that moral reform does not take place just through the knowledge of principles, but also through the power of sustained and various exhortation. According to Stowers, all diatribe contains an interplay between rebuke (ἐλεγκτικός) and encouagement (προτρεπτικός)[169]. He points in particular to Epictetus, who uses logical proofs, paradigms, and sayings, thus creating a theoretical framework, but who most of all engages in combinations of rebuke and encouragement. Therefore, in diatribe the author intentionally diversifies his attack in order to increase his chances of striking a responsive chord. In his introduction to Epictetus' Discourses, Arrian notes how persuasive Epictetus was in person: "let those who read these words be assured of this, that when Epictetus himself spoke them, the hearer could not help but feel exactly what Epictetus wanted him to feel"[170]. Epictetus would overwhelm his hearers with logic, stories, and sharp rebuke and encouragement. This is the best way to persuade, for, as Aristotle remarks, not many people are susceptible to arguments from reason alone[171].

The Pastorals participate in the diatribe style of argumentation by being eclectic and diverse in the range of materials from which arguments are built and by organizing those arguments loosely. By using the analogy of

---

[167] Aristotle *Rhetoric* 1356a1–20. Aristotle criticizes former treatments of rhetoric because "they say nothing about enthymemes which are the body of proof, but chiefly devote their attention to matters outside the subject; for the arousing of prejudice, compassion, anger, and similar emotions has no connection with the matter in hand ..." (1354a14–18).

[168] Seneca *Epistulae morales* 94.39.

[169] Stowers, *The Diatribe and Paul's Letter to the Romans*, finds this element in nearly all diatribes (pp. 48–78), so that he defines the genre in those terms: "The diatribe is not the technical instruction in logic, physics, etc., but discourses and discussions in the school where the teacher employed the 'Socratic' method of censure and protreptic" (p. 76). Stowers (p. 57) depends on E. G. Schmidt for the demonstration that censure and protreptic "are not distinct methods, but parts of one process" (E. G. Schmidt, "Die drei Arten des Philosophierens," *Philologus* 106 [1962]: 16–28).

[170] Epictetus *Preface* (Arrian to Lucius Gellius).

[171] Aristotle *Rhetoric* 1355a24–29.

diatribe the author's method of organizing becomes more comprehensible. He may use diverse materials and the focus of argument may shift about, but this does not mean that he lacks method[172]. Previous analyses of the author's method seem to be correct in emphasizing that the author combines distinct types of material[173]. Bartsch detects a church order, along the lines of that from which Polycarp drew and upon which the *Didascalia Apostolorum* is based, underlying 1 Timothy and Titus[174]. The author's use of household codes and virtue and vice lists is obvious. Most commentators detect liturgical fragments or hymns of various kinds. He clearly depends upon legends about Paul's life. Hanson believes the author's use of scripture depends upon traditional midrashim or haggada[175]. All of this is interspersed with direct and implied imperatives. This eclecticism seems analogous to the eclecticism of diatribe. And yet the argumentation in the Pastorals is not simply diatribe, for in Epictetus, Seneca, et al., the argument focuses upon one question or topic at a time. Diatribe may be eclectic and informal but it is also focused and topical. The argumentation in the Pastorals is not. For instance, Cancik has shown that Seneca moves from well defined theoretical sections into equally distinct parenetic sections[176]. The Pastorals on the other hand intersperse theory and parenesis, oftentimes alternating from sentence to sentence. Thus in the Pastorals the relationship among the pieces of argument and the movement from piece to piece is based on different grounds.

The best analogy for understanding the author's method is the tendency in both Epictetus and Seneca to argue in terms of contrast. Both authors frequently contrast proper and improper behavior. This contrast is accomplished by exhortation, descriptions, and positive and negative paradigms. Their ethic expresses itself as a choice between competing modes of behavior: one chooses between the road to wisdom and the one to folly.

The author of the Pastorals' method of composing and organizing his

---

[172]Verner, *The Household of God*, pp. 112–25, and Fiore, "The Function of Personal Example in the Socratic and Pastoral Epistles," pp. 398–417, provide helpful analyses of the parenetic style of the author. Both argue that his method should be classified as diatribe. Verner focuses on how the author's parenesis relates to tradition and order, while Fiore details how the author builds his arguments out of diverse materials; but both detect coherence.

[173]See Falconer, *The Pastoral Epistles*, and Hanson, *The Pastoral Epistles*, for analyses of the different kinds of material.

[174]Hans-Werner Bartsch, *Die Anfänge urchristlicher Rechtsbildungen: Studien zu den Pastoralbriefen* (Hamburg: Herbert Reich, 1965); J. Elliott, "Ministry and Church Order in the New Testament," *Catholic Biblical Quarterly* 32 (1970): 367–91, believes the Pastorals conform to a literary genre, to which 1 Peter also belongs, which he calls "advice to church leaders."

[175]Anthony Tyrrell Hanson, "The Foundation of Truth: 1 Timothy 3.15" and "The Apostates: 1 Timothy 2.19–21," in *Studies in the Pastoral Epistles*, pp. 5–20, 29–41; *The Pastoral Epistles*, p. 45.

[176]Cancik, *Untersuchungen zu Senecas epistulae morales*, notes, for example, that epistle 76 has a separate doxographic section in the middle of the letter (pp. 18–19) and that epistle 74 builds upon the doxography in epistles 71–73, and thus is mostly parenetic, though it too has separate doxographic and parenetic sections (pp. 27–28).

arguments is determined by his understanding of two competing life-style in the church. He counterposes his own version of the Christian life to that of his opponents. 1 and 2 Timothy begin with inductive paradigms which provide the author with reliable principles from which he can argue, and then each shifts back and forth between positive and negative accounts of how one relates to these principles. Titus lacks the initial Pauline paradigm but it does manifest this shift from positive to negative and back. Although each letter addresses a distinct theme or a different aspect of the author's concerns, the letters do not make sustained arguments which pick up parts of the problem one at a time, but rather interlace accounts of these two life-style. All of this is done within the peculiar shape he gives to the Pauline letter form.

D. Conclusion

The thesis of this chapter is that eclecticism does not equal chaos. The author's method of argumentation may appear aesthetically wooden and disorganized but he does have a method which is logically grounded and coherent. The form of his arguments was shown to have many analogues with the theory and praxis of his contemporary ethicists. The first two books of Aristotle's *Rhetoric* provided categories which adequately explained the logical relationship among individual propositions. Of course, the author had not read Aristotle, but rather Aristotle was describing how ethical logic functions. The validity of using Aristotle's categories resides ultimately in whether his categories successfully describe the logic in the Pastorals. It is my judgment that they do. It was necessary to supplement Aristotle's description of paradigmatic argument with illustrations from Greco-Roman diatribe, since paradigms had grown in importance and complexity by the author's day. Given these analytical tools there is nothing incoherent or unrecognizable in the author's arguments. He does not show the fluidity and flexibility which characterizes most diatribe but he participates in the eclecticism and logical forms of his contemporaries. He follows the norms for ethical argument of his day.

This analysis indicates that the author interrelates his material and that it is incorrect to fragment the Pastorals into groups of material having autonomous functions. For instance, statements about God and Jesus have ethical implications which the author explicitly details. Thus this analysis provides the foundation for the next chapter wherein the theological and ethical system of the author is examined and found to be consistent.

Chapter III

The Cosmological and Ethical System

This chapter attempts to demonstrate that the author of the Pastorals articulates a cogent and consistent ethical system which addresses the ethical questions of both Christians and non-Christians, proffering to both groups a carefully-wrought ethical option. This system participates in the language and canons of Greco-Roman philosophical ethics, co-opting what it considers valuable and indispensible, and providing unique answers to traditional ethical aporiae by incorporating the ethic into a Christian cosmology. In so doing the author makes an appeal to Greco-Roman readers that the good life they long for exists only within the doors of the Christian church. At the same time he addresses factions within his own church which he considers unorthodox, imposing upon them a rigorous moral standard, and insisting upon the necessity of the virtuous life. In order to make this double appeal the author must do more than simply insist upon good behavior; he must do more than parrot the language of Greek philosophy, for that is a commonplace. Most everyone agrees that virtues are better than vices. He must, in fact, make the virtuous life possible, even necessary, by articulating a cosmology and an anthropology in which virtue is achievable and essential. That is to say, reliable warrants, manifest knowledge of good and evil, unimpeachable ethical resources, the anthropological ability, and sufficient motivation must all be woven into the system before virtue can exist. And his system contains them all. To accomplish this, he grounds his ethic in the workings of God's plan for salvation, linking his ethical claims to cosmological and Christological assertions. Moreover, since the Christian cult plays a key role in that plan, membership in that cult is a prerequisite for the ethical life. Yet membership is not enough. Once baptized, one must choose which teachers, which authorities, to obey; in short one must be properly educated and trained in the ethical life. In the end this is a cultic ethic in that it exists only within the framework of the Christian cult and even then only within a particular part of the cult.

Dibelius' famous accusation that the Pastorals surrender to bourgeois ethics is true only in the sense that virtue comprises the very heart of the salvation process, and the language used to describe that virtue is the language of common Stoic ethics[1]. But it is surely not a surrender in the

---

[1] Dibelius actually referred to the "Ideal christlicher Bürgerlichkeit" and admitted that "Dies

sense that the author abandons something uniquely Christian in order to make his religion palatable to Greek tastes. Virtue for him is the highest standard. In fact, the key to God's plan resides in the virtuous life: God saves only on the basis of virtue, at least in the final judgment. Thus ethics and theology are one in the same, handmaidens, partners which cannot be separated. The epiphany Christology which undergirds the ethics provides the cosmological links, the anthropological power, and the primary motivation for making the ethic persuasive. Our purpose here is to unravel the cosmological and anthropological connections to the ethic and thus to discover the inner logic of the system. We will find that the author does indeed possess a consistent system which makes an argument to Christians and non-Christians alike.

A. The Opponents

When we moved from Greco-Roman pseudepigraphical letters to Christian ones, the major sociological change we noticed was the increased importance of doctrinal controversy. Disagreements over orthodoxy, continuous accusations of heterodoxy and apostasy, and the overwhelming desire to locate one's own ideas in a mythic past constitute the dominant occasion for Christian pseudepigraphical letters. They seem to grow out of theological and cultic debate[2]. Furthermore, the Pastorals themselves seem to receive their major impetus from just such a controversy. Therefore, it is methodologically appropriate to begin where the author began, with the problem, with the danger his opponents presented, to analyze the author's evaluation of them, and then to track his elaborate response.

After a Pauline-style prescript, the letter of 1 Timothy begins with a proem which contains a theme statement for the letter.

> As I urged you when I was going to Macedonia, to remain in Ephesus so that you may charge certain persons not to teach any different doctrine, nor to occupy themselves with myths and endless genealogies which promote speculation rather than God's plan which is in faith (1 Tim. 1.3—4).

So also the proem in the letter to Titus contains the exhortation to appoint elders who are able to rebuke those who contradict the sound teaching, because —

---

alles aber wird nicht als vulgäre Ethik reproduziert, sondern mit christlichen Gedanken neu motiviert und um der Kirche willen befohlen." Dibelius, *Die Pastoralbriefe*, pp. 24—25.

[2]Most striking in this regard were *3 Corinthians*, where the letter attributes the arrival of the heterodox teachers, Simon and Cleobius, as the occasion for its being written, and the *Epistula Petri*, where James preserves the sacred documents from heterodox hands.

there are many insubordinate men, empty talkers and deceivers especially those of the circumcision, who must be silenced; they are upsetting whole families by teaching for shameful gain what they should not teach (Tit. 1.10–11).

In addition to these two theme statements all three letters are peppered with warnings about false teachers. The author takes the time to describe them in some detail and to enumerate carefully what action should be taken against them. Their presence dominates the letters to such an extent that they appear to be the immediate occasion for writing the letters. It is heterodox teaching and especially its negative impact on the community in the eyes of the author which moved him to write. When we probe for insights into the state of affairs in the author's church, it is first of all doctrinal and ethical conflict we discover. Thus Easton declares, "But the Pastorals were written primarily to meet a grave emergency. ... The Pastor wrote first of all to protect the faith and the morals of the church against a corrupting invasion of 'false teaching' "[3].

Although we cannot be certain or detailed in our reconstruction of the historical situation which gave occasion to these letters, at least within the fiction of the letters the conflict between orthodoxy and heresy dominates. Although we have seen that conflict and controversy are a common element to pseudepigraphical letters (especially Christian ones), they are certainly not a necessary element. This would suggest that the depiction of heresy is historical and not just a part of style. Furthermore, a striking dualism runs through the Pastorals between adherence to the proper traditions and falling away, between virtues and vices, between good order and wild speculation, and between ordained church leaders and unattached busybodies. And, in fact, in the preceding chapter we noticed that the literary style is effected by this dualism. Thus, an ethical and salvific dualism structures both the form and content of the author's argumentation, so that it appears the author forges and articulates his ethic contra a specific and historical faction in his church. He views them as heterodox, as full of every vice, and thus as a real danger to the salvation offered by the cult. A major goal of his ethic, and thus of the fiction of the Pauline letter, is to promulgate an ethic and a view of Christian salvation in distinction from that promulgated by these opponents. Therefore, since his ethic is forged polemically, we shall investigate who these opponents were and what they believed, before we try to unravel the ethical system counterposed to them.

1. The Author's Portrait of His Opponents

Our goal as stated above is somewhat too optimistic since all we can in fact ever hope to know is how our author understood these opponents.

---

[3] Easton, *The Pastoral Epistles*, p. 2.

All we have is his portrait of them. This points to a major problem in many studies of the opponents in the Pastorals, which do not take seriously enough the creativity of the author in painting this portrait[4]. His ostensive goal is to cast his own conflicts back in time to Paul's own day. To do that, he takes two different tacks. In one, he simply has Paul make predictions about the future; in those cases we can be confident that the specifics come from the author's own day. In the other, the details merge with the fiction of the letter so that the opponents become Paul's own opponents or the opponents of Timothy and Titus. In such cases we stand on less solid ground, because the author seems to be acquainted with facts or legends about Paul's life and may be getting his specifics from traditional material which does not apply directly to his own time[5]. Furthermore, it might be that the opponents of Timothy and Titus are the author's opponents while those of "Paul" are not. However, the tendency to see them all as paradigms — even Jannes and Jambres are illustrative paradigms for those who oppose Timothy (2 Tim. 3.8–9) — suggests that all the portraits should be combined into one picture and that the resultant picture is of the author's own opponents. Only by examining how the opponents are portrayed in these three moments, namely, in Paul's day, in Timothy and Titus', and in the author's, can we be certain how the genre functions in describing them.

There are only three instances in the Pastorals where "Paul" refers to his own opponents in a direct way while not warning Timothy and Titus against them[6]. The three specific comments about Paul's opponents are similar in their sparseness. In 1 Tim. 1.19–20 we read that "Some have rejected the faith and good conscience ($\sigma\upsilon\nu\epsilon\iota\delta\eta\sigma\iota\nu$) and have suffered shipwreck ($\dot\epsilon\nu\alpha\upsilon\dot\alpha\gamma\eta\sigma\alpha\nu$) concerning the faith. Among whom are Hymenaeus and Alexander, whom I have handed over to Satan ($\pi\alpha\rho\dot\epsilon\delta\omega\kappa\alpha\ \tau\tilde\omega\ \Sigma\alpha\tau\alpha\nu\tilde\alpha$) in order that they might learn not to blaspheme ($\ddot\iota\nu\alpha\ \pi\alpha\iota\delta\epsilon\upsilon\vartheta\tilde\omega\sigma\iota\nu\ \mu\grave\eta\ \beta\lambda\alpha\sigma\varphi\eta\mu\epsilon\tilde\iota\nu$)." We get even less information in 2 Tim. 1.15 where "Paul" declares that "All who are in Asia have turned away from me ($\dot\alpha\pi\epsilon\sigma\tau\rho\dot\alpha\varphi\eta\sigma\dot\alpha\nu\ \mu\epsilon$), among whom are Phygelus and Hermogenes." This same kind of thing is said in 2 Tim. 4.10 where "Paul" reports that "Demas has abandoned me ($\dot\epsilon\gamma\kappa\alpha\tau\dot\epsilon\lambda\iota\pi\epsilon\nu$), loving the present age." And in the same section Timothy is told in 4.14–15 that "Alexander the cop-

---

[4]I can find no commentary which takes seriously the creativity of the author in composing this portrait. G. Haufe, "Gnostische Irrlehre und ihre Abwehr in den Pastoralbriefen," in *Gnosis und Neues Testament*, ed. K. W. Tröger (Gütersloh: Mohn, 1973), p. 335, speaks of the "Ketzerporträt" which the author counterposes to the "Apostelbild," but he does not pursue the distinction into the problems posed by the genre.

[5]See excursus "Information about Persons" in Dibelius-Conzelmann, *The Pastoral Epistles*, pp. 127–29, and MacDonald, *The Legend and the Apostle*.

[6]Most of the negative descriptions in the Pastorals do not specify whose opponents they might be. However, since these references always occur within larger admonitions to Timothy or Titus, they will be treated as references to the opponents of Timothy and Titus. See below for the specific passages.

persmith did me great harm (πολλά ... κακὰ ἐνεδείξατο)." Timothy is admonished to be on guard for him, because he is rigorously opposed to our teachings (λίαν γὰρ ἀντέστη τοῖς ἡμετέροις λόγοις). Here we encounter an instance where Paul and Timothy share the same opponent. And finally, at the close of the section, during "Paul's" reminiscence about his first defense, he remarks again that all deserted him (πάντες με ἐγκατέλιπον).

These remarks are striking most of all for their lack of concrete information. All we really learn is that Paul had opponents and what their names were. The accusation about conscience and especially the charge of being opposed to the sound teaching will recur in other descriptions of later opponents, showing that the author intends nothing specific in this about Paul's opponents as distinct from his own. The author's intention seems limited to affirming that all church leaders experience opposition and abandonment since even Paul did so.

The import of giving specific names is uncertain. They certainly lend verisimilitude, but it is possible that they do more. Alexander, the coppersmith, is most likely the same person we encounter in Acts 19.33. Moreover, many of the names in 2 Timothy recur in the *Acts of Paul* and perhaps even originated from names in Colossians and Philemon[7]. Thus the author was cognizant of legends about Paul and may have pulled names from those legends. On the other hand, the names we cannot locate in those legends may have had some significance to the author's readers and we can imagine that the author's opponents were connected somehow with those names. But I know of no reliable way of adjudicating whether this is so on independent grounds[8]. The pseudepigraphical letter as a genre

---

[7] The *Acts of Paul* mentions, as enemies of Paul, Demas and Onesiphorus, incorrectly designating the latter as the coppersmith, and attributes to them the belief that the resurrection has already happened (*Acts of Paul* 3. 1, 14). Onesiphorus is described as meeting Paul in Iconium (*Acts of Paul* 3.2), Luke comes to Rome from Gaul and Titus from Dalmatia in order to meet Paul (11.1). Schneemelcher confesses that Harnack was correct in admitting that reliable means are lacking for distinguishing legend and fact in these stories; see Schneemelcher, *New Testament Apocrypha*, 2: 333. The author of the Pastorals may have gotten most of these names from canonical letters. Colossians mentions Tychicus (Col. 4.7), Mark (Col. 4.10), Luke and Demas (Col. 4.14). Philemon mentions Mark, Demas, and Luke (Philem. 24). Prisca and Aquila occur in Acts 18.2, 18; Rom. 16. 3; 1 Cor. 16.19. Trophimus is mentioned in Acts 20.4; 21.29. Erastus occurs in Rom. 16.23. And Alexander is probably the Alexander of Acts 19.33—34. On the curious relationship between the Pastorals and the *Acts of Paul* see J. Rohde, "Die Pastoralbriefe und Acta Pauli," *Studia Evangelica* 5, ed. F. L. Cross, Texte und Untersuchungen 103 (Berlin: Akademie Verlag, 1968), pp. 303—10, who I think greatly overreads the similarities. For a more adequate treatment see MacDonald, *The Legend and the Apostle*.

[8] The correct location of these names constitutes an ancient debate in Pastoral scholarship. For a comparison of approaches see F. Spitta, "Über die persönlichen Notizen im zweiten Briefe an Timotheus," *Theologische Studien und Kritiken* 51, 1 (1878): 582—607 and Harrison, *The Problem of the Pastoral Epistles*, pp. 121 ff., who both think the notes are genuine, against Norbert Brox, "Zu den persönlichen Notizen der Pastoralbriefe," *Biblische Zeitschrift* 13 (1969): 76—94, and Dibelius-Conzelmann, *The Pastoral Epistles*, pp. 127—28, who think they are not.

is certainly capable of any of these devices and requires none of them.
Thus we are left speculating.

Of course, our uncertainty in this area does not negate the original observation that the author's intention does not seem to be historical curiosity or fidelity in describing Paul's actual opponents, but instead he merely
wants to include Paul in the experience of opposition, in itself certainly
historically true. This evidence indicates that the portrait he paints does
not come from Paul's day, and not from unknown legends, but from opponents of his own day whom he knows firsthand.

This conclusion is reinforced by our inability to detect any signigicant
differences between those descriptions of opponents that occur in prophecy, which manifestly refer to the author's own day, and those that occur
in admonitions to Timothy and Titus, which conceivably belong to the
past. It is one portrait we get.

There are three major prophecy passages. In 1 Tim. 4.1f. the spirit declares that in the last days people will turn away from (ἀποστήσονται) the
faith, will adhere to deceitful spirits and the teachings of demons (πνεύμα-
σιν πλάνοις καὶ διδασκαλίαις δαιμονίων) with the hypocrisy of liars
whose consciences are seared, will forbid marriage (κωλυόντων γαμεῖν),
and will abstain from food (ἀπέχεσθαι βρωμάτων). The admonition to
Timothy, which follows, to avoid godless and old women's myths (τοὺς ...
βαβήλους καὶ γραώδεις μύθους) should perhaps be included in this list.
In 2 Tim. 3.1f. "Paul" attaches a typical vice list to these persons, a list
which seems to be mostly stock in content. However, at the end of the
vice list the accusation is added that these persons enter households and
capture weak women (αἰχμαλωτίζοντες γυναικάρια). Further, they are
of one type with Jannes and Jambres. They have corrupted their minds
(κατεφθαρμένοι τὸν νοῦν) and are unapproved in the faith (ἀδόκιμοι περὶ
τὴν πίστιν). 2 Tim. 4.3 mentions people with itching ears (κνηθόμενοι
τὴν ἀκοήν), who do not put up with good teachers but select those that
say what they want to hear and who turn from the truth and pursue
myths.

The opponents against which Timothy and Titus are warned receive a
similar description. In 1 Tim. 1.3f. they teach heterodoxy (ἑτεροδιδασκαλεῖν ... προσέχειν μύθοις), and their behavior produces speculation
(ἐκζητήσεις) rather than God's plan of salvation (οἰκονομία θεοῦ). Not
only do they produce speculation but they pursue empty words (ματαιο-
λογίαν). They wish to be teachers of the law, but in fact they do not
understand it. In 1 Tim. 6.3 a variety of vices is applied to them: they are
conceited, envious, blasphemous, and so on. Naturally, they are opposed
to the sound teaching and have turned away from the truth. And once
again the accusation of speculation and dispute over words is raised (ζητήσεις καὶ λογομαχίαι).The same collection of terms occurs in Tit. 1.10f.,
where they have turned away from the truth, pursue Jewish myths, claim
to know God, but deny God with their deeds. Their Jewishness is highlighted (μάλιστα οἱ ἐκ τῆς περιτομῆς) and they are again accused of up-

setting families. Finally the theme of empty talk is raised once more (ματαιολόγοι).

The admonition to Timothy which begins at 2 Tim. 2.14 repeats many of the same themes, interspersing them within stringent warnings. By way of a strong metaphor, their teaching is compared to a gangrene which eats its way into the community. Once again, they upset the faith of many. The author also gives them names, repeating the Hymenaeus, who is "Paul's" opponent in 1 Tim. 1.20, and adding the name Philetus. Therefore, these figures, within the fiction of the letter, bridge the gap from Paul to Timothy and Titus (as does Alexander in 2 Tim. 4.14). We cannot know whether they were known figures in the author's own day. In any case, Hymenaeus, Philetus, and Alexander belong to the larger era of the letter, being of danger to both Paul and Timothy. The author also includes in this passage an important and much debated accusation of gnostic-sounding dogma: they hold that the resurrection has already happened.

In addition to these descriptive accounts of opponents, the letters contain numerous warnings about kinds of behavior, employing the same language used in these descriptive passages. For example, Titus is admonished in Tit. 3.9 to avoid foolish controversies and genealogies and battles over the law (μωρὰς δὲ ζητήσεις καὶ γενεαλογίας καὶ ἔρεις καὶ μάχας νομικάς). And Timothy in 2 Tim. 2.14f. is warned not to dispute over words (μὴ λογομαχεῖν) and to avoid profane, empty talk (τὰς δὲ βαβήλους κενοφωνίας). Finally the description of young widows who violate their first pledge picks up this same language. In 1 Tim. 5.11f. these widows become idle, run about from house to house, and turn towards Satan.

When all these accounts are pieced together, they produce one consistent picture. The fact that forbidding marriage and abstaining from food occurs only in a prophecy passage, while wishing to be teachers of the law occurs only in one passage describing Timothy's opponents, is not sufficient to draw a line between the two groups, since all the rest of the terms are repeated in essence in both places. Paul, Timothy, and Titus, along with the present-day church, all face the same danger, and the author does not engage in subtle temporal distinctions. In fact, the unification of the three time periods contributes directly to the success of the genre. "Paul" in speaking to his representatives, Timothy and Titus, speaks at the same time, without any need for hermeneutic, to the author's own church.

2. Identity

When all these scattered details and calumniations are gathered into one place, a consistent and rather full picture results. The numerous attempts to identify these opponents as Marcionites or proto-Montanists have not been successful[9]; however, this inability to put a tag on them from later

---

[9]In many ways we have not progressed much beyond the judicious and thorough investigations

second or third century heresies does not mean in Dibelius-Conzelmann's terms that "the author attempts to characterize his opponents as broadly as possible, in order to create an apologetic 'vademecum' for all sorts of anti-gnostic conflicts"[10]. Nor is it necessary to separate all these details into different groups as though the author confronts three or four distinct heresies. All these ideas are quite at home in ancient Judaism and in the early church; thus Haufe is correct in arguing that they belong to one basic group[11].

The extensive research which has been done on the meaning and provenance of all these ideas simplifies our task in identifying these opponents and does not need to be repeated here. Their Jewishness is unmistakable not only because of the direct accusation of Jewish myths, and of being of the circumcision, but also because of their anchoring their thought in scripture. Moreover, μῦθος and γενεαλογίαι, which they pursue, are popular Jewish concerns at this time, whatever the terms mean exactly[12]. Their gnostic coloring can be detected in their claiming the resurrection has already happened, for although this doctrine could be a Paulinism in the opponents' eyes, it becomes a frequent doctrine of later gnostics[13]. To this can be added, of course, the warning against "gnosis falsely so-called"[14]. Falconer has also shown the magical provenance of some of

---

of Heinrich Julius Holtzmann, *Die Pastoralbriefe* (Leipzig: Wilhelm Engelmann, 1880), pp. 126–59, who admitted to the mixed character of the opponents. This is so even though we have a less naive view of gnosticism than the one which informed Holtzmann's work. Wilhelm Lütgert, *Die Irrlehrer der Pastoralbriefe*, Beiträge zur Förderung christlicher Theologie 13, 3 (Gütersloh: Bertelsmann, 1909) gives in many ways the classic investigation of their gnostic roots. For the delicacy of the problem see Brox, *Die Pastoralbriefe*, pp. 31–42, and Dibelius-Conzelmann, *The Pastoral Epistles*, pp. 65–67. For the most thorough and competent treatment of the whole problem see Haufe, "Gnostische Irrlehre und ihre Abwehr in den Pastoralbriefen."

[10]Dibelius-Conzelmann, *The Pastoral Epistles*, p. 66.

[11]Haufe, "Gnostische Irrlehre und ihre Abwehr in den Pastoralbriefen," p. 325–39.

[12]On the possible gnostic background of these terms see Brox, *Die Pastoralbriefe*, pp. 34–36, who relies heavily on Irenaeus' remarks in *Adversus Haereses* 1.30.5, 9. Jeremias, *Die Briefe an Timotheus and Titus*, p. 13, and Haufe, "Gnostische Irrlehre und ihre Abwehr in den Pastoralbriefen," p. 329, detail the Jewish roots of the terms.

[13]See the collection of evidence in Brox, *Die Pastoralbriefe*, p. 36. James M. Robinson, ed., *The Nag Hammadi Library: In English* (New York: Harper & Row, 1977), pp. 4–5, in his introduction to the collection, referring to 2 Tim. 2.16–18, declares, "This view, that the Christian's resurrection has already taken place as a spiritual reality, is advocated in the *Treatise on Resurrection*, the *Exegesis on the Soul*, and the *Gospel of Philip* in the Nag Hammadi Library!" Although all three documents certainly contain the idea, it is not couched in the same terms we find in the Pastorals.

[14]Because Irenaeus picks up this phrase, applying it to his gnostic contemporaries, and because of the equally infamous name "antitheses," with its connections to Marcion, the gnostic shadings of the opponents seems unmistakable. Of course, few people would join F. C. Baur or Campenhausen in placing the Pastorals at the end of the second century (Baur, *Die sogenannten Pastoralbriefe des Apostels Paulus aufs neue kritisch untersucht* [Stuttgart: Cotta, 1835] and Hans von Campenhausen, "Polycarp von Smyrna und die Pastoralbriefe," in *Aus der Frühzeit des Christentums* [Tübingen: J. C. B. Mohr (Paul Siebeck), 1963], pp. 197–252). See Brox, *Die Pastoralbriefe*, p. 32, and Dibelius-Conzelmann, *The Pastoral Epistles*, p. 92, on the dubiousness of iden-

these terms[15]. Obviously, the designation of γόητες in 2 Tim. 3.13 comes from magic, but also Jannes and Jambres, who are connected typologically to these opponents, were often treated as Egyptian magicians. Less clearly, Falconer finds parallels between the confrontation of Paul and Barnabas with the Jewish magician Elymas in Acts 13.6—12 and the description of the heretics in 2 Tim. 3.1—9[16]. Within the penumbra of magic fall the terms φρεναπάται, πλανάω, and the image of them making their way into households and capturing weak women[17]. Of course, this language applies equally well to sophists, Cynics, and busy-bodies[18]. Sophists, Cynics, busybodies, and magicians share one thing in particular; they create instability, undermining the established social order, by introducing radical ideas or injecting powers beyond the control of the authorities[19]. In particular, Malherbe believes that this language, when coupled with the polemical use of ἀλαζόνες and ὑγιής, indicates the Cynic tendencies of these opponents[20]. Finally, MacDonald has traced the connection between Pauline legends in the Pastorals and those in the *Acts of Paul*. In the latter the elevation of women constitutes a major concern and

---

tifying Marcionites in all this. Easton, *The Pastoral Epistles*, p. 170, for instance, suggests that if if does refer to Marcion it is a later gloss. However, Bauer, *Orthodoxy and Heresy in Earliest Christianity*, pp. 221—26, places them after Polycarp, because of their antignostic tendencies. And Helmut Koester, *Introduction to the New Testament*, Hermeneia — foundations and facets (Philadelphia: Fortress Press, 1982), 2:305, puts them in the milieu of Polycarp.

[15]Falconer, *The Pastoral Epistles*, pp. 39—52. Falconer actually finds three heresies: magic, asceticism, and logomachies based on myths and genealogies. He finds the basic origin of these heresies in the Judaism of Asia Minor and Crete.

[16]Ibid., p. 43.

[17]On the connection of these terms to magic see Morton Smith, *Jesus the Magician* (San Francisco: Harper & Row, 1978), pp. 68—80, and Alan F. Segal, "Hellenistic Magic: Some Questions of Definition," in *Studies in Gnosticism and Hellenistic Religions*, presented to Gilles Quispel on the occasion of his 65th birthday, ed. R. van den Broek and M. J. Vermaseren (Leiden: E. J. Brill, 1981), pp. 349—75.

[18]Traducements against the sophists in antiquity are of course legion. We might highlight Plato in this regard, especially in the *Protagoras, Gorgias*, and *Sophist*. Plutarch gives a concise condemnation of busybodies in his diatribe "On Being a Busybody." And Lucian of Samosata parodies the Cynics in his *Death of Peregrinus*. For other examples of condemnation of the Cynics see Abraham J. Malherbe, "Medical Imagery in the Pastoral Epistles," in *Texts and Testaments*, ed. W. Eugene March (San Antonio: Trinity University Press, 1980), pp. 19—35.

[19]This helps explain why the Roman emperors periodically banished the philosophers from Rome and why magic was against the law. On the latter see M. Smith, *Jesus the Magician*, p. 75. On the role of Cynics in these tensions between philosophers and the emperors see Donald R. Dudley, *A History of Cynicism* (Hildesheim: Georg Olms, 1967), pp. 125—42. Instructive in this regard is the trial of Apollonius of Tyana before Domitian, where he is accused of four things: he dresses differently, people call him a god, he caused trouble in Ephesus by predicting a plague, and finally he is said to practice human sacrifice, or, in other words, magic (Philostratus *Life of Apollonius* 8.5). We might sum up the charges as looking like a Cynic and practicing magic. Apollonius' defense, according to Philostratus, apart from denying any association with magic, consists of insisting that his behavior is philosophically motivated and cannot possibly endanger the emperor (8.7).

[20]Malherbe, "Medical Imagery in the Pastoral Epistles," pp. 19—35.

this elevation occasioned problems with the church hierarchy. From this MacDonald concludes that the opponents in the Pastorals were primarily women or people concerned with the status of women[21].

Our author appears to be perturbed most of all by the instability fostered by these people. The accusation of vice may not be entirely unfounded, even though Karris has demonstrated that vice lists of this kind are mostly stock, a way of casting aspersions upon enemies, which have no real applicability in their details[22]. On the other hand, the sophists, Cynics, and magicians who are the most frequent targets for such attacks did not have quiet virtue at the focal point of their lives. The accusation may be stock but it is not nonsense, because the peaceable ethic common to Stoics, Platonists, and the Pastorals was not accepted by everyone in antiquity[23]. Thus, although we certainly cannot declare that these opponents killed their mothers and fathers[24], we might admit that the quiet virtues and rigid church hierarchies were not particularly important to them.

These opponents probably did not call themselves sophists, busybodies, or magicians, since for the most part these are all terms of derision. Most likely they would have considered themselves good Paulinists. Haufe, Mac-Donald, and others have clearly demonstrated that the peculiar direction taken by these people found its inspiration in the Pauline corpus or the Pauline legends[25]. They would certainly not accept the accusation of vice or κενοφωνία or ματαιολογία, and other terms of emptiness, vanity, or hypocrisy; but they might well have accepted ζητήσεις, μῦθοι, γενεαλογία, and perhaps even λογομαχία[26]. The author's portrait suggests that his opponents were speculative, creative theologians. They appear to have searched scripture, struggled to understand the stumbling block of the resurrection, and been willing to subject their results to the rigors of public debate. They were also having enormous success.

The author portrays them as deviating from established tradition, but

[21]MacDonald, *The Legend and the Apostle.*

[22]Robert J. Karris, "The Background and Significance of the Polemic of the Pastoral Epistles," *Journal of Biblical Literature* 92 (1973): 549—64.

[23]Of the groups closest to the general cultural milieu of the author, certainly the Cynics, gnostics, and certain apocalyptic groups would not evaluate these gentle, communal virtues with the same high regard as our author.

[24]The vice catalogues collected and analyzed by Anton Vögtle, *Die Tugend— und Lasterkataloge im Neuen Testament*, Neutestamentliche Abhandlungen 16.4—5 (Münster: Aschendorff, 1936) and Erhard Kamlah, *Die Form der katalogischen Paränese im Neuen Testament*, Wissenschaftliche Untersuchungen zum Neuen Testament 7 (Tübingen: J. C. B. Mohr [Paul Siebeck], 1964) illustrate how these terms can often compound into exaggeration. The role of these catalogues in the Pastorals will be examined below.

[25]Haufe, "Gnostische Irrlehre und ihre Abwehr in den Pastoralbriefen," and MacDonald, *The Legend and the Apostle.*

[26]Plato uses ζήτησις positively as an "inquiry" or "investigation" (Liddell & Scott, *Greek-English Lexicon*, s.v. ζήτησις). Myths and genealogies of course have perfectly benign meanings in Judaism and elsewhere. See excursus, "Myths and Genealogies," in Dibelius-Conzelmann, *The Pastoral Epistles*, pp. 16—17.

this is part of the fiction of the letter. The author wants them to appear as a minority who by their creativity have undermined what Paul handed down originally. But, as we shall see below, it is the author himself who concocts the exact features of this tradition in the letters. The Pauline tradition ($\pi\alpha\rho\alpha\vartheta\acute{\eta}\kappa\eta$), as the author manufactues it, did not exist in this exact form until the letters were written. We can assume extant traditions in the form of liturgy, the Pauline letters, the Old Testament, and other legends and sayings, all of which inform the author, but the idiosyncratic reading given this traditional material in the Pastorals is the result of the author's own creative act. Thus he is opposing his creative reading to theirs. Furthermore, there are hints, as we shall see below, that it is the author and not his opponents who constitutes the minority and thus in some sense the heterodox group. Not only does the author expressly record their success in misleading "some," but he carefully paints a picture of Paul and Timothy as abandoned church leaders. Paul's acknowledgment that all have abandoned him may, in fact, reflect the minority status of the author.

It is usual to ascribe to the opponents some form of spiritual enthusiasm[27]. The ascription may well be correct. The typical background to the doctrine that the resurrection has already happened is belief in spiritual power in the present and the immediate, personal lordship of Jesus[28]. When the author opposes to this a Christology in which Jesus has no direct contact with the church at all, it may be that he is banishing Jesus from the scene in response to what he regards as over-zealous spiritualism. $\zeta\eta\tau\acute{\eta}\sigma\epsilon\iota\varsigma$ and $\dot{\epsilon}\kappa\zeta\eta\tau\acute{\eta}\sigma\epsilon\iota\varsigma$, which the author uses pejoratively in the sense of speculation and controversy, can also mean simply investigation and inquiry[29]. In this latter sense it might be a term the opponents themselves

---

[27]The reason for this nearly ubiquitous tendency is twofold. First, the inchoate hints in the Pastorals link up with the late second and third century debates with gnosticism. See Brox, *Die Pastoralbriefe*, pp. 32—39, for a sketch of these links. Less anachronistic is the tendency to see analogies between the heterodox of the Pastorals to the heterodox in Colossians. When this is done, the detection of spiritual enthusiasm in Colossians is imported into the Pastorals. See essays in *Conflict in Colossae*, ed. and trans. Fred O. Francis and Wayne A. Meeks, Sources for Biblical Study 4 (Missoula: Scholars Press, 1975).

[28]For example, the *Treatise on Resurrection*, which is basically an argument for the fact that the resurrection happens now in baptism and not after death, combines both ideas. "Then indeed as the apostle said (Rom. 8.17; Eph. 2.5—6), 'We suffered with him, and we arose with him, and we went to heaven with him.' Now if we are manifest in this world wearing him, we are that one's beams, and we are embraced by him until our setting, that is to say, our death in this life. We are drawn to heaven by him, like beams by the sun, not being restrained by anything. This is the spiritual resurrection which swallows up the psychic in the same way as the fleshly" (in *Nag Hammadi Library*, ed. Robinson, p. 51). We are perhaps pushing analogies too far in intimating this kind of Lordship Christology for the opponents in the Pastorals. It is, of course, quite possible that their asceticism and peculiar doctrine of the resurrection did not result in Jesus being so immediately present in the church. They may, for instance, have taken the frequent gnostic position of having Jesus sitting atop a whole row of archons, far away from the individual. Perhaps this is what myths and genealogies mean.

[29]See p. 124, n. 26.

used. They may have concerned themselves with the rigors of theological inquiry, with puzzling out the difficulties in Pauline theology and with a detailed and aggressive hermeneutic of the Old Testament. The terms μῦθοι and γενεαλογίαι do not necessarily imply the outrageous systems of later gnostics, even though the author connects them with emptiness and speculation (μάταιοι, ξητήσεις)[30]. If this picture of creative theological inquiry along with a dynamic spiritualism based upon a lordship Christology is accurate, then we can understand both the accusation of asceticism and the indifference to the quieter virtues. They are not unethical but super-ethical; asceticism is more their style than the more corporate virtues which contribute to the harmony of the community. In fact, it is their negative impact upon the harmony and unity of the community which upsets our author most of all[31]. He believes they are producing in the church an unethical life-style in which personal knowledge and fascination with sophisticated theologies have superseded concern for the more traditional virtues. The proper church taxis is being overthrown: women are even teaching men. And since for the author, as we shall see, quiet virtues and traditional hierarchies form the heart of the salvation process, the eschatological status of many Christians is in jeopardy.

Thus he says in 1 Tim. 6.3—5:

> If anyone teaches other things and does not adhere to the sound words of our Lord Jesus Christ and the teaching which is in accordance with piety, he is conceited, understanding nothing, sick from speculation and debates over words (νοσῶν περὶ ξητήσεις καὶ λογομαχίας) which produce envy, strife, blasphemy, evil suspicians, the constant irritation of men who have destroyed their minds and are bereft of the truth, who consider religion to be an opportunity for profit.

And in Tit. 3.9, after noting that attention to good works is good and useful to human beings (καλὰ καὶ ὠφέλιμα τοῖς ἀνθρώποις), he counterposes as the opposite the opinion that foolish speculation and genealogies and strife and battle over the law are useless and empty (μωρὰς δὲ ξητήσεις καὶ γενεαλογίας καὶ ἔρεις καὶ μάχας νομικὰς περιίστασο, εἰσὶν γὰρ ἀνωφελεῖς καὶ μάταιοι). λογομαχία is useful for nothing (ἐπ οὐδὲν χρήσιμον) and destroys those who hear it (2 Tim. 2.14). It is a gangrene which consumes the community, perverting its faith (2 Tim. 2. 17, 18).

The theological result of these creative theologians is that they breed factions, controversy, and ultimately vice. Thus while they are disapproved (ἀδόκιμοι) for good works[32], the faithful teacher is approved (δόκιμος) and equipped (ἄρτιος) for good works[33]. And God's plan of

---

[30]Tit. 3.9; also in combinations at 1 Tim. 1.6; Tit. 1.10.

[31]For example, the description in 2 Tim. 2.14—19 of the heretics employs the images of a gangrene eating into the body, of the faith of some being upset (ἀνατρέπειν), and, on the other side, of the strong foundation of God.

[32]2 Tim. 3.8; Tit. 1.16.

[33]ἄρτιος, 2 Tim. 3.17; δόκιμος, 2 Tim. 2.15.

· salvation requires that one produce good deeds and manifest virtues. The opponents are undermining the good order of the church, and in regard to the dualism of being saved or not being saved they fall into the latter category and entice others after them. His problem with his opponents is not speculation in itself or creativity, since in many ways he is just as creative; his problem is that their activity produces a pattern of behavior which he considers improper and inadequate for the church.

3. The Author's Response

In order to portray the author's response to this theological and cultic crisis, which he perceived as lethal to his church, we must anticipate the more detailed study which follows[34]. However, for purposes of clarity a brief outline of the author's complex and subtle reaction will indicate how the shape of the heresy influenced the content of the ethical system promulgated in the letters and inspired the historical fictions which mold the pseudepigraphical letter which he writes. For instance, we cannot appreciate the effectiveness of the fiction of succession or of the peculiar Pauline portraits unless their polemical and argumentative slant is comprehended.

The author's basic strategy against these opponents is to employ the dualism of virtue and vice, placing them among the vices, and by a variety of methods to put a lid on theological speculation. To speculation he counterposes the good order of God's plan with its sound teachings; to their lordship Christology he counterposes an epiphany Christology in which Jesus has no immediate or direct contact with the Church; and to their spiritual enthusiasm he opposes a spirit which is dispensed only in baptism and which expresses itself through virtues. While his opponents capture women and apparently encourage them to join in the speculation and proselytizing process, the author subjects women to the authority of men, not allowing them to teach adult males but only children and younger women. While these opponents inspire debate, controversy, strife, zeal after knowledge, perhaps even intellectual excitement, he tries to inspire a peaceful, quiet life, where communal virtues dominate, where church members submit completely to the doctrinal and moral authority of certain bishops and elders, and where there is zeal after good works.

For all the theological and ethical sensitivity of our author, his boldest stroke is the absolute authority he conveys upon the authorized church leaders. God in this plan for saving people has funneled the salvation process through these leaders; there is no access to salvation except by way of

---

[34]The specifics of that study are outlined but not detailed here. In large part, the rest of this chapter is devoted to filling out this picture. For citations and analysis of the summary which immediately follows, see the appropriate sections below.

these cultic authorities. With Jesus out of the picture for the present, only these leaders can be trusted; they alone possess the knowledge and cultic gifts necessary for salvation. Further speculation about Christological puzzles is unnecessary, for these leaders possess the traditions, the sound teachings; they know the truth; they know God's plan for salvation. Thus speculation is not needed but rather obedience and trust. Furthermore, the ability to conform to the requisite virtues can only be acquired by way of baptism, which is within the exclusive provenance of these same leaders. Furthermore, the education and training necessary for the virtuous life can only be found in the sober schooling of these leaders and not in the useless and vain debates of their opponents. Thus the road to salvation is not through knowledge but through obedience to church authorities and through the quiet virtues which result.

The conclusion often drawn from this, that our author merely plays church politics by opposing the claims of one group of persons to the claims of another without taking the theological problems seriously, is not accurate[35]. As we shall see, he does indeed bestow absolute authority upon one faction, but he does this in a highly creative and original way. He first of all grounds their authority in Paul's authority through the fiction of the pseudepigraphical letter, using the genre with creativity and diversity. At the same time he articulates a theological system which provides a series of warrants and authorities for the requisite ethic. This system anchors his ethic in a consistent Christological framework, in an anthropological structure dependent upon the cult, and in an education process also dependent upon the cult. He employs along the way authoritative standards from his peculiarly Christian traditions ($\pi\alpha\rho\alpha\vartheta\eta\kappa\eta$) as well as canons and forms of argument from Greco-Roman ethics. On top of that the fiction of the Pauline letter and the details of God's plan contained therein are inseparable. The persuasiveness of his theology depends directly upon the persuasiveness of his pseudepigraphical techniques. He writes a history of Paul's activities which successfully conveys the entrusted traditions with their capacity to produce salvation to the present day church. Without this specific behavior of Paul, documented in the letters, the author's theological system crumbles, because the exclusive and reliable ($\pi\iota\sigma\tau\delta\varsigma$) authority of the church also crumbles. Pseudepigraphy and theology are welded together. If the fiction of the letters is not believed by its readers, then the theology of the letters loses its reliable status. To the theological creativity of his opponents he opposes his own theological creativity.

---

[35]Hanson, *The Pastoral Epistles*, p. 25, declares, "Against this teaching, the author, as we have seen, did not on the whole employ argument but abuse." Brox, *Die Pastoralbriefe*, p. 39, contrasts the Pauline carefulness in addressing his opponents' positions in order to refute them to the stock rebuke by the author of the Pastorals.

B. Christology and Ethics

1. Scholarship

When A. T. Hanson declared in 1968 that "the author of the Pastorals had no theology of his own. He is a purveyor of other men's theology," he echoed the prevailing opinion of modern scholarship of that time[36]. Subjected to intense comparison to the more dynamic theology of Paul and to the more sophisticated speculations of later church fathers, the argumentation in the Pastorals looked fragmented, chaotic, and pedestrian in comparison[37]. Defenders of authenticity saw in the Pastorals either an older Paul concerned with unforeseen heresies and perhaps debilitated by a faded intensity or a matured and mollified Paul who had recognized the need for firm church structures and explicit ethical norms[38]. But even advocates of non-Pauline authorship detected no theologian behind these letters but a churchman, who is assaulted by heresy and profligacy and responds as he must — with a rigid dogmatism, taken from church liturgy or early catechisms, and with strict ethical norms, taken from popular Greek ethics, resulting in an unsystematic collage of liturgy, hymns, misapprehended Paulinisms, and Greek ethics[39]. There were few attempts to

---

[36]A. T. Hanson, "The Significance of the Pastoral Epistles," in *Studies in the Pastoral Epistles* (1960), p. 110. In Hanson's recent commentary, *The Pastoral Epistles* (1982), p. 38, even though he has changed his mind about some things, he still asserts, "This gives us the key to the author's Christology. He does not have any doctrine of his own, but makes use of whatever comes to him in the sources which he uses."

[37]Hans Windisch, "Zur Christologie der Pastoralbriefe," *Zeitschrift für die neutestamentliche Wissenschaft* 34 (1935): 213—38, provided the most thorough and systematic analysis of the Christology of the Pastorals and ended by insisting that the author possesses no cogent system. Among scholars who disbelieve Pauline authorship I can find no one before Brox who attributed consistency and system to the Pastorals. Even Easton, *The Pastoral Epistles*, and Dibelius-Conzelmann, *The Pastoral Epistles*, who give generally sympathetic readings, refuse to speak of system in regard to the Pastorals.

[38]J. N. D. Kelly, *The Pastoral Epistles*, Black's New Testament Commentaries (London: Adam & Charles Black, 1963), pp. 16—20, provides a judicious statement of this attitude, suggesting that as things now stand, the best solution, though even it is beset by problems, is that Paul wrote these late in life, after a second imprisonment, in order to address a specific heresy. Therefore, he couched his letters in polemical terms, emphasizing the structures and authorities always implicit in his thought. Moreover, Paul may have become more and more hellenized. The inability of defenders of authenticity to square the Pastorals with Paul has led to increased reliance upon the role of the secretary. For Jeremias the activity of the secretary expands to the point where Paul nearly disappears, suggesting the letters be written and then proofreading them afterwards (Jeremias, *Die Briefe an Timotheus und Titus*, esp. p. 10). Spicq gives a multifaceted account, detecting four separate categories of material in the letters: (1) clear Paulinisms, (2) slight changes, like an emphasis on church order resulting from the natural growth of the man midst a changing church, (3) obvious anomolies, coming out of the polemic against heresy, and (4) other anomolies, springing from the hand of the amanuensis (Spicq, *Les Épîtres Pastorales*, pp. 157—214).

[39]Thus, Easton, *The Pastoral Epistles*, p. 22, explains the curious form of Pauline thought in the Pastorals by insisting that "Despite his passionate admiration for Paul, he never really under-

take the Pastorals seriously on their own terms. Even those scholars who admitted non-Pauline authorship tended to concentrate their analysis of the Pastorals on determining what was borrowed from tradition and what was not, and then tracing out the original provenance of those traditions[40]. In defense of the author they suggested that the problems of the author's day did not call for inspiration or real creativity; they called for moderation, clear ethical norms, and definitive church standards[41]. Thus the author was depicted as a good churchman, using whatever would persuade, borrowing at his pleasure from a wide variety of sources, and combining it all in cut-and-paste fashion into his letters without integrating them into a coherent system. In fact, he could not systematize these diverse elements because he did not possess a system. And he cannot use Paul's system because he did not understand Paul. All he really has of his own is a sense of piety which expresses itself in commonplace ethics, and he casts about wherever he can for doctrinal pieces to buttress his ethics[42]. Therefore, although scholarship did enormous and invaluable work

---

stood him." Although most scholars adhering to non-Pauline authorship dissect the letters into various layers of tradition and other sources, Falconer's treatment epitomizes this effort. He slices the material into six sections: a Pauline letter, Pauline-based material, a Christian fragment on church order, a Christian prophecy, an authoritative tractate on Christian purity and church order, and finally redactions by the editor of the Pastorals. This last comes in terms of short verses and half-verses used to glue the stuff together. It is noteworthy that he calls the author throughout the commentary the "editor" (Robert Falconer, *The Pastoral Epistles* [Oxford: Clarendon Press, 1937]). It is also interesting that Hanson insists that "This is not to suggest that he was a mere magpie, one who collected any bits of liturgy or confession within his grasp and strung them together like beads on a string, quite unaware of their mutual incompatibility" ("The Significance of the Pastoral Epistles," *Studies in the Pastoral Epistles*, p. 111). Unfortunately, all that Hanson means by this is that the author's theological principles are not mutually incompatible (he finds only 2 Tim. 2.19—21 and 1 Tim. 2.5 suspect). He does not mean that ethics, church order, and theology fit into a system.

[40]Once again, there are innumerable examples of scholars tracing out and delimiting the Pauline influence on the Pastorals, but perhaps the aggressiveness of Hanson, *The Pastoral Epistles*, will illustrate adequately this phenomenon. In his appendix (p. 199) he lists twenty-one places in the Pastorals where he thinks the author is "editing" Pauline material. Also Spicq throughout his commentary, *Les Épîtres Pastorales*, takes care to note all analogies to other Pauline letters. Of course, more recently, Trummer has reploughed much of this ground, insisting that the only way to understand the Pastorals is as part of the ongoing Pauline traditions, but also by giving some attention to the power of pseudepigraphy he provides a somewhat more enlightening reading of how the author interprets Paul (*Die Paulustradition der Pastoralbriefe*).

[41]Thus the apology of Ernest Findlay Scott, *The Pastoral Epistles*, The Moffat New Testament Commentaries (London: Hodder and Stoughton, 1936), p. xxxvii: "He has been accused by some modern critics of substituting a 'bourgeois religion' for the authentic gospel. It is just here, however, that we can perceive the lasting service which he rendered to Christianity. He wrote in the time when the first wave of enthusiasm had spent itself .... If the Church was to survive it must transform itself into an organized society, and make terms with earthly conditions which would endure, perhaps, for ages to come ...."

[42]For the emphasis on εὐσέβεια and its cognates see Falconer, *The Pastoral Epistles*, pp. 30—39. Hanson defends this technique on the author's part by noting "that in thus purveying other people's theology the author is simply following his own declared principles. He repeatedly empha-

in detailing the historical milieu of nearly every significant motif in the Pastorals, the theological system promulgated by the letters themselves remained undetected because it was assumed it did not exist. "There is a diversity of Christological perspectives which must not be combined to reconstruct 'the' Christology of the Pastorals."[43]

In many ways Norbert Brox simply extended this tendency to perceive fragmentation and incoherence in the Pastorals. For instance, he continuously insisted that the Pastorals present less an "independent, original theology" than "instructions for practical Christianity"[44]. In his introduction to his commentary in 1968, he quotes with approval all the careful apologies of previous scholars for this practical, non-Pauline (and thus non-theological) slant to the author's work[45]. In spite of this, in other ways Brox laid the groundwork for the more creative readings which have followed him. Brox had immersed himself in the study of ancient pseudepigraphy and this should have prepared the way for him to detect creativity on the author's part when he took the genre in hand[46]. Unfortunately, Brox did not pursue the implications which his presuppositons allowed him. Perhaps decades of contrary scholarship discouraged him, but we have also seen that his study of pseudepigraphy focused upon the psychology of the author and the historical impingements upon him, so that he ignored the literary dimensions. Thus he may not have been attuned to literary conventions and the possibilities of genre. In any case, Brox does not perceive the unity of theology, ethics, and genre which I think exists. However, he does point the way. For example, he speaks cautiously of the "epiphany Christology" in the letters and of "portraits" of Paul, Timothy, and Titus as coming from the hand of the author[47]. These few hints about theological creativity on the author's part have inspired a series of systematic investigations of the Pastorals. However, no scholar has picked up at the same time the equal hints about the capacities of pseudepigraphy to make certain kinds of arguments; in fact, no one has even gone as far as Brox did, even though Brox had taken only a few hesitant steps. There-

---

sizes throughout all three Epistles that Timothy and Titus are to guard carefully the sacred tradition and hand it on intact. As several editors have pointed out, the last thing that the author of the Pastorals would have wanted was to be 'an original theologian' " ("The Significance of the Pastoral Epistles," p. 112).

[43]Dibelius-Conzelmann, *The Pastoral Epistles*, p. 9.

[44]Brox, *Die Pastoralbriefe*, p. 50.

[45]Brox highlights both the changing circumstances of the church and the natural development of Pauline thought (*Die Pastoralbriefe*, pp. 52–53).

[46]Without reminding ourselves of his encyclopedic investigations we can simply note the short analysis of early Christian pseudepigraphy in the introduction to his commentary, which he uses as a springboard into the Pastorals (*Die Pastoralbriefe*, pp. 60–66).

[47]Brox, *Die Pastoralbriefe*, pp. 51, 72–77. I believe it is Brox's suggestion of a creative "Paulusbild" which actually marks his greatest contribution. Yet even here, Brox does not pursue the possibility that the author is aggressively creating tradition and not just handing it on with minor adjustments.

fore, in Brox's wake have come a variety of theological inquiries which ignore the literary factors.

Of the more recent studies of the theology of the Pastorals the most helpful for our purposes are those of Oberlinner, Trummer, Lips, and Hasler[48]. Although the focus of each is different, they agree in wanting to address the Pastorals on their own terms. By doing this, a great deal of progress has been made in tracing out the intricacies of the theological system in the Pastorals. Each of these studies has contributed significantly to our understanding of the provenance of the theological ideas of the author and the manner in which these ideas interrelate with each other. In addition to this shared contribution, the idiosyncratic focus of each of these studies has clarified certain problems. Although I do not always agree with the results, Oberlinner and Trummer have both taken great care to distinguish what is merely tradition passed on uncritically and what is the author's own[49]. Lips' study focuses upon the organizational concepts in the Pastorals, and many of the details of the author's attitude toward church officers which Lips explicates are built into my own argument[50]. Finally, in my opinion, Hasler has managed to escape from the Pauline shadow better than anyone else, and his short study of the Christology of the Pastorals marks a major advance[51].

Despite my appreciation and reliance upon these studies, all of them suffer from the same malaise. They do not take literary questions seriously enough. This attitude betrays itself in two predominant ways. First, they ignore the unique capacities of the pseudepigraphical letter for conveying certain kinds of information and making certain kinds of arguments. Therefore, the import of the various fictions concocted in the letters for supporting and giving content to the ethic is ignored. Secondly, the various theological and Christological statements are pulled individually from

---

[48]Oberlinner, "Die 'Epiphaneia' des Heilswillens Gottes in Christus Jesus," pp. 192–213; Trummer, *Die Paulustradition*; Lips, *Glaube, Gemeinde, Amt*; Hasler, "Epiphanie und Christologie in den Pastoralbriefen," pp. 193–209.

[49]Without a doubt Trummer presents the single most thorough analysis of this relationship, though I am more sympathetic to Oberlinner's treatment, since he perceives more creativity in the author of Pastorals. Oberlinner begins his essay with a nod to Trummer's work, but proceeds quite differently from Trummer. Trummer tried to distinguish first what was Pauline and what was not and then to analyze what is not. Oberlinner begins by looking at the peculiar shape of the theology of the Pastorals and then notes how the Pauline tradition is taken up into this new framework. In this way I think he reaches a better understanding of the dynamics between tradition and creativity in the Pastorals. Trummer, *Die Paulustradition*; Oberlinner, "Die 'Epiphaneia' des Heilswillens Gottes in Christus Jesus."

[50]Lips begins his study with a careful and mostly accurate exposition of the "Glaubensverständnis" of the Pastorals, then fits the concepts of office and ordination into this system. What is most helpful for us is his ability to combine the author's concepts of succession and official authority with his religious notions. See esp. Lips, *Glaube, Gemeinde, Amt*, pp. 265–78.

[51]I would only quibble seriously with Hasler's assertion that all salvation takes place on the other side after judgment, with believers in the present having only the promise. See Hasler, "Epiphanie und Christologie in den Pastoralbriefen," pp. 207–9.

their contexts and are woven into a new system. None of these studies attempts to understand the author's method of argumentation or the literary shape of the letters. Therefore, the elaborate interplays among ethical statements, Christological statements, and other dicta are ignored.

Consequently the last thing that is needed at this point is another investigation of the theology and Christology of the Pastorals which confines itself to the explicit theological statements in the letters, divorced from their literary context, or which ignores the logical connections between theological and ethical statements. Scholarship has spent most of its time since Holtzmann working out the implications of the individual theological and Christological propositions in the Pastorals, but the relationship of those propositions to the rest of the material in the letters, such as the duty lists for elders, remains unexplored. The following analysis attempts to demonstrate how the seemingly disparate elements of the letters combine into a consistent theological and ethical system without repeating all the detail work already done on these separate elements. We will be looking for the inner logic of the system.

It will be clear from what follows that the theological and ethical system outlined here depends upon a specific way of reading the letters. In my opinion the author's system can be comprehended only if one is aware of how he uses the pseudepigraphical letter to create certain fictions and of how he constructs connections among theological, ethical, and biographical statements by way of enthymematic and paradigmatic logic. That is to say, the previous two chapters proffer heuristic tools with which to organize the Pastorals into a coherent system. It will not be our procedure to proceed in commentary fashion through the letters, detailing the argumentative structure of each pericope, but rather to analyze and organize the results of just such a reading. So what follows is an analysis of the author's theological system and not his method of argumentation.

2. The Cosmological Framework of the Ethic

All three of the Pastorals contain theme statements in the proem of the letters. 1 Tim. 1.3—4 introduces the contrast between God's plan of salvation (οἰκονομία θεοῦ) and the empty speculation of the opponents. The purpose of the letters and the task enjoined upon church leadership is to produce (παρέχειν) God's plan. The tendency in scholarship to debate whether οἰκονομία means "God's plan of salvation" or "the education of men by God for salvation," the difference between plan and active management, is an unnecessary and misleading split. οἰκονομία in the Pastorals means both to have a plan and to execute it[52]. Thus the Pastorals assume as a basic theme the existence of a plan of God for salvation which is being executed by the letters and ultimately by the church leadership. This plan is being "produced."

The salutation in Titus contains a noticeable expansion over the Pauline form and provides further information about this plan. Picking up the

terms πίστις, ἐπίγνωσις, εὐσέβεια, and hope for eternal life, all of which
are concepts for describing God's plan, the author adds that this was promised by the unlying God before time began, and that it was revealed
(ἐφανέρωσαν) at the proper time in the preaching act. Thus the οἰκονομία θεοῦ is God's pre-existent plan of salvation for creation which has
now been revealed[53]. As we shall see, it was Jesus who revealed it, and
Paul and his followers who continue this revelation. And, we might add, it
is the author himself who works out its specific form for the first time.

The proem of 2 Timothy gives further details about this plan, when a
series of formulaic propositions is used to buttress the thematic statement
to rekindle leadership gifts (2 Tim. 1.3–14). Paul himself is painted in
such a fashion as to be a paradigm of this type of leader, but the author
also provides theological warrants in the form of theological formulae
used as enthymematic premises. The participial style and the traditional
schema of the propositions in vv. 9 and 10 indicate to many scholars that
the author is citing a piece of tradition, although there is no agreement
about how extensive the citation is, what its original provenance was, and
what the author changes or adds[54]. For our purposes we need not pursue
further attempts to draw the line between tradition and the author, because, even if this is a citation, the author fully agrees with it. I can discover no tension between the theology articulated here and the theology
of the rest of the letter. In fact, the specific terms σώζω, χάρις, πρὸ
χρόνων αἰωνίων, φανερόω, ἐπιφάνεια, destroying death, and bringing
life and immortality to light are basic and recurring concepts for the author. Thus if he is citing, he is persuaded by what he cites. "Paul" anchors
his ability to not be ashamed of the witness (μαρτύριον) of the Lord in
the power of God:

---

[52]I am not asserting here the poetic use of language in the Pastorals, as though the author were
consciously playing with the ambiguity between two separate meanings of the term. The warnings
from students of semantics that words almost always mean one thing is to the point. What I am asserting is that οἰκονομία can mean this one idea, which combines both existence of a plan and
its actuality. Bauer, Arndt, and Gingrich, A Greek-English Lexicon, lists three meanings for οἰκονομία : (1) management, office, (2) arrangement, plan, (3) training. They even place 1 Tim.
1.4 under "training." And Spicq, Les Épîtres Pastorales, p. 26, emphasizes the educative quality
of the term. The closest parallels to the use of the term in the Pastorals occur in Ignatius Letter to
the Ephesians 18.2; 26.1, where it clearly means "God's plan of salvation" which is taking place,
in Eph. 1.10; 3.9, which may in fact be the source of the term for the Pastorals, where this plan
was preordained before the foundation of the world, was once hidden and is now revealed and taking force (the Pastorals assert the same things about this plan), and in Epictetus 3.24.92 where
τεταγμένη οἰκονομία is the "ordered process of nature." I contend that the term always (or nearly so) has a dynamic dimension except where it refers to a specific office.

[53]The analogies to Eph. 1.10; 3.9 are obvious.

[54]"Most editors believe that these two verses constitute a liturgical fragment introduced by
the author into his text at this point, though there is wide disagreement as to the original nature
of the fragment. Easton, followed by Holtz, believes it was a hymn; Gealy says either a hymn or a
baptismal confession (or one made at ordination); D-C [Dibelius-Conzelmann] call it 'a kerygmatic
formula'; Dornier says it is a confession of faith; Hasler suggests a baptismal hymn" (Hanson, The
Pastoral Epistles, p. 122).

who saved us and called us to a holy calling,
not according to our works, but according to his own plan
($\pi\rho\acute{o}\vartheta\epsilon\sigma\iota\nu$) and grace,
which was given to us in Christ Jesus before time began,
and has now been revealed ($\varphi\alpha\nu\epsilon\rho\omega\vartheta\epsilon\tilde{\iota}\sigma\alpha\nu$) through the
appearance ($\dot{\epsilon}\pi\iota\varphi\alpha\nu\epsilon\iota\alpha\varsigma$) of our savior Christ Jesus,
who destroyed death and brought to light life and
immortality through the gospel (2 Tim. 1.9–10).

Then "Paul" locates his own activity as preacher, apostle, and teacher in this salvation schema ($\epsilon\iota\varsigma$ $\ddot{o}$ $\dot{\epsilon}\tau\acute{\epsilon}\vartheta\eta\nu$ $\dot{\epsilon}\gamma\acute{\omega}$)[55].

The theological propositions in this passage provide further information about this plan of salvation. First of all, it is God who authors the plan and carries it out through Jesus. Jesus has an essential though clearly subordinate role (this subordination of Jesus to God is carried out consistently in the letters)[56]. God is the primary savior. In fact, the author's vision of God as savior, creator, giver of grace, who includes every person in the plan, explains a great deal about the author's ethics and the general positive tone of the letters. Secondly, the key historical moment of the plan is the epiphany of Jesus. This is the only time in the New Testament where $\dot{\epsilon}\pi\iota\varphi\acute{\alpha}\nu\epsilon\iota\alpha$ is specifically linked with the historical appearance of Jesus – it usually refers to his parousia[57]. "Paul" builds his apostolic activity upon the specifics of this first epiphany, and though the letters do not use $\dot{\epsilon}\pi\iota\varphi\acute{\alpha}\nu\epsilon\iota\alpha$ again in this exact way (the verb is used) they do provide more extensive information about the impact of this first epiphany. Thus the cosmological origins of God's plan eventually issue into historical dimensions by moving through Jesus into Paul and his traditions.

In order to understand the ethical system of the author these cosmological links must be traced. His conceptions of who God is, who Jesus is, what they have done and will do, determine in a definite way the life-style of the Christian. God's plan has two sides – cosmological and ethical. Frequently the two contribute separate elements in the same enthymeme. And as the above citation demonstrates, the author's cosmology focuses first of all on the nature and activity of God and secondly on the activity of Jesus. Each of these will be investigated in turn.

a) *God as Creator and Savior*

Perhaps the most striking theological idiosyncrasy of the Pastorals is the frequent application of the epithet $\sigma\omega\tau\acute{\eta}\rho$ to God: of the eight instances in the New Testament where $\sigma\omega\tau\acute{\eta}\rho$ is applied to God six are in the Pas-

---

[55] 2 Tim. 1.11–12.

[56] See Hasler, "Epiphanie und Christologie in den Pastoralbriefen," pp. 200–1.

[57] Ibid., p. 199. However, verbal forms occur in 1 Tim. 3.16 and Tit. 2.11, both of which clearly refer to the incarnation.

torals[58]. Jesus, of course, is also called σωτήρ four times, and in using this title for Jesus the Pastorals participate in a growing tendency in early Christianity[59]. But the primary savior in the Pastorals is God, with Jesus being savior largely by assisting God in revealing the plan of salvation[60]. The extensive studies done on σωτήρ in the Greco-Roman world and the excellent summary of that work in Dibelius-Conzelmann demonstrate that, although the term σωτήρ eventually became a general epithet for all kinds of gods and demi-gods, an identifiable and specific set of ideas is most commonly associated with the term[61]. The Jewish tendency, seen in the Septuagint, Philo, and other Hellenistic Jewish writings, to attach σωτήρ to God emphasizes God's role as giver of life, as creator and sustainer[62]. The primary Greco-Roman use is to refer to a specific act of a deity wherein salvation or life or rescue is effected by the intervention of the god[63]. This occurs in the emperor cult and elsewhere, frequently in conjunction with the term ἐπιφάνεια, so that a deity "appears" and by that epiphany effects salvation, and thus is termed savior[64]. Often this epiphany determines more than the safety of an individual, as when the emperor, the savior, appears and inaugurates a general time of salvation. Thus savior becomes a designation for a deity who rules and manages an era and domain of salvation. As Bultmann and Lührmann have argued, this linkage of a savior to an epiphany is an ancient phenomenon in which the god typically revealed his ἀρεταί and δυνάμεις (virtues and powers)[65]. These ἀρεταί revealed in such instances do not of course compare to the virtues of the Pastorals, because the general understanding of virtue had

---

[58]Lk. 1.47; Jude 25; 1 Tim. 1.1; 2.3; 4.10; Tit. 1.3; 2.10; 3.4.

[59]2 Tim. 1.10; Tit. 1.4; 2.13; 3.6. For an analysis of the development of the concept of Jesus as Savior in post-canonical early Christianity see Wilhelm Bousset, *Kyrios Christos*, trans. John E. Steely (Nashville: Abingdon Press, 1970), pp. 310–17.

[60]So Brox, *Die Pastoralbriefe*, pp. 232–33. However, Oberlinner points out how unique the use of σωτήρ is in the Pastorals as compared to the rest of the New Testament. Even the many analogues to the Septuagint and the emperor cult and the frequent linkage with ἐπιφάνεια do not entirely predict the usage in the Pastorals (Oberlinner, "Die 'Epiphaneia' des Heilswillens Gottes in Christus Jesus," pp. 196–203).

[61]Dibelius-Conzelmann, *The Pastoral Epistles*, pp. 100–101.

[62]Dibelius-Conzelmann, *The Pastoral Epistles*, pp. 100–101, cite numerous examples from the Septuagint and Hellenistic Judaism, as does Spicq, *Les Épîtres Pastorales*, pp. 315–316. Spicq argues that even if the emperor cult and other Greco-Roman ideas have influence on the author of the Pastorals, this influence is radically transformed by its association with Jewish ideas. In my opinion, the idea of the creator God also being savior produces a distinct Jewish transformation of the "intervention" ideas of the Greco-Roman world.

[63]In tracing these ideas everyone still depends on Wendland's programmatic study (Paul Wendland, "Σωτήρ," *Zeitschrift für die neutestamentliche Wissenschaft* 5 (1904): 335–53).

[64]The linkage with ἐπιφάνεια and the analogies to ruler cult appear in Wendland, "Σωτήρ,' and Dibelius-Conzelmann, *The Pastoral Epistles*, pp. 100–101. But also see Ernst Lohmeyer, *Christuskult und Kaiserkult* (Tübingen: J. C. B. Mohr [Paul Siebeck], 1919); E. Pax, ΕΠΙΦΑΝΕΙΑ *Ein religionsgeschichtlicher Beitrag zur biblischen Theologie* (Munich: Zink, 1955). Cf. discussion in Hanson, *The Pastoral Epistles*, pp. 186–88.

[65]Bultmann-Lührmann, "ἐπιφάνεια," TDNT, 9:8–11.

changed by this time from its original connection with power to an emphasis on the quieter virtues of justice and prudence[66]. In any case, all of
these implications in the term savior seem to be in force in the Pastorals.
It is linked with "epiphany"; it inaugurates a new time of salvation; and
it touches upon the Jewish idea of God as creator and giver of life. There
are even instances where it has become a mere title without any direct or
at least explicit connection with salvific action (1 Tim. 1.1; Tit. 1.3; 2.
10). Our intention here, as stated above, is not to plough again through
debates over the correct provenance of theological predicates in the Pastorals, but to try to understand how the theological propositions influence
the larger ethical system of the author. Thus we must investigate what
role God as savior can play in an enthymematic argument.

The title "savior" occurs with "God" twice in the formulaic salutations,
in 1 Timothy and Titus, although the usage in Titus may be more than
formulaic, since the salutation with its expansion to include a short description of the plan of salvation is so unusual[67]. As we shall see, the Christological and cultic dimensions of God's plan of salvation receive their ful-
lest treatment in the letter to Titus. Thus it is no surprise that the other
two occurrences of God as savior in Titus are specifically linked to detailed expressions of the plan of salvation. In Tit. 2.11 the title is used to
describe God as the author of Jesus' first epiphany, which makes possible
the ethical life and lays the basis for coming judgment. In Tit. 3.4 the title
is linked in an enthymeme with the plan of salvation, although here the
emphasis is upon its cultic dimensions in the act of baptism and the anthropological transformation resultant from baptism. The details of these
two citations will be investigated more fully below since these are helpful
passages for learning the details of the plan, but at this point we can conclude that God is called savior because God authors and brings to fruition
this plan of salvation.

This connection between the title savior and God's ability to save receives further treatment in 1 Tim. 4.10 where God's capacity as savior is
employed in an enthymeme to establish the value of training for the
ethical life. As we shall see, the author believes not only that virtues require rigorous and constant pursuit but also that their achievement is
possible within the Christian cult. Here the author is enjoining training
in piety ($\gamma\acute{\upsilon}\mu\nu\alpha\zeta\epsilon$ $\delta\grave{\epsilon}$ $\sigma\epsilon\alpha\upsilon\tau\grave{o}\nu$ $\pi\rho\grave{o}\varsigma$ $\epsilon\dot{\upsilon}\sigma\acute{\epsilon}\beta\epsilon\iota\alpha\nu$) which is not of little use
($\pi\rho\grave{o}\varsigma$ $\dot{o}\lambda\acute{\iota}\gamma o\nu$) but helpful ($\dot{\omega}\varphi\acute{\epsilon}\lambda\iota\mu o\varsigma$) to humans. It is helpful because it
is acceptable to God. He concludes his exhortation by remarking, "in
these things we labor and work, because we hope in a living God, who is

---

[66]For a history of the change in meaning of $\dot{\alpha}\rho\epsilon\tau\acute{\eta}$ from Homer to Aristotle, and of how the
quieter virtues win out over notions of power see Arthur W. H. Adkins, *Merit and Responsibility*,
Midway reprint (Chicago: University of Chicago Press, 1975).

[67]The expansion over the shorter form suggests the hand of the author rather than a more elaborate tradition.

savior of all people, especially of believers (ὅς ἐστιν σωτὴρ πάντων ἀνθρώπων, μάλιστα πιστῶν)." That is to say, the ethical life which forms the heart of the Christian life-style has its motivation and its possibility in the saving character of God. Ethics is tied to cosmology and the connecting of the two is accomplished through the modes of inference of enthymematic arguments.

In 1 Tim. 2.3 "Paul" again enjoins the virtuous life which he terms "quiet and peaceful" (ἵνα ἤρεμον καὶ ἡσύχιον βίον διάγωμεν ἐν πάσῃ εὐσεβείᾳ καὶ σεμνότητι) and which he justifies enthymematically on the grounds that such a life is good and acceptable to God our savior (τοῦτο καλὸν καὶ ἀπόδεκτον ἐνώπιον τοῦ σωτῆρος ἡμῶν θεοῦ). This repeats the train of thought expressed in 1 Tim. 4.10, but an additional purpose can be detected in this instance. The larger literary section is one where "Paul" encourages that prayers be made for all people and for all in authority, including secular leadership. As we shall see, one of the major themes of 1 Timothy is the relationship of orthodox Christians to those on the outside, whether they be heterodox Christians or non-Christians. The noun savior in 2.3 anticipates the verbal form in 2.4. Peaceful and friendly behavior towards outsiders, along with the ethical life, is grounded in God our savior, "who wishes all people to be saved and to come into a knowledge of the truth (ὅς πάντας ἀνθρώπους θέλει σωθῆναι καὶ εἰς ἐπίγνωσιν ἀληθείας ἐλθεῖν)." Therefore, God's attitude towards all people is paradigmatic for the attitude of the Christian towards outsiders. This paradigmatic role functions logically as a premise in the enthymeme. The logic says that just as God has the salvation of outsiders at heart, so should Christians be peaceful and solicitous towards them. Once again an enthymeme links theological propositions to ethical conclusions.

The author's use of the verbal form (σῴζειν) to fill out the specifics of God's function as savior indicates that we should include an analysis of the various ways the author employs σῴζειν. The noun and the verb are specifically connected in 1 Tim. 2.3–4, as we saw, but they are also expressly linked in Tit. 3.4–5. As we have already noted in this passage, God as savior manages salvation through the cultic act of baptism which produces an anthropological transformation through the gift of the spirit[68]. Thus it is no surprise that σῴζειν is used to articulate what God is doing in baptism: "Not from works which we have done in righteousness, but on the basis of his own mercy (κατὰ τὸ αὐτοῦ ἔλεος) he saved us through the bath of regeneration (ἔσωσεν ἡμᾶς διὰ λουτροῦ παλιγγενεσίας) and the renewal of the holy spirit (ἀνακαινώσεως πνεύματος ἁγίου)." Thus, the God of the Pastorals is a merciful God who saves via cultic acts and the

---

[68]On the baptismal dimensions of this passage see A. T. Hanson, "Elements of a Baptismal Liturgy in Titus," *Studies in the Pastoral Epistles*, pp. 78–96. Hanson also links the presence of Haustafeln in the Pastorals to this baptismal liturgy, noting parallels in Colossians, Ephesians, and 1 Peter. Cf. M. E. Boismard, "Une Liturgie Baptismale dans la Prima Petri," *Revue Biblique* 63 (1956–57): 182ff.

new anthropoligical possibilities provided by the spirit. The primary cosmological context of the Pastorals becomes one of salvation; consequently, σῴζειν is used in a variety of ways. In 1 Tim. 2.15, for instance, after a series of warnings about women who exceed their proper authority and elevate themselves above or make themselves equal to men, the author permits God's capacity for salvation to apply even to them: "but they will be saved through childbearing." The now familiar enthymematic linkage between ethical injunctions and the plan of salvation, specifically between ideas of grace and calling, inaugurated by Jesus at his epiphany, occurs in 2 Tim. 1.9. As we have already seen, this passage as a whole gives cosmological warrant to the exhortation to renew oneself in leadership. 1 Tim. 4.16 also uses the verbal form to provide a theological premise to an enthymeme which concludes with an exhortation for good leadership: "doing these things (exercising proper leadership) you will save yourself and those who hear you." And we may include in this list "Paul's" remark in 2 Tim. 4.18 that God alone stood by him at his first defense, will save (ῥύσεται) him from every evil work, and will save (σώσει) him for his heavenly kingdom.

To this diverse list we can add Christ's own accomplishments as savior. This inclusion is not in my opinion a mixing of categories, even though Jesus has a specific and limited role, because the primary import of salvation language in the Pastorals is not to draw lines between God and Jesus but to articulate the author's general view of his cosmos as one in which a process of salvation is taking place. Every occurrence of salvation, every link in the chain, is part of the plan of salvation, whether it is referred for its immediate cause to God or Jesus or church leaders or cultic acts. We have already noticed in 1 Tim. 4.16 that the author describes correct performance of the duties of a church leader as producing salvation for both the leader and all who hear him. As we shall see, this is not a careless remark, for in many ways those church leaders who are behaving properly become the one essential element in realizing salvation in the author's day. Jesus receives the title savior only in the midst of descriptions of the plan of salvation and only when the effects of his epiphany are being described. In fact, the three major passages in the Pastorals which paint the details of the salvation schema, the cosmological side of the οἰκονομία θεοῦ, are 2 Tim. 1.9–10; Tit. 2.11–14; and Tit. 3.4–7. And it is only there, in those passages, plus the expanded salutation in Titus, where the salvation schema is also played out, that Jesus is called savior. When we look at what Jesus accomplishes in these epiphanies, which we will do below, his impact appears to focus upon the ethical life, making virtues possible, providing teaching standards for virtue, and rewarding virtue on judgment day. Thus Jesus saves, because virtues save. Jesus is also attached to the verbal form one time in 1 Tim. 1.15 where it is declared that "Christ Jesus came into the world to save sinners" of whom Paul is the foremost. The author paints Paul as the prototype of all sinners, whom, as we have seen, God wants to be saved and thus wants church members, who were once sinners themselves, to be solicitous and gentle towards sinners. Therefore, Jesus' accommodation to sinners embodies God's own, both of which together encourage mercy towards sinners by church members.

The ultimate impression produced by this aggregate of ideas is that the theological epithet of savior along with its verbal form determines directly the content and direction of the ethical and ecclesiastical life-style promulgated in the letters. Again, we must admit that theology and ethics are intimately connected. σωτήρ and σώζειν occur most frequently within enumerations of the salvation schema as premises to enthymemes. They apply directly to the leadership pattern enjoined in the letters, both when Paul is saved either amidst distress and abandonment or forgiven in spite of his sins, and when leaders by leading properly save themselves and those who hear them. Likewise, as the inductive paradigm concludes, all sinners are saved. In fact, God and Christ as saviors manifest great concern and sympathy for everyone, Christian or not, for all were once alike in sin. Because of this friendliness on God's part, church members in imitation of God are to reprove opponents only in the hope of reincorporating them within the orthodox fold. Even women, ensnared by these heretics or themselves heretics, who contrary to nature have placed themselves above men, can be saved and thus should be admonished gently. Finally the whole ethical life is grounded in the savior concept, because it is solely by way of virtue that God saves.

Although the specifics of how cosmological concepts determine ethical content are important, the general tone of all these arguments is striking. In Tit. 3.4, where we have already noticed the linkage of savior with ideas of grace worked out in baptism, the salvation schema is introduced as revealing God's kindness (χρηστότης) and love of mankind (φιλανθρωπία). The first epiphany of Jesus revealed to the world something essential about the nature·of God which has shaped the author's whole attitude towards the world. God's dealing with the world and with human beings is based upon χρηστότης and φιλανθρωπία. Thus God has instigated the plan of salvation with the intention to save all. And while the author puts great stock in the intricacies of this plan, especially upon the role of the cult and its leadership, the general positive evaluation of God as savior, who entertains χρηστότης and φιλανθρωπία towards humanity, bestows an aura of hope, accommodation, peacefulness, and belonging to the author's basic outlook. He lives in a friendly cosmos, a cosmos which contains within it processes of salvation. There are helpful forces in the world, placed there as part of God's management, forces which can be contacted and drawn upon if one lives properly within the Christian cult. As much as anything else this positive regard for the cosmos explains why quiet virtues could be embraced so wholeheartedly. Pursuit of a quiet, peaceful life, in which every human is a potential equal, where the social virtues of εὐσέβεια, φρόνησις, σωφροσύνη are pursued, makes sense only when the world and a human's present-day life have essential value. It does not have to be said that such a positive attitude towards the world and life in it was not the only option in the Greco-Roman world. In fact, both the apocalyptic and gnostic world views, which lay close at hand for the author, did not admit such things. That the stress laid upon these ideas betrays a contrary point of view among the author's opponents is uncertain though probable. In any case, God, the savior, by bringing to the fore God's kindness and concern for humanity in the workings of the plan of salvation, gives cosmological warrant to quiet virtues and a peaceful life.

The positive aura pervades other parts of the letters. We have already encountered language about God's grace applied to Paul as a sinner (1 Tim. 1.12–17), and have seen the distinction between works which win salvation and the free gift of God (2 Tim. 1.9). Furthermore, the emphasis on election, being chosen for salvation for no discernible reason (Tit. 1.1: 3.4–7) along with the admonition to reprove opponents ἐν πραΰτητι, since they too may be destined for salvation, illustrates that this image of God as being kind and concerned for all people surfaces in a variety of ways. As might be expected, God is also creator (1 Tim. 6.13). And since God's character is one of friendliness, creation itself is a friendly place, where one should live at peace and not according to ascetic revulsion. Thus the author excoriates his opponents who misunderstand the nature of creation by practicing abstinence from certain foods, which in the author's mind should be accepted with prayer as rightful parts of God's creation (1 Tim. 4.3). He is arguing that everything in creation comes from God's hands and consequently participates in the goodness of God. God's kindness pervades the cosmos.

b) *The First Epiphany of Jesus*

The plan of salvation, the character of which comes from God's nature and which contains within it all the necessary powers to effect salvation, has now, according to the author, been revealed in its specifics and set loose as a working force in the world. Thus the salutation in Titus locates the origin of the plan at the beginning of time or before time began (πρὸ χρόνων αἰωνίων) in God's initial intentions for the cosmos; it was promised long ago, but only now has broken loose at the proper time (καιροῖς ἰδίοις) (Tit. 1.3; 1 Tim. 2.6). The moment of revelation of both the existence and power of this plan lies in the first epiphany of Jesus. This is made clear in 2 Tim. 1.9–10, which we have mentioned before but now must investigate in more detail.

τοῦ σώσαντος ἡμᾶς καὶ καλέσαντος κλήσει ἁγίᾳ, οὐ κατὰ τὰ ἔργα ἡμῶν ἀλλὰ κατὰ ἰδίαν πρόθεσιν καὶ χάριν, τὴν δοθεῖσαν ἡμῖν ἐν Χριστῷ Ἰησοῦ πρὸ χρόνων αἰωνίων, φανερωθεῖσαν δὲ νῦν διὰ τῆς ἐπιφανείας τοῦ σωτῆρος ἡμῶν Χριστοῦ Ἰησοῦ, καταργήσαντος μὲν τὸν θάνατον φωτίσαντος δὲ ζωὴν καὶ ἀφθαρσίαν διὰ τοῦ εὐαγγελίου,

[God] who saved us and called us to a holy calling not according to our works but according to his own plan and grace, which was given to us in Christ Jesus before time began, but has now been revealed, through the epiphany of our Savior Christ Jesus, who destroyed death and brought to light life and immortality through the gospel.

Without repeating the observations we have already drawn from this passage, we must reiterate at least that God's plan, his grace, has suddenly been revealed at Jesus' first epiphany. Consequently, part of the Christological function of the first epiphany is one of epistemology, to provide information heretofore unknown about the nature of God and God's intentions for the cosmos. Through the salvific impact of the first epiphany humans discover the single most significant aspect of God's dealings with them, namely, God possesses a plan for the salvation of people which is now breaking forth in its effective power. In a way the entire preceding discussion on the nature of God as savior hinges directly upon upon Jesus' epiphany, since without that epiphany not only would the plan still be held in abeyance but also the very existence of that plan would still be unknown. Yet there are obviously more than epistemological consequences from this epiphany; there are also, so to speak, ontic ones. The nature of reality is changed. As our passage puts it, death has been destroyed and immortality brought to light. We can assume, since Jesus apparently introduces for the first time this change in the cosmos, that immortality was not a possibility before his epiphany. The essential and unavoidable role of the Christian cult in providing salvation to the world will bear this out. Only now with Jesus' first epiphany is eternal life possible. Furthermore, we cannot ignore the peculiar phrase διὰ τοῦ εὐαγγελίου, which in effect claims that the actual working out of this ontic transformation is accomplished in the act of Christian preaching, specifically in Paul's preaching as contained in these letters. Therefore, when "Paul" adds in v.11 that he has been appointed preacher, apostle, teacher, he is insisting that the specific teachings handed down by him contain the cosmological powers of salvation. Those teachings, along with leadership models embodied in Paul, have been taken over by certain leaders in the author's own church. As the fiction of the letter puts it at this point, "Paul" boasts, "I am convinced that God is able to guard my traditions (παραθήκη) until that day (2 Tim. 1.12)." God will guard it by placing it in reliable hands; or so the fiction goes.

Although the effective power of Jesus' epiphany is mediated to believers only by way of cultic leaders, this mediation process, the embodiment of salvation forces in language, does not annul the cosmological power which is proffered in this epiphany[69]. The traditional terminology, which describes the results of this first epiphany as "saving sinners" (1 Tim. 1. 15) or Jesus in this epiphany as giving himself as a "ransom for all"

---

[69]The concept of a new age in which new possibilities arise with the appearance of the savior forms the most obvious parallel to language in the Pastorals. The battery of terms, ἐπιφάνεια, σωτήρ, μακαρία ἐλπίς, μέγας θεός, φιλανθρωπία, χρηστότης, which occurs in the Pastorals, also occurs in the emperor cult. This has led to the frequent suggestion that the Pastorals are consciously opposed to the emperor cult. See, for example, Dibelius-Conzelmann, *The Pastoral Epistles*, pp. 143–46; Wendland, "Σωτήρ"; Trummer, *Die Paulustradition*, p. 195; Hanson, *The Pastoral Epistles*, p. 187.

(ἀντίλυτρον ὑπὲρ πάντων) (1 Tim. 2.6), hints at the dimensions of power inherent in this process[70]. But the real key to understanding the cosmological and salvific forces which have been unleashed can be found in Tit. 3.4—7.

ὅτε δὲ ἡ χρηστότης καὶ ἡ φιλανθρωπία ἐπεφάνη τοῦ σωτῆρος ἡμῶν θεοῦ, οὐκ ἐξ ἔργων τῶν ἐν δικαιοσύνῃ ἃ ἐποιήσαμεν ἡμεῖς, ἀλλὰ κατὰ τὸ αὐτοῦ ἔλεος ἔσωσεν ἡμᾶς διὰ λουτροῦ παλιγγενεσίας καὶ ἀνακαινώσεως πνεύματος ἁγίου, οὗ ἐξέχεεν ἐφ᾽ ἡμᾶς πλουσίως διὰ Ἰησοῦ τοῦ σωτῆρος ἡμῶν, ἵνα δικαιωθέντες τῇ ἐκείνου χάριτι κληρονόμοι γενηθῶμεν κατ᾽ ἐλπίδα ζωῆς αἰωνίου.

But when the kindness and love of humanity of God our savior appeared, not from works which we did in righteousness, but according to his mercy, he saved us through the bath of regeneration and the renewal of the holy spirit, which he poured out upon us richly through Jesus Christ our savior in order that being justified by that grace we might become heirs in accordance with hope for eternal life.

Once again, we do not need to repeat what we have already discussed in regard to this passage; but rather let us highlight the connection made among Jesus' epiphany, baptism by the cult, and the reception of a powerful and transforming spirit. An anthropological transformation, described as the reception of a spirit, is bestowed most immediately via baptism but ultimately via Jesus' first epiphany[71]. This transformation, which enables baptized persons to perform ethical deeds non-baptized people cannot perform, has a cosmological referent; but it is not available everywhere in the cosmos. Part of God's management of this plan is the restriction of access to the spirit to the cultic act of baptism. Thus he places cosmological power into the hands of cultic leaders. In order to possess this spirit, one must appear before the church leaders and become subject to them.

Although the spirit plays a crucial role in the ethical system of the Pastorals, it would be misleading to categorize the ethics of the Pastorals as life in the spirit, especially if one means by that what it means in Pauline ethics. In the Pastorals the spirit is not a guide but an enabler[72]. Paul seemed to believe that by walking in the spirit the specifics of ethical behavior will automatically become clear. In fact, Paul hesitates over inculcating moral rules because the spirit provides the content of action in each instance[73]. The spirit in the Pastorals possesses no such ability. The con-

---

[70]On the roots of the terms see Hanson, "Elements of a Baptismal Liturgy in Titus," pp. 78—96.

[71]This is, of course, the commonplace notion of baptism in early Christianity. See for example Oscar Cullmann, *Baptism in the New Testament*, trans. J. K. S. Reid (Chicago: H. Regency Co. 1950) or James L. D. Dunn, *Baptism in the Spirit* (Philadelphia: Westminster Press, 1970).

[72]This is pointed out by E. Schweizer, "πνεῦμα," TDNT, 6:445. See also discussion in Lips, *Glaube, Gemeinde, Amt*, pp. 212—23.

[73]See the survey of nineteenth and twentieth century interpretations of Paul's ethics in the appendix of Victor Paul Furnish, *Theology and Ethics in Paul* (Nashville: Abingdon Press, 1968), pp. 242—79. Furnish notes very few exceptions to this reading of the Pauline ethic in the history of scholarship, even though he himself denies it, believing the spirit to be a bestower of power and not a guide (p. 231).

tent of ethical behavior is puzzled out in other ways. Other than this passage, two others in the Pastorals illustrate this specialized understanding of the role of the spirit. The occurrences in 1 Tim. 3.16, where the spirit serves to designate that realm which is opposed to the realm of the flesh, and in 1 Tim. 4.1, where the author employs language traditional to prophetic discourse[74], do not show enough of the author's hand to assist our understanding. But in 2 Tim. 1.14 the concept of the spirit as enabler is clear. "Paul" has been defining the nature and importance of the entrusted traditions, enjoining Timothy to preserve them, and he concludes with the admonition "to guard the good traditions through the holy spirit which dwells in us (τὴν καλὴν παραθήκην φύλαξον διὰ πνεύματος ἁγίου τοῦ ἐνοικοῦντος ἐν ἡμῖν)."

Here the spirit endows its recipient with abilities necessary for successful participation in the management of God's plan (οἰκονομία θεοῦ)[75]. The spirit does not provide the content of the tradition, the preceding verses do that; rather the spirit is the giver of power. It is not surprising that the author treats the spirit in this manner, since he is really returning to its most frequent meaning in the Greco-Roman world; it is Paul who is idiosyncratic in this regard[76]. 2 Tim. 1.7 further clarifies the author's understanding of the role of the spirit, where after introducing the theme of the letter, which is to renew and maintain proper leadership even when abandoned and pressed, the author proffers the spirit as the power which enables one to do just that.

> On account of this I remind you to rekindle the gifts of God which are in you through the laying on of my hands. For God did not give us a spirit of timidity but of power and love and moderation (πνεῦμα ... δυνάμεως καὶ ἀγάπης καὶ σωφρονισμοῦ).

From the foregoing discussion we should anticipate "a spirit of power," but the virtues of love and moderation are a new addition. The spirit hereby becomes an ethical enabler; it bestows the ability to perform the requisite virtues[77].

Therefore, in these two passages the spirit is introduced as a necessary prerequisite for the two most important tasks incumbent upon the church — to preserve Paul's traditions and to live the ethical life[78]. Thus the humdrum-sounding duties which the author assigns his church leaders and all members turn out to have cosmological connections. The Christological event of Jesus' first epiphany, which proffered theretofore non-existent

---

[74]On the "prophetic" style of this passage see Spicq, Les Épîtres Pastorales, pp. 494—96.

[75]Lips detects the specificity and exclusivity of the gifts here, noting that the spirit gives officers, not general Christians, the abilities necessary for office (Lips, Glaube, Gemeinde, Amt, pp. 206, 213, 217, 219).

[76]Schweizer, "πνεῦμα," TDNT, 6:424—37.

[77]This means I disagree with Lips' understanding mentioned above. Cf. Brox, Die Pastoralbriefe, p. 229, who agrees with Lips, to Dibelius-Conzelmann, The Pastoral Epistles, who speak (more correctly, I think) of the Christian in general.

[78]The first of these tasks may be limited to officers but the second confronts every believer.

possibilities, is mediated through proper church officials as a cosmological power, the spirit, which in turn produces the quiet virtuous life.

The single most informative passage in the Pastorals for establishing this thoroughgoing connection between Christology and ethics occurs in Tit. 2.11–14. It is no coincidence that the letter of Titus provides two essential passages, since the letter itself stands out in the three letter corpus as an exploration of the relationship among good leaders, bad leaders, ethics, and Christology. The author in some ways employs a different genre for Titus, for he derives his warrants from cosmological (Christological) claims rather than from inductive paradigms or a mythical past. Thus the cosmological presuppositions which underlie 1 and 2 Timothy, but which remain mostly unstated and assumed, come to the fore.

Ἐπεφάνη γὰρ ἡ χάρις τοῦ θεοῦ σωτήριος πᾶσιν ἀνθρώποις, παιδεύουσα ἡμᾶς ἵνα ἀρνησάμενοι τὴν ἀσέβειαν καὶ τὰς κοσμικὰς ἐπιθυμίας σωφρόνως καὶ δικαίως καὶ εὐσεβῶς ζήσωμεν ἐν τῷ νῦν αἰῶνι, προσδεχόμενοι τὴν μακαρίαν ἐλπίδα καὶ ἐπιφάνειαν τῆς δόξης τοῦ μεγάλου θεοῦ καὶ σωτῆρος ἡμῶν Ἰησοῦ Χριστοῦ, ὃς ἔδωκεν ἑαυτὸν ὑπὲρ ἡμῶν, ἵνα λυτρώσηται ἡμᾶς ἀπὸ πάσης ἀνομίας καὶ καθαρίσῃ ἑαυτῷ λαὸν περιούσιον, ζηλωτὴν καλῶν ἔργων.

For the grace of God the savior has appeared to all people, teaching us that denying impiety and worldly passions we might live soberly and righteously and piously in this age, waiting for the blessed hope and epiphany of the glory of the great God and our savior Jesus Christ, who gave himself for us, in order that he might redeem us from all lawlessness and cleanse for himself a special people who are zealous for good deeds.

The Christological work which our author accomplishes is not one of a kind with second or third century Christologies, which seek to answer speculative questions about the metaphysical status of the father and the son; this is not an historic moment on the way to Chalcedon. But we must not leap to the conclusion that no Christological argument is being made. The Christological focus of the author is not upon the heavens but upon the earth; or more accurately, Christology for the author lives in ethics. The argument is clearly stated. Jesus appeared in order to teach his people how to live ethically. He has no real impact other than creating people who are zealous for good deeds and successful in pursuit of them.

The author assumes, as most ethicists do, an implicit dualism between the moral life and the non-moral life. It turns out that his description of the moral life is colored extensively by his vision of the quiet, peaceful life within the cult, and thus he will focus predominantly upon the communal virtues which contribute to the health of the cult. But that is certainly not .surprising and in itself constitutes no great contribution to Greco-Roman or Christian ethics. Furthermore, some of the language employed here puzzles as much as it elucidates. Jesus has appeared, "teaching (παιδεύειν)" us to live the ethical life. There is no other mention in the letters of Jesus as teacher, and how he functions as such in the author's church is uncertain. Paul teaches, Timothy and Titus teach, present-day church leaders teach; thus it may be that Jesus' capacity as a teacher lives on through these persons, rather than through the sayings in

the gospels or other collections[79]. Perhaps the two methods do not ex-
clude one another. In any case, the author claims here that the cosmological warrant, upon which the ethical life and salvation are based, is not
only focused upon ethics but is dependent upon an education process.
This need for education and the dangers and tasks inherent in carrying it
out earn much of the author's attention in the letters. The exhortation to
teach, and to teach correctly not incorrectly, is repeated throughout the
letters. For instance, this passage concludes with the admonition, "speak
these things, exhort and reprove with all authority."

Throughout all these passages, the author uses the specifics of Jesus'
first epiphany as private topics from which propositions are derived.
These propositions are placed in enthymemes which connect them logically with ethical conclusions. When Pauline inductive paradigms are used,
the inductive logic also links cosmology and ethics. In this way the author
provides a functional Christology which details the impact of Jesus and
not a speculative Christology which investigates Jesus' metaphysical status.
Jesus has a functional role in the plan of salvation to provide both cosmological and anthropological warrants for the ethical life, which in
itself is the crux of salvation. We must also bow to the author's language
and admit that Jesus functions paideutically, even though the manner in
which he does that will only become clear as we investigate further the
fictions in the letters. In fact, Jesus' role as teacher is imbedded in the
many devices of the pseudepigraphical letter. The author employs some of
the most frequent and well-known terms in the Greek world for describing
this Christological event. His usage of ἐπιφάνεια, δόξα, the common
hendiadys of God and savior, the phrase "great God," and various terms
for cleansing is typical religious discourse for his day[80]. The author uses
this language as logical and theological support for his ethics. Because
Jesus has come, there now exists a people who are "zealous for good
deeds." The language of good deeds and the concept of being δόκιμος,
ἀδόκιμος, ἄρτιος, for good deeds recur throughout the letters. In fact,
the entire ethical focus of the letters, including the virtue and vice lists,
the duty lists for elders, deacons, widows, slaves, and others, must be
drawn into this Christological framework. Duty lists become prescriptions for salvation, vice lists become proscriptions, because they have
such a central role in God's plan of salvation and because they are grounded in Christology.

c) *The Second Epiphany of Jesus*

Tit. 2.11—14 mentions another Christological event: those members of

---

[79]I say this with some hesitation recalling Helmut Koester, "Apocryphal and Canonical Gospels," *Harvard Theological Review* 73 (1980): 105—130, who demonstrates how widespread, diverse, and complex the Jesus traditions (including his sayings) were in the early church.

[80]See Dibelius-Conzelmann, *The Pastoral Epistles*, pp. 143—46.

the cult who are properly equipped for good deeds are waiting for Jesus' second epiphany. No details are given here about this second epiphany other than its linkage with hope, but the letters provide content to that second epiphany elsewhere. It will complete the cosmological framework of the ethic, providing the proper motivation necessary to a persuasive ethic.

We have already noticed the future referent of some of the salvation language, for instance, when "Paul" expresses confidence that God *will* save him and when he advises that women *will* be saved through child-bearing. The salvific effect of Jesus occurs on two levels, this life and the life to come. The second epiphany of Jesus will present Jesus as judge who weighs in balance the ethical and non-ethical thrust of people's lives. The future context of salvation shows itself in several ways. "Paul" wishes for Onesiphorus, who supported Paul in his troubles and thus represents as an illustrative paradigm the church member who aligns his allegiances correctly, "mercy on the day of the Lord" (2 Tim. 1.18). On the other side of the ethical and organizational fence, the Lord is invoked to repay for his deeds the coppersmith Alexander, who is rigorously opposed to Paul and the sound teachings (2 Tim. 4.18). Again, the opponents are relegated to the same fate as that of Jannes and Jambres (illustrative paradigms) who opposed Moses and thus opposed the truth (2 Tim. 3.8). The author obviously participates in the general apocalyptic framework of early Christianity with its inheritance of the judgmental language of Judaism[81]. This probably comes to him by way of his Christian heritage and not by way of direct contact with Jewish apocalypses. There will be a judgment day and Jesus will be the judge. It is a major motivational force. Thus, logically Jesus' second epiphany can be premise in an enthymeme with an imperative conclusion.

I adjure you before God and Christ Jesus who will judge the living and dead (τοῦ μέλλοντος κρίνειν ζῶντας καὶ νεκρούς) and by his epiphany and his kingdom (τὴν ἐπιφάνειαν καὶ τὴν βασιλείαν αὐτοῦ), preach the word ... (2 Tim. 4.1).

Once again Jesus' parousia is not called by the usual terms in the New Testament but by the Greek religious term ἐπιφάνεια[82]. But the content of what happens at first glance is the same as it is throughout early Christianity: it is the day on which Jesus will judge the living and the dead. The author occasionally uses the more frequent terminology, such as "the

---

[81]Windisch, "Zur Christologie der Pastoralbriefe," pp. 213–38, found these concepts as evidence for a more primitive apocalyptic and thus more primitive (more primitive than Paul) Christology in the Pastorals. Brox, *Die Pastoralbriefe*, pp. 161–66, agrees. But cf. Hasler, "Epiphanie und Christologie in den Pastoralbriefen," pp. 199–201, who sees it more as a development.

[82]Dibelius-Conzelmann, *The Pastoral Epistles*, p. 104, claim "parousia" is actually the later term. Cf. Brox, *Die Pastoralbriefe*, pp. 299–301. On the background of the term see Pax, ΕΠΙΦΑΝΕΙΑ, and D. Lührmann, "Epiphaneia: Zur Bedeutungsgeschichte eines griechischen Wortes," *Tradition und Glaube*, ed. G. Jeremias (Göttingen: Vandenhoeck & Ruprecht, 1971), pp. 185–99.

day of the Lord," but offers nothing new to the early Christian imaginings about judgment day[83]. However, the standard which Jesus relies upon for judgment, though certainly not unique in early Christianity, is highly functional and indicative of the moral force of the letters. Jesus judges on the basis of virtues and vices[84]. Yet, since adherence to correct teaching produces virtue and running after false teaching produces vice, Jesus also judges on the basis of orthodoxy. And, to push it further, because sound teaching and empty teaching relate to church politics, Jesus also judges on the basis which faction in the church one chooses to follow. Thus Onesiphorus is accorded mercy for following Paul and "our" teaching ($\dot{\eta}\mu\epsilon\tau\acute{\epsilon}\rho\omega$ $\lambda\acute{o}\gamma\omega$). Nothing is said about Alexander's life of virtue or vice; he is simply on the wrong side of the organizational fence.

Consequently the expectation of future judgment becomes a major warrant in the letters. This is particularly the case when the author addresses the puzzling paradox of his opponents' success. They look like the ones on the right side not the wrong, so the author appeals to the popular motif that judgment will reveal hitherto hidden facts about people[85]. "The sins of some people are clear, going before them into judgment, but some they follow; and likewise good works are clear and those of another kind cannot remain hidden" (1 Tim. 5.24). He argues also that just as the nature of Jannes and Jambres eventually became manifest so will the nature of those who like them oppose the truth ($\dot{\eta}$ $\gamma\dot{\alpha}\rho$ $\ddot{\alpha}\nu\omega\alpha$ $\alpha\dot{\upsilon}\tau\tilde{\omega}\nu$ $\ddot{\epsilon}\kappa\delta\eta\lambda\omega\varsigma$ $\ddot{\epsilon}\sigma\tau\alpha\iota$ $\pi\tilde{\alpha}\sigma\iota\nu$, $\dot{\omega}\varsigma$ $\kappa\alpha\dot{\iota}$ $\dot{\eta}$ $\dot{\epsilon}\kappa\epsilon\acute{\iota}\nu\omega\nu$ $\dot{\epsilon}\gamma\acute{\epsilon}\nu\epsilon\tau\omega$) (2 Tim. 3. 9)[86]. Faced with the inescapable affront that his opponents have more influence than he does, the author uses a common argument for those who possess an apocalyptic arsenal: on the day of the Lord his orthodoxy will be proven. Of course, this is not his major argument on behalf of his orthodoxy but merely one he makes because the weapon is there.

Equally frequent as the idea of punishment is the idea of reward. The author uses the rewards of the next life as a major positive motivational force. The most striking instance is bound up with the fiction of the letter, where "Paul" at the end of 2 Timothy articulates assurances about his own end. His confidence in this regard results from the fidelity with which he has completed his tasks ($\tau\dot{o}\nu$ $\kappa\alpha\lambda\dot{o}\nu$ $\dot{\alpha}\gamma\tilde{\omega}\nu\alpha$ $\dot{\eta}\gamma\acute{\omega}\nu\iota\sigma\mu\alpha\iota$, $\tau\dot{o}\nu$ $\delta\rho\acute{o}\mu\omega\nu$ $\tau\epsilon\tau\acute{\epsilon}\lambda\epsilon\kappa\alpha$) and the ultimate orthodoxy of his stance ($\tau\dot{\eta}\nu$ $\pi\acute{\iota}\sigma\tau\iota\nu$ $\tau\epsilon\tau\acute{\eta}\rho\eta\kappa\alpha$)[87]. Only others who can make the same claim towards their

---

[83]Oberlinner, "Die 'Epiphaneia' des Heilswillens Gottes in Christus Jesus," pp. 200–3.

[84]Only defenders of authenticity have, for the most part, admitted the connection between this second epiphany and ethics, though they, of course, read the connection in Pauline terms, as the inbreaking of the endtime. So Jeremias, *Die Briefe an Timotheus und Titus.* I know of no systematic treatment of the second epiphany as a motivational force for the ethic.

[85]This motif may in fact go back to the Jesus traditions: for example, Lk. 11.42; 12.2; Mt. 10. 26; 23.23.

[86]Hanson, *The Pastoral Epistles,* p. 147, sees the author conversing with a widespread "haggada" on Ex. 8.18–19, or perhaps Wis. 15.18–16.1.

[87]Dibelius-Conzelmann, *The Pastoral Epistles,* p. 121, and Brox, *Die Pastoralbriefe,* p. 266,

own tasks, who can correctly claim orthodoxy, and who agree with the author and adhere to the doctrines inculcated in the letters, can stand with Paul confidently facing this second epiphany. But if one is orthodox, obedient, and faithful, as Paul was, one's confidence ought to be great.

> Finally, the crown of righteousness (ὁ τῆς δικαιοσύνης στέφανος) is set aside for me, which the Lord, the righteous judge, will give to me on that day, and not only to me but to all who have loved his epiphany (πᾶσι τοῖς ἠγαπηκόσι τὴν ἐπιφάνειαν αὐτοῦ) (2 Tim. 4.8).

The "Lord" in this passage, the righteous judge, since this is the one who will appear, must refer to Jesus not God. The heavenly rewards are laid aside not only for Paul but — showing the power of Paul as the source of an inductive paradigm — also for all who, like Paul, have loved his epiphany. Therefore, the author includes *all* orthodox and ethical Christians within the umbrella of heavenly rewards. However, the author's way of designating these people is curious: "all who have loved his epiphany" is not a highly precise way of making a description of who is included and who is not[88]. As we have noted, the author's description of who is saved and who is not is filled out, both here and elsewhere, by his description of Paul's prototypical behavior. Since ἐπιφάνεια is singular and not plural, we must wonder whether the first or second epiphany is meant. Certainly the general context argues for the second epiphany, but it is possible that the author does not intend to distinguish here which one[89]. He may simply be placing the Pauline pattern of behavior within its Christological framework (he needs a premise for the enthymeme) and thus wants to remind his readers of the cosmological realities on which his cultic ethic is based. In any case Jesus is depicted as the righteous judge who will dispense heavenly rewards to those who have followed Paul correctly. The second epiphany, here at least, seems not to provide content to the ethic but motivation. Therefore, the logical form of these enthymemes must be built upon the inherent desirability of salvation.

The depth at which this motivation moves in the letters becomes clear in the elaborate argument made in 2 Tim. 2.8—13. In this enthymematic argument a two-layered connection is established between Christological ideas and personal behavior. As far as I can discover it is unanimous among scholars that the series of four couplets in vv. 11—13 are a quotation of some sort, whether a hymn, a hymnic fragment, or a liturgical formula[90]. We must hesitate to contradict such unanimity, especially since

---

find this one-sided emphasis on success and rewards to be quite unPauline. Contrary to many who see this passage as evidence of authenticity, they see it as the opposite.

[88]Spicq, *Les Épîtres Pastorales*, p. 808, emphasizes the frequency in the Greco-Roman world of this terminology.

[89]Actually, I know of no commentator who thinks this passage refers to the first epiphany.

[90]"The four lines that follow in vv. 11b–13a are undoubtedly a quotation from an early Christian hymn. The theology implied in the hymn is thoroughly Pauline, indeed more thoroughly Pauline than is the theology of the author of the Pastorals himself" (Hanson, *The Pastoral Epistles*, p. 132).

the couplets manifest a liturgical rhythm. Therefore, even though the author might be capable of writing such a hymn himself, we should conclude that he is quoting from his liturgical traditions. Nevertheless, this piece of tradition is normative for the author, because the doctrines therein agree in every detail with the author's own theology[91]. In each of the couplets a specific ethical behavior is made the immediate cause of a corresponding Christological behavior. We recognize the form of inference as cause and effect. This link between ethics and cosmology is such an essential notion for the author that his hand in the formulation of these couplets would not be surprising. This possibility is enhanced by the specific terms which the couplets employ.

εἰ γὰρ συναπεθάνομεν, καὶ συζήσομεν.
εἰ ὑπομένομεν, καὶ συμβασιλεύσομεν.
εἰ ἀρνησόμεθα, κἀκεῖνος ἀρνήσεται ἡμᾶς.
εἰ ἀπιστοῦμεν, ἐκεῖνος πιστὸς μένει, ἀρνήσασθαι
    γὰρ ἑαυτὸν οὐ δύναται.
If we died with him, we shall also live with him;
if we endure, we shall rule with him;
if we deny [him], he also will deny us;
if we are faithless, he remains faithful
    for he is not able to deny himself (2 Tim. 2.11–13).

Every motif in these couplets is a common one in the letters. The entire letter of 2 Timothy is shadowed by Paul's death, his faithfulness under that spectre, and the rewards which will ensue. The letter of 2 Timothy emphasizes the difficulties incumbent upon a church leader, enjoins endurance in the face of such troubles, and promises rewards: the letter is a letter to beleagured church leaders. The act of denial is of course a recurrent motif associated with the problem of heresy. The author agrees with the doctrine of the third couplet, that those who deny Jesus or the sound teaching will not enjoy salvation. Finally the fourth couplet with its extended three-member form (the enthymeme is thus complete) entertains one of the most important concepts in the Pastorals and treats it just as the rest of the letters do. Essential to the persuasivensss of the author's ethical system is his assertion that certain things are reliable (πιστός) πιστός in the Pastorals means reliability, faithfulness, and trustworthiness[92]. The author applies the term to statements of doctrine, especially with the affirmation formula "πιστὸς ὁ λόγος"[93]. He associates it with

---

[91]Houlden, The Pastoral Epistles, p. 119, points out how beautifully the piece is incorporated into the argument of the letter: "However, it cannot be claimed that it is seriously out of line with the cast of thought displayed in the rest of these writings.... Faithfulness is a prime virtue in these works.... The movement of the thought of the piece supports the view that it is an integral part of the writing rather than a quotation inserted."

[92]This is of course the most common meaning of the term. See Bultmann, "πίστις, κτλ.," TDNT, 6:174–228; L. P. Foley, "Fidelis, Faithful," Catholic Biblical Quarterly 1 (1939): 163–65.

[93]See Dibelius-Conzelmann, The Pastoral Epistles, pp. 28–29; Brox, Die Pastoralbriefe, pp. 112–14; George W. Knight, The Faithful Sayings of the Pastoral Epistles (Kampen: J. R. Kok, 1968).

proper teachings (Tit. 1.9); he uses it to describe certain kinds of behavior and certain kinds of people; and here he designates Jesus himself as πιστός[94]. If the things which are πιστοί are not ultimately and irrevocably so, then the foundation of his ethical system begins to crumble.

Therefore, the series of four couplets articulates beautifully the ethical and cosmological connections which lie at the heart of the author's theology. The logical structure of cause and effect indicates the theological logic. Proper ethical behavior, with its cultic colorings, issues in rewards, while improper behavior earns punishment. Yet in the midst of this ethical freedom with its contingencies and uncertainties, certain things are fast, concrete, immovable, reliable (πιστός). Among those things which are πιστοί is Jesus. Whether the author learned this point of view from his traditions, which is a real possibility, or wrote this piece of doctrine himself, is uncertain.

But this is only half of the connection made in this passage. In order for the cosmological-ethical connections believed in by our author to gain a hearing in his church and thus acquire power and influence, this theology must be anchored in reliable roots. The ability of these teachings to persuade and thus to save resides in the believability of the fiction of Pauline origins. "Paul" reminds Timothy of the facts of Jesus' first epiphany in traditional language. The historical forces issuing from this epiphany result in the preaching of the gospel or "my gospel" as "Paul" calls it. For the sake of this gospel, Paul undergoes sufferings and wears chains like a criminal. But as "Paul" says, "On account of this, I endure everything, for the sake of the elect, in order that they might receive salvation which is in Christ Jesus with eternal glory" (2 Tim. 2.10). The role of the teacher and preacher in the salvation process could not be more succinctly put. Unless the saving message is preached by reliable preachers then salvation will not occur. Furthermore, the teaching and preaching functions of church leaders have direct Christological foundations. The peculiar series of connections among the historical events of Jesus' first epiphany, the gospel which results, the preachers who preach that gospel, and the whole cosmological framework of this process is made believable (no small task) by a number of fictions made possible to the author through the pseudepigraphical genre. The historical and cosmological implications of these fictions about what Paul, Timothy, and Titus did as part of God's plan result in the astonishing state of affairs where certain designated church leaders speak with cosmological authority. What they say is πιστός.

Since the author needs to validate the teachings of his faction beyond any question, the cosmological authorization of these teachings is asserted in a variety of ways. For instance, we have already noticed that it is Jesus' teaching which is preserved, not just anyone's. "Paul" expresses confi-

---

[94]On the word group πίστις, πιστός, κτλ. in the Pastorals see Lips, *Glaube, Gemeinde, Amt*, pp. 25–53.

dence that "he [God] is able to guard my traditions until that day" (2 Tim. 1.12). And even more to the point, at the end of 1 Timothy, where the author is reiterating the main themes of the letter, he commands the task of preserving tradition with a series of cosmological references.

> I command you before God who gives life to everything and before Christ Jesus who confessed the good confession before Pontius Pilate to keep the commandment unstained and beyond reproach until the epiphany of our Lord Jesus Christ, which the blessed and only sovereign will show at the proper time, the king of kings, the lord of lords, who alone has immortality and dwells in inapproachable light, whom no person has ever seen or is able to see, to him be honor and eternal power. Amen (1 Tim. 6.13–16).

Without becoming inundated by the rich details of this passage, we should take note of the connective links between the act of preserving tradition and the cosmological propositions[95]. That is to say, the cosmological assertions provide premises for the enthymematic argument in specific and limited ways. Jesus' own behavior in speaking the truth under duress is paradigmatic for later church leaders, who are also under duress. The judgmental power of God and Jesus is brought to the fore not only by the imperatival form of the commandment but also by the direct mention of the second epiphany with its connotations of rewards and punishments. Finally the whole passage accelerates into a hymn of praise to the king of kings and lord of lords, intimating thereby that the preserving of the pure traditions is also an act of praise to this wonderful God.

d) *Summary*

At this point we are able to gather some of these observations on the theology of the author and offer a few conclusions.

(1) A plan of salvation exists and has existed for all time, in which God intends the salvation of all people and which is now producing its benefits through the actions of Jesus and the subsequent actions of a series of Christians.

(2) God, in being acclaimed as savior and creator, is a friendly God who has good intentions for all of creation. Thus the cosmos itself is a friend not an enemy.

(3) Jesus as savior participates in this kindness of God and inaugurates the key moment of God's plan of salvation in his first epiphany.

---

[95]Nearly every commentator treats this section (incorrectly I think) as an awkward intrusion into the logic of 1 Timothy. "But on the whole, the section appears to be an intrusion between vs. 10 and 17" (Dibelius-Conzelmann, *The Pastoral Epistles*, p. 87). "There has been considerable discussion among commentators as to what sort of source the author is drawing on in this section. One view, defended by H. Windisch, Falconer, Jeremias, Spicq, Holtz, Pax, and Kelly, is that it originally formed part of an (adult) baptism address. Another view is that it comes from an ordination address. This is supported by Käsemann, D-C [Dibelius-Conzelmann], J. Roloff, Barrett, Brox, and Hasler. A third view is that it could be a personal confession by an individual Christian" (Hanson, *The Pastoral Epistles*, p. 110).

(4) The positive conceptions about the essence of God and Jesus have direct ethical implications, wherein quiet virtues find a rightful place in this good world. Because the cosmos is oriented towards salvation, a feeling of peace and security pervades the letters.

(5) Jesus at his first epiphany revealed the existence of God's plan of salvation, articulated the proper content of the Christian life through his teachings and the ethical standards imposed thereby, and provided a means for realizing this ethical standard with the gift of the spirit, which is mediated to the individual through the cultic act of baptism.

(6) Jesus at his second epiphany dispenses rewards and punishments on the basis of virtues and vices, noting who has been orthodox and thus moral and who has not. A further standard is imposed upon church leaders who have specialized duties, which are embodied and illustrated by the paradigmatic actions of Paul, Timothy, and Titus.

(7) Ethics forms the heart of the plan of salvation in that God saves by making virtue possible and by rewarding it in the hereafter. This necessary ethic has a double foundation in the cosmological propositions about God and Jesus and in the ecclesiastical assertions about the reliability of certain teachings, certain leaders, and Paul.

(8) The author employs both paradigms and enthymemes, with their capacity for creating logical connections between premises and conclusions, to create the interplay between his theological and ethical ideas.

(9) It is possible that pieces of this theological system were structured in response to contrary positions held by opponents. We cannot of course ever be certain about the origin of a person's ideas, but a few possibilities suggest themselves, especially because the conflict between orthodoxy and heterodoxy appears to be so important to the author and because some of the author's ideas are directly opposite to those he attributes to his opponents. If the author's primary argument with his opponents centers upon life-style and ethics, there are two primary theological moves the author makes which enable him to counteract the dangers of his opponents. First of all, he banishes Jesus from the scene. Tendencies towards spiritualism, asceticism, and distaste for the quieter virtues can be encouraged and strengthened by a lordship Christology. In the place of the uncontrollable presence and authority of Jesus speaking in visions, the author inserts an epiphany Christology where Jesus is relegated to two appearances, one in the past and one in the future, with no present contact. Contact with Jesus comes through adherence to correct doctrine, which in turn comes through obedience to the leaders of the author's faction in the church. In Jesus' place stand his designated representatives. Secondly, quiet virtues constitute the sole means of salvation. Knowledge, spiritualism, ascetic practices, and even baptism are to no avail if the quiet virtues are not practiced. Thus the theological sophistication, the aggressive inquiry into theological puzzles, and the dramatic asceticisms of his opponents are useless. God's plan of salvation, the entire purpose of creation, and the impact of Jesus himself, all focus upon living a quiet and

peaceful life which successfully practices the more communal Greco-Roman virtues, producing health and peace in the church.

(10) Finally, in this system salvation occurs on two-levels — in this life and the life to come. Virtues not only are the prerequisite for eternal life; they also provide the best life in this world. The virtuous life, according to the common cliche, is the only life worth living[96]. Since God and God's creation are both good, there are positive forces available to humans for life in the world. The author places high value on this life and not just the life to come.

γύμναζε δὲ σεαυτὸν πρὸς εὐσέβειαν. ἡ γὰρ σωματικὴ γυμνασία πρὸς ὀλίγον ἐστὶν ὠφέλιμος. ἡ δὲ εὐσέβεια πρὸς πάντα ὠφέλιμός ἐστιν, ἐπαγγελίαν ἔχουσα ζωῆς τῆς νῦν καὶ τῆς μελλούσης.

Train yourselves for piety, for bodily training is of little value, but piety is useful in every way, having the promise of life now and in the future (1 Tim. 4.7b—8).

Piety (εὐσέβεια), a religious life-style which the author carefully describes in the letters, is the best way to live the present life as well as being the ticket to eternal rewards[97]. The primary purpose of the letter is, after all, to describe "how one should behave in the house of God" (1 Tim. 3.15). We now turn to the author's description of this ethical life.

C. A Cultic Ethic

1. Greco-Roman Ethics

The author of the Pastorals does not desist in his effort to construct a workable ethic with these cosmological connections but creates a complex of warrants for his ethic which are both specific and historical. The author's tendency to relate his conception of God and Jesus and what they do to specific ethical injunctions shows that he is attuned to the need for providing warrants to his parenesis. But, in comparison to other Greco-Roman ethical systems, the probative force of the cosmological assertions

---

[96]Although this dictum certainly has roots in Socrates, Plato, and Aristotle, it was really the Stoics who highlighted it and popularized it. See Diogenes Laertius 7.87—132, for a discussion of the Stoic attitude towards virtue: "That is why Zeno was the first (in his treatise *On the Nature of Man*) to designate as the end (τέλος) 'life in agreement with nature', which is the same as the virtuous life (κατ' ἀρετὴν ζῆν), virtue being the goal towards which nature guides us" (Diogenes Laertius 6.11, 12). On the relationship of Cynics and Stoics on virtue: J. M. Rist, *Stoic Philosophy* (Cambridge: Cambridge University Press, 1969), pp. 54—80. On Stoics: Max Pohlenz, *Die Stoa: Geschichte einer geistigen Bewegung* (Göttingen: Vandenhoeck & Ruprecht, 1949), pp. 32—36, 111—58; F. H. Sandbach, *The Stoics* (New York: W. W. Norton & Co., 1975), pp. 28—68.

[97]On εὐσέβεια: Werner Foerster, "Εὐσέβεια in den Pastoralbriefen," *New Testament Studies* 5 (1959): 213—18; Falconer, *The Pastoral Epistles*, pp. 30—39; and Spicq, *Les Épîtres Pastorales*, pp. 482—92.

in the Pastorals is significant but not sufficient. Their insufficiency results from both their distance from the individual (there is no anthropological connection) and their generality. The author's perception of God and Jesus as saviors cannot produce specific standards of behavior. At best, these ideas cast a positive and non-ascetic light on his ethic by giving him an affirmative stance towards life and the world; thus at times he is able to adjudicate ethical questions by bouncing them off this general concept — ascetic practices do not accord with belief in a friendly cosmos. But an appeal to the nature of the cosmos is too general and subject to misinterpretation to be a servicable warrant for all the minutiae of the ethical life. He needs guidelines which are both more specific and controllable.

The general retreat of logic and physics in Greco-Roman ethics[98] does not indicate that ethicists ceased to create logical and physical warrants for their parenesis. The demise of logic and physics related more to their status as self-contained disciplines; in fact, A. A. Long has remarked that "No one today would readily accept the view that logic in the mature Stoic system ranks below physics and ethics in importance"[99]. We have already seen that Seneca and Epictetus use logic, even if they do not devote much attention to it as a separate discipline. In fact, logic and physics have not disappeared but have been incorporated into ethics. Thus we have the Stoic assertion that there is no difference in the three disciplines of logic, ethics, and physics[100]. The use of enthymemes and paradigms illustrates how logic was taken up into the discipline of ethics; moreover, many of the premises of these logical forms are derived from the discipline of physics. Thus the practitioners of diatribe do not attempt to prove their logical or physical theories, as must be done when they are separate disciplines; but, nevertheless, they incorporate logical presuppositions and physical propositions into their arguments. Logic and physics did not die; they were transformed.

What has changed is the nature of the warrant with which the ethic is supplied. Although A. A. Long argues that Stoics still used dialectic to discover the truth[101], one cannot find in extant Stoic sources the kind of dialectical assault which Socrates manages in the Platonic dialogues. The Platonic forms waiting at the end of dialectic do not exist in the theories of these ethicists; therefore, other methods of discovering standards must

---

[98]On the general tendency: Paul Wendland, *Die hellenistisch-römische Kultur* (Tübingen: J. C. B. Mohr [Paul Siebeck], 1912), pp. 41–52, 75–91, 106–115 (Wendland notes that ethics and "Wissenschaften" became increasingly divorced from one another, p. 54); W. W. Tarn and G. T. Griffith, *Hellenistic Civilization* (New York: Meridian Books, 1974), pp. 325–26. This division of philosophy into three parts is traditionally attributed to Zeno (Diogenes Laertius 7.39). On the Stoics: Pohlenz, *Die Stoa*, pp. 277–366, esp. pp. 293–99; A. A. Long, "Dialectic and the Stoic Sage," in *The Stoics*, ed. John M. Rist (Berkeley: University of California Press, 1978), pp. 101–24.

[99]Long, "Dialectic and the Stoic Sage," p. 116.

[100]Diogenes Laertius 7.40.

[101]Long, "Dialectic and the Stoic Sage," pp. 101–21.

be used. Long declares that the wise man replaced the Platonic form in Stoic epistemology[102]. If this is true, we can understand why paradigms come to the fore. But Greco-Roman ethicists appeal to other standards than just the wise man; they create a complex of logical, cosmological (physical), and anthropological warrants for their ethics.

In order to better understand the care with which the author of the Pastorals creates standards and resources for the ethical life, I shall enlist two analogies from the Greco-Roman world where different ethical systems are built. Although Epictetus is idiosyncratic in some ways, he believed the basic structure of his system to be orthodox Stoicism in a way which Seneca did not. He provides a workable example of an elaborately structured Greek ethic close in time to the Pastorals. The author of 4 Maccabees faces the problem of how to be Jewish in a Greek world, a problem analogous to what the author of the Pastorals confronted. His attempt to hold on to the Jewish law and to live the Greek virtues at the same time parallels the attempt in the Pastorals to incorporate Greek virtues into the Christian cult. Thus Epictetus and 4 Maccabees demonstrate how ethical systems similar to that of the Pastorals might be constructed.

The parenetic style of the diatribes of Epictetus typifies the cluttered and disorganized look of Greco-Roman ethical writings. Not only does he use an extensive array of diatribe-style questioning with imaginary interlocutors, objections, and false conclusions, but also provides in generous portions the usual argumentative forms of protreptic, namely, paradigms of past heroes or of himself, analogies, quotations from famous texts, sayings from the sages, cosmological propositions about the nature of God or the laws of the cosmos, and even logical deductions which approach the rigor of formal syllogisms[103]. Yet with all this jumble of elements Epictetus consistently substantiates his ethical exhortations with valid and reliable warrants[104]. He makes the virtuous life possible first of all by a series of cosmological-anthropological connections wherein human capacities are anchored in the inviolable structure of the cosmos and the nature of God[105].

Without rehearsing the whole complex of ideas which make up Epictetus' ethical system, the basic outline of the system demonstrates sufficiently

---

[102]Ibid., p. 103.

[103]I know of no systematic study of the argumentative style of Epictetus along the lines of Cancik's work on Seneca. The best we have is Stowers, The Diatribe and Paul's Letter to the Romans, esp. pp. 53—58. But Stowers focuses on the role of the interlocutor. Aside from that, general studies on the diatribe style and basic introductions to Epictetus proffer the most help: Pohlenz, Die Stoa, pp. 327—41; M. Spanneut, "Epiktet," Reallexikon für Antike und Christentum, 5, pp. 599—681; P. E. More, Hellenistic Philosophies (Princeton: Princeton University Press, 1923), pp. 94—171. On the diatribe: see Stowers for a full bibliography.

[104]Long, "Dialectic and the Stoic Sage," points out that the early Stoics and Epictetus among the later ones, unlike the Cynics, did not eschew logic.

[105]Pohlenz, Die Stoa, pp. 327—41, details some of these physical and ethical connections.

how the ethic is structured[106]. Progress (προκοπή) in the ethical life results from the interplay of the preconceptions (προλήψεις), the external
impressions (φαντασίαι), the opinions (δόγματα), the reason (λόγος), and
finally the will (προαίρεσις or ἡγεμονικόν). An external event presents an
impression (φαντασία) to which a person appliés a preconception (πρόληψις) of what the nature of the thing is. This produces opinions (δόγματα), which in turn produce behavior. The problem is that one's preconceptions can be applied incorrectly, and thus erroneous opinions result,
and in turn deviant behavior is practiced. But the reason (λόγος) is able to
determine, through the processes of analysis, the correctness of how a preconception is applied and the soundness of the opinions which ensue.
The reason uses a variety of methods to do this, but the ultimate result
is that a person can indeed puzzle out what is virtuous behavior and what
is not. Finally, the προαίρεσις or the ἡγεμονικόν is free to choose what
opinions it will believe and consequently is free to choose whether to live
virtuously or not. All this accords with orthodox Stoic doctrines, and
Epictetus seems to be adhering faithfully to the tenets of his school in
his choice of terms and the meanings they have[107].

Epictetus creates a series of cosmological-anthropological connections
which give this system probative force. Part of God's providence (πρόνοια)
for the cosmos and for human beings is that people have been equipped
with certain abilities (δυνάμεις, παρασκευαί) and ideas (δόγματα, κανόν-
ες) which are ultimately reliable. The προλήψεις, the λόγος, and the
προαίρεσις all have cosmological origins which make their reliability unquestionable. The preconceptions in themselves are sound (πρόληψις
προλήψει οὐ μάχεται)[108]; errors emerge only in application. Their trustworthiness comes from their origin in God. The λόγος enjoys the same
status. Epictetus apparently acquired his version of the λόγος from that of
Chrysippus, which would mean that for Epictetus reason is a reliable process[109]. The λόγος can be untrained or underemployed but not innately
misleading. Therefore, given the unimpeachable reliability of the preconceptions and reason, the human being is theoretically able to reason out
the specifics of the virtuous life. It is possible to know what is good because God has outfitted humans with anthropological powers adequate

---

[106]The exposition which follows is a standard treatment of Epictetus. There is nothing original in it, unless it be some inadvertent misunderstanding on my part. Therefore, on what follows
see the standard works mentioned above.

[107]Epictetus' occasional use of the Airstotelian term, προαίρεσις, rather than the more common term among Stoics, ἡγεμονικόν, has been seen as a conscious modification of the Stoic concept of the predetermined Stoic will: See Pohlenz, Die Stoa, pp. 332–33; M. Dragona-Monachou,
"Prohairesis in Aristotle and Epictetus. A comparison with the concept of intention in the philosophy of action," Philosophia 8–9 (1978–79), pp. 265–310.

[108]Epictetus 1.22.1.

[109]There is some debate on the origin of this idea in Epictetus: see Rist, Stoic Philosophy, pp.
228–29, 186–87.

to the task. The third anthropological power ($\delta\acute{u}\nu\alpha\mu\iota\varsigma$) is the will ($\pi\rho o\alpha\acute{\iota}$-$\rho\epsilon\sigma\iota\varsigma$, $\dot{\eta}\gamma\epsilon\mu o\nu\iota\kappa\acute{o}\nu$), which is so free and beyond compulsion that not even Zeus, who gave the will to humans, can assault successfully its freedom. No one can make a person assent to what he or she does not think is true. Thus Epictetus grounds his ethic first of all in three anthropological absolutes, which enjoy their status due to their cosmological connections.

Beyond the anthropological-cosmological warrants and a few other cosmological assumptions which we shall not investigate here, Epictetus, as we noted above, also uses in abundant measure the most frequent warrant in Greco-Roman ethics — the paradigm ($\pi\alpha\rho\alpha\delta\epsilon\acute{\iota}\gamma\mu\alpha\tau\alpha$ or $\tau\acute{u}\pi o\iota$)[110]. Even though Epictetus does not honor himself or any of his contemporaries with the designation of wise man, he does bestow the honor upon the heroes of his Stoic past, in particular upon Socrates, Zeno, and Diogenes. As is normally the case, the character ($\mathring{\eta}\vartheta o\varsigma$) of these figures becomes paradigmatic for anyone progressing towards wisdom. The paradigms are given content either by specific legends from their lives, e.g., Socrates' implacability in the face of death or Diogenes' indifference to externals, or by the process of applying their character to new situations, e.g., asking oneself how Socrates would behave in a particular situation. Thus Socrates teaches one not only how to approach death as a wise man but how to approach any danger. These idealized figures function in a third way by providing reliable sayings or maxims. Some of these sayings have canonical status, such as Socrates' dictum, "Anytus and Meletus can kill me, but they cannot harm me,"[111] while others function more like proverbs, to elucidate and clarify.

Even when only scratching the surface of Epictetus' ethic as we have done here, it is clear that he provides his protreptic with a variety of warrants. These warrants are imbedded in the parenesis, scattered about without elaborate introductions. Oftentimes they are seemingly introduced without design. But as we have seen, this cluttered and careless look, which is so characteristic of ethical argument of this time, belies the rigor and order which underlie the system. Finally, considering the primacy of the individual, divorced from any indispensible community other than the cosmos, it is not surprising that all the warrants in Epictetus' system are portable. They can be taken along into exile. The anthropological-cosmological warrants go wherever the body goes or wherever the cosmos exists. And the paradigms from Stoic teachings can of course be learned anywhere. Even though education is a prerequisite to becoming wise and

---

110On the range of these terms see Adolf Lumpe, "Exemplum," *Reallexikon für Antike und Christentum*, 6:1229—57. On their treatment in rhetorical theory: J. Bennett Price, " 'Paradeigma' and 'Exemplum' in Ancient Rhetorical Theory," Dissertation, University of California, Berkeley, 1975 (Ann Arbor: University Microfilms, 1982).

111Epictetus 1.29.19; 2.2.15; 3.23.21; *Ench.* 53.

Epictetus himself devoted much of his life to his school, this community is a tool not a goal and could be discarded when the goal is reached. Ultimately, Epictetus grounds his ethic in a series of warrants which are part of the structure of the cosmos and are thus available to any individual.

The ethical similarities between 4 Maccabees and the Pastorals with their shared predilection for Greek ethical terminology, the use of εὐσέ-βεια, of the cardinal virtues, of paradigms, and even the larger attempt to speak with one voice out of two different traditions, from Judaism and Greco-Roman ethics for the author of 4 Maccabees and from Christianity and Greco-Roman ethics for the author of the Pastorals, have encouraged many comparisons between the two systems[112]. Without delving into the intricacies of the rather delicate argument of 4 Maccabees on the relationship of Jewish πολιτεία to the Greek way of life or into the problems of a genre which pretends to be a dialogue answering the question of whether reason (λογισμός) can control the passions (πάϑος) but which is over-whelmed by the bulk and insistence of its illustrative paradigms, we can still sketch the basic outline of the ethical system[113].

The author attempts to co-opt the terms, goals, and canons of Greco-Roman ethical theory by placing them within the framework of Jewish piety. By doing this, the law (νόμος) becomes the one unimpeachable canon in the system, with the more traditional Greek notions in service to it[114]. The author agrees with his contemporary ethicists that the virtuous life is the best life, that reason must control the passions for this life to be possible, and further that reliable warrants must undergird any such system[115]. Beyond that, he completely transforms the usual look of such ethical theories by introducing the law into the mix.

The author of 4 Maccabees articulates a series of anthropological-cosmological connections similar to what we found in Epictetus.

> When God fashioned man he implanted in him emotions and inclinations; but at the same time he enthroned intellect (νοῦς), through the agency of the sense, as the sacred guide of all. To

---

112A. T. Hanson, "An Academic Phrase: 1 Timothy 3.16a," *Studies in the Pastoral Epistles*, pp. 21—28: "The author of the Pastorals has lifted this word from 4 Maccabees.... He is, we maintain, deliberately copying 4 Maccabees" (pp. 22, 23). Others who do not assume that the author has actually read *4 Maccabees* note parallels. Cf. Falconer, *The Pastoral Epistles*, pp. 32—33; Dibelius-Conzelmann, *The Pastoral Epistles*, p. 39.

113On introductory questions see Moses Hadas, ed. and trans., *The Third and Fourth Books of Maccabees* (New York: Harper and Brothers, 1953), pp. 91—141; A. Dupont-Sommer, *La Quatrième Livre des Machabées*, Bibliothèque de L'école des Hautes Études, 274 (Paris: H. Champion, 1939); R. B. Townsend, "The Fourth Book of Maccabees" in R. H. Charles, *The Apocrypha and Pseudepigrapha of the Old Testament*, Vol 2 (Oxford: Clarendon Press, 1913), pp. 653—85; Paul L. Redditt, "The Concept of 'Nomos' in Fourth Maccabees," *Catholic Biblical Quarterly* 45 (1983): 249—270.

1144 Macc. 1.13f.

115The proposition to be tested in this diatribe is whether ὁ εὐσεβὴς λογισμός can control the passions. After each account of a martyrdom the author appends a note that this ability to surrender to death proves the proposition.

the intellect he gave the law; and he who lives subject to it shall reign over a realm of temperance, and justice, and goodness, and courage[116].

λογισμὸς μὲν δὴ τοίνυν ἐστὶν νοῦς μετὰ ὀρθοῦ λόγου προτιμῶν τὸν σοφίας βίον. σοφία δὴ τοίνυν ἐστὶν γνῶσις θείων καὶ ἀνθρωπίνων πραγμάτων καὶ τῶν τούτων αἰτιῶν. αὕτη δὴ τοίνυν ἐστὶν ἡ τοῦ νόμου παιδεία, δι' ἧς τὰ θεῖα σεμνῶς καὶ τὰ ἀνθρώπινα συμφερόντως μανθάνομεν. τῆς δὲ σοφίας ἰδέαι καθεστήκασιν φρόνησις καὶ δικαιοσύνη καὶ ἀνδρεία καὶ σωφροσύνη. κυριωτάτη δὲ πάντων ἡ φρόνησις, ἐξ ἧς δὴ τῶν παθῶν ὁ λογισμὸς ἐπικρατεῖ.

Reason, then, is the intellect choosing with correct judgment the life of wisdom; and wisdom is knowledge of things human and divine and of their causes. Such wisdom is education in the law, through which we can learn things divine reverently and things human advantageously. The types comprised in wisdom are prudence, justice, courage, and temperance. Of these, prudence has the greatest authority of all, for it is through it that reason rules over the emotions[117].

The method of argumentation, the specific definitions of reason and wisdom and the elevation of φρόνησις above the other virtues are typical Hellenistic ideas, but all of this is transformed by the presence of the law, which rings a false note in this Greek scale. Furthermore, the law does not enter as an equal but as the ruling idea[118]. Unlike what we see in most Greco-Roman ethics, there is no need to puzzle out the content of the ethical life, because the law states clearly and unequivocally what one should do. The task is not knowledge, as it is in the post-Socratic tradition, but obedience. Consequently the normal function of reason (λογισμός) is severely limited, because it no longer inquires or investigates but only dominates the passions[119].

This unusual combination of ideas requires that two propositions be proved beyond all doubt: first, that obedience to the law produces the virtuous life, and, secondly, that reason can indeed control the passions. The first proposition is proved by the method by which many such basic tenets are proved in Greco-Roman ethical theories. It is not proved at all; it is simply asserted. It is in that sense a "special topic" from which enthymemes can be derived. Similarly Epictetus does not prove by dialectical reasoning that the προλήψεις, the λόγος, or the προαίρεσις are what he claims they are. At best he uses enthymemes built upon special topics; at a minimum he uses rhetorical appeals[120]. The author of 4 Maccabees says, "We [the Jews] believe that God has established the law, and

---

[116]4 Macc. 2.21–23. Translation by Hadas, *Fourth Maccabees*.

[117]4 Macc. 1.15–20. Translation by Hadas, *Fourth Maccabees*.

[118]Paul L. Redditt, "The Concept of 'Nomos' in Fourth Maccabees," points out this dominance of the law over other concepts (pp. 251–54, 262).

[119]Redditt, "The Concept of 'Nomos' in Fourth Maccabees," notes that λογισμός is subordinate to νόμος, adding, "Reason, as seen above, does not operate in 4 Maccabees as an independent agent left free to follow its own devices" (pp. 258–59).

[120]It is possible, of course, that Epictetus provided more elaborate arguments in his school. The *Discourses* recorded by Arrian seem to assume more formal procedures elsewhere, and perhaps in his classroom lectures he introduced more strictly logical examinations. Long, "Dialectic and the Stoic Sage," pp. 119–21, notes that although Epictetus claimed no expertise in logic, he treated it as a necessary instrument.

.we know that the creator of the world, in giving us the law, has conformed it to our nature"[121]. This is a statement of faith not a proof. He then moves from this general proposition to the narrative containing the illustrative paradigms of the martyrs. In this way the final proof of his final statement about the law depends on the persuasiveness of the paradigms of the martyrs. The second proposition is stated as a question not as a belief statement, but it is proved the same way. The illustrative paradigms of Antiochus, the seven brothers, and their mother are regarded as affirmative proofs. For example, the author concludes after his account of the martyrdom of Antiochus, "If, then, an aged man despised the tortures unto death, we must acknowledge that religious reason ($\dot{o}$ $\epsilon\dot{v}\sigma\epsilon\beta\dot{\eta}\varsigma$ $\lambda o\gamma\iota\sigma\mu\dot{o}\varsigma$) is leader over the passions"[122]. Similar statements follow each account of martyrdom[123]. Thus his paradigms vindicate his theory.

What is important in all this for our understanding of the Pastorals is that the author does not believe he can merely enjoin the virtues or in his case appeal to the law; rather he takes great care to establish reliable warrants and to prove, according to rhetorical canons, the reliability of those warrants. The fact that his warrants are in many ways unique to him does not negate his method. Special topics do not frequently pass from author to author, and different religious or philosophical schools keep allegiance to different sets of wise men.

Even the Cynics, the ultimate individualists, who on the surface are pure ethicists without a theoretical base[124], appeal to two specific warrants[125]. The first is the appeal to the proposition that virtue is $\kappa\alpha\tau\dot{\alpha}$ $\varphi\dot{v}\sigma\iota\nu$ (in accordance with nature). This is treated as a first principle ($\dot{\alpha}\rho\chi\dot{\eta}$); it is not explained, explored, or proved even in the loose manner we find in Stoics who make the same appeal[126]. Yet it is a warrant and

---

121 4 Macc. 5.25. Redditt translates against Hadas: "The Creator of the world had the best in view for us according to nature" ($\kappa\alpha\tau\dot{\alpha}$ $\varphi\dot{v}\sigma\iota\nu$ $\dot{\eta}\mu\tilde{\iota}\nu$ $\sigma\upsilon\mu\pi\alpha\vartheta\epsilon\tilde{\iota}$ $\nu o\mu o\vartheta\epsilon\tau\tilde{\omega}\nu$ $\dot{o}$ $\tauo\tilde{v}$ $\kappa\dot{o}\sigma\muo\upsilon$ $\kappa\tau\dot{\iota}\sigma\tau\eta\varsigma$) (Redditt, "The Concept of 'Nomos' in Fourth Maccabees," p. 257).

122 4 Macc. 7.16.

123 4 Macc. 6.31−34; 13.1−4; 16.1.

124 Diogenes Laertius declares, "They [the Cynics] are content then like Ariston of Chios, to do away with the subjects of Logic and Physics and to devote their whole attention to Ethics" (6.103). As Malherbe, "Cynics," *The Interpreter's Dictionary of The Bible*, Suppl. Vol., pp. 201−3, puts it, "The Cynic rejects all supraindividual points of view. He shows no interest in providence, but stresses his own free will and his own accomplishment without recourse to any physical or logical theory. His interest is solely in ethics." Furthermore, we search in vain for any real examination of their ethical canons. In our extant Cynic sources, there are no discussions of what $\varphi\dot{v}\sigma\iota\varsigma$ is exactly, why living $\kappa\alpha\tau\dot{\alpha}$ $\varphi\dot{v}\sigma\iota\nu$ is good or even possible, or why particular modes of behavior are virtuous and others are not. All these things are assumed to be self-evident. $\varphi\rho\dot{o}\nu\eta\sigma\iota\varsigma$ is a virtue: there is no need to prove it.

125 On what follows see Malherbe, "Cynics," pp. 201−3; Donald R. Dudley, *A History of Cynicism* (Hildesheim: Georg Olms, 1967); R. Helm, "Kynismus," *Pauly-Wissowa, Real-Encyclopädie der classischen Altertumswissenschaft* 12 (1924): 3−24.

126 Rist, *Stoic Philosophy*, p. 62, says, "The difficulty is that he [Diogenes] gives no justification for his use of the words 'nature' and 'natural'; nor does he attempt to explain why it is good

functions as such in their protreptic. More important however is the use of inductive and illustrative paradigms. The Cynic epistles give canonical status to a select group of ancient Cynics (Socrates, Zeno, Chrysippus, and others). Not only do these Cynics provide content to the ethical life, serving as inductive paradigms which should be imitated, they also serve as illustrative paradigms, providing proof that the ethical life is possible[127]. These paradigms constitute the real theoretical and logical foundation of Cynic ethical theory. While the Cynics expressly reject the fields of physics and logic as pedantic and useless, the confirmatory function of those disciplines is replaced by the paradigms. Thus even the Cynics supply warrants to their ethics, by recounting the deeds and sayings of their virtuous ancestors.

In order to create a serviceable and persuasive ethic, Greco-Roman ethicists constructed systems which provided individuals with standards and abilities to meet those standards. These systems not only have cosmological warrants but are flexible enough to provide detailed instructions for the minutiae of the ethical life. The general cosmological assertions in the Pastorals, which are built upon ideas of God as savior and creator, are not sufficient to do this. What the ethic in the Pastorals needs is something corresponding to Epictetus' cosmological-anthropological theories or even the extensive prescriptions of the law in 4 Maccabees. The cosmological-anthropological interaction created by the reception of the spirit through the act of baptism is a step in the right direction, but it is an insufficient one. The spirit does not provide content to the ethic; it provides the ability to perform the requisite standards. In this sense it is comparable to the reason in 4 Maccabees, which is stripped of its more common office of investigation and adjudication and assigned the limited task of enabling obedience to the law. The author of the Pastorals must somehow place into the hands of every individual a reliable method of determining what is εὐσέβεια and what is not. In itself the author's conception of God's plan of salvation is only an assertion that God does indeed have such a plan. The mere existence of this plan produces minimal ethical content or direction. However, in the details of the realization and management of this plan, the author moves deep into the specifics of daily life. With a series of steps beginning in God's original plan, moving through the first epiphany of Jesus, then through Paul, Timothy, Titus, and further through certain church officers, and ending in the individual church member, this divine plan places into the hands of every believer the necessary standards for the virtuous life and the ability to meet those standards. In order to understand how these warrants and guidelines are furnished, we must submerge ourselves deeper into the intricacies of the system.

2. The Entrusted Traditions

When investigating the extent of the cosmological basis of the author's ethics, we suggested that eventually the workings of the plan of salvation produce church officers who speak with cosmological authority. This laying of the mantle of cosmic reliability upon church leaders constitutes the author's basic solution to the problem of ethical warrants. He places all necessary authority into the hands and mouths of living church officers. Thus for an individual to find ethical guidance he or she need only consult this select group of people. This rather astonishing solution is accomplished by a series of fictions which the pseudepigraphical genre permits the author. He weaves together three fictions: the existence of a Pauline tradition (παραϑήκη) with its sound teachings, the realization of a life-style modelled upon Paul's paradigmatic behavior, and a process of transmission or succession which brings these two standards out of the sacred Pauline past into the fabric of his own church. Each of these elements enjoys a secure place in the workings of God's plan and consequently is reliable and effective. In the end, they all take shape in the deeds and teachings of orthodox church officers.

The short peroration in 1 Timothy 6.20, in summing up the major theme of the letter, declares that Timothy must "guard the traditions" (παραϑήκην). The reader is of course to understand that Timothy, in accord with the fiction of the letter, scrupulously carried out that injunction. Again in 2 Tim. 1.12—14 the reliable transmission of the traditions is asserted by detailing the action of Timothy, Paul, and ultimately God, in guarding its preservation. Timothy is again enjoined to guard the traditions, this time with reference to the spirit bestowed upon him as part of his office. The passing of these traditions, from Paul to Timothy to others, falls under the purview of God; it is part of God's management of the plan of salvation (οἰκονομία ϑεοῦ), so that Paul can declare, "I am convinced that he is able to guard my traditions until that day."

The many competent inquiries into the background and function of παραϑήκη in the Pastorals have clearly demonstrated that the concept comes out of legal terminology in which a deposit of some kind was entrusted to another, placing the latter under legal obligation[128]. Further, the term outgrew its legal provenance and was frequently used to establish the reliability of transmission processes for words and ideas[129]. Therefore,

---

to behave naturally. Certainly he does not attempt to justify his talk about nature by introducing physical theories." Malherbe, "Cynics," p. 201, agrees: "They felt no need to explain what 'nature' was, nor why it is good to live κατὰ φύσιν."

[127] See citations in first chapter.

[128] The legal provenance of this term is examined by C. Spicq, "Saint Paul et la loi des dépôts," *Revue Biblique* 40 (1931): 481—502. Cf. J. Rauft, "Depositum," *Reallexikon für Antike und Christentum* 3, p. 781. This assumes that παραϑήκη is identical to the Attic παρακαταϑήκη; on which see W. Hellebrand, "Parakatatheke," *Pauly-Wissowa, Real-Encyclopädie der classischen Altertumswissenschaft* 36 (1949): 1186—1202. See also K. Wegenast, *Das Verständnis der Tradition bei Paulus und in den Deuteropaulinen,* Wissenschaftliche Monographien zum Alten und Neuen Testament 8 (Neukirchen: Neukirchener Verlag, 1962), pp. 132—44; Brox, *Die Pastoralbriefe,* pp. 235—36; Lips, *Glaube, Gemeinde, Amt* pp. 266—70, and the bibliography there.

[129] Dibelius-Conzelmann, *The Pastoral Epistles,* cite Herodotus 9.45; Pseudo-Isocrates *Ad*

the author of the Pastorals is not replacing the dynamic term παράδοσις with the static term παραϑήκη[130], but is specifying the reliable status of his traditions with the nuances of trustworthiness and obligation inherent to the term παραϑήκη. He supplements the abilities of his term παραϑήκη with the fiction of succession. As we shall see below, the sound teaching of the Lord is handed down untarnished from Paul to Timothy and Titus and then to selected church officers. This fiction demonstrates the complete credibility of the doctrines of the letters. Divorced from the fiction of succession, the concept of tradition might appear to be static or suspect; but its function in the Pastorals is the exact opposite. Its very existence is a fiction created by the author. There never was, of course, a deposit of teachings and moral standards of this kind which was handed down in this fashion. The παραϑήκη comes into existence out of the author's own creativity. He picks and chooses from his theological environment; he weaves various ideas into a coherent system; then he thrusts the whole collection back into a fictional past. This in turn, from the point of view of the letters, is handed down carefully from this sacred past to his own day. Of course, the pseudepigraphical genre permits (for appearances sake) the author to turn the real creation process of the traditions on its head.

Hermann von Lips' helpful study of the crucial role of ordination and office in the Pastorals has pointed out that the peculiar idea of succession in the Pastorals establishes the reliability of both the officers who hold office and the doctrines they teach[131]. Lips believes that part of this succession process was the gift of a particular spirit, one reserved for church officers, which came with ordination and enabled the ordained to perform the special tasks of office[132]. Paul is portrayed in such a way that he himself embodies this double aspect of sound doctrine and office. In 1 Tim. 1.11, for example, his message receives substantiation (τὸ εὐαγγέλιον ... ὃ ἐπιστεύϑην ἐγώ '), while in 2 Tim. 1.10–11 it is his office (. . . τοῦ εὐαγγελίου, εἰς ὃ ἐτέϑην ἐγὼ κῆρυξ καὶ ἀπόστολος καὶ διδάσκαλος). Finally 1 Tim. 1.12 includes both aspects (πιστόν με ἡγήσατο ϑέμενος εἰς διακονίαν)[133]. The rite of ordination and conscious imitation of Paul's behavior by later officers keep Paul's peculiar leadership pattern alive. Lips offers the following schema:[134]

Demonicum 22; Philo *Det. pot. ins.* 65. See Lips, *Glaube, Gemeinde, Amt*. pp. 266–70, for further examples.

[130]Hans von Campenhausen, "Lehrerreihen und Bischofsreihen im zweiten Jahrhundert," in *In Memoriam Ernst Lohmeyer*, ed. Werner Schmauch (Stuttgart: Evangelisches Verlagswerk, 1951), pp. 244ff. Dibelius-Conzelmann, *The Pastoral Epistles*, p. 92, n.31, state that Campenhausen believed the gnostics had contaminated the term παράδοσις so the author used παραϑήκη to stress inviolability.

[131]Lips, *Glaube, Gemeinde, Amt*, pp. 265–78.

[132]Ibid., pp. 206–22.

[133]Ibid., p. 275.

[134]Ibid., p. 273.

Paul	ἀπόστολος	κῆρυξ	διδάσκαλος
Timothy		κηρύττειν	διδάσκειν
and Titus			
Officers			διδάσκειν

Paul enjoys unique status as apostle; but his role as teacher, which is a designation original to the Pastorals, is imitated by Timothy and Titus and then by the church officers. The intermediate position of Timothy and Titus is reflected in their being preachers like Paul but unlike later church officers, who "teach" only what has already been preached. Whether this schema holds up completely or not, the insertion of the term διδάσκαλος into the portrait of Paul and its subsequent repetition indicate that not only is pattern of teaching handed down but also pattern of behavior[135].

In addition to creating the concept of Pauline tradition and the fiction of its transmission, the author also creates its content[136]. This is a necessary concomitant to the fiction of the pseudepigraphical letter. The letter portrays Paul as handing over these traditions to Timothy and Titus. Yet readers would not be able to detail what παραθήκη is just from hearing the term[137]. They cannot consult anything exterior to the letters themselves unless it be the mouths of those ethical church officers. And, if they could, it would undermine the author's attempt to endow these officers with singular authority. The παραθήκη itself must be created by the author and thus come into existence for the first time in the teachings of the letters. The doctrines and portraits in the Pastorals are the παραθήκη. There is no other source.

The Pastorals designate the doctrinal content of the Pauline tradion as sound teaching (ὑγιαίνουσα διδασκαλία). The prevailing tendency among scholars is to underline the healing connotation of ὑγιής in the author's use of this term; and thus sound teaching would be read as teaching which makes a person whole[138]. However, Dibelius-Conzelmann emphasize the rational aspects of the term; and Malherbe places the term in a polemical context, with ὑγιής distinguishing the orthodox from the heterodox[139].

---

135 1 Tim. 5.17 refers to "elders" who both preach and teach, thus casting some doubt on Lips' schema.

136 Trummer, *Die Paulustradition der Pastoralbriefe*, p. 221, understands the παραθήκη as the author transforming and re-interpreting the Pauline traditions which came down to him, ending with a non-Pauline content. This is certainly the most balanced and pervasive view of what happened and I do not want to contradict it so much as to emphasize the aggressiveness of the transformation and the non-Pauline character of the results.

137 In this I want to disagree strongly with Hanson, *The Pastoral Epistles*, p. 26, who remarks " ... the author never explicitly expounds what the paratheke is."

138 Kelly, *The Pastoral Epistles*, p. 50. "It expresses his conviction that a morally disordered life is, as it were, diseased and stands in need of treatment, viz., by the law, whereas a life based on the teaching of the gospel is clean and healthy" (Easton, *The Pastoral Epistles*, p. 234).

139 Dibelius-Conzelmann, *The Pastoral Epistles*, pp. 24—25: "Therefore one must not read into these passages an originally poetic viewpoint, e.g., that the word "sound," "healthy," is intended to describe the power of the gospel to bring healing and life. Nor is it possible to be content with the assumption that the expressions in question were coined for purposes of the heresy polemic."

Like so many such discussions, the hard distinctions among the various nuances of the term cannot be maintained. ὑγιής is one word and its penumbras include various shades of meaning. Moreover, the Pastorals at one time or another seem to use ὑγιής with all the connotations noted above. Without exploring any further the linguistic labyrinth surrounding this term, we can proceed to an investigation of how it functions in the letters[140].

The recurrent focus on heterodoxy in 1 Timothy is reflected in the definition given to sound teaching. At the conclusion of a brief vice list applied to the heterodox in 1 Tim. 1.9–11, the author attaches the following generalization: "and whatever else is opposed to the sound teaching (τῇ ὑγιαινούσῃ διδασκαλίᾳ), according to the gospel of the glory of the blessed God, with which I have been entrusted." The sound teaching is whatever is Pauline, and anything opposed is vice. Once the concept of a pure doctrine is introduced, the author immediately links it with its syzygy, the concept of succession. In 1 Tim. 1.12 "Paul" asserts that Christ Jesus appointed him for his service, and then in v. 18 Timothy is commissioned by Paul to his office by being entrusted with these teachings (ταύτην τὴν παραγγαλίαν παρατίθεμαί σοι). The content of these instructions is quite diverse, as the context shows. But leaving aside those details, we can perceive immediately that the author binds together doctrines and succession through the fiction of what Paul said and did.

Lips has already pointed out the importance of 1 Tim. 2.7, where Paul is appointed as apostle, preacher, and teacher[141]. To his observations we should add that the placement of this sentence in the letter immediately following a doctrinal hymn is significant. The "into which (εἰς ὅ)" of Paul's appointment can only refer to the doctrinal assertion in 1 Tim. 2. 5–6; he is the witness of the salvation event produced by Jesus' epiphany. Once again doctrine and office are linked. We should recall at this point that Lips also detects the concept of succession lurking in the phraseology of this verse, so that doctrine, office, and succession are bound together.

Timothy's intermediary role is continuously emphasized in his passing on these sound teachings which Paul entrusted to him. In 1 Tim. 4.6 Timothy is advised that "If you instruct the brothers with these things (ταῦτα ὑποτιθέμενος), you will be a good servant of Christ Jesus, nourished by the words of faith and good teaching which you have followed (ἐντρεφό-

---

For an analysis of the many ways the term has been understood see Malherbe, "Medical Imagery in the Pastoral Epistles," pp. 19–35. Malherbe agrees with Dibelius that the rational connotations dominate over the medical ones, but then proceeds to show how the term was frequently used in polemics, especially against Cynics. Brox, Die Pastoralbriefe, pp. 107–8, also sees it primarily as a polemical term.

[140]Lips, Glaube, Gemeinde, Amt, treats ὑγιής, πίστις, διδασκαλία, ἀλήθεια, εὐαγγέλιον, κήρυγμα, μαρτύριον, εὐσέβεια as a collection of terms placed in close relation by the author, which mutually interpret each other.

[141]Lips, Glaube, Gemeinde, Amt, p. 275.

μενος τοῖς λόγοις τῆς πίστεως καὶ τῆς καλῆς διδασκαλίας ᾗ παρηκο-
λούθηκας)." Again in 1 Tim. 4.11 he is instructed to "command these
things and teach them (παράγγελλε ταῦτα καὶ δίδασκε)." And finally 1
Tim. 4.15—16 reads, "Attend to these things, in these things be (ταῦτα
μελέτα, ἐν τούτοις ἴσθι), in order that your progress might be manifest
to all. Take hold of yourself and the teachings, remain in them (ἔπεχε
σεαυτῷ καὶ τῇ διδασκαλίᾳ, ἐπίμενε αὐτοῖς), for doing this you will
save yourself and those who hear you." These commandments, assuming
they are obeyed, create the appearance of a process of transmission which
results in Paul's own orthodoxy taking shape in the author's day. Paul
consciously hands over the sound teaching. Timothy adheres to them, rejecting anything contrary. He in turn teaches them to others. Ultimately
this process produces salvation (τοῦτο γὰρ ποιῶν καὶ σεαυτὸν σώσεις
καὶ τοὺς ἀκούοντάς σου)[142]. God's plan of salvation, which intends salvation for all who are chosen, works its power by way of this fictional process of transmission.

The content of the entrusted tradition is enumerated by the letters
themselves. When Timothy is encouraged to teach ταῦτα, this refers to the
things expressed in the letters. Therefore, the three injunctions in chapter
4 of 1 Timothy reflect back upon the collection of material in chapters
1—3 and even include the material in chapter 4. The entrusted tradition
consists of all the doctrinal and parenetical forms in the letters. This
would include (1) virtue and vice lists, (2) household codes, (3) paradigms
of Paul, Timothy, and Titus, (4) positive and negative illustrative paradigms,
(5) direct imperatives, and (6) pieces of theological doctrine.

The pseudepigraphical genre presents Paul as the author of these diverse elements and consequently validates certain doctrines and a certain
life-style for the author's church. The series of cultic instructions in 1
Tim. 5.1ff. articulates the content of the entrusted traditions with great
specificity. "Do not rebuke an older man (5.1)." "Honor widows who are
real widows (5.3)." "Let a widow be enrolled if . . . (5.9)." "Let elders
who rule well be considered worthy of double honor (5.17)." "No longer
drink only water (5.23)." "Let all who are under the yoke of slavery regard their masters as worthy of all honor (6.1)." All these imperatives not
only describe but also attempt to produce a life-style. The entrusted
tradition, therefore, includes doctrinal material with Christological formulae, all the cosmological details of the plan of salvation, a variety of parenetic forms, and descriptions of the proper life-style. Each of these
devices becomes an ethical warrant, with each functioning in a different
way.

Although the author himself is enjoying a great moment of creativity
in composing these traditions, within the fiction of the letter, he depicts
its origin as the very opposite of contemporary creativity. Timothy and

---

[142]1 Tim. 4.16.

Titus do not tamper with the sound teaching and, of course, neither do their successors, if they are faithful. Furthermore, the genre permits a reader to circumvent the doctrinal uncertainties of his own day by giving him a look behind the processes of history. The true teaching which was handed down can be identified easily, because the reader has access to Paul's letters (the Pastorals) in which he articulated this sound teaching. This means that the fiction of succession does more than validate certain teachings, since a pseudepigraphical letter without the concept of succession could validate these teachings; it also gives credibility and unimpeachable authority to the teachers who adhere to these teachings. In short, as Lips has claimed, office, doctrine, and succession are wedded together. And this is accomplished efficiently and smoothly through the unique capacities of the pseudepigraphical letter.

If possible, 2 Timothy underlines the connection among these ideas even more than 1 Timothy does. This is immediately apparent in the proem of 1.3–14, where the entrusted tradition, which includes doctrines and life-style, receives extensive validation in autobiographical reminiscences of "Paul." In 1.6 "Paul" reminds Timothy to rekindle the gifts which are his through the laying on of Paul's hands. Then the ethical dimensions of the spirit are asserted, followed by a major piece of doctrine which we have investigated above (2 Tim. 1.9–10). Finally, all this is confirmed by the author's theory of tradition and its transmission.

> Into which I have been placed as preacher and apostle and teacher. On account of which I suffer these things; but I am not ashamed, for I know whom I have trusted and I am convinced that he is able to guard my traditions until that day. You have a prototype of the sound teachings, which you have heard from me in the faith and love which is in Christ Jesus. Guard the good traditions through the holy spirit which dwells in you (2 Tim. 1.11–14).

Not only does "Paul" insist upon his own fidelity to his duty of handing down the correct teachings, but, when he appeals to God's active role in this process, he implies the subsequent success of Timothy in preserving them. These fictional events, which in themselves would be sufficient for authenticating the traditions, derive additional support in the appeal to divine activity. The concept of the spirit provides a rhetorical frame for this account by both introducing and concluding the section. Thereby, as Lips has pointed out, the special gifts concomitant to ordination play an essential role in the transmission of the traditions[143]. The difficult task of preserving these traditions intact, a task necessary to the effectiveness of God's plan, obtains cosmological assistance by way of the spirit, which dwells in those assigned the job of transmission and preservation.

The penultimate leg of the transmission process is documented with the direct commandment in 2 Tim. 2.2 of "Paul" to Timothy: "and what you have heard from me in the presence of many witnesses, entrust these things

---

[143]Lips, *Glaube, Gemeinde, Amt*, pp. 265–78.

to faithful men (ταῦτα παράθου πιστοῖς ἀνθρώποις) who are capable of teaching others." The care with which each step is verified is manifest. Timothy passes on only what he has heard directly from Paul. This is not hearsay and does not depend on literary records vulnerable to editing. This is a confidant's information, secrets passed on behind the public face of history. The letters are between confidants. Yet despite this intimacy the author introduces the legal warrant that these things were spoken before many witnesses, implying thereby an additional authentication without specifying who those witnesses were. Timothy in turn passes these traditions on to reliable, trusthworthy men (not women). The virtue lists which are associated with the elders and deacons throughout the letters are further attempts to substantiate the reliability of those who received the entrusted traditions from Timothy.

Finally, the traversing of the last barrier is intimated in the facility (διδακτικόν) of these leaders for teaching others[144]. This facility is the final leg of the journey from God's plan conceived at the beginning of time to the presence of the individual church member. These people must be taught correctly by the elders and deacons capable of such. This explains why teaching and education occupy so much of the author's attention in the letters.

The inclusion of a particular life-style or pattern of behavior in the process of transmission, which we detected in 1 Timothy, is also described in 2 Timothy. The proem gives the first suggestion of this when it alludes to the faith which existed in Timothy's mother and grandmother and now surely exists in him (2 ·Tim. 1.5). Although these relationships reflect more the author's concern with educational activities in his church than his particular idea of succession, the possibility of something so allusive and ineffable as faith being repeated in subsequent generations illustrates our author's capacity for believing that a life-style could be transmitted through time by a process of imitation[145]. He generates the illusion of such a transmission primarily by his construction of paradigms worthy of imitation, but he also explicitly enunciates his theory in 2 Tim. 3.10–11.

> Now you have observed (παρηκολούθησας) my teaching, my conduct (ἀγωγή), my plan, my faith, my patience, my love, my endurance, my persecutions, my sufferings, which happened to me at Antioch, Iconium, and Lystra; whatever persecutions I endured, the Lord saved me from them all.

Then, as we would now expect, he exhorts Timothy to "Remain in what you have learned and believed, knowing from whom you have learned (σὺ δὲ μένε ἐν οἷς ἔμαθες καὶ ἐπιστώθης, εἰδὼς παρὰ τίνων ἔμαθες)" (2 Tim. 3.14). Paul's particular life-style, here painted by way

---

[144]1 Tim. 3.2; 2 Tim. 2.24.

[145]On the difficulties of squaring this account of Timothy's family with Acts 16.1–3 or with seeing this as a comment on Jewish-Christian relations see Brox, *Die Pastoralbriefe*, pp. 226–27. Brox refers helpfully to 1 Tim. 3.15.

of "autobiographical" statements, becomes an integral part of Timothy's knowledge and thus shapes his teaching. The Pauline life-style will re-emerge in the author's own church. The author assumes that the virtues realized by Paul can also be realized in his own day, because all the necessary warrants and powers for such an ethical life are present in the cult.

Titus repeats this same set of ideas. In fact, the theme statement in Tit. 1.5 declares the purpose of Titus' stay in Crete to be the appointment of elders, as directed by Paul. These elders are selected by their ethical behavior (imtimating their general reliability and orthodoxy), by their success in managing their own houses (intimating their ability to rule the church), and by their capacity to reprove the heterodox and exhort with the sound teachings (intimating their ability to inculcate the proper life-style in others)[146]. The injunction to teach the proper teachings recurs in Tit. 2.1 and 2.15. Furthermore, the transmission of the proper life-style is embodied in the linkage of Titus as a paradigm with his adherence to the sound teachings in Tit. 2.7—8. All this is woven into the larger argument in the letter in which parenesis is placed in parataxis to theological doctrines by way of enthymematic arguments.

3. Summary

The preceding analysis yields several conclusions.

(1) The author has created a Pauline tradition, which, when coupled with the fiction of succession, is faithfully transmitted from Paul to the author's own day.

(2) The author authenticates this process of succession with three devices: (a) a theory of ordination with its concomitant leadership charisma, (b) the validation of the people who participate in this relay by means of virtue lists and assertions of their fidelity, (c) the autobiographical reminiscences of "Paul" in which he asserts his own reliability, coupled with his injunctions to Timothy and Titus to do likewise.

(3) The entrusted traditions consist primarily of sound teachings, which include the entire range of theological doctrines and protreptic forms occurring in the letters. Moreover, a life-style, which is in part depicted in the teachings with the many direct injunctions and virtue and vice lists, but which receives its fullest portrait in the paradigmatic patterns of Paul, Timothy, and Titus, is transmitted by its linkage with succession patterns and also by the continued existence of the letters.

(4) Ethical church officers become the focal point of the transmission of the entrusted traditions, because they embody the correct life-style and proclaim the sound doctrine.

---

[146]Tit. 1.6—11.

(5) The letters themselves provide a further canon by which reliable officers can be discovered, tested, and authenticated.

(6) The author has created the requisite warrants for his ethic by furnishing the individual Christian with two unimpeachable warrants: his ethical church officers and the letters themselves. Thus his warrants include both the wide diversity of argumentative forms collected in the letters and the ongoing teachings of the proper church officers.

D. The Content of the Ethic

When "Paul" declares to Timothy at 1 Tim. 3.14—15 that he is writing to him, hoping to come to him soon, but if delayed, in order that "you might know how it is necessary to behave in the house of God" (ἵνα εἰδῇς πῶς δεῖ ἐν οἴκῳ ϑεοῦ ἀναστρέφεσϑαι), the author is in effect summarizing the purpose of the letters. Circumventing the fiction, we can conclude that Paul will never show up; but in his stead the author has provided instructions for proper behavior in the letters themselves. Consequently, the letters primarily contain protreptic material of various kinds. We have noted above that the effectiveness of God's plan of salvation eventually depends upon the question of whether virtue is realized. The author provides a series of warrants for this position, but he also takes pains above all to describe the ethical life. His parenetic style is an issue in itself, which we have already discussed, but in order to comprehend the basic structure of his ethical system it is necessary to examine the core material the author uses to build this structure.

1. Virtues and Vices[147]

Virtue and vice lists in the Pastorals are imbedded within larger parenetic sections, functioning more as single limbs in ethical arguments and less as

---

[147]On what follows I am leaning heavily upon the standard works of virtue and vice lists: Anton Vögtle, *Die Tugend – und Lasterkataloge im Neuen Testament*, Neutestamentliche Abhandlungen 16.4—5 (Münster: Aschendorff, 1936); Siegfried Wibbing, *Die Tugend— und Lasterkataloge im Neuen Testament und ihre Traditionsgeschichte unter besonderer Berücksichtigung der Qumran-Texte*, Beiheft zur Zeitschrift für die neutestamentliche Wissenschaft 25 (Berlin:,Töpelmann, 1959); Erhard Kamlah, *Die Form der katalogischen Paränese im Neuen Testament*, Wissenschaftliche Untersuchungen zum Neuen Testament 7 (Tübingen: J. C. B. Mohr [Paul Siebeck], 1964); Burton Scott Easton, "New Testament Ethical Lists," *Journal of Biblical Literature* 51 (1932): 1—12; Johannes Thomas, "Formgesetze des Begriffskatalogs im Neuen Testament," *Theologische Zeitschrift* 24 (1968): 15—28; M. Jack Suggs, "The Christian Two Ways Tradition: Its Antiquity, Form and Function," in *Studies in New Testament and Early Christian Literature*, Essays in Honor of A. P. Wikgren (Leiden: E. J. Brill, 1972), pp. 60—74.

self-evident, self-contained species of protreptic[148]. This is so even though the connection among the various members of the argument is typically accomplished by parataxis, not hypotaxis. Furthermore, we do not encounter the stark juxtaposition of virtue lists to vice lists which occurs in Galatians, the Didache, and other Christian documents influenced by ideas of the two ways[149]. Kamlah has argued persuasively that the hard contrasting of virtues to vices, frequent in the Greco-Roman world, reflects to varying degrees the dualistic cosmology of Iran and the east, from which he believes such lists originated[150]. The cosmological and ethical dualism of Qumran is illustrative of this connection. However, we have seen that the cosmology of the Pastorals is as far from dualism as it could possibly be, with God being declared creator and savior of all. At the same time, nearly every ethical system which proffers prescriptions and proscriptions has dualistic undertones. The Pastorals clearly draw a solid line between the life of virtue and the life of vice. This dualism on the ethical level may not reach into the godhead, but it does reach into the basic structure of God's plan of salvation. God's plan is inherently and inescapably dualistic, and this dualism is played out in every moment of the pro-

---

[148] Unfortunately, I know of no systematic analysis of how these lists function in the larger ethical arguments of the Pastorals. Lists occur at 1 Tim. 1.9—10; 3.1—7, 8—10, 11—12; 4.12; 6.4—5, 11; 2 Tim. 2.22, 24, 25; 3.2—5, 10; Tit. 1.7—8, 10; 2.2—5, 12; 3.3. A glance at these shows how problematic it becomes in the Pastorals to even determine what is a "list" and what is not, much less to understand how lists are used. The best treatments of their argumentative function are given by Kamlah, Die Form der katalogischen Paränese im Neuen Testament, pp. 198—200, and Vögtle, Die Tugend— und Lasterkataloge im Neuen Testament, pp. 51—56, 170—78, 237—43. Kamlah traces the role of the lists in the general argumentative structure of 1 and 2 Timothy, emphasizing their polemical and paideutic role. Vögtle detects levels of usage in the Pastorals, depending on how much the author has transformed the lists from the traditional form. Although he also detects polemical and paideutic functions, he emphasizes their articulation of "Pflichtenlehren." In any case, both detect great freedom in the author's usage; the classic pattern is broken down. We will see this same "breakdown" in the author's use of household codes. In fact, codes and ethical lists seem to run together and become nearly indistinguishable. See also Dibelius-Conzelmann, The Pastoral Epistles, who detail the background of each of these terms and the author's idiosyncracies against tradition throughout the commentary. However, they do not investigate the argumentative status of the material.

[149] See Suggs, "The Christian Two Ways Tradition: Its Antiquity, Form and Function," who traces the dualism out of Jewish (Qumran) traditions with its cosmological links to the strictly ethical dualism of the Didache. At an intermediate position comes Gal. 5.17—24. On which see Betz, Galatians, pp. 278—90, who remarks: "They do not represent vices and virtues in the sense of Greek ethics, but describe phenomena or manifestations of the powers of evil ("the works of the flesh") and of the Spirit ("the fruit of the Spirit")." To use Betz's terms: the lists in the Pastorals do represent vices and virtues in the sense of Greek ethics and not manifestations of cosmic powers.

[150] Kamlah, Die Form der katalogischen Paränese im Neuen Testament, pp. 39—175, locates the origins of this dualism in Iran then traces it into Judaism and Greco-Roman philosophy. But cf. Hans Conzelmann, 1 Corinthians, trans. by James W. Leitch, Hermeneia (Philadelphia: Fortress Press, 1975), pp. 101—2, who disagrees: "It is mistaken to speak of a 'dualistic structure' of the catalogues. What is dualistic is not the catalogue, but the contrasting of catalogues within the framework of a dualistic, eschatological view of salvation." On the dualism in Qumran see Wibbing, Die Tugend— und Lasterkataloge im Neuen Testament.

cess. There is sound teaching and deceptive teaching; there is fidelity and apostasy to the sound teaching; there are positive and negative paradigms, people who embody orthodoxy or heresy; there are reliable teachers and unreliable; there are virtues and vices. In short, there is a dualism of salvation which can be detected most clearly in the contrast between virtues and vices. The fictions of succession, the reliable doctrines, and even the reliable teachers all have one goal, namely, to produce the ethical life in believers, because virtue inherently provides the best possible life. Given all this, it is no surprise that the author uses virtues and vices to give content to this ethic.

Since the ethical terminology of the Pastorals comes directly out of the general culture, the virtue and vice lists may function apologetically[151]. The cardinal virtues, three of the four, are employed in adverbial form in Tit. 2.11 to describe what kind of life Jesus teaches the Christian to live[152]. The specific ethical terms in the virtue and vice lists are all common to other extra-Christian lists, although the exact combination of terms reflects Christian sensibilities. But there is nothing here to which a non-Christian could not be expected to give ready assent. Even the author's favorite terms, like εὐσέβεια, ὑγιής and its cognates, πιστός, and σώφρων and its cognates, which occur in a variety of contexts scattered throughout the letters, are each natural to Greco-Roman parenesis[153]. Although the final selection of ethical terms is shaped somewhat by the author's concern for an ethic which focuses upon community life, the au-

---

151 Betz, *Galatians*, p. 282, remarks, " ... the catalogues sum up the conventional morality of the time. Christianity was interested in that morality to the extent that Christian existence should not be 'against the conventions.' ... The primary function was to make clear that Christian ethical life should roughly conform to the moral conventions of the time." The missionary aspect of these lists is emphasized throughout by Vögtle, *Die Tugend— und Lasterkataloge im Neuen Testament*. On the larger role of ethics in Christian missionary propaganda see Adolf Harnack, *The Mission and Expansion of Christianity in the First Three Centuries*, trans. and ed. James Moffatt (1908; New York: Harper & Bros., 1961), pp. 205—18, who believes that ethics came to the front whenever Christians sought to proselytize outsiders. Christians typically claimed not only high moral standards but the power to meet them. The parallels to the Pastorals are obvious, though Harnack does not mention the letters.

152 In the expression σωφρόνως καὶ δικαίως καὶ εὐσεβῶς only ἀνδρεία is lacking. The four virtues were enumerated in classical form by Plato in *Protagoras* 349, 359, and though Aristotle changed the mix somewhat, the Stoics pretty much kept to the classical combination. Of course, even Plato sometimes complexified the mix by making σωφροσύνη a kind of harmony (Plato *Republic* 3.389; 4.440f.; *Laws* 3.696).

153 See Vögtle, *Die Tugend— und Lasterkataloge im Neuen Testament*, who in the "Griechisches Wortverzeichnis," pp. 248—53, lists all these terms as they occur in various lists. Although we have discussed εὐσέβεια and ὑγιής elsewhere, in terms of frequency of occurrence σώφρων and its cognates are the most numerous: 1 Tim. 2.9, 15; 3.2; 2 Tim. 1.7; Tit. 1.8; 2.2, 4, 5, 6, 12. In fact, of the sixteen occurrences of σώφρων and it cognates in the New Testament ten are in the Pastorals. On this term, see Ulrich Luck, "σώφρων, κτλ.,' TDNT, 7:1097—1104; Spicq, *Les Épîtres Pastorales*, p. 289, n. 4. The political dimensions of this term with the implication that it promotes harmony in the state, in the community, in the soul, make it a logical choice for the author of the Pastorals, who wants to emphasize cooperative virtues rather than ascetic ones.

thor is co-opting for his own system the highest ethical ideals of his culture. In so doing he pronounces an apology for his community, since he
is asserting that the ideal ethical life to which the majority of his culture
aspires is available only within the doors of the Christian church. However,
the author is competing for a fund of values which dominated the tone
of most Greco-Roman philosophy and ethics and for which many others
were competing. We have seen, for instance, that the author of 4 Maccabees makes the same claim, by arguing that the Greek ethical ideal is available only through the special powers of the law[154]. Thus the author of
the Pastorals will have to make additional arguments, beyond simply incorporating this terminology into his system, by demonstrating what tools
the Christian cult provides which are not available elsewhere.

The virtue and vice lists also have a polemical function[155]. This polemical role is manifest from the basic dualistic structure of virtues versus
vices. As we noted above, this dualistic structure emerges from the dualism of salvation and runs throughout all the ethical standards and warrants. The polemic occurs because the author places his opponents on the
side of vice. In fact, the two major vice lists in the letters are used to describe these opponents. In 2 Tim. 3.1f. "Paul" predicts the character of
the heterodox who will arise in the last days and paints them with vices.
In 1 Tim. 1.9–10 the vices are depicted as a necessary result of being
heterodox. Whether this polemic is justified is uncertain, although the
Greco-Roman world produced more than one philosophical or religious
group which eschewed the quiet virtues. In any case, the author shapes
his argument by placing virtues at the heart of the salvation process, and
thus, by situating his opponents in the realm of vice, he asserts not only
their individual destruction but also their danger, uselessness, and decep-
tiveness to the rest of the community.

Of course, the virtue and vice lists also have a paideutic function[156].

---

[154] 4 Maccabees, in fact, shows the same kind of apologetic or missionary interest in this. In 4
Maccabees this interest is of course much more explicit, especially in the contest between the Jewish and the Greek way of life.

[155] As we noted above the polemical aspect of these lists is noted by most commentators:
Brox, *Die Pastoralbriefe*, pp. 106–7, 253–54; Dibelius-Conzelmann, *The Pastoral Epistles*, pp. 6–
7; Easton, "New Testament Ethical Lists," pp. 1–12; Vögtle, *Die Tugend– und Lasterkataloge im
Neuen Testament*, pp. 54, 170–74. Kamlah believes we need to distinguish two kinds of catalogues,
with only the dualistic kind, emerging from Iranian cosmology, being essentially polemical. The
parenetic type is mostly paideutic (*Die Form der katalogischen Paränese im Neuen Testament*, esp.
pp. 214–15). Suggs, "The Christian Two Ways Tradition," p. 73, finds that dualistic catalogues are
not primarily apologetic, polemical, or even educational, thereby rejecting the categories offered
here. He thinks it is part of the process of identification, necessary to every youthful community:
"it serves the distinction between 'we' and 'they' ...."

[156] The educational function of this material is also commonly noted by commentators:
Dibelius-Conzelmann, *The Pastoral Epistles*, pp. 6–7, 50–51; Vögtle, *Die Tugend– und Lasterkataloge im Neuen Testament*, pp. 62–73, 170–78, 237–43. Dibelius-Conzelmann in noting the
use of virtue lists in honorary inscriptions remark, "By listing the virtues of the person being
honored, their intention was to inspire posterity to similar accomplishment." But on the educa-

They describe the ethical life with its hard contrast between virtue and vice, and they demonstrate the essential and inescapable role which virtues must play in the process of salvation. As we have already seen, this is done first of all by framing the ethical life with the two epiphanies of Jesus, with the first teaching and enabling one to live virtuously and the second dispensing reward and punishment on the basis of virtue and vice. In this way every believer is placed under the ethical requirements enjoined in the letters, but the author also uses these lists to establish a special urgency for church leaders to meet these requirements. In Tit. 1.6f. a virtue list is applied to bishops as a prerequisite to office, suggesting that only the virtuous can be selected as bishop. This culminates in the assertion that these ethical leaders will adhere to the sound doctrine and thus will be able to teach correctly and refute the heterodox, as though this were just another virtue. With the reliable teacher thus described with a list of virtues, the author immediately contrasts them with the undisciplined, deceivers, and empty talkers who are upsetting whole families. Again in 1 Tim. 3.1f. a virtue list is applied to the bishop as part of the prerequisites for office. However, in 3.8f. deacons and women attract virtue lists, which are shorter but seem to function in the same way as the lists for bishops. In fact, the short lists may simply be a cue for the larger lists, as though the author was saying that ethical standards apply to these people as well without bothering to detail a complete list. It turns out that every virtue list in the Pastorals occurs in such duty lists for bishops, elders, deacons, and women. This certainly agrees with the author's placing of church leadership in such an essential position in the plan of salvation. The fidelity of the leadership is necessary for the salvation of themselves and everyone else; consequently, they must embody in their own deportment the standards they enjoin upon the rest of the church. This is not simply to avoid hypocrisy on their part but to authenticate their status as ethical warrants and paradigms. We recall that the author places two sources of ethical warrants within reach of the believers: the letters and church leaders. Therefore, a church member must be able to lay his or her hands upon good standards by observing the officers. The ethical system of the author would be undermined and perverted if church officers manifested vices and not virtues. The paideutic function of these lists thus occurs on two levels: first, in the reading of the letters the ethical life is described, and, secondly, church officers who

---

tional aspects see above all Kamlah, *Die Form der katalogischen Paränese im Neuen Testament*, pp. 176–214, who in his analysis of the New Testament catalogues emphasizes that parenesis is the primary context and purpose of this material and notices constant baptismal imagery in the material. Suggs, "The Christian Two Ways Tradition," follows this connection with baptismal catechesis, as does Betz, *Galatians*, pp. 284–85, both referring primarily to Galatians and the *Didache*. Holtz, *Die Pastoralbriefe*, who sees eucharistic allusions everywhere in the Pastorals, actually places these lists in a baptismal context (esp. p. 226).

adhere to these standards are not only able to teach with the sound doctrine but to present themselves as τύποι to the rest of the church.

Finally, the central role of virtue in the salvation process means that
these virtue lists are double-pronged for the officers themselves. They are
first of all standards for performing their offices, for relating to the rest
of the church. But they are also the personal standards requisite for them
as individuals, if they are to receive favorable judgment at the second
epiphany[157]. The officers in this sense are believers like anyone else. Virtues provide them with the best life here, but they also constitute their
ticket to heavenly rewards. Therefore, the virtue lists are indeed pre-
requisites for office; but they are also prescriptions for personal salvation,
explicitly applied to the officers but implicitly to any believer.

2. Household codes[158]

The Haustafeln or household codes also display the three-fold function of
apologetic, polemic, and paideia[159]. The traditional shape of Haustafeln
has undergone considerable transformation in the Pastorals[160]. The three
syzygies of parent-child, husband-wife, and master-slave with the double
exhortation to the dominant partner to rule well and to the subordinate
to submit willingly, which can be traced back to Aristotle and which occurs in more traditional form in Col. 3.18–4.1; Eph. 5.21–6.9; and to a
lesser degree in 1 Pet. 2.11–3.7, are lacking in the Pastorals[161]. In fact it

---

[157]Dibelius-Conzelmann, *The Pastoral Epistles*, p. 50, contrary to most commentators, deny
that these lists are duty lists or are couched especially for leaders: "In the catalogue of their duties,
why are particular requirements for office not specified, but instead qualities which for the most
part are presupposed for every Christian?"

[158]This analysis depends especially on David L. Balch, *Let Wives Be Submissive: The Domestic
Code in 1 Peter*, Society of Biblical Literature Monograph Series 26 (Chico, Calif.: Scholars Press,
1981) and James E. Crouch, *The Origin and Intention of the Colossian Haustafel*, Forschungen
zur Religion und Literatur des Alten und Neuen Testaments 109 (Göttingen: Vandenhoeck &
Ruprecht, 1972). But see also Karl Weidinger, *Die Haustafeln: Ein Stück urchristlicher Paränese*,
Untersuchungen zum Neuen Testament 14 (Leipzig: J. C. Hinrichs, 1928); Martin Dibelius, *An die
Kolosser, Epheser, an Philemon* (Tübingen: J. C. B. Mohr, 1913), esp. excursus on Col. 4.1; Eduard
Lohse, *A Commentary on the Epistles to the Colossians and to Philemon*, trans. William R. Poehl-
mann and Robert J. Karris, Hermeneia (Philadelphia: Fortress Press, 1971), pp. 154–63; Phillip
Carrington, *The Primitive Christian Catechism: A Study in the Epistles* (Cambridge: Cambridge
University Press, 1940); Wolfgang Schrage, "Zur Ethik der neutestamentlichen Haustafeln," *New
Testament Studies* 21 (1975): 1–22; Verner, *The Household of God*.

[159]Balch, *Let Wives Be Submissive*, pp. 106–8, divides scholarship into three options on the
function of household codes: parenesis (Dibelius and Weidinger), social repression (Schroeder and
Crouch), and mission (Selwyn and Schroeder), to which he adds his own — apologetic. Of course,
he admits the relationship between mission and apologetic is intimate, but insists they are not identical.

[160]Weidinger, *Die Haustafeln*, p. 53; Hanson, "Elements of a Baptismal Liturgy in Titus";
Dibelius-Conzelmann, *The Pastoral Epistles*, pp. 6–7.

[161]On the roots in Aristotle see Balch, *Let Wives Be Submissive*, esp. pp. 33–45. This structure is traced in all the major studies listed above with only slight alterations. See, e.g., Balch, *Let*

is problematic where Haustafeln begin and end in the Pastorals, because the traditional structure has been fragmented and the pieces have been scattered about into the midst of different parenetic forms throughout the letters. Nevertheless, the importance of this material to the author is unmistakable from the attention he devotes to it; 1 Tim. 2.8–15, 5.1–6.2; Tit. 2.1–10; 3.1–2 are pieces of Haustafeln, and similar language is interspersed throughout the letters. Therefore, we can conclude that, although the traditional structure of such material is broken, the standard of good order in the community is taken from these three traditional pairs[162]. Using Haustafeln in this fashion is not unique to the Pastorals, since both the Didache and Polycarp do much the same thing[163].

David L. Balch in his study of the household code in 1 Peter has demonstrated the apologetic function of this material[164]. Balch shows that to many eyes the proper maintenance of the dominance of parent, husband, and master over their counterparts comprised part of the framework of society itself. To overturn this dominance-and-subordination pattern was seen as a revolt against society. Furthermore, Balch shows that religious groups frequently suffered the specific accusation of reversing the proper order of things[165]. Thus when the Pastorals enjoin parents to rule children well[166], when women are put in their proper place, namely, in subordination to men[167], and when slaves are discouraged from disobedi-

---

Wives Be Submissive, p. 1, and Lohse, *Colossians and Philemon*, pp. 154–57. For a comparison of the Pastorals' form to those of 1 Peter and Ephesians see Hanson, *Studies in the Pastoral Epistles*, esp. pp. 87–89. For a comparison between the Pastorals and the *Didache* see Dibelius-Conzelmann, *The Pastoral Epistles*, p. 6.

[162]The border between what was traditional and what comes from the author's own hand is nearly impossible to draw; we cannot, in fact, even be very confident about the original shape of the tradition. J. Elliot, "Ministry and Church Order in the New Testament," *Catholic Biblical Quarterly* 32 (1970): 367–91, believes that the literary shape of the Pastorals accords with a known genre best called "advice to church leaders." On the other hand, Hans-Werner Bartsch, *Die Anfänge urchristlicher Rechtsbildungen: Studien zu den Pastoralbriefen* (Hamburg: Herbert Reich, 1965), believes the Pastorals had access to an already existing church document on church order; as did Ephesians, 1 Peter, Ignatius, *Didache*, and *Barnabas*. Hanson, *The Pastoral Epistles*, p. 43, and Falconer, *The Pastoral Epistles*, p. 73, also see written sources. Dibelius-Conzelmann, *The Pastoral Epistles*, p. 6–7, and Easton, *The Pastoral Epistles*, pp. 16–17, do not so much reject written sources as they see considerable eclecticism and creativity in the use of such traditions. I think the best approach is to keep the three options in mind, as we see in full form in Eph. 5.21–6.9 and Col. 3.18–4.1, since we can be fairly confident about our author's knowledge of this schema, and interpret the Pastorals against that pattern.

[163]Dibelius-Conzelmann, *The Pastoral Epistles*, p. 6, refer to an "amalgamation of church order and rules," finding the only meaningful parallels (especially with the anti-heretical cast of the material) in Polycarp and the *Didache*. See Hans von Campenhausen, "Polykarp von Smyrna und die Pastoralbriefe," in *Aus der Frühzeit des Christentums* (Tübingen: J. C. B. Mohr [Paul Siebeck], 1963), pp. 192–252.

[164]Balch, *Let Wives Be Submissive*, pp. 63–121.

[165]Ibid., pp. 65–80. Balch focuses on the accusations made against Judaism and the Dionysus and Isis cults and how the apologetic responses were couched in terms of these household rules.

[166]1 Tim. 3.4–5, 12.

[167]1 Tim. 2.11–12; Tit. 2.5.

ence[168], the author is not just modelling church relationships upon the pattern of society's proper social hierarchies, he is also making an apology about the impact of the Christian cult upon society at large. He is sensitive throughout the letters to the relationship between the cult and outsiders. Bishops must have a good reputation with outsiders[169]; women must be subordinate and ethical so that outsiders will not traduce the community[170]; prayers are made for people in authority, and obedience to secular authorities is required[171]; and finally the author aspires to the quiet, dignified life at peace with neighbors[172]. These strictures fall most heavily upon women, whom the author's opponents had apparently encouraged towards more freedom, for they are left in total subordination to men, permitted to have authority only over younger women or children and required to express their virtues in terms of domestic tasks like bearing and raising children[173]. The needs of the cultic community also provide them with service opportunities beyond their focus upon their own house, but this is hardly a liberation[174]. Nevertheless, every member of the cult is assigned a well-defined role in the hierarchy, not just women, slaves, and children, but also younger men[175], older men[176], younger women[177], older women[178], widows[179], deacons[180], bishops[181], and even elders with double duty[182]. A pecking order is established, as well as a series of responsibilities, wherein each member by playing his or her role contributes to the overall health of the community.

The Pastorals also use this standard of good order polemically. Without rehearsing the evidence gathered earlier, we should recall that the major accusation, beyond living a life of vice, which the author makes towards his opponents is that they produce disorder and disharmony in the

---

[168] 1 Tim. 6.1–2; Tit. 2.9.
[169] 1 Tim. 3.7; Tit. 1.6.
[170] 1 Tim. 5.14.
[171] 1 Tim. 2.1–2; Tit. 3.1.
[172] 1 Tim. 2.2; Tit. 3.2.
[173] 1 Tim. 2.15; Tit. 2.3–5.
[174] The possibility of an order of widows and the question of its status is the most provocative topic in this regard. Certainly Ignatius *Smyrnaeans* 13.1; Ignatius *Polycarp* 4.1; and Polycarp *Philippians* 4.3 evidence the likelihood of such a formal order. The most comprehensive argument supporting the existence of such an order in the Pastorals can be found in J. Ernst, "Die Witwenregel des Ersten Timotheusbriefes," *Theologie und Glaube* 59(1969): 434–45. For more moderate views cf. Brox, *Die Pastoralbriefe*, pp. 185–87; Hanson, *The Pastoral Epistles*, pp. 37–38; Dibelius-Conzelmann, *The Pastoral Epistles*, pp. 73–76.
[175] 1 Tim. 5.1; Tit. 2.6.
[176] 1 Tim. 5.1; Tit. 2.2.
[177] 1 Tim. 5.2; Tit. 2.4–5.
[178] 1 Tim. 5.2; Tit. 2.3.
[179] 1 Tim. 5.3–5, 9–16.
[180] 1 Tim. 3.8–10, 12–13.
[181] 1 Tim. 3.1–6; Tit. 1.6–9.
[182] 1 Tim. 5.17.

church[183]. They mislead women[184], upset whole households[185], including the household of the church, by introducing speculation and controversy rather than God's plan of salvation[186]. At this point we can better understand the danger of such results, for it destroys the system of order by which the church must function if salvation is to be made available. This high regard for good order is reflected even in the terminology of the vices, which are applied to these heterodox teachers, illustrating that the specific terms in these ethical lists are not collected carelessly. The list at 2 Tim. 3.1f., beyond general accusations of wildness and implacability (ἄστοργοι, ἄσπονδοι, ἀκρατεῖς, ἀνήμεροι), which have obvious negative implications for someone's value to communal life, includes the charge of being disobedient to parent (γονεῦσιν ἀπειθεῖς). The accusation in 1 Tim. 1.9–10 is even more focused upon their danger to proper order. They are lawless (ἄνομοι), disobedient (ἀνυπότακτοι), and even kill their mothers and father (in a bit of hyperbole). They are in short the immediate enemies of church and social order. The term ἀνυπότακτοι articulates the idea of order and disorder succinctly. The group of terms, τάξις, τάγμα, and τάσσω, often designate the lining up in proper rank by an army or the proper positioning of oneself in the cosmos or in any relationship[187]. The Pastorals employ the term ὑποταγή to refer to the subordinate position of women, children, and slaves. Women are to learn ἐν ὑποταγῇ to men (1 Tim. 2.11), and bishops are to keep their children ἐν ὑποταγῇ (1 Tim. 3.4). Since ὑποταγή with its linkage to concepts of a hierarchy of order evokes the position of subordination, women and children are thus being reminded to remember their place. The verbal form ὑποτάσσεσθαι is used for admonishing slaves to obey their masters (Tit. 2.9) and all Christians to obey the secular authorities (Tit. 3.1). Every member of the community is assigned a position in this taxis; consequently, when the author's opponents are accused of being ἀνυπότακτοι, they are not only being condemned for being out of position but for undermining the taxis of the church.

Lips and Balch have furnished us with analyses of this pattern of order in the church, which they feel is based on analogies to the common arrangements and management structures of households in the Greco-Roman world[188]. Lips has shown that both the terms and the hierarchical

---

[183] 1 Tim. 1.4; 2.8; 6.4–5; 2 Tim. 2.14, 16, 23; Tit. 3.9–11.

[184] 1 Tim. 3.6.

[185] 1 Tim. 2.18; 3.6; Tit. 1.11.

[186] 1 Tim. 1.4.

[187] On the wide range of these terms see Gerhard Delling, "τάσσω, κτλ.," TDNT, 8:1–49. One can be subject to such things as the gods or the virtues, but it usually refers to being subject to another person. It can also mean to draw up behind in rank or to subject beneath. See also Liddell and Scott, *Greek-English Lexicon*, s.v. τάσσω.

[188] For the most comprehensive analysis of the philosophical topic, "Concerning Household Management," see Balch, *Let Wives Be Submissive*, pp. 23–62. Balch presents a full bibliography of ancient texts and modern studies, though he draws out the specific parallels only to 1 Peter.

structure used to express this taxis in the Pastorals are modelled on the terms and structures used for the management and arrangements of Greco-Roman households (οἰκονομία). In fact, the duties which fall upon the οἰκονόμος of the οἶκος θεοῦ are analogous to those for the οἰκονόμος of any household, as are the duties of women, slaves, younger men and women, and children. It is no accident that the terms οἰκονόμος and οἰκονομία have their major usage in designating secular managers and managements of households. Nor is it an accident that the church is called οἶκος θεοῦ (1 Tim. 3.15). Moreover, ὑποτάσσεαθαι, ὑποταγή, ἐπιταγή, ἀντιλέγοντες, ἀνυπότακτοι, προΐστασθαι, ἐπιμελεῖσθαι, παραγγέλλειν, πειθαρχεῖν, along with the parenetic terms, διδάσκειν, ἐλέγχειν, παι-δεύειν, ἐπιτιμᾶν, κτλ., have coinage in discussions of households and occur as well in the Pastorals[189]. Lips' linguistic and conceptual evidence is convincing, especially when combined with the phenomenological parallels suggested by Balch. Furthermore, the Pastorals themselves expressly articulate this link between the house and the church.

> He [a bishop] must rule (προΐστασθαι) his own household well, keeping his children submissive (ἐν ὑποταγῇ) with all dignity; for if he does not know how to rule his own household, how can he care for (ἐπιμελήσεται) the church of God (ἐκκλησία θεοῦ) (1 Tim. 3.4–5).

"Let deacons be husbands of one wife, who rule (προϊστάμενοι) their children and households well" (1 Tim. 3.12). "I wish young widows to marry, to bear children, to rule households (οἰκοδεσποτεῖν), and to give no opportunity to the enemy to revile us" (1 Tim. 5.14). "Let all who are under the yoke of slavery regard their masters as worthy of all honor, so that the name of God and teaching may not be blasphemed" (1 Tim. 6.1)[190].

The apologetic role of this material is manifest in 1 Tim. 5.14 and 6.1 (quoted above) and reflects the milieu of criticism and skepticism towards new cults and their impact upon social order, as documented by Balch. But the apology is not purely rhetorical, an attempt to avoid traducements by putting on fancy dress, because the Pastorals co-opt for the real structure of their church government the standards and patterns most acceptable in the Greco-Roman world. The οἰκονομία of the οἶκος θεοῦ is not based upon the idiosyncratic patterns detectable in other early Christian communities, where the spirit and eschatological ideas produce a community ruled by prophets, apostles, and anyone moved by the spirit[191]. Those communities would be in disorder (ἄτακτοι). Perhaps the

---

Lips' study is much briefer, concentrates more on linguistic phenomena, and details all the parallels he can find to the Pastorals (*Glaube, Gemeinde, Amt*, pp. 121–50).

[189]See complete listing of terms in Lips, *Glaube, Gemeinde, Amt* pp. 132–35.

[190]For further evidence see ibid., pp. 143–50.

[191]Hans von Campenhausen, *Ecclesiastical Authority and Spiritual Power in the Church of the First Three Centuries*, trans. J. A. Baker (Stanford: Stanford University Press, 1969); Eduard Schweizer, *Church Order in the New Testament* (Naperville, Ill.: Alec R. Allenson, 1961); Bengt Holmberg, *Paul and Power: The Structure of Authority in the Primitive Church as Reflected in the Pauline Epistles* (Philadelphia: Fortress Press, 1980). For an analysis of the roles of office in

author's opponents wanted to return to or maintain non-hierarchical patterns, but the author does not. Just as he co-opted the ideal of the virtuous life for his own ends, he also co-opts the concept of good order and employs it as the basic social structure of his community. This is sociologically significant, for it shows that the author does not surrender to these standards by allowing them in the side door or by using them to disguise idiosyncratic cultic patterns. Instead, by using these standards of the household as the foundation upon which salvation depends, the author betrays the fact that he is a natural and comfortable member of his culture.

The full implications of the accusation in 1 Tim. 1.3–4 can now be comprehended. Paul left Timothy in Ephesus so that he could command certain people to cease promulgating heterodoxy and adhering to myths and genealogies, "which produce speculation (ἐκζητήσεις) rather than God's plan (οἰκονομία θεοῦ) which is in faith." The οἰκονομία θεοῦ entertains a double reference, evoking both God's method of managing the cosmos and God's method of managing the church. Cosmic order and cultic order come together with the cultic order being a moment in the cosmic, albeit a necessary moment for the effectiveness of the cosmic plan. The disorder engendered by the speculations and freedoms practiced by these heterodox teachers assaults directly the taxis of the church; and, by so doing, these heterodox teachers threaten the salvific structure of the cosmos itself. Unless the proper taxis of the community is maintained, with ethical officers enjoying obedience and honor, the ethical warrants proffered by their example and by their teachings are not mediated to the individual believers; and, consequently, salvation will not occur.

The ethic, which issues from warrants proffered only by the cult and which focuses its virtues upon the maintenance of the proper taxis in the church, is less an individual ethic and more a communal one. This does not mean that the community itself is saved on judgment day and that individuals enjoy heavenly rewards only by being card-carrying members of the cult. In fact, the author would deny that baptism into the cultic community is sufficient for salvation. The individual is judged as individual on the basis of virtues and vices. However, the virtues, which are required, are not ascetic ones which demonstrate private powers (ἀρεταί) but public ones which show one's value (ὠφέλιμος) to the community. The predominance of meekness and gentleness, as opposed to implacability and aggressiveness, illustrates the cultic orientation of these terms. But even more telling is the inescapable fact that every warrant necessary to the virtuous life, to εὐσέβεια, lies in the hands of select bishops and elders. God's plan of salvation subsumes the individual to the authority of the cult.

---

the Pastorals see Hanson, *The Pastoral Epistles*, pp. 31–38, and Lips, *Glaube, Gemeinde, Amt*, esp. pp. 106–21, 147–60, 206–65. Lips, Campenhausen, and Schweizer more or less agree in distinguishing the leadership style and pattern from earlier models.

To these virtue and vice lists and his delineation of community order, which inculcate an ethical life focusing upon communal life, the author adds a diverse array of parenetic forms, in order to fill out his portrayal of the content of the ethical life. Inductive paradigms built upon Paul's life, as we have seen, depict patterns of behavior and standards which are supposed to shape the life of all subsequent Christians. To a lesser degree positive illustrative paradigms built upon Timothy, Titus, Onesiphorus, and others also give definition to this life. These are, of course, balanced by negative illustrative paradigms, which define the nature of the ethical life by drawing the borderline which should not be crossed. Beyond these paradigms, the author also provides positive and negative descriptions, such as the positive group of elements in 1 Tim. 3.1–7 which lists the pre-requisites for a bishop and the negative prophecy in 2 Tim. 3.1–9 which describes the nature of disobedient people in the last days. These descriptions, in fact, include virtues and vices, propositions about orthodoxy and heterodoxy, evaluations of certain people and certain behavior on the community, imperatival instructions, and doctrinal warrants. The logical form of these accounts is both enthymematic and paradigmatic.

The paideutic function of these descriptions can be seen in the juxta-position of a negative and a positive description in 1 Tim. 4.1–10[192]. The negative description is presented as a prophecy by the spirit about the apostates of the later days. The apostates wander after deceptive spirits ($\pi\nu\epsilon\acute{u}\mu\alpha\tau\alpha$ $\pi\lambda\acute{a}\nu o\iota$) and the teachings of demons; therefore, we can infer that their own teachings would be demonic and deceptive. They practice asceticism, which the author believes contradicts the friendly nature of God's cosmos. Thus the negative description contains two major elements: these people adhere to and promulgate the wrong teachings, and they practice the wrong life-style. Similarly, the positive description contains these same elements, only in opposite terms. It is presented more directly as an exhortation to Timothy in imperatival form with descriptive elements appended. He is enjoined to impose the correct teachings upon his brothers, while it is noted that he has long been nourished by these teachings himself and has continuously eschewed the opposite teachings. He trains himself not in the ascetic practices of forbidding marriages or foods but towards piety. His training is contrasted with that of the ascetics with the maxim: "For bodily training is of little value, but piety is useful in every way, having the promise of life now and to come." To this assertion is attached a cosmological warrant. Therefore, the author delineates a con-trast between the life-style of the heterodox and that of the orthodox. In so doing, he employs once again all the ethical warrants which his system supplies and which we have encountered in other contexts, putting them in both enthymematic and paradigmatic arguments.

---

[192]We should recall here the discussion in the preceding chapter on the tendency in diatribe to argue in terms of ethical contrasts.

We have argued above, on the basis of this and other evidence, that the author's church endured at least two sets of opinions about what is ethical and what is not. The negative descriptions imply the presence of opponents who owned different positions on sound teaching, virtue, doctrine, and certainly church government. The author takes surprising pains to articulate the contrasts. He defends his own version first of all with the fiction of the letter, but he also enters into debate with his opponents, even though the shape of the debate is determined by genre considerations[193]. For instance, he specifically rejects the asceticism of his opponents, not just by the fiat of having Paul reject it and banishing it from the realm of sound teaching, but also by appeals to cosmological principles, to logic, and to the bar of what is useful ($\dot{\omega}\varphi\acute{e}\lambda\iota\mu o\varsigma$) to communal life[194]. Admittedly the fiction of the letters bestows cosmological authority upon his version and thus in some ways undermines or overwhelms the seriousness of these debates; nevertheless, the author does engage his opponents' point of view, taking care to articulate their position and to refute it according to acceptable norms. This rather humane tactic agrees with the author's expressed opinion that rebuke should be exercised only in a spirit of gentleness so that the heterodox can be saved.

When all these elements are totalled up, a fairly clear picture of the correct life-style emerges. The outline is complete, and the details can be filled in by the bishops and elders as the occasion arises. Warrants and standards are available for learning how to live correctly, if one accepts the author's fiction. But in a way this is only half of the problem, for in contrast to the Socratic tradition, knowing what to do does not ensure being able to do it. The cult will provide powers for that task, just as it provides warrants.

E. Outfitted for Good Works

1. Baptism

The old Socratic dictum that knowing the good inevitably led to doing the good no longer held probative force in the empire. The question of

---

[193]Brox, *Die Pastoralbriefe*, p. 39, agreeing with Hasler, declares (incorrectly I think) that the author does not combat the false teachings but only the false teachers. In my opinion, he does both.

[194]1 Tim. 4.3—5, 7—9. Cf. 1 Tim. 6.3—10, where the danger of the love of money is analyzed with some care, using a variety of theological warrants. It is true that in 2 Tim. 2.18 the doctrine that the resurrection has already happened is not analyzed but rather the teachers of the doctrine are placed outside God's community. Of course, the many speculations of which that doctrine is a part are combatted throughout the letters by the incessant demand for order.

whether the virtuous life is possible or whether a true wise man exists became a constant topic of discussion among Greco-Roman ethicists[195]. Even for a person like Epictetus, for whom success in the moral realm is the only worthy goal of life, the possibility of achieving wisdom is problematic. For instance, we noted above that he does not accord himself the honor of being completely wise, of having reached the goal, for he confesses that he still pampers his body too much for a true wise man[196]. He does of course claim that the past had produced true wise men among the Stoic and Cynic pantheon[197], but that does not lessen the fact that the problem was pressing for him. And we noticed that the author of 4 Maccabees claims that no Greek or Roman can be virtuous, because the virtuous life is conceivable only in dependence on the Jewish law[198]. Without gathering more evidence we may assume that providing standards was not always a sufficient grounding for an ethical system; there must be a further argument made demonstrating how those standards can be met.

We have seen that the author of the Pastorals creates warrants and standards for his ethic through the peculiar position of the cultic leaders and their possession of the entrusted traditions. He draws a full picture of the virtuous life, so that no one who admits the claims of his letters can deny knowing what the standards are. One need only read the letters or consult the cultic leaders. Nevertheless, the question remains of whether one can meet those requirements.

The paradigms of Paul, Timothy, and Titus, with their fidelity to the sound teaching and their completion of the tasks assigned them, function first of all by proving the possibility of success[199]. The positive illustrative paradigm of Onesiphorus does much the same. But the author supplies further arguments by furnishing two tools or powers or resources which increase the possibilities: baptism and education.

Lips has argued cogently that Timothy and Titus are able to fulfill their special assignments because of the spirit which was given them in ordination[200]. The same spirit is by inference to be imposed upon subsequent

---

[195] For a clear introduction to a complex subject see Pohlenz, *Die Stoa*, pp. 153—58; G. B. Kerford, "What Does the Wise Man Know?" in *The Stoics*, ed. John M. Rist (Berkeley: University of California Press, 1978), pp. 125—36. Sandbach, *The Stoics*, p. 44, asserts that after Chrysippus it became orthodox Stoicism to regard wisdom as an unattainable ideal. See Seneca *Letters to Lucilius* 1.24: "What I mean, Lucilius, is this: the good is not to be found in any person whatever in any age whatever." But Seneca frequently speaks of the *vir bonus* as though he existed; e.g., the dialogue "On Providence" examines the question of why bad things happen to good men without ever questioning the existence of such men.

[196] Epictetus 4.1.151—52.

[197] Ibid., 1.4.24; 1.9.22; 1.12.23; 1.24.6—10; 1.29.16—19; 4.1.152—59.

[198] 4 Maccabees 2.23.

[199] See the discussion in the preceding chapter on inductive paradigms.

[200] Lips, *Glaube, Gemeinde, Amt*, pp. 206—65. Lips concentrates on the χάρισμα bestowed in 1 Tim. 4.14 and 2 Tim. 1.6. These are obviously ordination texts. He includes πνεῦμα because 2 Tim. 1.7 includes it. On Lips' opinion on the relationship of the spirit to baptism and to all believers see pp. 260—63.

church leaders and thereby empowers them to complete the special requirements of leadership. The χάρισμα or the πνεῦμα is an enabler, which
at least applies to church officers. We also noted earlier that the author
believes that the spirit is not a guide in the Pauline sense but a superhuman power which enables one to do things normally beyond reach.
This is of course the prevalent understanding of πνεῦμα in the Greco-
Roman world. Further, the author connects this spirit with baptism, making it a gift available to every individual, to every single member of the
cult[201]. This connection with baptism is crucial for the persuasiveness of
his ethic. The task of every member of the cult is ethically oriented, and,
with the spirit in hand, every member has a unique capacity for meeting
those ethical tasks. The spirit, as the special gift of the cultic act of baptism, provides a unique answer to how the ethical life is possible[202].

The key passage is Tit. 3.4—7, which we have consulted before in different contexts. Here we note that "[God] saved us through the bath of
regeneration (διὰ λουτροῦ παλιγγενεσίας) and the renewal of the holy
spirit (ἀνακαινώσεως πνεύματος ἁγίου), which he poured out upon us
richly." This doctrinal proposition unites the three concepts of baptism,
the spirit, and regeneration[203].

Dibelius-Conzelmann have argued that παλιγγενεσία, meaning renewal,
should be understood in the context of the mysteries[204]. It refers there
and in other places to the renewal which occurs after death, but it also on
occasion designated the mystical renewal which occurs in the cultic acts
of the mysteries. "It is clear that the term rebirth is closely connected
with the transfer of vital powers in the cult."[205] The mystical transition

---

[201]Including all Christians under the power of the spirit is done on the basis of Tit. 3.4—7.
Every major commentator admits the baptismal background of this language. For the most detailed
analysis see Hanson, "Elements of a Baptismal Liturgy in Titus."

[202]The connections between baptism and parenetic forms in the Pastorals are complex. The re-
lation of household codes to baptism is probable: see discussions and bibliography in Balch, *Let
Wives Be Submissive*, pp. 11—14; Hanson, *Studies in the Pastoral Epistles*, pp. 86—91. Most schol-
ars also connect virtue and vice lists to baptism: Kamlah, *Die Form der katalogischen Paränese im
Neuen Testament*, pp. 176—216, who detects baptismal allusions scattered throughout the lists;
Carrington, *The Primitive Christian Catechism*; Betz, *Galatians*, p. 285, notes the importance of
Did. 7.1, "Concerning baptism: Having first repeated all these things [the virtue and vice lists in
Did. 1—6] .... " These connections, when coupled with the evidence below, indicate that the gift
of the spirit which comes in baptism was a crucial moment in the author's ethic. We might say
that he prefers to argue in the syles most closely aligned with baptismal exhortations.

[203]Hanson, *Studies in the Pastoral Epistles*, pp. 84—89, wants to greatly extend the seminal
concepts related to baptism in this passage, but he certainly would include these three. Hanson
believes that comparisons with 1 Peter and Ephesians suggest a baptismal liturgy in skeletal form
which extends from Tit. 2.1 through 3.8. He does not think the author copied either 1 Peter or
Ephesians but relies on a traditional pattern of baptismal liturgy peculiar to Asia Minor.

[204]Dibelius-Conzelmann, *The Pastoral Epistles*, pp. 148—50. Cf. Joseph Dey, ΠΑΛΙΓΓΕΝΕ-
ΣΙΑ, *Ein Beitrag zur Klärung der religionsgeschichtlichen Bedeutung von Tit. 3.5*, Neutestamentliche Abhandlungen 17,5 (Münster: Aschendorff, 1937); Friedrich Büchsel, "γίνομαι, κτλ.,"
TDNT, 1:686—89. See Dibelius–Conzelmann, *The Pastoral Epistles*, p. 150, n. 20, for further
bibliography.

[205]Dibelius-Conzelmann, *The Pastoral Epistles*, p. 149.

which occurs through παλιγγενεσία places the participant into immediate contact with heavenly realities of some kind. Usually these realities would insure immortality by bestowing special knowledge or by creating a new person who exists in the spiritual realm rather than the physical. In much the same way παλιγγενεσία in the Pastorals provides the novitiate with immediate contact with heavenly realities by bestowing the spirit. And though we cannot quite say that a new person is born by this process, we can say that an anthropological transformation takes place which makes the person more powerful than before. The fact that the author subsumes this transformation to his ethical system, with the spirit enabling the ethical life, does not negate the equally important fact that an anthropological transformation dispensed by the cult is a prerequisite.

Curiously Dibelius-Conzelmann assert that the exclusivity implied in the mysteries by the term rebirth is not in force in the Pastorals, because "rebirth is . . . not solely available to certain individual mystics, but is the fundamental event and experience of all Christians"[206]. But this is to miss the direction of the argument. Exclusivity results from the very fact that rebirth is the "fundamental event and experience of all Christians" and, we must add, only Christians. With this move, the cultic control is made complete. The ethic becomes totally a cultic ethic, for not only are the warrants and standards only accessible within the cult but the ability to meet those standards only comes from participating in a ritual dispensed at the discretion of that cult. There is no virtue outside of the church doors.

The role of the spirit, therefore, appears to be an argument directed as much at outsiders as insiders[207]. Even though it is doubtful that the author spun this concept of the spirit out of his own head, since it appears to have been a fairly traditional idea in early Christianity, its peculiar function in his ethical system probably comes from the author[208]. Recalling that membership in the cult is not alone sufficient for salvation in the author's eyes, since virtue must be achieved or all is for naught, we may infer that possession of the spirit in itself is not enough. Perhaps his opponents, with their doctrine of the resurrection already having occurred, articulated a higher concept of the spirit in which its possession insured immortality, as rebirth does in the mysteries or gnosis among the gnostics[209].

---

[206]Ibid., p. 150.

[207]At the same time, the author reminds Timothy that he has the spirit and what kind of spirit he has. Thus in a way the distinction is a false one, for everyone needs to be told what the spirit is and how it enters a human life.

[208]I am not arguing that the connection of the spirit with baptism or with Christian ethics is unique, since that is a common early Christian linkage, but that the manner in which these ideas are incorporated into his system is, if not unique, at least different from the rest of the New Testament.

[209]Cf. *The Treatise on the Resurrection*, where possession of the turth and the spirit insures life. In many ways, of course, this is a Pauline doctrine: Albert Schweitzer, *The Mysticism of Paul*

The author has co-opted the ethical and social ideals of the Greco-Roman world. The virtues he enjoins and the taxis he exhorts are consistent with the commonplace ethics of his day, even if he colors them with a communal hue. Therefore, the ideal life to which most of his contemporaries would aspire is claimed to be in the possession of the church. But more than that, by structuring a plan of salvation in which all the reliable warrants are in the hands of the cult and then by proposing that the cultic ritual of baptism bestows the ability to realize the ethic, the author makes a radical claim of exclusivity. Only the baptized and obedient Christian can live the life most people want to live. Thus, to extend the argument a bit, if a citizen of the Roman empire read this letter and accepted the fiction, logically he or she should then submit both to baptism and to the moral and social authority of the Christian cult.

2. Education

When Plutarch essays to demonstrate that virtue is teachable, he is addressing one of the most popular topics in Greco-Roman philosophy[210]. The insistence that virtue is teachable and in fact can be acquired in no other way sits at the heart of the school tradition, because the dynamic of teacher-student, which determines so much of the structure of the Platonic and Stoic schools in the empire, presupposes that virtue can and must be taught[211]. Even the Cynics, who place so much emphasis on the power of nature, do not take the option proffered and rejected in Aristotle that virtue could be innate, but rather create teacher-student relationships and insist upon training and learning[212]. Education ($\pi\alpha\iota\delta\epsilon\iota\alpha$) is the constant and necessary companion to ethics. Therefore, it is certainly no surprise that the Pastorals with their concentration upon ethics should also proclaim a doctrine of education.

---

the Apostle, trans. William Montgomery (New York: Seabury Press, 1968), pp. 160—68, who cites, among others, Rom. 8.11; 2 Cor. 1.22; 1 Cor. 15.45—49.

[210]Plutarch, "Can Virtue Be Taught?" Diogenes Laertius 2.121, 122, attributed to Crito a diatribe entitled, "That Men are not made Good by Instruction," and to Simon one entitled, "That Virtue cannot be Taught." The most focused discussion in Plato on the teachability of virtue occurs in the *Meno* but the value of education and inquiry is a necessary presupposition to Plato's whole project. Werner Jaeger, *Paideia: The Ideals of Greek Culture*, Vol. 2, trans. Gilbert Highet (New York: Oxford University Press, 1943).

[211]Wendland, *Die hellenistisch-römische Kultur*, pp. 75—91; Émile Bréhier, *The Hellenistic and Roman Age*, The History of Philosophy, trans. Wade Baskin (Chicago: University of Chicago Press, 1965), pp. 98—126.

[212]Diogenes Laertius 6.105: "They [the Cynics] hold, further, that virtue can be taught, as Antisthenes maintains in his 'Heracles,' and when once acquired cannot be lost." For the school setting of Cynics see p. 161, n. 125 above but also Stowers, *The Diatribe and Paul's Letter to the Romans*, on Teles and Bion (pp. 50—53) and Maximus of Tyre (pp. 67—68). Stowers argues that even the street preacher model for Cynics is accommodated to school patterns (p. 77). Certainly the Cynic Epistles are incomprehensible without appreciation of this educational pattern.

The importance of teaching for the author of the Pastorals has already attracted our attention in the fiction that Paul's teaching role is passed down and continued in the author's church. Paul, Timothy, Titus, and living officers are all designated as teachers[213]. One of the prerequisites of bishops and elders, which occurs in the virtue lists, is that they be διδακτικοί[214]. And Timothy, Titus, and those appointed by them are continuously commanded to teach[215]. The basic term διδασκαλία occurs fifteen times in the letters; and to this must be added an array of cognates: διδάσκειν, διδάσκαλος, ἑτεροδιδασκαλεῖν, διδακτικός, νομοδιδάσκαλος, and διδαχή. If the weight of the material in the letters corresponds to the amount of activity in the author's church, then most of its energy is spent in teaching. Teaching takes two forms: either that of the heterodox teachers (ἑτεροδιδασκαλεῖν)[216], who upset whole households and produce vices, or that of the selected church officers, who teach the sound doctrines (ὑγιαίνουσα διδασκαλία)[217]. The latter is, of course, grounded in the fiction of succession, where the teacher, Paul, instructs the teacher, Titus, to appoint elders, who can in turn teach with the sound teachings and rebuke the heterodox[218].

The author recognizes the danger of his opponents by the heterodoxy of what they teach and the disruptions to the community which result. The author denigrates their success among the members of the church by combining a popular ancient maxim with prophetic language: "For the time is coming when people will not endure the sound teaching, but having itching ears they will accumulate teachers for themselves which suit their own likings" (2 Tim. 4.3). In the same vein the one activity of women which upsets the author more than anything else is that they should dare to teach men. It is not to be allowed (1 Tim. 2.12).

Lips has analyzed the various terms, πίστις, ἀλήθεια, εὐαγγέλιον, διδασκαλία, and εὐσέβεια, and concludes that the author combines them in a unique way. The combination focuses upon the aspect of knowledge inherent to these ideas and consequently upon the teachability of faith[219]. This knowledge has a high moral dimension and is dependent upon the realization of this knowledge in ethical deeds[220]. For our purposes, Lips' analysis demonstrates that all the key terms the author uses to describe his understanding of faith connect to the dynamics of teaching.

---

[213]Only Paul receives the noun (1 Tim. 2.7; 2 Tim. 1.11), but the verb is applied to others (e.g., 1 Tim. 4.11; 6.2; 2 Tim. 2.2; Tit. 2.1).

[214]1 Tim. 3.2; 2 Tim. 2.2, 24.

[215]1 Tim. 4.6, 11, 16; 5.17; 6.2; 2 Tim. 3.16; 4.2; Tit. 2.1. Of course this list is misleadingly sparse since it refers only to διδάσκαλος and its cognates. In fact, the author uses a wide, variety of didactic terms. See below.

[216]1 Tim. 1.3; cf. 1 Tim. 1.10; 4.1; Tit. 1.11.

[217]2 Tim. 4.3; Tit. 1.9; 2.1. Cf. 1 Tim. 6.3; 2 Tim. 1.13.

[218]2 Tim. 2.2; Tit. 1.5.

[219]Lips, Glaube, Gemeinde, Amt, pp. 25—87.

[220]Ibid., p. 87.

The teaching model even invades the literary structure of the letters. For instance, the letter to Titus opens with an injunction to appoint elders who can teach and who adhere to the sound teachings, then proceeds (Tit. 1.9b–16) to analyze the heterodox teaching, the heterodox teachers, and their impact, and then moves to the positive injunction to Timothy to teach according to the sound doctrine, adding a description of what that entails and accomplishes (1 Tim. 2.1–10). Apparently, the polarity between good teaching and bad determines the literary structure of the chapter, with the two teaching options displayed in separate sections as contrary interpretations of the nature of church office.

The exigencies of teaching influence the diatribe style of the letters as well. Stowers' work on the diatribe has shown that the primary setting of the diatribe is not that of Dio Chrysostom, the streetcorner preacher, but that of Epictetus, the schoolmaster[221]. All the major practitioners of diatribe in the Hellenistic era, with the possible exception of Philo, betray a school background. Admittedly there was, on occasion, no extant school in which these diatribes were proclaimed, but even then the paideutic model of teacher addressing student is imported into the framework of the diatribe[222]. This teacher-student pattern transcends the limits of genre, for when Seneca is writing his diatribe-style letters to Lucilius, he creates an external framework of a teacher-student relationship, imitating the school setting of the diatribe[223].

As we have seen, the parenetic pattern which repeats itself in all these diatribes is based upon the concerns of rhetoric, which endeavors to persuade rather than syllogistically prove. The Socratic method of persuasion, which established the pattern for diatribe, was that of rebuke or censure

---

[221]Stowers, *The Diatribe and Paul's Letter to the Romans*, pp. 48–78. In this assessment of the milieu of the diatribe, Stowers must take strong exception to most previous scholarship. Stowers traces the concept of the itinerate preacher and the streetcorner as the catalyst for diatribe to Wilamowitz (p. 51), but demonstrates the classroom setting for all major exponents of diatribe, with the possible exception of Philo.

[222]Stowers, ibid., believes Teles, Epictetus, Musonius, and Plutarch wrote their diatribes specifically for the classroom, while Die Chrysostom, Maximus of Tyre, and Seneca, none of whom were attached to a school, imported the classroom style, especially the teacher-student relationship.

[223]Seneca's relationship to the diatribe is a much controverted issue, depending in large part on how one defines the genre. Stowers speaks of a growing consensus that Seneca used the diatribe style if not the genre (ibid., pp. 69–70). But, as he himself admits, the relationships among διάλεξις, διάλογος, and διατριβή are subtle, and scholars are not in agreement on their individual definitions or the borders between them. See Cancik, *Untersuchungen zu Senecas epistulae morales*, pp. 46–58, for a discussion of this problem relative to Seneca and for further bibliography. Cancik believes Seneca only called his work *dialogi* because Latin had no other term. For our purposes this confusion over terms and specific genre does not present a real problem since Seneca's style is manifestly a combination of "diatribe" (diatribe as defined as that genre or style which Teles, Musonius, Epictetus, Seneca et al. employ) and the philosophical letter. Thus our uncertainty over what genre tag to apply does not undermine the deep stylistic analogies to the Pastorals, which combine "diatribe" with the Pauline letter.

(ἐλεγχός) coupled with encouragement (προτρεπτικός)[224]. Stowers quotes Epictetus, who attributes the origin of his teaching style to Socrates.

> He, then who can show to each man the contradiction which causes him to err, and can clearly bring home to him how he is not doing what he wishes, and is doing what he does not wish, is strong in argument, and at the same time effective in both encouragement (προτρεπτικός) and refutation (ἐλεγκτικός)[225].

Thus two parenetic methods alternate in these diatribes: that of rebuke and that of encouragement.

The Pastorals impose this same dual task upon Timothy, Titus, and church officers. The similarities are striking. At Tit. 1.9 "Paul" instructs (παρακαλεῖν) Titus to appoint elders who can both encourage (παρακαλεῖν) with the sound teaching and rebuke (ἐλέγχειν) those who are opposed. These two parenetic styles recur throughout the letters, though the exact terms fluctuate. At 1 Tim. 5.3 Timothy is instructed not to rebuke (ἐπιπλήσσειν) older men but to encourage (παρακαλεῖν) them as fathers. And those inside the community who are not expressly part of the apostasy can also feel the sting of rebuke, for at 1 Tim. 5.20 Timothy is enjoined to rebuke (ἐλέγχειν) publicly all who sin. On the other side, the opponents at 2 Tim. 2.25 are to be instructed with meekness (ἐν πραΰτητι παιδεύειν), so that they can repent and enjoy salvation. The teaching itself is termed a παράκλησις at 1 Tim. 4.13. Women are encouraged (παρακαλεῖν) to domesticity at Tit. 2.6, 15. And Paul encourages (παρακαλεῖν) Timothy at 1 Tim. 1.3 and the whole church at 1 Tim. 2.1. The fluidity of this terminology is no hindrance to making parallels with other diatribes, since no one adheres strictly to technical terminology in Hellenistic parenesis. Epictetus certainly does not limit himself so προτρεπτικός and ἐλεγκτικός[226]. For a nice summary we can refer to 2 Tim. 4.2: "Paul" articulates the teaching task with a series of imperatives, κήρυξον τὸν λόγον, ἐπίστηθι εὐκαίρως ἀκαίρως, ἔλεγξον, ἐπιτίμησον, παρακάλεσον, κτλ.

To this range of evidence illustrating the author's fondness for language about teaching and instruction must be added evidence of the author's concern for the other side of the teacher-student dynamic. Scattered throughout the letters is a series of terms describing the learning process in positive terms: μανθάνειν, ἀκούειν, ἐπιγινώσκειν, ἀκοή, νοῦς, ἐπίγνωσις ἀληθείας, κτλ. On the negative side occurs a similar collage: ἀνατρέπειν, ἀποτρέπειν, ἐκτρέπειν, ἀποστρέφειν, ἐκστρέφειν, ἀρνεῖσ-

---

[224]Schmidt, "Die drei Arten des Philosophierens," pp. 14—28.

[225]Epictetus 2.26.4. Stowers, The Diatribe and Paul's Letter to the Romans, pp. 57—75, traces the use of this two-sided dynamic and the changes of terminology associated with it through the major exponents of diatribe, concluding that diatribe as a genre should be defined as "discourses and discussion in the school where the teacher employed the 'Socratic' method of censure and protreptic" (p. 76).

[226]See for example, ἐπιτιμᾶν (Epictetus 3.23.93—94) or the list of terms at 3.21.19.

ϑαι, κτλ. With these terms and others the author paints two portraits of what can happen in the learning process, one of learning, gaining knowledge, and accepting the proper authorities, the other of opposition, turning away, perversion of the truth, and rebellion.

We have already noticed detailed descriptions of the teaching process (1 Tim. 4.11—16 and Tit. 2.1f.), and the author also depicts the learning process in detail. 2 Tim. 3.14—17 is shaped by the fiction of Paul reminding Timothy of his childhood upbringing[227]:

> But as for you, continue in what you have learned, knowing from whom you learned it and how from childhood you have been acquainted with the sacred writings which are able to make you wise for salvation through faith in Christ Jesus. All scripture is inspired by God and profitable for teaching (διδασκαλία), for reproof (ἐλεγμός), for correction (ἐπανόρθωσις), for education (παιδεία) in righteousness, so that the man of God may be complete, equipped for every good work.

Even if Timothy does fit adequately this imagined childhood, this passage is less concerned with the legends of Timothy than with the author's theory of education processes in his church. The claim that the ultimate purpose of education is for salvation results from its ostensive ability to produce virtue. And we note again the language of rebuke and correction. The introduction of scripture as a major pedagogical device is consonant with the author's own use of scripture, even though scripture on occasion functions more as a mine of paradigms (2 Tim. 3.8)[228], or as a book of proverbs (1 Tim. 5.18)[229], than as a proscriptive and prescriptive document. On the other hand, the author does appeal to scripture and exhorts its reading in the church[230].

The elevation of scripture to the status of being one of the major ped-

---

[227] According to Acts 16.1—3, Timothy's mother was Jewish and his father was Greek. Brox, *Die Pastoralbriefe*, pp. 226—27, suggests that the author has mishandled the legends in his desire to portray the good results of Christian parents raising Christian children. Cf. Hanson, *The Pastoral Epistles*, p. 120.

[228] Hanson, *The Pastoral Epistles*, p. 147, sees this passage as a haggada based on Ex. 8.18—19 and connects it with the accusation of magic. See Hanson, *Studies in the Pastoral Epistles*, pp. 25—28, where he traces the legend in contemporary Jewish literature, especially Wis. 15.18—16.1. For an analysis of these legends see H. Odeberg, "Ἰάννης and Ἰαμβρῆς," TDNT, 3:192—93. The existence of extensive haggada on Jannes and Jambres explains why the author chose them.

[229] This passage comes from Deut. 25.4 and is used in the identical context by Paul in 1 Cor. 9.9. Hanson, *The Pastoral Epistles*, p. 102, insists "it had become a stock proof-text to show that the ordained ministry is entitled to some financial reward."

[230] See Hanson, *Studies in the Pastoral Epistles*, pp. 42—55, and, *The Pastoral Epistles*, pp. 151—52. Hanson has done the most thorough analysis of the author's use of scripture and concludes that he does not allegorize (contra Hasler) or use it as a handbook of ethics but rather follows Pauline typology. As far as that goes, it is certainly correct, though I do not think "typology" is the best term for describing the author's method. The Old Testament is not the source of the author's ethic nor does he allegorize it; however, neither does he use Pauline-style typology unless one means by that only that Jannes and Jambres are negative τύποι. Classical typological exegesis is certainly more than that. See Goppelt, *Typos*; G. W. H. Lampe and K. J. Woolcombe, *Essays on Typology* (Naperville, Ill.: Alec Allenson, 1957); James D. Smart, *The Interpretation of Scripture* (Philadelphia: Westminster Press, 1961).

agogical tools of the church raises the question of what the "sound teaching" consists[231]. At a minimum we can assume that the teachings contain everything in the letters. This includes objective items such as doctrines, ethical standards, and portraits of the proper life-style, along with the less objective and more dynamic processes of education, which are divided into protreptic and rebuke on the teaching side and into obedience and rebellion on the learning side. In this way the letters mirror the educational activity of the church. If this is so, then the observation that the Pastorals are catechetical manuals for church leaders is correct, because they detail how the teaching must take place, not just implicitly but explicitly[232]. "Until I come, attend to the public reading of scripture, to preaching, to teaching" (1 Tim. 4.13). "Let elders who rule well be considered worthy of double honor, especially those who labor in preaching and teaching" (1 Tim. 5.17). Furthermore, the many imperatives, by their constant repetition and universal validity, break through the fiction of the letters and become living commandments. Thus when "Paul" commands Timothy and Titus to teach, preach, exhort, comfort, encourage, rebuke, correct, educate (using all the different terms noted above), those imperatives reach the ears of the author's contemporaries. This overriding of the fiction is aided by the fiction itself when living church leaders are portrayed as fulfilling those imperatives.

In spite of these conclusions, the sociological information in the letters is limited. They are telling only one side of the story. In fact, although the author deals at great length with the rowdiness of heresy, he is painting an idealized picture of his church. Therefore, the pedagogical processes may look quite different in practice from what we see frozen in literary form. Unfortunately, I know of no good way to bridge the gap from subjective, fictionalized letters to sociological realities not mentioned in the text. All we can say about the church is what the letters say, and then only with hesitations. Thus, we can repeat, the teaching consists at a minimum of everything in the letters. We encountered earlier a similar need for ephectic judgment when evaluating the factual reliability of the letters in their depiction of the authority structures in the church. In fact, the bishop-elder-deacons structure, which the author advocates, with ordained officers rather than spirit-inspired people having all the teaching and preaching authority, may have very little to do with the actual state of affairs in his church. We have noted several indications that he is an abandoned leader who is promulgating an authority structure as he wishes it could be rather than as it is. Thus the portrait of the church painted here,

---

[231]Lips' careful analysis of διδασκαλία and its relationship to other terms in the letters does not fully address this question (*Glaube, Gemeinde, Amt*, pp. 29–53). Dibelius-Conzelmann, *The Pastoral Epistles*, p. 92, suggest correctly, "The content of the 'deposit' can be derived naturally from the epistle."

[232]Brox, *Die Pastoralbriefe*, pp. 9–12; Elliott, "Ministry and Church Order in the New Testament."

with its carefully arranged taxis, its school-like setting, and its pursuit of the quiet, virtuous life, may be drawn more from the imagination than from reality.

Nevertheless, the author treats his church more like a school than a cult. Just as Seneca does, he fabricates for himself a teacher-student relationship in the pedagogical dynamics between Paul, the teacher, and Timothy and Titus, the students. He employs the school-oriented diatribe style, admittedly without imaginary interlocutors or rhetorical objections and false conclusions, and combines it with the Pauline letter form and his own pseudepigraphical designs. More than anything else, of course, church leaders in the Pastorals teach. This is especially the case when we remember that all the parenetic styles employed in the letters, from enthymemes to doctrinal citations, to paradigms, to protreptic, belong to the teacher's arsenal. The cult becomes a school which teaches the ethical life and a place where students train in the virtues.

This attitude towards the cult is a natural outgrowth of the emphasis on ethics. Education and ethics go hand in hand. This linkage shows itself in the implicit stances the author takes toward several traditional ethical topics. The traditional question of whether virtue can be taught is certainly answered in the affirmative. According to the canons of Greco-Roman ethical theory, to assert this means concomitantly that one must accept the notions of progress ($\pi\rho o\kappa o\pi\acute{\eta}$) and training ($\check{\alpha}\sigma\kappa\eta\sigma\iota\varsigma$, $\gamma\upsilon\mu\nu\acute{\alpha}\zeta\epsilon\iota\nu$)[233]. Aristotle limits the acquisition of virtue to three options: either it is innate, a part of nature, and thus cannot be taught; or it is a gift of the gods and also cannot be taught; or it is acquired through learning and training, in which case it must be taught[234]. When Aristotle opts for the last, he admits as a necessary adjunct the need for teachers, for rigorous training, and for gradual progress towards virtue[235]. This notion of gradual progress becomes an essential idea to Stoicism, even though the Stoic doctrine that all sins are equal is not easily harmomized with it[236]. Seneca and Epictetus, as we have noted, both regarded themselves not as wise men but as men making progress[237].

Therefore, it is logically consistent for the author of the Pastorals, if he accepts the principle that virtue can be taught, to also accept the notions of progress and training. And he clearly adheres to both ideas. When "Paul" encourages Timothy to orthodoxy in 1 Tim. 4.15, he does

---

233 On the Socratic and Platonic roots of this concept see Jaeger, *Paideia*, 2:46–76, 166–73. See Plato, especially the *Meno*. On these terms: Gustav Stählin, "$\pi\rho o\kappa o\pi\acute{\eta}$," TDNT, 6:703–19; Hans Windisch, "$\check{\alpha}\sigma\kappa\acute{\epsilon}\omega$," TDNT, 1:494–96; Albrecht Oepke, "$\gamma\upsilon\mu\nu\acute{o}\varsigma$," TDNT, 1:773–74.

234 Aristotle *Nicomachean Ethics* 1099b1–24.

235 Ibid., 1103a14–b25.

236 On $\pi\rho o\kappa o\pi\acute{\eta}$ in the Stoics see Pohlenz, *Die Stoa*, esp. 154 (citations in 2 [1949]: 83); Sandbach, *The Stoics*, p. 48. One of Epictetus' discourses (1.4) was entitled $\pi\epsilon\rho\grave{\iota}$ $\pi\rho o\kappa o\pi\tilde{\eta}\varsigma$. On the relationship of the notion of progress to the doctrine that all sins are equal, see Rist, *Stoic Philosophy*, pp. 81–96.

237 Seneca *Epistulae morales* 26, 27; Epictetus 4.1.151.

so "in order that your progress might be manifest to all (ἵνα σου προκοπὴ φανερὰ ᾖ πᾶσιν)." He even entertains the idea of negative progress, presumably a falling away by people who were once orthodox and ethical but are becoming heterodox and profligate. In 2 Tim. 2.16 godless chatter leads (προκόπτειν) one to impiety (ἀσέβεια); in 2 Tim. 3.9 the author's opponents will not make much progress (οὐ προκόψουσιν ἐπὶ πλεῖον); and in 2 Tim. 3.13 evil people and magicians progress to the worse (προκό-ψουσιν ἐπὶ τὸ χεῖρον). The author imposes the same dualism upon the concept of training: at 1 Tim. 4.7 "Paul" admonishes Timothy, "Train (γύμναζε) yourself in piety, for bodily training is of little value, but piety is useful in every way. . . ." To this explicit citation can be added all the admonitions to learn, to hold fast, to be nourished, which denote the activity of someone in progress.

By using this school language the author is not abandoning all contact with traditional organizational patterns in the Pauline churches, replacing them with organizational models from philosophical schools. His use of the traditional terms for officers, namely, bishops, elders, deacons, the references to widows, the presence of evangelists in the community, his adherence to sacramental notions of baptism and ordination, and the permanence of the envisioned fellowship emerge from old patterns in the Pauline churches. And the results certainly do not look like the Academy. But at the same time he is shaping the traditional organizational forms along lines more sensitive to the exigencies of teaching. The taxis which results, with certain people officially designated as the only reliable source of good teaching, who are required as part of the honor of office to rule, to rebuke, to encourage, in short to behave as Epictetus does with his pupils, and with everyone else required to obey, to listen, and to learn, is a conducive setting for education. The credibility of this hierarchy is built on the elaborate fiction of the entrusted traditions and the fiction of succession; and just as the ethical system crumbles if the fiction is detected so does the structure of this cultic school. Without the fiction one is free to follow those teachers who appear to be wisest, and apparently for most people that meant choosing those creative, speculative, aggressive people who were the author's opponents. The letters give credibility to the teaching office of specific bishops and elders by linking them with Paul and his authority. Therefore, the author is attempting to crown certain teachers, who were being ignored by large portions of the church, with a pedagogical authority which they were not able to accrue on their own through the force of argument. He does this through the opportunities for rewriting history afforded him by the genre of the pseudepigraphical letter.

The author thus makes a separate ethical argument to outsiders and insiders. To outsiders he claims that the virtuous life they dream of is theirs only within the walls of the church, because only there can one undergo the anthropological rebirth of baptism, which bestows the superhuman powers of the spirit, and because only in the cult can one have immediate access to the rightful heirs of sound teaching, which is grounded in God's plan of salvation. To insiders he makes a quite different argument, although one part of it is the same. Baptism is not enough. Education is necessary. And salvation comes from successfully living the virtues. Thus, in itself, possession of the spirit or membership in the cult or even a mystical rebirth with its new knowledge provides no ticket to salvation. These things are means to the end and not the end itself. All the gifts must issue in virtues or they are useless. Therefore, the author proposes to every Christian that the task before him or her is to go into training ($\gamma\nu\mu\nu\acute{\alpha}\zeta\epsilon\iota\nu$) for piety and therein to make progress ($\pi\rho\sigma\kappa\sigma\pi\acute{\eta}$) towards the virtues. The danger is that two kinds of progress are possible, one to the better and one to the worse. And in his church both are taking place. At this point he repeats the arguments he made to outsiders. In order to make the proper kind of progress one must adhere to the correct teachigs and teachers. He carefully designates which teachers those are by fiction of the letters. If that fiction is accepted, then church members have in hand teachers and teachings that can guide them through the perilous road to virtue. It is perilous because so many miss the mark ($\mathring{\alpha}\sigma\tau\sigma\chi\epsilon\tilde{\iota}\nu$), wander after the teachings of demons and deceitful spirits, sear their consciences, suffer shipwreck in the faith, and earn condemnation on judgment day. If there is a question as to which teachers are orthodox, there is one recourse which is totally reliable, namely, to consult the letters themselves. By comparing teachers to the teachings and descriptions of proper teachers in the letters, the orthodox can be distinguished from the heterodox. The spirit is not enough, for there are misleading, evil spirits abroad; one must identify the Pauline traditions, which are authenticated by God, hold to them, and not move. Once there, one can learn in safety and confidence, and make much progress.

3. Good Works

Foerster defines $\epsilon\mathring{\upsilon}\sigma\acute{\epsilon}\beta\epsilon\iota\alpha$ as "Ordnungen, die das Zusammenleben tragen und die die Götter schützen"[238]. According to Dibelius-Conzelmann, $\epsilon\mathring{\upsilon}\sigma\acute{\epsilon}\beta\epsilon\iota\alpha$ is the completion of cultic duties and general behavior which is pleasing to the gods, which in the case of the Pastorals means maintaining good order and realizing the virtues[239]. Lips contends that these relational meanings overlook the knowledge component, noting that $\epsilon\mathring{\upsilon}\sigma\acute{\epsilon}\beta\epsilon\iota\alpha$ is connected in the letters to $\gamma\nu\tilde{\omega}\sigma\iota\varsigma$ and $\delta\iota\delta\alpha\sigma\kappa\alpha\lambda\acute{\iota}\alpha$[240]. The author uses this common term from Greco-Roman religious and ethical circles to describe the life-style which God's plan of salvation produces. Commentators

---

238 Foerster, "Εὐσέβεια in den Pastoralbriefen," pp. 213—18. Foerster emphasizes the relational aspects of the term, connecting it with the maintenance of order in the church.

239 Dibelius-Conzelmann, *The Pastoral Epistles*, p. 39.

240 Lips, *Glaube, Gemeinde, Amt*, pp. 76—86.

are certainly correct in pointing out both the religious and ethical dimensions to the term. Exactly what the author means is therefore no puzzle at all, because he takes great care to describe the life-style he envisions. All the parenetic and descriptive passages fill out the meaning of εὐσέβεια. The ideal is stated clearly in 1 Tim. 2.2, where prayers are prescribed "in order that we may lead a quiet and peaceful life with all piety and dignity (ἵνα ἤρεμον καὶ ἡσύχιον βίον διάγωμεν ἐν πάσῃ εὐσεβείᾳ καὶ σεμνό-τητι)"[241]. The author's predilection for σώφρων and its cognates, especially σωφροσύνη, also expresses the peculiar ethical emphasis of the author[242]. He wants a temperate life, where communal virtues that contribute to upbuilding the fellowship are emphasized over ascetic or private ones, where temperance, good order, obedience to proper authorities, and moral progress predominate, and where creativity, debate, and social freedom are controlled and limited. It is an ethic which is built upon the ideal of communal life, for not only do the warrants come out of the community but the ethic which results relates back to the community. Thus temperance dominates over asceticism and obedience over creativity.

The purpose of inculcating such a sober life-style is that this is the life-style which produces salvation. Good works, the quiet virtues, the life-style modelled on Paul and practiced in the community, will get one a favorable judgment at the second epiphany. In the end everything depends upon the question of whether one practiced good works or not. Everything else is a means to that end.

At the first epiphany Jesus "cleanses for himself a selected people, who are zealous for good works (ζηλωτὴν καλῶν ἔργων)" (Tit. 2.14). Redemption and selection for cultic membership originates in Jesus, who produces, via the medium of baptism with its gift of the spirit, an anthropological transformation which reorients one towards good works[243]. Cos-

---

[241]Foerster points out   that the connection made here between εὐσέβεια and σεμνότης is a normal one in Greek literature (" Εὐσέβεια in den Pastoralbriefen," p. 216). Dibelius-Conzelmann, *The Pastoral Epistles*, pp. 38—39, note that 1 Clement 61 makes the connection between prayers for rulers and the peaceful life that ensues. That the author is embuing quiet and peace with autonomous religious feelings and not just longing for cessation from persecution is indicated by the many parallels cited by Dibelius-Conzelmann..The Jewish parallels are particularly striking. See also Brox, *Die Pastoralbriefe*, pp. 174—77.

[242]Tit. 2.12 links σωφρόνως, δικαίως, and εὐσεβῶς. On σώφρων see p.173, n.153, above. The Platonic discussions of σωφροσύνη are interesting for understanding the Pastorals. The *Charmides*, which is devoted to answering the question, "what is σωφροσύνη?" finds no definition adequate, proferring τὰ ἑαυτοῦ πράττειν and γνῶθι σαυτόν as the best suggestions (*Charmides* 161b, 164d). In the *Gorgias* (507, 508) Plato gives an etymological definition: σωφροσύνη is the σωτηρία (keeping) of φρόνησις. But in the *Republic* (3.389) and the *Laws* (3.696) Plato develops the political dimensions of the term: σωφροσύνη is the ruling over and harmony among the elements of the soul and the ruling over and harmony among members of the state. This communal dimension seems to be in force in the Pastorals.

[243]The linkage of baptism, the spirit, and good deeds is of course a frequent one in early Christianity (cf. Eph. 2.10). On the roots in Paul see Betz, *Galatians*, pp. 32—33.

mological and cultic events must occur before one can begin to make progress towards virtue, but once those occur the education process takes over. The conclusion of the author's short description of Timothy's own upbringing articulates the goal of all the teaching activity in the church. It is done "in order that the man of God might be complete (ἄρτιος), equipped (ἐξηρτισμένος) for every good work." ἄρτιος means first of all "complete," but it also can be rendered "suitable or adequate to the tasks at hand"[244]. This latter meaning expresses the intention of the author that education prepare one for the duties required. ἐξαρτίζειν also means "to complete," but in the passive it is usually rendered "to be prepared or furnished"[245]. Moulton and Milligan cite examples where it means "supplied" with necessary goods or even "equipped" for ethical behavior[246]. The goal of the education process is to outfit the church member with all the tools necessary for meeting the ethical tasks incumbent upon him or her. This means more than providing the superhuman spirit with its unique powers; the church must also provide all the standards and warrants necessary to an ethical system. We have seen how the author does this through the fiction of the Pauline traditions and its transmission. Furthermore, we have seen how diverse his warrants prove to be, with the author employing the vast array of parenetic devices common to Greco-Roman ethics. All this is done in order to equip the believer for good works. Those who follow the prescriptions laid out by the author will be approved on judgment day, while those who do not will be disapproved[247].

F. Conclusion

(1) A faction within the author's church, which was having success in converting the fellowship to its way of thinking and living, impelled the author to write the Pastorals. He portrays these people as engaging in fruitless theological speculation, as encouraging disorder and disharmony in the fellowship, and as being ascetic but not virtuous. He polemicizes against them by painting them with numerous vices, by designating them as apostates from sound teachings, by associating them with legendary enemies of Paul, and by excluding them from salvation.

(2) To this improper mode of living the author counterposes his own vision of the Christian life, replacing speculation with doctrinal traditions and authorities, disorder with a strict community hierarchy, and asceticism with communal virtues. These competing life-styles, as they play off

---

[244]Gerhard Delling, "ἄρτιος," TDNT, 1:475—76.
[245]Liddell and Scott, *Greek-English Lexicon*, s.v. ἐξαρτίζω.
[246]Moulton and Milligan, *The Vocabulary of the Greek New Testament*, s.v. ἐξαρτίζω.
[247]2 Tim. 2.15; 3.8; Tit. 1.16.

one another, produce a dualism in his ethic, his mode of argumentation, and his method of composing the letters.

(3) In order to create warrants for his ethic and authorities for his argument with opponents, the author uses the pseudepigraphical letter to rewrite the history of his church, so that his own faction and vision can enjoy apostolic support. Thus he fabricates the two fictions of the Pauline traditions and their successful transmission into the care of church officers of his day. This furnishes the community with two unquestionable resources to which it can turn for ethical and religious guidance: the letters themselves and the church officers.

(4) In his attempt to make his ethical system workable yet under the control of cultic authorities, the author treats the reception of the spirit through baptism as a necessary empowerment and the subsequent education of believers by the proper officers as a necessary tutelage for positive progress towards virtue. Given the fiction of the Pauline traditions and these two cultic controls, the author furnishes the believer with the requisite tools for realizing the virtuous life.

(5) Every detail of this schema is designated by the author as part of God's plan of salvation for people. God's role as creator and savior, along with Jesus' function as teacher, redeemer, and judge at his epiphanies, provides cosmological grounding and motivation for the virtuous life.

Conclusion

The hermeneutic of the Pastorals offered here is based on historical judgments about the proper literary and philosophical milieu of the letters. In an effort to moderate the arbitrariness of the hermeneutical structures imposed upon the letters analogies were drawn only from documents of similar genre and the same time period. Thus the observation that the letters are pseudepigraphical suggested an inquiry into the form and function of other ancient pseudepigraphical letters. Similarly, the observation that the letters make ethical arguments in the diatribe style led to an examination of other Greco-Roman ethical arguments. These analogies were put forward as propositions to be tested. What if the Pastorals use the genre of the pseudepigraphical letter in the following ways? What if the paratactical argumentation in the letters contains a logical structure of the kind Aristotle describes? What if the eclecticism and diversity of ethical warrants in the letters contribute to the persuasiveness of the ethical system? These propositions did more than offer a stance or attitude towards the material, for they provided structures by which the diverse materials in the Pastorals could be organized. For instance, we have done more than simply claim the letters are logically coherent, because we have tried to demonstrate that the argumentation in the letters makes deduction in good enthymematic form and induction in paradigmatic form. Again, the analogue of other Greco-Roman ethical systems building warrants and motivations permitted us to detect an inner coherence in the diverse argumentative forms. And the analysis of other pseudepigraphical letters provided a basis for linking the act of deception with the ethical system so that the system itself crumbles if the deception is detected. That is to say, these were not intended to be benign analogies but hermeneutical probes through which we perceived order and coherence where none was apparent. Therefore, the hermeneutic offered here was intentionally aggressive.

The validity of this hermeneutic resides in an aesthetic judgment concerning whether the imposed structures are appropriate or even inherent to the text. We are not attempting here a school exegesis whereby self-justifying categories, such as Marxist ones, are used to critique a text. We tried not to beat the text out of shape. To the contrary, it was the text itself which was perceived as the final standard; it was not ourselves but the text we were trying to unpack. A conscious effort was made to reject incompatible structures. Therefore, the success of this hermeneutic can only be evaluated by taking the reading given here, returning to the text, and seeing if it works. It is my judgment that this reading of the Pastorals works well.

Given this reading, the Pastorals become an important moment in early Christian thought. Even if we cannot claim great theological insight for the author of the Pastorals, his version of Pauline theology as a cultic, ethical system exerted enormous influence on the early church[1]. Paul's letters were interpreted in diverse ways and the battle over Paul and what he meant became a focal point in doctrinal controversy[2]. The moderate, authoritarian, and ethical rendition of Paul given in the Pastorals provided the "orthodox" camp with a comfortable version of Paul which could be counterposed to gnostic readings. Although I do not think Polycarp was the author, he shares with the Pastorals an ethical, non-speculative view of Christianity; and, when Irenaeus uses the Pastorals in his polemic against heretics, it marks the success of the author's attempt to deceive and to promulgate his peculiar reading of Paul. Thus the Pastorals provided a non-threatening lens through which orthodoxy could read Paul.

The author's eventual success resulted from his ability to combine a well-disguised pseudepigraphical letter format with a plausible and non-controversial interpretation of Paul. His persuasiveness was more literary and political than theological, for he provided orthodoxy not with a new theological stance but with a portrait of Paul which agreed with the or-thodox point of view. By using the letter genre he was able to fictionalize Pauline history and Pauline thought so that Paul's authority but not his complexity was placed in the orthodox camp.

Thus the Pastorals are mildly interesting for their cogent ethical system and their effective use of the pseudepigraphical letter, but historically very important as a telling moment in the battle between the authority structures of orthodoxy and the theological diversity and creativity in the church. Here, authority and ethics dominate inquiry.

When Bultmann evaluated the theology of the Pastorals in his *Theology of the New Testament* he noted that, even though "the eschatological tensions that Paul knew" was mostly lost, the "paradox of Christian exist-ence . . . is here grasped"[3]. He suggested that the Pastorals are an ade-quate though certainly not a profound expression of Christian existence.

---

[1] For the history of post-Pauline thought and the role of the Pastorals in that history see Andreas Lindemann, *Paulus im ältesten Christentum: Das Bild des Apostles und die Rezeption der paulinischen Theologie in der frühchristlichen Literatur bis Marcion*, Beiträge zur historischen Theologie 58 (Tübingen: J. C. B. Mohr [Paul Siebeck], 1979).

[2] Pagels, *The Gnostic Paul*, details the gnostic exegesis of Paul. MacDonald, *The Legend and the Apostle*, shows that competing interpretations of Paul constituted a basic disagreement be-tween the author and his opponents. MacDonald details further how the author of the Pastorals and the orthodox camp successfully project their own interpretation of Paul upon the early church, so that non-orthodox readings of him are forced to the fringes of the church.

[3] Rudolf Bultmann, *Theology of the New Testament*, trans. Kendrick Grobel (New York: Charles Scribner's Sons, 1955) 2:185.

Bultmann, in fact, grades it much higher than most other scholars do, because he at least detected some theology of some kind. If, then, the rendition given here of the theology of the Pastorals is accurate, what voice should this theology have in Christian circles today? Does the charge. of deception eliminate its right to speak?

The Pastorals identify for us the innate flaw in Johannine and Pauline theologies: the spirit does not behave as it must to make those theologies work. This critique is reminiscent of the Stoic criticism of Cynic thought. For as the Stoics complain that the Cynic appeal to "life according to nature" is inadequate, so might the author of the Pastorals complain that an appeal to "life in Christ" or "life in the spirit" gives insufficient direction. It makes one wonder whether his opponents, who may have believed in a more aggressive version of the spirit, are not the true heirs of Pauline thought. The Pastorals proffer, in contrast to this spirit-ethic, clear ethical norms and reliable authorities. These three letters then are the ordained clergy's trump cards. Given the theological fact that Jesus is not accessible and that the spirit keeps relatively quiet, these letters suggest that the ordained and educated clergy can provide a version of Christianity that is reasonable and moral. This version is actually closer to what mainline western churches practice today than anything in Paul and John. So in a sense the question above was improperly framed, because this voice is already the loudest and it is Paul and Matthew and some others whose voices need amplification.

The embarrassment of pseudepigraphy strikes at the heart of scriptural authority. The vehemence of conservative scholars who resist the whole notion of pseudepigrapha in the canon is well-founded, for to admit it would be to admit that the canon is not what they want it to be. However, if the canon is just another moment in tradition, the first among many attempts by Christians to debate their various versions of the religious life, then a pseudepigraphon could be an explicable and valid voice in the debate. Admittedly, in a pseudepigraphon the prejudices and weaknesses of the author and the humanness of the theology therein are displayed so openly that they cannot be ignored. But then all theology is human and prejudiced and flawed. It is just here, in the face of such duplicity, that we must admit it at the outset.

Pseudepigraphy represents one mode of response to the predicament of second-generation theology. Theological warrants must come from somewhere, especially when the diversity of opinions about the character of the Christian life was, to some minds at least, out of control. The church's inability to adjudicate these debates created an urgent need for unimpeachable warrants. The Old Testament can be read many ways; the spirit can and does produce contrary prophecies; reason can split an issue from many angles; but the immediate voice of an apostle can circumvent these predicaments and provide one rudder in these theological meanderings.

Finally, this analysis of three ancient letters indicates that ethical argumentation, despite its disorganized appearance, follows recognizable logical forms; and, thereby, this study suggests that further research along these lines into other ethical documents, ancient and modern, might be fruitful.

Bibliography

Adkins, Arthur W. H. *Merit and Responsibility.* Midway reprint, Chicago: University of Chicago Press, 1975.

Aland, Kurt, "The Problem of Anonymity and Pseudonymity in Christian Literature of the First Two Centuries." *Journal of Theological Studies* 12 (1961): 39–49.

Allan, John, A. "The 'in Christ' Formula in the Pastoral Epistles." *New Testament Studies* 10 (1963): 115–21.

Alonso-Schökel, Luis. "Narrative Structures in the Book of Judith." Protocol of the Colloquy of the Center for Hermeneutical Studies in Hellenistic and Modern Culture. Berkeley: Center for Hermeneutical Studies, 1975.

Arnhart, Larry. *Aristotle on Political Reasoning: A Commentary on the "Rhetoric."* Dekalb, Ill.: Northern Illinois University Press, 1981.

Bahr, Gordon J. "Paul and Letter Writing in the First Century." *Catholic Biblical Quarterly* 28 (1966): 465–77.

Bailey, John A. "Who Wrote II Thessalonians?" *New Testament Studies* 25 (1975): 131–45.

Balch, David L. *Let Wives Be Submissive: The Domestic Code in 1 Peter.* Society of Biblical Literature Monograph Series 26. Chico, Calif.: Scholar Press, 1981.

Balz, H. R. "Anonymität und Pseudepigraphie im Urchristentum." *Zeitschrift für Theologie und Kirche* 66 (1969): 403–36.

Bardy, Gustave. "Faux et fraudes littéraires dans l'antiquité chrétienne." *Revue d'histoire ecclésiastique* 32 (1936): 5–23, 275–302.

Barnett, Albert E. *Paul Becomes a Literary Influence.* Chicago: University of Chicago Press, 1941.

Barrett, C. K. *The Pastoral Epistles.* The New Clarendon Bible. Oxford: Clarendon Press, 1963.

——. "Pauline Controversies in the Post-Pauline Period." *New Testament Studies* 20 (1944): 229–45.

Bartsch, Hans Werner. *Die Anfänge urchristlicher Rechtsbildungen: Studien zu den Pastoralbriefen.* Hamburg: Herbert Reich, 1965.

Bauer, Walter. *Orthodoxy and Heresy in Earliest Christianity.* 2d ed. English ed. edited by Robert Kraft and Gerhard Krodel. Philadelphia: Fortress Press, 1971.

Bauer, Walter; Arndt, William F.; and Gingrich, F. Wilbur. *A Greek-English Lexicon of the New Testament and Other Early Christian Literature.* Translated and adapted from 4th ed. Chicago: University of Chicago Press, 1957.

Baur, F. C. *Die sogenannten Pastoralbriefe des Apostels Paulus aufs neue kritisch untersucht.* Stuttgart: Cotta, 1835.

Betz, Hans Dieter. *Galatians.* Hermeneia. Philadelphia: Fortress Press, 1979.

——. *Nachfolge und Nachahmung Jesu Christi im Neuen Testament.* Beiträge zur historischen Theologie 37. Tübingen: J. C. B. Mohr (Paul Siebeck), 1967.

Bitzer, Lloyd. "Aristotle's Enthymeme Revisited." In *Aristotle: The Classical Heritage of Rhetoric.* Edited by Keith V. Erickson. Metuchen: Scarecrow Press, 1974.

Blumenthal, A. von. "ΤΥΠΟΣ und ΠΑΡΑΔΕΙΓΜΑ." *Hermes* 63 (1928): 391–414.

Boismard, M. E. "Une Liturgie baptismale dans la Prima Petri." *Revue biblique* 63 (1956–57): 182ff.

Boman, Thorleif. *Hebrew Thought Compared with Greek.* Translated by Jules L. Moreau. Philadelphia: Westminster Press, 1960.

Boobyer, G. N. "The Indebtedness of 2 Peter to 1 Peter." In *New Testament Essays: Studies in Memory of T. W. Manson.* Edited by A. Higgins. Manchester: Manchester University Press, 1959.

Bousset, Wilhelm. *Kyrios Christos.* Translated by John E. Steely. Nashville: Abingdon Press, 1970.

Bréhier, Émile. *The Hellenistic and Roman Age.* Translated by Wade Baskin. The History of Philosophy. Chicago: University of Chicago Press, 1965.

Brockington, Leonard H. "The Problem of Pseudonymity." *Journal of Theological Studies* 4 (1953): 15–23.

Brox, Norbert. *Falsche Verfasserangaben. Zur Erklärung der frühchristlichen Pseudepigraphie.* Stuttgarter Bibelstudien 79. Stuttgart: Katholisches Bibelwerk, 1975.

——. "Lukas als Verfasser der Pastoralbriefe." *Jahrbuch für Antike und Christentum* 13 (1970): 62–77.

——. *Die Pastoralbriefe.* Regensburger Neues Testament. Regensburg: F. Pustet, 1969.

——. "Προφητεία im ersten Timotheusbrief." *Biblische Zeitschrift* 20 (1976): 229–32.

——. "Zu den persönlichen Notizen der Pastoralbriefe." *Biblische Zeitschrift* 13 (1969): 76–94.

——. "Zur pseudepigraphischen Rahmung des ersten Petrusbriefes." *Biblische Zeitschrift* 19 (1975): 78–96.

——. *Pseudepigraphie in der heidnischen und jüdisch-christlichen Antike.* Wege der Forschung. Vol. 484. Darmstadt: Wissenschaftliche Buchgesellschaft, 1977.

Burkert, W. "Hellenistische Pseudopythagorica." *Philologus* 105 (1961): 17–28.

Campenhausen, Hans von. *Ecclesiastical Authority and Spiritual Power in the Church of the First Three Centuries.* Translated by J. A. Baker. Stanford: Stanford University Press, 1969.

——. *The Formation of the Christian Bible.* Translated by J. A. Baker. Philadelphia: Fortress Press, 1972.

——. "Lehrerreihen und Bischofsreihen im zweiten Jahrhundert." In *In Memoriam Ernst Lohmeyer.* Edited by Werner Schmauch. Stuttgart: Evangelische Verlagswerk, 1951.

——. "Polykarp von Smryna und die Pastoralbriefe." *Aus der Frühzeit des Christentums.* Tübingen: J. C. B. Mohr (Paul Siebeck), 1963.

Cancik, Hildegard. *Untersuchungen zu Senecas epistulae morales.* Spudasmata 18. Hildesheim: Georg Olms, 1967.

Candlish, J. S. "On the Moral Character of Pseudonymous Books." *The Expositor,* ser. 4 (1891), pp. 91–107, 262–79.

Carrington, Phillip. *The Primitive Christian Catechism: A Study in the Epistles.* Cambridge: Cambridge University Press, 1940.

Charles, R. H. "Eschatology." *Encyclopaedia Biblica.* Vol. 2 (1901), cols. 1335–92.

Clarke, M. L. *Rhetoric at Rome: A Historical Survey.* 1953, reprint; New York: Barnes & Noble, 1966.

Conzelmann, Hans. *1 Corinthians.* Translated by James W. Leitch. Hermeneia. Philadelphia: Fortress Press, 1975.

Cope, E. M. *An Introduction to Aristotle's Rhetoric.* London: Macmillan, 1867.

Crem, Theresa M. "The Definition of Rhetoric according to Aristotle." In *Aristotle: The Classical Heritage of Rhetoric.* Edited by Keith V. Erickson. Metuchen: Scarecrow Press, 1974.

Crouch, James E. *The Origin and Intention of the Colossian Haustafel.* Forschungen zur Religion und Literatur des Alten und Neuen Testaments 109. Göttingen: Vandenhoeck & Ruprecht, 1972.

Cullmann, Oscar. *Baptism in the New Testament.* Translated by J. K. S. Reid. Chicago: H. Regnery, 1950.

DeBoer, Willis Peter. *The Imitation of Paul: An Exegetical Study.* Kampen: J. H. Kok, 1962.

Deissmann, Adolf. *Light from the Ancient East: The New Testament Illustrated by Recently Discovered Tests of the Graeco-Roman World.* 4th ed. Translated by Lionel R. M. Strachan. Grand Rapids, Mich.: Baker Book House, 1978.

DeLacy, Philip. "The Logical Structure of the Ethics of Epictetus." *Classical Philology* 38 (1943): 112–25.

Dey, Joseph. ΠΑΛΙΓΓΕΝΕΣΙΑ. *Ein Beitrag zur Klärung der religionsgeschichtlichen Bedeutung von Tit. 3.5.* Neutestamentliche Abhandlungen 17, 5. Münster: Aschendorff, 1937.

Dibelius, Martin. "Επίγνωσις ἀληθείας." *Botschaft und Geschichte* 2. Tübingen: J. C. B. Mohr (Paul Siebeck), 1956.

——. *An die Kolosser, Epheser, an Philemon.* Handbuch zum Neuen Testament 12. 3rd ed. Tübingen: J. C. B. Mohr, 1953.

——. *Die Pastoralbriefe*. Handbuch zum Neuen Testament 13. 2d ed. Tübingen: J. C. B. Mohr (Paul Siebeck), 1931.

Dibelius, Martin, and Conzelmann, Hans. *The Pastoral Epistles*. Translated by Philip Buttolph and Adela Yarbro. Hermeneia. Philadelphia: Fortress Press, 1972.

Döring, Klaus. *Exemplum Socratis: Studien zur Sokratesnachwirkung in der kynisch-stoischen Popularphilosophie der frühen Kaiserzeit und im frühen Christentum*. Hermes, Zeitschrift für klassische Philologie, Einzelschriften 42. Wiesbaden: Franz Steiner, 1979.

Doty, William G. "The Classification of Epistolary Literature." *Catholic Biblical Quarterly* 31 (1969): 183–99.

——. *Letters in Primitive Christianity*. Philadelphia: Fortress Press, 1973.

Dragona-Monachon, M. "Prohairesis in Aristotle and Epictetus. A Comparison with the Concept of Intention in the Philosophy of Action." *Philosophia* 8–9 (1978–79): 265–310.

Dudley, Donald R. *A History of Cynicism*. 1937, reprint; Hildesheim: Georg Olms, 1967.

Dunn, James L. D. *Baptism in the Spirit*. Philadelphia: Westminster Press, 1970.

Dupont-Sommer, André. *La Quatrième Livre des Machabées*. Bibliothèque de L'École des Hautes Études 274. Paris: H. Champion, 1939.

Düring, Ingemar. "Aristotle's Use of Examples in the *Topics*." In *Aristotle on Dialectic: The Topics*. Proceedings of the Third Symposium Aristotelicum. Edited by G. E. L. Owen. Oxford: Clarendon Press, 1968.

Easton, Burton Scott. "New Testament Ethical Lists." *Journal of Biblical Literature* 51 (1932): 1–12.

——. *The Pastoral Epistles*. New York: Charles Scribner's Sons, 1947.

Elliott, J. "Ministry and Church Order in the New Testament." *Catholic Biblical Quarterly* 32 (1970): 367–91.

Erickson, Keith V. , ed. *Aristotle: The Classical Heritage of Rhetoric*. Metuchen: Scarecrow Press, 1974.

Ernst, J. "Die Witwenregel des Ersten Timotheusbriefes." *Theologie und Glaube* 59 (1969): 434–45.

Exler, Francis Xavier J. *The Form of the Ancient Greek Letter of the Epistolary Papyri*. 1923, reprint; Chicago: Chicago Area Publishers, 1976.

Falconer, Robert. *The Pastoral Epistles*. Oxford: Clarendon Press, 1937.

Fiore, Benjamin. "The Function of Personal Example in the Socratic and Pastoral Epistles." Ph.D. dissertation, Yale University, 1982. Ann Arbor, Mich.: University Microfilms, 1983.

Foerster, Werner. "Εὐσέβεια in den Pastoralbriefen." *New Testament Studies* 5 (1959): 213–18.

Foley, L. P. "Fidelis, Faithful." *Catholic Biblical Quarterly* 1 (1939): 163–65.

Francis, Fred O., and Meeks, Wayne A., eds. and trans. *Conflict in Colossae*. Sources for Biblical Study 4. Missoula, Mont.: Scholars Press, 1975.

Funk, Robert W. "The Apostolic 'Parousia': Form and Significance." In *Christian History and Interpretation: Studies Presented to John Knox*. Edited by W. R. Farmer, C. F. Moule, and R. R. Niebuhr. Cambridge: Cambridge University Press, 1967.

Furnish, Victor Paul. *Theology and Ethics in Paul*. Nashville: Abingdon, 1968.

Goppelt, Leonard. *Typos, the Typological Interpretation of the Old Testament in the New*. Translated by Donald H. Madvig. Grand Rapids, Mich.: Wm. B. Eerdmans, 1982.

Grimaldi, William M. "The Aristotelian *Topics*." In *Aristotle: The Classical Heritage of Rhetoric*. Edited by Keith V. Erickson. Metuchen: Scarecrow Press, 1974.

——. "A Note on the Πίστεις in Aristotle's *Rhetoric*, 1354–1356." *American Journal of Philology* 78 (1957): 188–92.

Gudemann, Alfred. "Literary Frauds among the Greeks." *Classical Studies in Honour of Henry Drisler*. New York: Macmillan, 1894.

Gulley, Norman. "The Authenticity of the Platonic Epistles." In *Pseudepigrapha I: Pseudopythagorica — Lettres de Platon — Littérature pseudépigraphique juive*. Fondation Hardt, Entretiens sur l'antiquité classique, 18. Vandoeuvres-Genève: Fondation Hardt, 1972.

Guthrie, Donald. "The Development of the Idea of Canonical Pseudonymity in New Testament Criticism." In *Vox Evangelica*. Edited by Ralph P. Martin. London: Epworth Press, 1962.

——. *The Pastoral Epistles: An Introduction and Commentary*. Tyndale New Testament. Grand Rapids, Mich.: Wm. B. Eerdmans, 1957.

Hadas, Moses. *Hellenistic Culture.* The Norton Library. New York: W. W. Norton, 1959.

Hadas, Moses, ed. and trans. *The Third and Fourth Books of Maccabees.* New York: Harper & Bros., 1953.

Haefner, Alfred E. "A Unique Source for the Study of Ancient Pseudonymity." *Anglican Theological Review* 16 (1934): 8–15.

Hanson, Anthony Tyrrell. *The Pastoral Epistles.* The New Century Bible Commentary. Grand Rapids, Mich.: Wm. B. Eerdmans, 1982.

——. *The Pastoral Letters.* The Cambridge Bible Commentary on the New English Bible. New York: Cambridge University Press, 1966.

——. *Studies in the Pastoral Epistles.* London: S. P. C. K., 1968.

Harnack, Adolf. *The Mission and Expansion of Christianity in the First Three Centuries.* Translated and edited by James Moffatt. New York: Harper & Bros., 1962.

Harris, R. Baine, ed. *The Significance of Neo-Platonism.* Studies in Neo-Platonism: Ancient and Modern, Vol. 1. Norfolk, Va.: Old Dominion University Press, 1976.

Harrison, P. N. *The Problem of the Pastoral Epistles.* London: Oxford University Press, Humphrey Milford, 1921.

Harward, J. *The Platonic Epistles.* Cambridge: Cambridge University Press, 1932.

Hasler, Victor. "Epiphanie und Christologie in den Pastoralbriefen." *Theologische Zeitschrift* 33 (1977): 193–209.

Haufe, G. "Gnostische Irrlehre und ihre Abwehr in den Pastoralbriefen." In *Gnosis und Neues Testament.* Edited by K. W. Tröger. Berlin: Evangelische Verlagsanstalt, 1973, pp. 325–39.

Hauser, Gerald. "The Example in Aristotle's *Rhetoric*: Bifurcation or Contradiction?" In *Aristotle: The Classical Heritage of Rhetoric.* Edited by Keith V. Erickson. Metuchen: Scarecrow Press, 1974.

Hellebrand, W. "Parakatatheke." *Pauly-Wissowa, Real-Encyclopädie der klassischen Altertumwissenschaft* 36 (1949): 1186–1202.

Hellwig, A. *Untersuchungen zur Theorie der Rhetorik bei Platon und Aristoteles.* Hypomnemata; Untersuchungen zur Antike und zu ihrem Nachleben, Vol. 38. Göttingen: Vandenhoeck & Ruprecht, 1970.

Helm, R. "Kynismus." *Pauly-Wissowa, Real-Encyclopädie der classischen Altertumswissenschaft,* Vol. 12 (1924), 3–24.

Hengel, Martin. "Anonymität, Pseudepigraphie und 'Literarische Fälschung' in der jüdisch-hellenistischen Literatur." In *Pseudepigrapha I: Pseudopythagorica — Lettres de Platon — Littérature pseudépigraphique juive.* Fondation Hardt, Entretiens sur l'antiquité classique, 18. Vandœuvres-Geneve: Fondation Hardt, 1972.

Hennecke, Edgar, and Schneemelcher, Wilhelm, eds. *New Testament Apocrypha.* Translated by A. Higgins et al. English ed. edited by R. Mcl. Wilson. 2 vols. Philadelphia: Westmister Press, 1963–1965.

Hijmans, B. L. ΆΣΚΗΣΙΣ: *Notes on Epictetus' Educational System.* Assen: Van Gorcum, 1959.

Hitchcock, F. R. Montgomery. "Tests for the Pastorals." *Journal of Theological Studies* 30 (1929): 272–79.

Holmberg, Bengt. *Paul and Power: The Structure of Authority in the Primitve Church as Reflected in the Pauline Epistles.* Philadelphia: Fortress Press, 1980.

Holtz, Gottfried. *Die Pastoralbriefe.* Theologischer Handkommentar zum Neuen Testament 13. Berlin: Evangelische Verlagsanstalt, 1972.

Holtzmann, Heinrich Julius. *Die Pastoralbriefe, kritisch und exegetisch bearbeitet.* Leipzig: W. Engelmann, 1880.

Houlden, J. L. *The Pastoral Epistles.* Pelican New Testament Commentaries. New York: Penguin Books, 1976.

Jaeger, Werner. *Early Christianity and Greek Paideia.* Oxford: Oxford University Press, 1961.

——. *Paideia: The Ideals of Greek Culture.* Vol. 2. Translated by Gilbert Highet. New York: Oxford University Press, 1943.

Jeremias, Joachim. *Die Brief an Timotheus und Titus.* Das Neue Testament Deutsch 9. Göttingen: Vandenhoeck & Ruprecht, 1975.

Jewett, Robert. "The Redaction of 1 Corinthians and the Trajectory of the Pauline School." *Journal of the American Academy of Religion,* Supplement, Vol. 44 (1978).

Kamlah, Ehrhard. *Die Form der katalogischen Paränese im Neuen Testament*. Wissenschaftliche Untersuchungen zum Neuen Testament 7. Tübingen: J. C. B. Mohr (Paul Siebeck), 1964.

Karlsson, Gustav. "Formelhaftes in Paulusbriefen?" *Eranos* 54 (1956): 138—41.

Karris, Robert J. "The Background and Significance of the Polemic of the Pastoral Epistles." *Journal of Biblical Literature* 92 (1973): 549—64.

—. "The Function and Sitz im Leben of the Paraenetic Elements in the Pastoral Epistles." Ph.D. dissertation, Harvard University, 1970.

—. *The Pastoral Epistles*. New Testament Message 17. Wilmington, Del.: Michael Glazier, 1979.

Käsemann, Ernst. "An Apologia for Primitive Christian Eschatology." In *Essays on New Testament Themes*. Translated by W. J. Montague. Studies in Biblical Theology. Naperville, Ill.: Alec R. Allenson, 1964.

Kelly, J. N. D. *A Commentary on the Pastoral Epistles*. Black's New Testament Commentaries. London: Adam & Charles Black, 1963.

Kennedy, George Alexander. *The Art of Persuasion in Greece*. Princeton: Princeton University Press, 1963.

—. *The Art of Rhetoric in the Roman World, 300 B.C. — A.D. 300*. Princeton: Princeton University Press, 1972.

Kerford, G. B. "What Does the Wise Man Know?" In *The Stoics*. Edited by John M. Rist. Berkeley: University of California Press, 1978.

Klöpper, D. A. "Zur Christologie der Pastoralbriefe (1 Tim. 3,16)." *Zeitschrift für wissenschaftliche Theologie* 45 (1902): 339—61.

—. "Zur Soteriologie der Pastoralbriefe." *Zeitschrift für wissenschaftliche Theologie* 47 (1904): 57—88.

Knight, George W. *The Faithful Sayings in the Pastoral Epistles*. Kampen: J. H. Kok, 1968.

Koester, Helmut. "Apocryphal and Canonical Gospels." *Harvard Theological Review* 73 (1980): 105—30.

—. *Introduction to the New Testament*. Vol. 1: *History, Culture, and Religion of the Hellenistic Age*. Vol. 2: *History and Literature of Early Christianity*. Hermeneia — foundations and facets. Philadelphia: Fortress Press, 1982.

Koskenniemi, H. *Studien zur Idee und Phraseologie des griechischen Briefes bis 400 n. Chr*. Annales Academiae Scientiarum Fennicae, Ser. B, Vol. 102, 2. Helsinki: Suomalaisen Tiedeakatemian, 1956.

Kümmel, Werner Georg. *Introduction to the New Testament*. Founded by Paul Feine and Johannes Behm. Translated by A. J. Mattil. 14th ed. New York: Abingdon, 1966.

Lampe, G. W. H., and Woolcombe, K. J., eds. *Essays on Typology*. Naperville, Ill.: Alec R. Allenson, 1957.

Liddell, H. and Scott, R. *Greek-English Lexicon*. Revised by H. S. Jones and R. McKenzie. Oxford: Clarendon Press, 1968.

Lienhard, Joseph T. "A Note on the Meaning of ΠΙΣΤΙΣ in Aristotle's Rhetoric." *American Journal of Philology* 87 (1966): 446—54.

Lindemann, Andreas. *Paulus im ältesten Christentum: Das Bild des Apostels und die Rezeption der paulinischen Theologie in der frühchristlichen Literatur bis Marcion*. Beiträge zur historischen Theologie 58. Tübingen: J. C. B. Mohr (Paul Siebeck), 1979.

Lips, Hermann von. *Glaube, Gemeinde, Amt: Zum Verständnis der Ordination in den Pastoralbriefen*. Forschungen zur Religion und Literatur des Alten und Neuen Testament. Vol. 122. Göttingen: Vandenhoeck & Ruprecht, 1979.

Lock, Walter. *The Pastoral Epistles*. The International Critical Commentary. New York: Charles Scribner's Sons, 1924.

Lohmeyer, Ernst. *Christuskult und Kaiserkult*. Tübingen: J. C. B. Mohr (Paul Siebeck), 1919.

Lohse, Edward. *A Commentary on the Epistles to the Colossians and to Philemon*. Translated by William R. Poehlmann and Robert J. Karris. Hermeneia. Philadelphia: Fortress Press, 1971.

Long, A. A. "Dialectic and the Stoic Sage." In *The Stoics*. Edited by John M. Rist. Berkeley: California Press, 1978.

Lührmann, D. "Epiphaneia: Zur Bedeutungsgeschichte eines griechischen Wortes." In *Tradition und Glaube*, FS für K. G. Kuhn. Edited by G. Jeremias. Göttingen: Vandenhoeck & Ruprecht, 1971.

Lumpe, Adolf. "Exemplum." *Reallexikon für Antike und Christentum*, 6:1229–57.

Lütgert, Wilhelm. *Die Irrlehrer der Pastoralbriefe*. Beiträge zur Förderung christlicher Theologie, 13, 3. Gütersloh: W. Bertelsmann, 1909.

McBurney, James H. "The Place of the Enthymeme in Rhetorical Theory." In *Aristotle: The Classical Heritage of Rhetoric*. Edited by Keith V. Erickson. Metuchen: Scarecrow Press, 1974.

MacDonald, Dennis Ronald. *The Legend and the Apostle: The Battle for Paul in Story and Canon*. Philadelphia: Westminster Press, 1983.

McEleney, N. J. "The Vice Lists of the Pastoral Epistles." *Catholic Biblical Quarterly* 36 (1974): 203–19.

Malherbe, Abraham, J. "Ancient Epistolary Theorists." *Ohio Journal of Religious Studies* 5 (1977): 3–77.

——. "Cynics." *Interpreter's Dictionary of the Bible*. Supplementary Volume (1976), pp. 201–3.

——. *The Cynic Epistles*. Society of Biblical Literature Sources for Biblical Study 12. Missoula, Mont.: Scholars Press, 1977.

——. "Medical Imagery in the Pastoral Epistles." In *Texts and Testaments*. Edited by W. Eugene March. San Antonio: Trinity University Press, 1980.

——. *Social Aspects of Early Christianity*. Baton Rouge: Louisiana State University Press, 1977.

Meier, J. P. "Presbyteros in the Pastoral Epistles." *Catholic Biblical Quarterly* 35 (1973): 323–45.

Merk, O. "Glaube und Tat in den Pastoralbriefen." *Zeitschrift für die neutestamentliche Wissenschaft* 66 (1975): 91–102.

Merlan, P. *From Platonism to Neo-Platonism*. The Hague: N. Nijhoff, 1960.

Metzger, Bruce. "Literary Forgeries and Canonical Pseudepigrapha." *Journal of Biblical Literature* 91 (1972): 3–24.

Meyer, Arnold. "Religiöse Pseudepigraphie als ethisch-psychologisches Problem." In *Pseudepigraphie in der heidnischen und jüdisch-christlichen Antike*. Edited by Norbert Brox. Darmstadt: Wissenschaftliche Buchgesellschaft, 1977.

Mitton, C. Leslie. *The Epistle to the Ephesians*. Oxford: Clarendon Press, 1951.

Momigliano, Arnaldo. *The Development of Greek Biography*. Cambridge, Mass.: Harvard University Press, 1971.

More, P. E. *Hellenistic Philosophies*. Princeton: Princeton University Press, 1923.

Moulton, James Hope, and Milligan, George. *The Vocabulary of the Greek New Testament: Illustrated from the Papyri and Other Non-Literary Sources*. Grand Rapids, Mich.: Wm. B. Eerdmans, 1930.

Oberlinner, Lorenz. "Die 'Epiphaneia' des Heilswillens Gottes in Christus Jesus." *Zeitschrift für die neutestamentliche Wissenschaft* 17 (1980): 192–213.

Ochs, Donovan, J. "Aristotle's Concept of the Formal Topics." In *Aristotle: The Classical Heritage of Rhetoric*. Edited by Keith V. Erickson. Metuchen: Scarecrow Press, 1974.

Pagels, Elaine Hiesey. *The Gnostic Paul: Gnostic Exegesis of the Pauline Letters*. Philadelphia: Fortress Press, 1975.

Palmer, Georgiana Paine. "The ΤΟΠΟΙ of Aristotle's Rhetoric as Exemplified in the Orators." Ph.D. dissertation, University of Chicago, 1934.

Pax, E. ΕΠΙΦΑΝΕΙΑ: *Ein religionsgeschichtlicher Beitrag zur biblischen Theologie*. Munich: Zink, 1955.

Pedersen, J. *Israel: Its Life and Culture*. 2 vols. New York: Oxford University Press, 1926.

Penella, Robert J. *The Letters of Apollonius of Tyana*. Leiden: E. J. Brill, 1979.

Pohlenz, Max. *Die Stoa: Geschichte einer geistigen Bewegung*. Göttingen: Vandenhoeck & Ruprecht, 1949.

Price, J. Bennett. " 'Paradeigma' and 'Exemplum' in Ancient Rhetorical Theory." Ph.D. dissertation, University of California, Berkeley, 1975. Ann Arbor, Mich.: University Microfilms, 1982.

Pseudepigrapha I: Pseudopythagorica — Lettres de Platon — Littérature pseudépigraphique juive. Fondation Hardt, Entretiens sur l'antiquité classique 18. Vandoeuvre-Genève: Fondation Hardt, 1972.

Ramsay, W. M. "A Historical Commentary on the Epistles to Timothy." *Expositor*, Ser. 7–8 (1909–1911).

Raphael, Sally, "Rhetoric, Dialectic, and Syllogistic Argument: Aristotle's Position in 'Rhetoric' I–II." *Phronesis* 19 (1974): 153–67.

Ranft, J. "Depositum." *Reallexikon für Antike und Christentum* 3 (1957): 778–84.

Redditt, Paul L. "The Concept of 'Nomos' in Fourth Maccabees." *Catholic Biblical Quarterly* 45 (1983): 249–70.

Rist, John M. *Stoic Philosophy*. Cambridge: Cambridge University Press, 1969.

——, ed. *The Stoics*. Major Thinkers Series. Berkeley: University of California Press, 1978.

Rist, Martin. "Pseudepigraphy and the Early Christians." In *Studies in New Testament and Early Christian Literature: Essays in Honor of Allen P. Wikgren*. Edited by D. E. Aune. Leiden: E. J. Brill, 1972.

Robinson, H. Wheeler. "The Hebrew Conception of Corporate Personality." In *Werden und Wesen des Alten Testaments*. Beiheft zur Zeitschrift für die alttestamentliche Wissenschaft 66 (1936).

Robinson, James M., ed. *The Nag Hammadi Library: In English*. New York: Harper & Row, 1977.

Rohde, J. "Pastoralbriefe und Acta Pauli." In *Studia Evangelica* 5. Edited by F. L. Cross. Texte und Untersuchungen zur altchristlichen Literatur 103. Berlin: Akademie Verlag, 1968.

Russell, D. S. *The Method and Message of Jewish Apocalyptic*. The Old Testament Library. Philadelphia: Westminster Press, 1964.

Sandbach, F. H. *The Stoics*. New York: W. W. Norton, 1975.

Schlatter, Adolf. *Die Kirche der Griechen im Urteil des Paulus: Eine Auslegung seiner Briefe an Timotheus und Titus*. Stuttgart: Calwer Verlag, 1936.

Schleiermacher, Friedrich. *Sendschreiben an J. C. Gass: Über den sogenannten ersten Brief des Paulos an den Timotheos*. Berlin: Realschulbuchhandlung, 1807.

Schmidt, E. G. "Die drei Arten des Philosophierens." *Philologus* 106 (1962): 14–28.

Schrage, Wolfgang. "Zur Ethik der neutestamentlichen Haustafeln." *New Testament Studies* 21 (1975): 1–22.

Schweitzer, Albert. *The Mysticism of Paul the Apostle*. Translated by William Montgomery. New York: Seabury Press, 1968.

Schweizer, Eduard. *Church Order in the New Testament*. Naperville, Ill.: Alec R. Allenson, 1961.

Scott, Ernest Findlay. *The Pastoral Epistles*. Moffatt New Testament Commentary. London: Hodder & Stoughton, 1936.

Seaton, R. C. "The Aristotelian Enthymeme." *Classical Review* 28 (1914): 113–19.

Segal, Alan F. "Hellenistic Magic: Some Questions of Definition." In *Studies in Gnosticism and Hellenistic Religions*. Presented to Gilles Quispel on the occasion of his 65th birthday. Edited by R. van den Broek and M. J. Vermaseren. Leiden: E. J. Brill, 1981.

Smart, James D. *The Interpretation of Scripture*. Philadelphia: Westminster Press, 1961.

Smith, Morton. *Jesus the Magician*. San Francisco: Harper & Row, 1978.

——. "Pseudepigraphy in the Israelite Tradition." In *Pseudepigrapha I: Pseudopythagorica — Lettres de Platon — Littérature pseudépigraphique juive*. Fondation Hardt, Entretiens sur l'antiquité classique 18. Vandoeuvres-Genève: Fondation Hardt, 1972.

Solmsen, Friedrich. "The Aristotelian Tradition in Ancient Rhetoric." In *Aristotle, The Classical Heritage of Rhetoric*. Edited by Keith V. Erickson. Metuchen: Scarecrow Press, 1974.

——. *Die Entwicklung der Aristotelischen Logik und Rhetorik*. Berlin: Weidmannsche Buchhandlung, 1929.

Spanneut, M. "Epiktet." *Reallexikon für Antike und Christentum* 5 (1962): 599–681.

Speyer, Wolfgang. "Echte religiöse Pseudepigraphie." In *Pseudepigrapha I: Pseudopythagorica — Lettres de Platon — Littérature pseudépigraphique juive*. Fondation Hardt, Entretiens sur l'antiquité classique 18. Vandoeuvres-Genève : Fondation Hardt, 1972.

——. *Die literarische Fälschung im heidnischen und christlichen Altertum: Ein Versuch ihrer Deutung*. Handbuch der klassischen Altertumswissenschaft. Vol. 1, Pt. 2. Munich: C. H. Beck, 1971.

——. "Religiöse Pseudepigraphie und literarische Fälschung." In *Pseudepigraphie in der heidnischen und jüdisch-christlichen Antike*. Edited by Norbert Brox. Wege der Forschung. Vol. 484. Darmstadt: Wissenschaftliche Buchgesellschaft, 1977.

Spicq, Ceslaus. *Les Épîtres Pastorales*. 2 vols. 4th ed. Études Biblique. Paris: J. Gabalda, 1969.

——. "Pèlerine et Vêtements (A propos de II Tim. iv, 13 et Act xx, 33)." In *Mélanges Eugène Tisserant*. Vatican City: Biblioteca apostolica vaticana, 1964.

——. "St. Paul et la loi des dépôts." *Revue Biblique* 40 (1931): 481–502.

Spitta, F. "Über die persönlichen Notizen im zweiten Briefe an Timotheus." *Theologische Studien und Kritiken* 51 (1878): 582–607.

Sprute, Jürgen. *Die Enthymemetheorie der aristotelischen Rhetorik.* Abhandlungen der Akademie der Wissenschaften in Göttingen. Göttingen: Vandenhoeck & Ruprecht, 1982.

Städele, Alfons. *Die Briefe des Pythagoras und der Pythagoreer.* Beiträge zur klassischen Philologie 115. Meisenheim am Glan: Anton Hain, 1980.

Stenger, W. "Timotheus und Titus als literarische Gestalten. Beobachtungen zur Form und Funktion der Pastoralbriefe." *Kairos* 16 (1974): 252—67.

Stowers, Stanley. *The Diatribe and Paul's Letter to the Romans.* Society of Biblical Literature Dissertation Series 57. Chico, Calif.: Scholars Press, 1981.

Strobel, August. "Schreiben des Lukas? Zum sprachlichen Problem der Pastoralbriefe." *New Testament Studies* 15 (1968—69): 191—210.

Suggs, Jack M. "The Christian Two Way Tradition: Its Antiquity, Form, and Function." In *Studies in New Testament and Early Christian Literature: Essays in Honor of Allen P. Wikgren.* Edited by D. E. Aune. Leiden: E. J. Brill, 1972.

Syme, Ronald. "Fraud and Imposture." In *Pseudepigrapha I: Pseudopythagorica — Lettres de Platon — Littérature pseudépigraphique juive.* Fondation Hardt, Entretiens sur l'antiquité classique 18. Vandoeuvres-Genève : Fondation Hardt, 1972.

Tarn, W. W., and Griffith, G. T. *Hellenistic Civilization.* New York: Meridian Books, 1974.

Thesleff, Holger. "Doric Pseudo-Pythagorica." In *Pseudepigrapha I: Pseudopythagorica—Lettres de Platon—Littérature pseudépigraphique juive.* Fondation Hardt, Entretiens sur l'antiquité classique 18. Vandoeuvres-Genève: Fondation Hardt, 1972.

——. *An Introduction to the Pythagorean Writings of the Hellenistic Period.* Acta Academiae Aboensis, Ser. A, Humaniora, Vol. 24, No. 3. Åbo: Åbo Akademi, 1961.

——. "Okkelos, Archytas, and Plato." *Eranos* 60 (1962): 8—36.

——. *The Pythagorean Texts of the Hellenistic Period.* Acta Academiae Aboensis, Ser. A, Humaniora, Vol. 30, No. 1. Åbo: Åbo Akademi, 1965.

Thomas, Johannes. "Formgesetze des Begriffskatalogs im Neuen Testament." *Theologische Zeitschrift* 24 (1968): 15—28.

Torm, Frederick. "Die Psychologie der Pseudonymität im Hinblick auf die Literatur des Urchristentums." In *Pseudepigraphie in der heidnischen und jüdisch-christlichen Antike.* Edited by Norbert Brox. Wege der Forschung, Vol. 484. Darmstadt: Wissenschaftliche Buchgesellschaft, 1977.

Trummer, Peter. *Die Paulustradition der Pastoralbriefe.* Beiträge zur Evangelischen Theologie 8. Frankfurt am Main: Peter Lang, 1978.

Verner, David C. *The Household of God: The Social World of the Pastoral Epistles.* Society of Biblical Literature Dissertation Series 71. Chico, Calif.: Scholars Press, 1983.

Vögtle, Anton. *Die Tugend- und Lasterkataloge im Neuen Testament.* Neutestamentliche Abhandlungen 16, 4—5. Münster: Aschendorff, 1936.

Wegenast, K. *Das Verständnis der Tradition bei Paulus und in den Deuteropaulinen.* Wissenschaftliche Monographien zum Alten und Neuen Testament 8. Neukirchen-Vluyn: Neukirchener Verlag, 1962.

Weidinger, Karl. *Die Haustafeln: Ein Stück urchristlicher Paränese.* Untersuchungen zum Neuen Testament 14. Leipzig: J. C. Hinrichs, 1928.

Weil, Eric. "La Place de la logique dans la pensée aristotelicienne." *Revue de metaphysique et de morale* 56 (1951): 283—315.

Wendland, Paul. *Die hellenistisch-römische Kultur.* 2nd and 3rd ed. Tübingen: J. C. B. Mohr (Paul Siebeck), 1912.

——. "Σωτήρ." *Zeitschrift für die neutestamentliche Wissenschaft* 5 (1904): 335—53.

Wibbing, Siegfried. *Die Tugend- und Lasterkataloge im NT und ihre Traditionsgeschichte unter besonderer Berücksichtigung der Qumran-Texte.* Beiheft zur Zeitschrift für die neutestamentliche Wissenschaft 25. Berlin: Töpelmann, 1959.

Wikramanayake, G. H. "A Note on the Πίστεις in Aristotle's Rhetoric." *American Journal of Philology* 82 (1961): 193—96.

Wilamowitz-Möllendorff, U. v. "Unechte Briefe." *Hermes* 33 (1898): 492—98.

Wilson, Stephen G. *Luke and the Pastoral Epistles.* London: S.P.C.K., 1979.

Windisch, Hans. "Zur Christologie der Pastoralbriefe." *Zeitschrift für die neutestamentliche Wissenschaft* 34 (1935): 213—38.

Index of Passages

Greek and Latin Authors

New Testament

Early Christian Literature

Index of Modern Authors

Index of Subjects

Index of Greek Words

Hermeneutische Untersuchungen zur Theologie

Herausgegeben von
Hans Dieter Betz · Gerhard Ebeling · Manfred Mezger

11
Norbert Schneider
*Die rhetorische Eigenart der
paulinischen Antithese*
1970. VII, 147 Seiten. Ln.

10
Martin Ferel
Gepredigte Taufe
1969. VIII, 265 Seiten. Ln.

9
Ernst Fuchs
Marburger Hermeneutik
1968. XI, 227 Seiten. Ln.

8
Jürgen Heise
Bleiben
1967. XI, 186 Seiten. Ln.

7
Gerd Schunack
*Das hermeneutische Problem
des Todes*
1967. XI, 318 Seiten. Br.

6
Dieter Nestle
*Eleutheria.
Band 1: Die Griechen*
1967. XI, 164 Seiten. Br.

5
Ulrich Duchrow
*Sprachverständnis und
biblisches Hören bei Augustin*
1965. XII, 284 Seiten. Ln.

4
Alfred Schindler
*Wort und Analogie in
Augustins Trinitätslehre*
1965. XI, 269 Seiten. Ln.

3
Friedrich Gogarten
Die Verkündung Jesu Christi
2. Auflage 1965.
568 Seiten. Ln.

2
Eberhard Jüngel
Paulus und Jesus
5. Auflage 1979. XI,
319 Seiten. Ln.

1
Gerhard Ebeling
Theologie und Verkündigung
2. Auflage 1963. XII,
146 Seiten. Ln.

J.C.B. Mohr (Paul Siebeck)
Tübingen